BUSY at MATHS

Fifth Class

Maths for Primary Schools

Orla Murtagh • Claire Leane • Tom Roche • Martin Kennedy
General Editor: Kevin Barry

CJFallon

Published by

CJ Fallon
Ground Floor – Block B
Liffey Valley Office Campus
Dublin 22

First Edition March 2015

ISBN: 978-0-7144-2070-7

The publishers gratefully acknowledge Kenn Nesbitt for permission to reproduce copyright material:

"My Teacher Ate My Homework" copyright Kenn Nesbitt. All rights reserved.
Reprinted by permission of the author.

Printed in Ireland by
Turner Print Group
Earl Street
Longford

BUSY at MATHS 5

Fifth Class

Introduction

Busy at Maths 5 provides the most effective **problem-solving** strategies to ensure that pupils are exposed to **real-life maths** in the classroom.

The series encourages **collaborative learning** and **pair/small group work**, and is supported by excellent **digital interactives** and **tutorials** for use on the interactive whiteboard.

Busy at Maths provides the latest teaching methods for primary schools. It embodies sound **constructivist** principles and draws clear links with the Project Maths approach used in secondary schools.

Busy at Maths 5 includes the following elements:

- A Pupil's Book
- A Shadow Book
- Integrated digital classroom resources
- An Individual Pupil Profile Term Assessment Record for each pupil
- An extensive Teacher's Resource Book for each class, including:
  - Fortnightly teaching schemes
  - 100 Photocopiable Masters to consolidate learning
  - Home/School Links
  - A wide selection of activities and games to encourage the constructivist approach

Contents

Chapter 1: Look back

LOOK BACK

1. Write the correct number under each abacus or notation board.

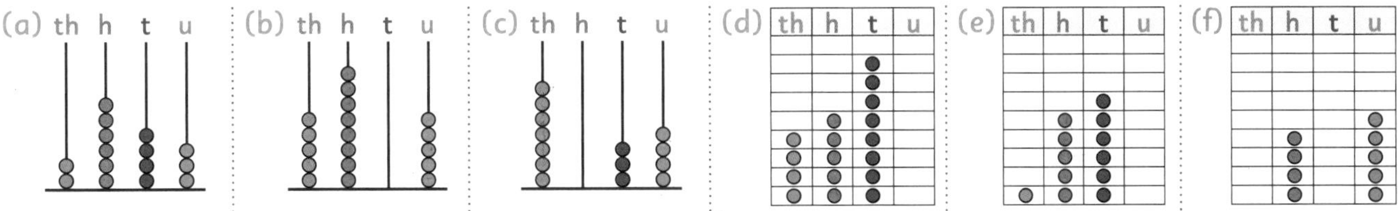

2. Write the missing numbers on each number strip.

(a)	2,561			2,564					2,569		
(b)	3,786			3,789						3,795	
(c)	6,892					6,897					6,902
(d)	8,995				8,999				9,003		

3. Write the value of the underlined **digit** in (i) figures and (ii) words.

(a) 2,1$\underline{4}$6 (b) 3,$\underline{7}$42 (c) 7,59$\underline{2}$ (d) $\underline{6}$,854 (e) 8,$\underline{7}$05 (f) $\underline{9}$,085

(g) 8,4$\underline{2}$9 (h) 9,$\underline{9}$99 (i) $\underline{5}$,555 (j) 2,00$\underline{7}$ (k) 4,3$\underline{9}$8 (l) 3,$\underline{8}$81

4. Write the **largest** and **smallest** four-digit numbers that can be made from these dice. Write the largest number first.

(a)

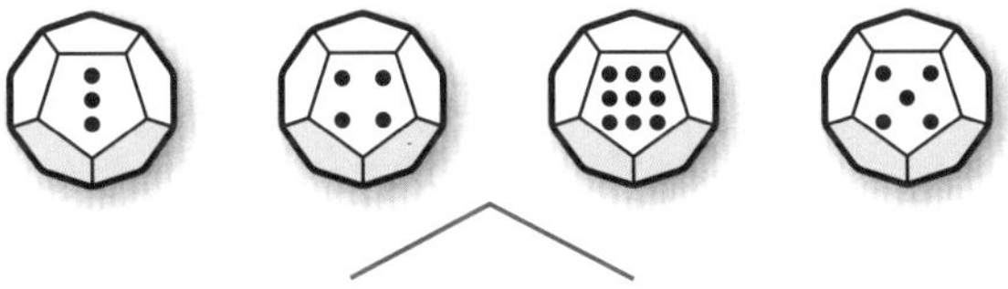

(b)

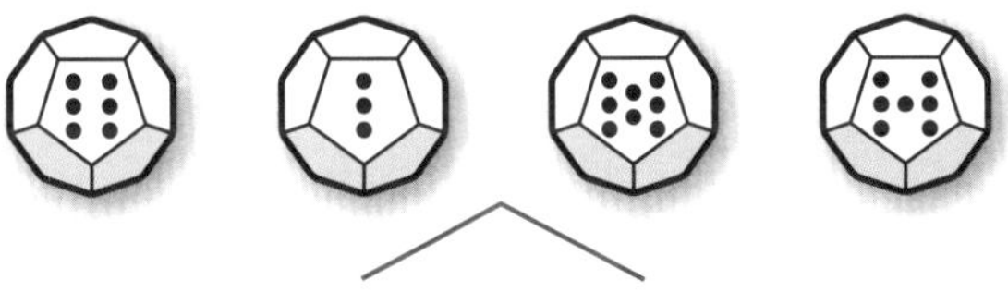

(c)

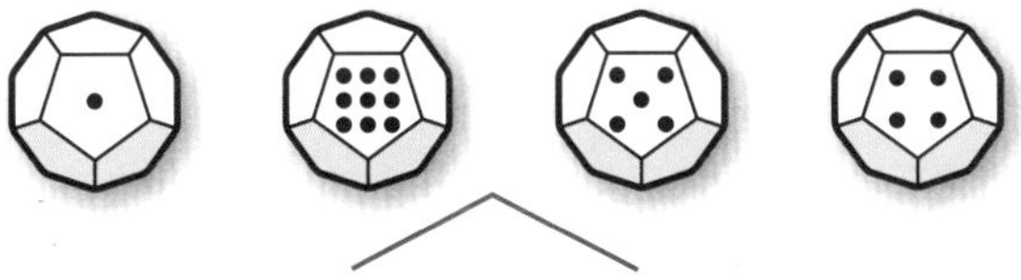

(d)

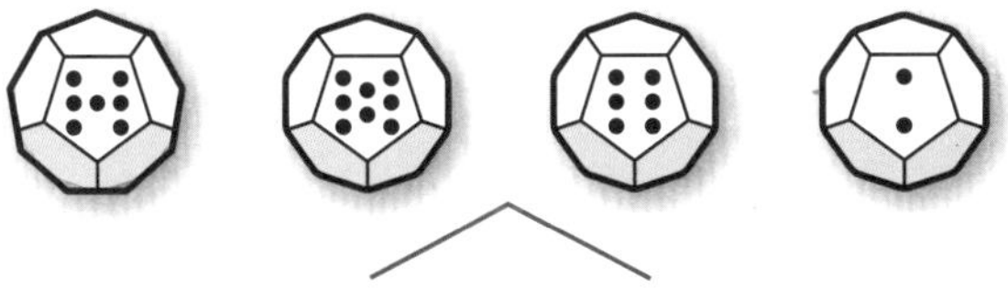

5. Complete these patterns.

(a) 4, 8, 12, ____, ____, ____, 28.

(b) 7, 14, ____, ____, 35, ____, ____.

(c) 18, 24, ____, ____, 42, ____, ____.

(d) 16, ____, 32, 40, ____, ____, ____.

(e) 27, ____, 45, 54, 63, ____, ____.

(f) 45, ____, 55, 60, ____, ____, 75.

(g) 72, 68, 64, ____, ____, ____, 48.

(h) 84, 77, ____, 63, 56, ____, ____.

(i) 480, 440, ____, 360, ____.

(j) 510, ____, 550, 570, ____.

(k) 2,300, 2,400, 2,500, ____, ____.

(l) 7,750, 7,550, 7,350, ____, ____.

6. Round these (i) to the nearest **10**; (ii) to the nearest **100**; (iii) to the nearest **1,000**.

(a) 3,216 (b) 4,715 (c) 3,199 (d) 5,876 (e) 6,549 (f) 9,351

(g) 7,999 (h) 7,550 (i) 5,087 (j) 2,001 (k) 8,556 (l) 7,448

Look back

1. Write the correct name under each 2-D shape.

hexagon rhombus parallelogram pentagon octagon

(a)  ________

(b) 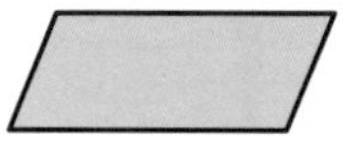 ________

(c) 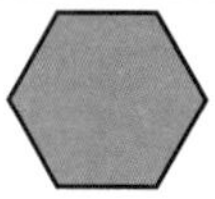 ________

(d) 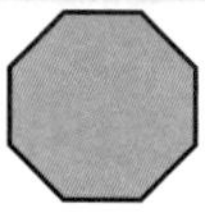 ________

(e) 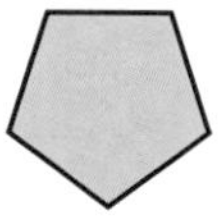 ________

2. Write the correct name under each 3-D shape.

prism pyramid sphere cuboid cylinder

(a)  ________

(b) 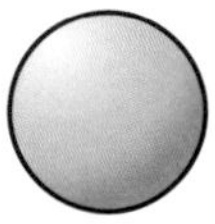 ________

(c)  ________

(d) 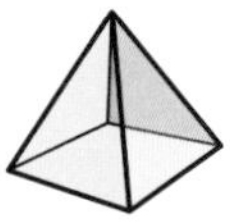 ________

(e) 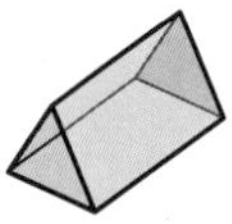 ________

3. Write the correct line names.

parallel diagonal horizontal

(a)  ________

(b) ________

(c)  ________

4. Write the correct angle name.

obtuse right acute

(a)  ________

(b)  ________

(c)  ________

5.

(a)	(b)	(c)	(d)	(e)	(f)
2,753	6,879	4,376	7,851	3,674	6,739
+ 4,135	− 2,634	+ 2,528	− 3,219	+ 4,193	− 2,475

6.

(a)	(b)	(c)	(d)	(e)	(f)
3,725	8,175	4,379	5,176	5,748	8,000
+ 4,862	− 6,931	+ 2,586	− 2,897	+ 2,575	− 2,874

7.

(a)	(b)	(c)	(d)	(e)	(f)
2,341	4,135	3,251	5,322	2,468	3,487
3,615	3,214	4,163	1,643	3,572	4,196
+ 2,032	+ 1,528	+ 1,274	+ 2,504	+ 1,748	+ 1,839

8. (a) 2,468 + 3,135 + 1,534 = ________ (b) 5,749 + 1,863 + 2,387 = ________

(c) (3,296 + 4,875) – 5,769 = ________ (d) (8,537 – 3,186) + 1,977 = ________

Challenge 1 8,243 adults attended a hurling match. If 4,869 women attended, how many men were at the match? ________

Challenge 2

A dairy produced 2,486l of milk in the morning and 3,729l in the evening. If 368l of the milk turned sour, how many litres of milk were not sour? ________ l

Look back

LOOK BACK

Complete the following multiplication and division tables.

1. (a) 5 × 2 = ____ (b) 6 × 3 = ____ (c) 4 × 7 = ____ (d) 8 × 6 = ____ (e) 5 × 9 = ____
(f) 9 × 8 = ____ (g) 10 × 5 = ____ (h) 8 × 8 = ____ (i) 7 × 9 = ____ (j) 8 × 7 = ____

2. (a) 12 ÷ 3 = ____ (b) 16 ÷ 2 = ____ (c) 24 ÷ 4 = ____ (d) 32 ÷ 8 = ____ (e) 54 ÷ 9 = ____
(f) 36 ÷ 6 = ____ (g) 48 ÷ 4 = ____ (h) 54 ÷ 6 = ____ (i) 63 ÷ 7 = ____ (j) 72 ÷ 8 = ____

3. (a) 57 × 3 (b) 74 × 4 (c) 86 × 5 (d) 125 × 2 (e) 238 × 6 (f) 537 × 7

4. (a) 45 × 16 (b) 72 × 17 (c) 86 × 24 (d) 68 × 39 (e) 95 × 43 (f) 99 × 68

5. (a) 176 × 6 (b) 249 × 8 (c) 379 × 7 (d) 254 × 32 (e) 189 × 28 (f) 176 × 54

6. (a) 6)48 (b) 7)63 (c) 8)64 (d) 5)185 (e) 3)501 (f) 4)984

7. (a) 4)173 ____ R ____ (b) 5)757 ____ R ____ (c) 6)921 ____ R ____ (d) 7)961 ____ R ____ (e) 8)994 ____ R ____

Challenge 1

Eggs are packed in trays of six.
How many trays are needed to pack 762 eggs? ____

Challenge 2

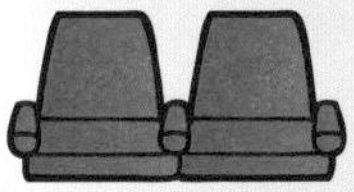

There are 54 rows of seats in a cinema. Each row has 78 seats.
How many seats are there altogether in the cinema? ____

8. Write the time shown on each clock in digital form (12-hour clock only).

(a)  ___ : ___

(b)  ___ : ___

(c)  ___ : ___

(d)  ___ : ___

(e)  ___ : ___

9.

	(a) hrs	mins	(b) hrs	mins	(c) hrs	mins	(d) hrs	mins	(e) hrs	mins	(f) hrs	mins
	4	27	3	39	7	56	6	25	5	47	9	32
	+ 3	18	+ 2	46	− 1	32	− 3	58	+ 2	39	+ 6	48

Challenge 3

A train left Dublin at 7:42. It arrived in Tralee at 10:34.
How long did the journey take? ____ hrs ____ mins

Look back

LOOK BACK

1. Write these amounts in cent.

(a) €2·46 = ____c (b) €3·15 = ____c (c) €9·07 = ____c (d) €14·27 = ____c

2. Write these amounts in euro (€).

(a) 346c = €____ (b) 876c = €____ (c) 1,234c = €____ (d) 1,975c = €____

3.

(a)	(b)	(c)	(d)	(e)	(f)
€3·46	€7·87	€4·75	€6·81	€5·78	€9·32
+ €2·23	− €5·26	+ €3·28	− €2·58	+ €2·65	− €6·57
€	€	€	€	€	€

4.

(a)	(b)	(c)	(d)	(e)	(f)
€4·58	€6·72	€9·63	€5·37	€8·86	€9·79
× 6	× 5	× 8	× 7	× 4	× 9
€	€	€	€	€	€

5. (a) 5)€6·75 € ____ (b) 4)€8·76 € ____ (c) 7)€8·26 € ____ (d) 6)€8·88 € ____ (e) 9)€7·11 € ____ (f) 8)€7·84 € ____

Challenge 1 If it costs €4·75 to rent a bicycle for a day, how much does it cost to rent it for a full week? € ____

Challenge 2 Six pineapples cost a total of €7·44. How much did each pineapple cost? € ____

6. What fraction of each shape is coloured (i) red; (ii) blue?

(a) 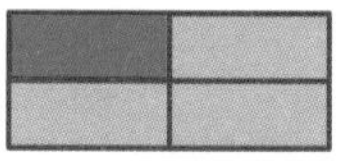

(b) 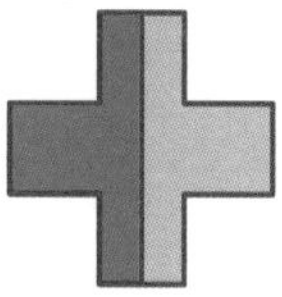

(c) 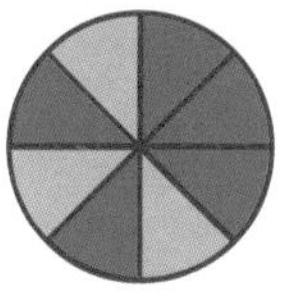

(d) 

(e) 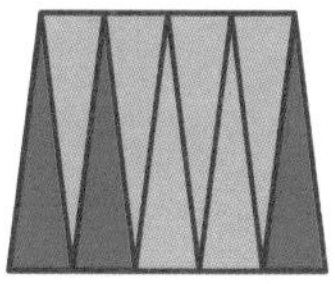

7. Write the correct sign (<, = or >) in each ◯.

(a) $\frac{1}{2}$ ◯ $\frac{1}{4}$ (b) $\frac{1}{4}$ ◯ $\frac{1}{10}$ (c) $\frac{3}{4}$ ◯ $\frac{7}{8}$ (d) $\frac{1}{4}$ ◯ $\frac{7}{12}$ (e) $\frac{2}{3}$ ◯ $\frac{6}{9}$ (f) $\frac{5}{6}$ ◯ $\frac{1}{12}$

8. (a) $\frac{1}{2}$ of 16 = ____ (b) $\frac{1}{4}$ of 20 = ____ (c) $\frac{1}{8}$ of 48 = ____ (d) $\frac{1}{9}$ of 72 = ____

9. Find the whole number if:

(a) $\frac{1}{3}$ = 7 ____ (b) $\frac{1}{8}$ = 4 ____ (c) $\frac{2}{3}$ = 6 ____ (d) $\frac{4}{5}$ = 16 ____ (e) $\frac{7}{9}$ = 21 ____

10. Write:

(a) 1 as a fraction of 4. (b) 3 as a fraction of 12. (c) 7 as a fraction of 56.

(d) 8 as a fraction of 12. (e) 20 as a fraction of 50. (f) 16 as a fraction of 20.

Challenge 3 Cian has 15c and Rowan has 35c. Write Cian's money as a fraction of Rowan's.

Look back

LOOK BACK

1. What decimal fraction of each shape is coloured (i) red; (ii) green?

(a)
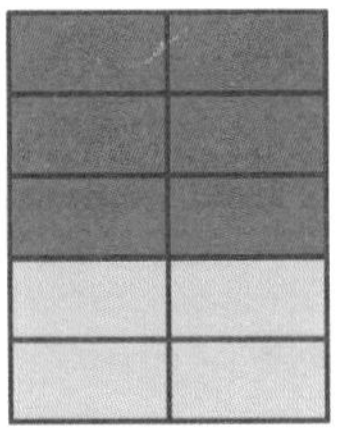
(i) ____ (ii) ____

(b)
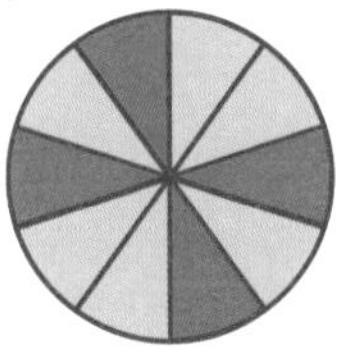
(i) ____ (ii) ____

(c)
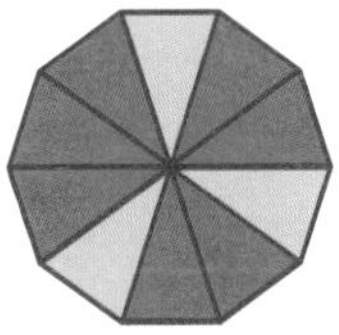
(i) ____ (ii) ____

(d)
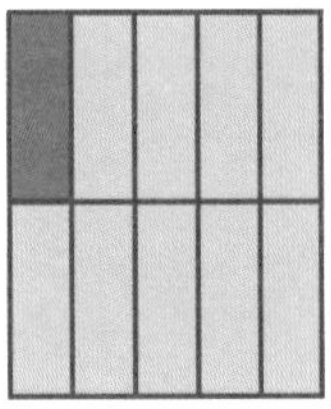
(i) ____ (ii) ____

(e)
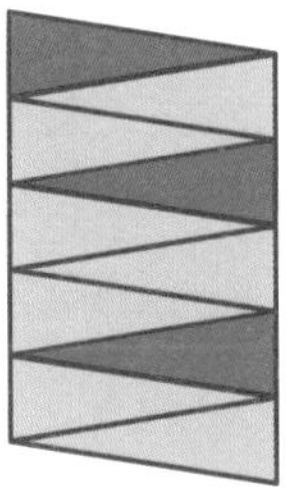
(i) ____ (ii) ____

2. Write the following in decimal fraction form.

(a) $\frac{3}{10}$ = ____ (b) $\frac{5}{10}$ = ____ (c) $\frac{9}{10}$ = ____ (d) $\frac{14}{100}$ = ____ (e) $\frac{29}{100}$ = ____

(f) $1\frac{4}{10}$ = ____ (g) $4\frac{7}{10}$ = ____ (h) $5\frac{8}{10}$ = ____ (i) $7\frac{41}{100}$ = ____ (j) $8\frac{74}{100}$ = ____

3. Complete these decimal number sequences.

(a) 0·4, 0·5, 0·6, ____, ____, ____, ____.
(b) 0·8, 0·9, ____, ____, 1·2, ____, ____.
(c) 0·47, 0·48, 0·49, ____, ____, ____.
(d) 0·76, 0·77, ____, 0·79, ____, ____, ____.
(e) 2·78, 2·79, ____, 2·81, ____, ____.
(f) 8·96, 8·97, ____, ____, ____, ____.

Complete the following.

4. (a) 1m = ____ cm (b) $\frac{1}{10}$m = ____ cm (c) $\frac{3}{10}$m = ____ cm (d) $\frac{1}{4}$m = ____ cm

(e) $\frac{1}{2}$m = ____ cm (f) $\frac{3}{4}$m = ____ cm (g) $1\frac{1}{2}$m = ____ cm (h) $3\frac{9}{10}$m = ____ cm

5. (a) $\frac{1}{4}$km = ____ m (b) $\frac{7}{10}$km = ____ m (c) $\frac{5}{10}$km = ____ m (d) $\frac{3}{4}$km = ____ m

(e) $\frac{1}{100}$km = ____ m (f) $\frac{75}{100}$km = ____ m (g) $1\frac{9}{10}$km = ____ m (h) $\frac{39}{100}$km = ____ m

6. (a) 1kg = ____ g (b) 0·1kg = ____ g (c) 0·75kg = ____ g (d) 0·5kg = ____ g

(e) 3·2kg = ____ g (f) 1·32kg = ____ g (g) 1·9kg = ____ g (h) 3·07kg = ____ g

7. (a) $\frac{1}{10}$l = ____ ml (b) $1\frac{1}{2}$l = ____ ml (c) $\frac{1}{5}$l = ____ ml (d) $\frac{4}{5}$l = ____ ml

(e) 0·3l = ____ ml (f) 0·75l = ____ ml (g) 1·25l = ____ ml (h) 3·49l = ____ ml

8. (a) 3·76m + 2·87m = ____ m (b) 8·71m − 2·39m = ____ m (c) 4·95l + 3·78l = ____ l (d) 9·32l − 5·78l = ____ l (e) 2·48kg + 6·73kg = ____ kg (f) 8·54kg − 3·99kg = ____ kg

9. (a) 4·83m × 4 = ____ m (b) 3·29l × 6 = ____ l (c) 7·68km × 8 = ____ km (d) 8·74kg × 9 = ____ kg (e) 7)8·89l ____ l (f) 8)9·76l ____ l

Challenge 1

A box of oranges weighs 5·86kg.
What is the total weight of eight such boxes of oranges? ____ kg

Challenge 2

A ball of ribbon is 8m 47cm long. If it is cut into seven equal pieces, what is the length of each piece? ____

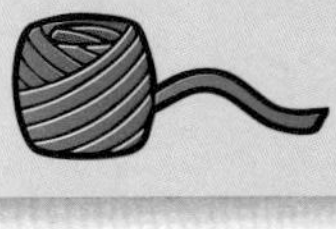

A quick look back 1

LOOK BACK

1. 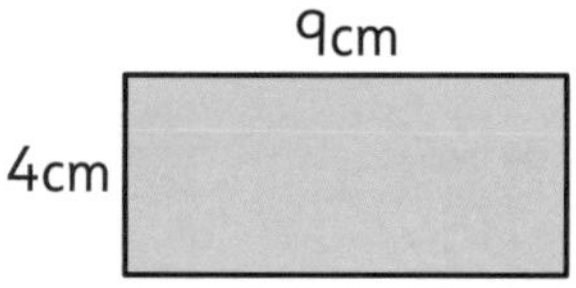

The perimeter of this rectangle is ____ cm.

2. 342 + 214 = ______

3. 798 – 126 = ______

4. Tick (✓) the pentagon:

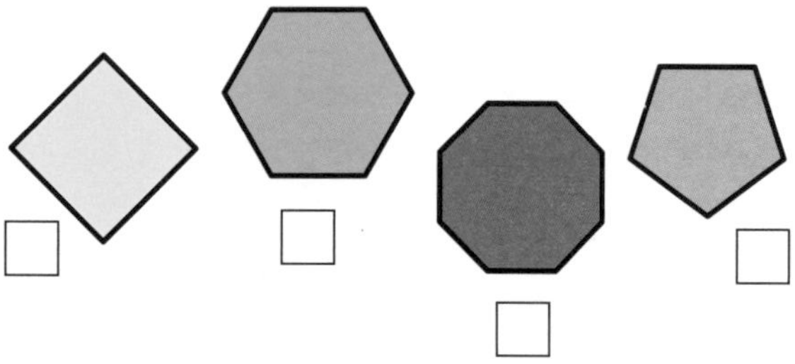

5. (8 × 6) + 4 = ______

6. $7\overline{)51}$

____ R ____

7. 18 × 9 = (10 × 9) + (____ × 9)

8. This pie chart shows the number of boys, girls and adults at a cinema. If there are 25 girls at the cinema, how many adults are there altogether?

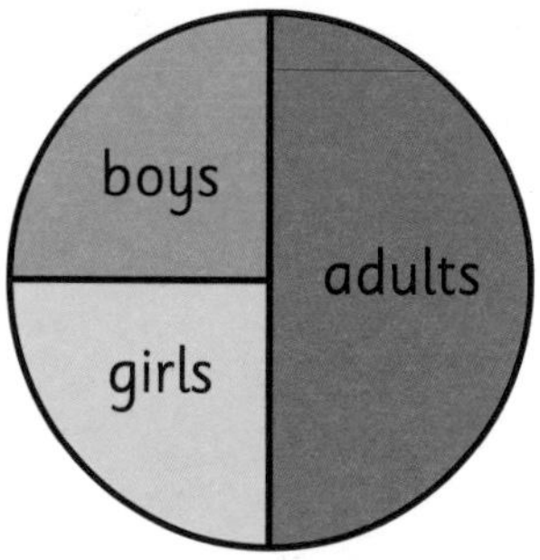

______

9. $\frac{1}{2} = \frac{\square}{8}$

10. What is $\frac{1}{9}$ of 36? ______

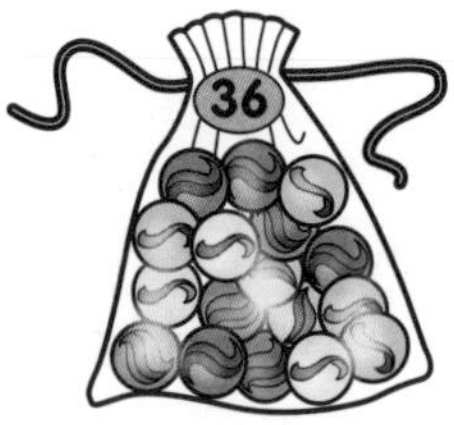

11. $\frac{1}{6}$ of a number is 7. What is the number? ______

12. What is $\frac{5}{12}$ of 24? ______

13. 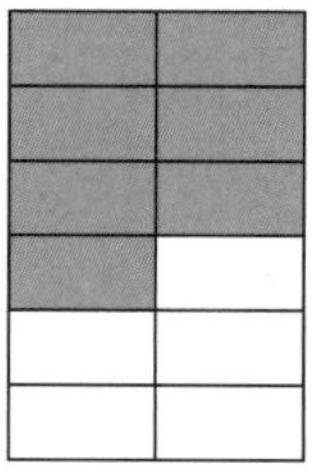

What fraction of this shape is coloured?

$\frac{\square}{\square}$

14. $\frac{76}{100} = \frac{\square}{10} + \frac{\square}{100}$

15. Write 3 units and 56 hundredths in decimal form.

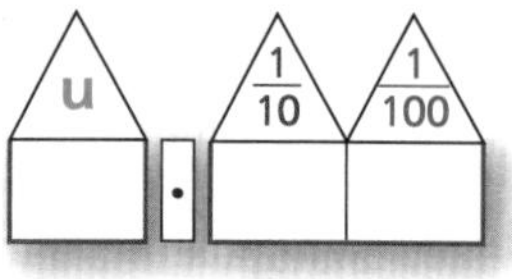

16. Make €1·58 using only five coins.

◯ ◯ ◯ ◯ ◯

17. 

Adam had €20. He bought the ball. How much money had he left?

€ ______

18. Colour the correct squares to complete the symmetrical pattern.

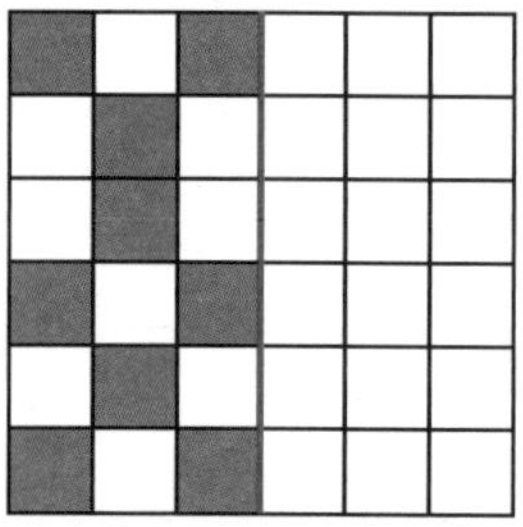

19. 

Write the time shown on this clock in digital form.

[:]

20. A cartoon started at 6:55. If it lasted for 45 minutes, it ended at

[:]

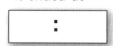

Chapter 2: Place value to 99,999

There were 34,516 people at a rock festival. That's tens of thousands! Let's record 34,516 on the abacus and notation board.

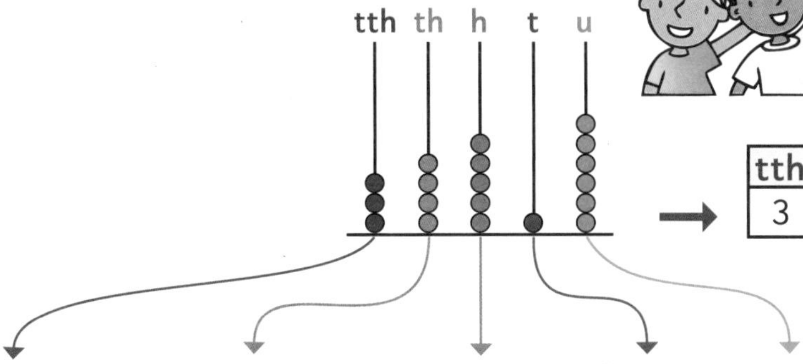

tth	th	h	t	u
3	4	5	1	6

3 ten thousands + 4 thousands + 5 hundreds + 1 ten + 6 units → number words

30,000 + 4,000 + 500 + 10 + 6 → expanded form

1. Write the correct number under each abacus.

(a) 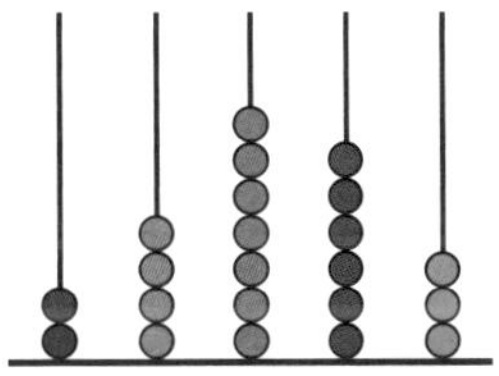

(b) 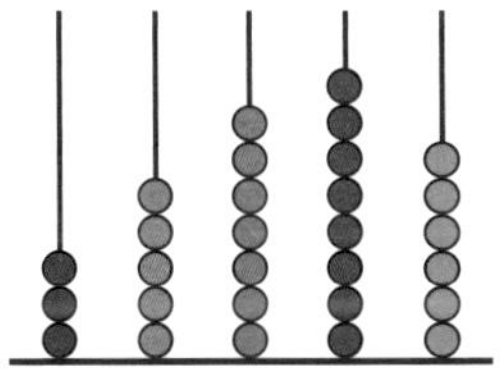

(c) 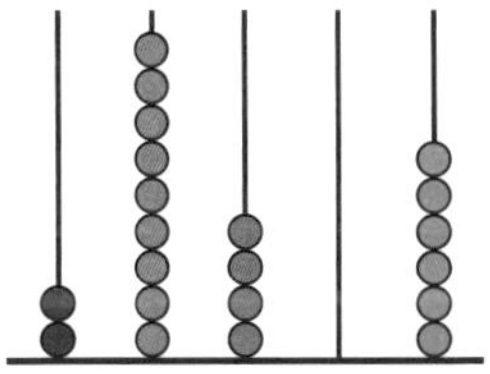

(d) 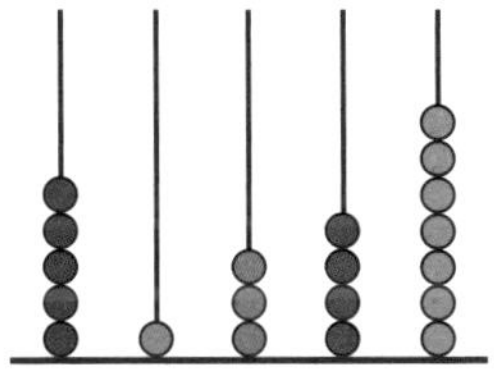

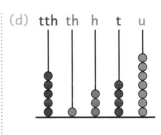

(e) 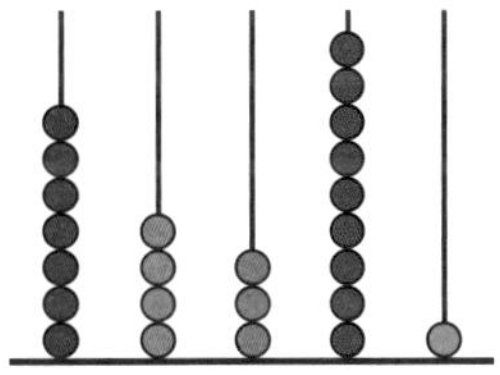

(f) 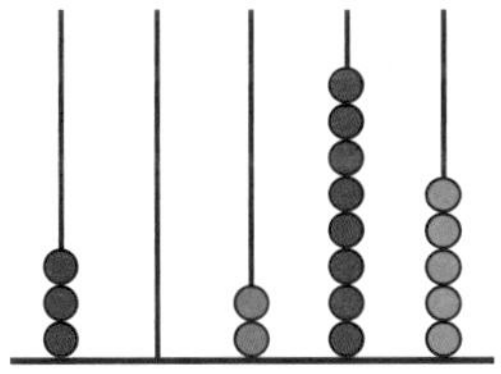

(g) 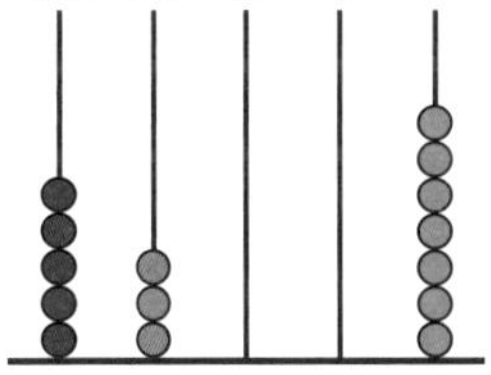

(h) 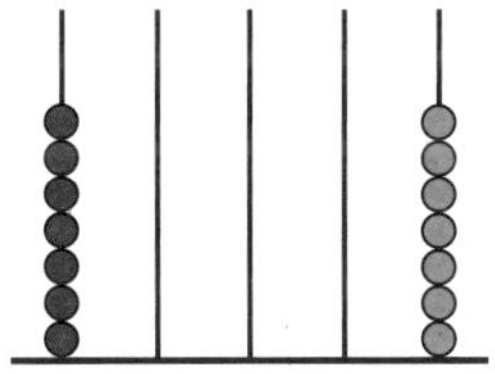

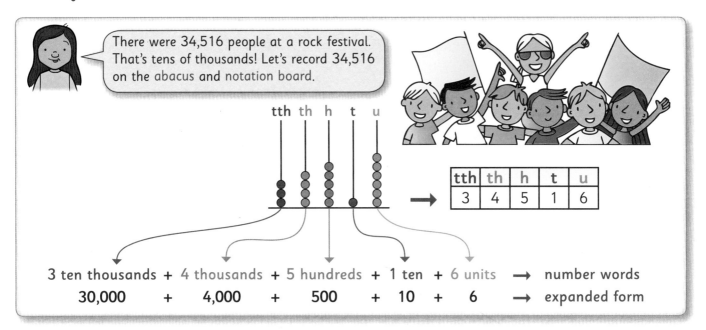

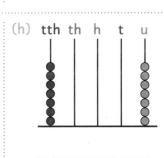

2. Show the following numbers on an abacus.

(a) 16,534 (b) 28,947 (c) 48,206 (d) 59,057 (e) 99,009

3. Write the following in (i) number words and (ii) expanded form.

(a)

tth	th	h	t	u
1	3	4	7	8

(b)

tth	th	h	t	u
3	6	9	0	5

(c)

tth	th	h	t	u
8	7	6	9	0

(d)

tth	th	h	t	u
7	0	0	5	6

(e) 48,322 (f) 52,003 (g) 72,119 (h) 80,603 (i) 60,606

Challenge

Write the five-digit number that has 3 in the hundreds place, 5 in the ten thousands place, 8 in the tens place, 0 in the thousands place and 7 in the units place. ____________

STRAND Number **STRAND UNIT/ELEMENT** *Place value*

LANGUAGE *Ten thousands, thousands, hundreds, tens, units, digits, numbers, abacus, notation board, smallest, greatest, largest, roman numerals*

Place value

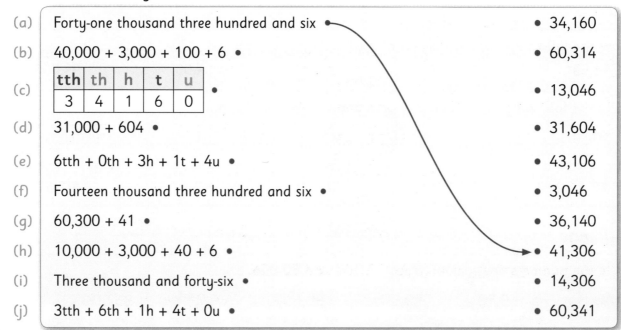

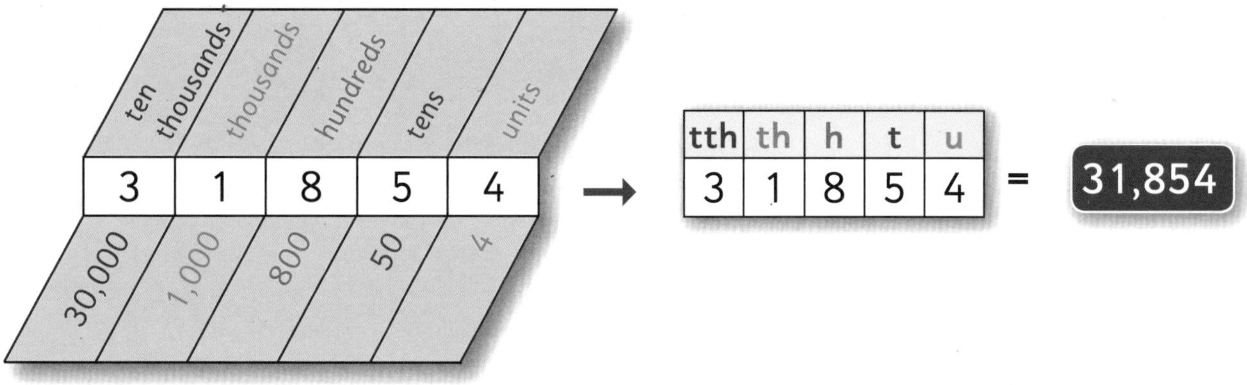

1. Write the value of the underlined digits in each of the following numbers in figures.

(a) 16,843 (b) 37,906 (c) 85,417 (d) 90,692 (e) 17,649

(f) 3,648 (g) 55,042 (h) 68,309 (i) 47,610 (j) 44,444

(k) 13,579 (l) 7,243 (m) 95,959 (n) 64,364 (o) 88,888

2. Write the following numbers in figures.

(a) Eighteen thousand three hundred and seventy-two: ____________

(b) Thirty-four thousand seven hundred and twenty-one: ____________

(c) Eighty-six thousand five hundred and ninety-six: ____________

(d) Forty-seven thousand and eight: ____________

(e) Sixty-three thousand: ____________

(f) Fifty-four thousand two hundred and two: ____________

(g) Seventy-eight thousand and sixty-three: ____________

(h) Eighty-nine thousand three hundred and twenty: ____________

3. Match the following.

(a) Forty-one thousand three hundred and six • • 34,160

(b) 40,000 + 3,000 + 100 + 6 • • 60,314

(c)

tth	th	h	t	u
3	4	1	6	0

• • 13,046

(d) 31,000 + 604 • • 31,604

(e) 6tth + 0th + 3h + 1t + 4u • • 43,106

(f) Fourteen thousand three hundred and six • • 3,046

(g) 60,300 + 41 • • 36,140

(h) 10,000 + 3,000 + 40 + 6 • • 41,306

(i) Three thousand and forty-six • • 14,306

(j) 3tth + 6th + 1h + 4t + 0u • • 60,341

Place value – Comparing numbers

1. Order the numbers of people attending the Cool Kidz rock concerts from **smallest** number to **largest** number.

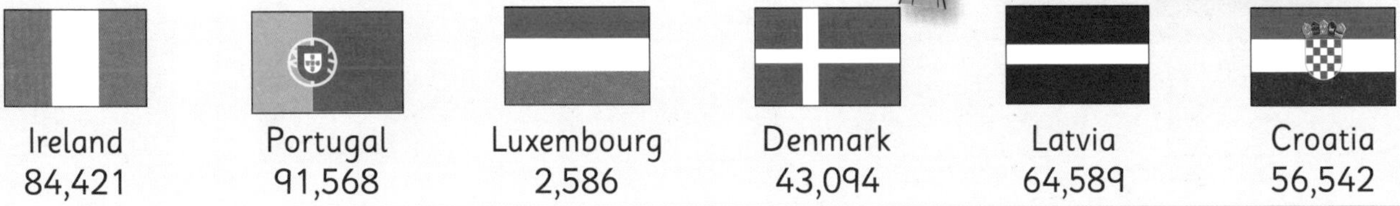

2. Put the following numbers in order of size starting with the **smallest**.

(a)	46,328	29,756	87,600	92,815	64,373	35,874	87,006
(b)	38,652	49,046	38,625	71,604	38,689	49,406	71,406
(c)	63,199	63,201	99,101	63,200	84,121	63,121	99,099

3. Order these classic cars from the **most** expensive to the **least** expensive.

4. Put the following numbers in order of size starting with the **largest**.

(a)	46,128	63,217	46,218	74,516	86,901	74,089	74,615
(b)	55,164	55,064	55,416	55,641	55,100	55,146	55,614
(c)	73,618	73,620	73,020	37,018	37,800	73,281	73,801

5. Complete the table.

	1,000 less	100 less	10 less		10 more	100 more	1,000 more	10,000 more
	5,278	6,178	6,268	6,278	6,288	6,378	7,278	16,278
(a)				12,594				
(b)				36,723				
(c)				58,165				
(d)				83,240				
(e)				86,108				
(f)				66,318				

6. Circle the numbers that are between 79,008 and 80,006.

79,006 79,801 80,001 80,600 79,999 86,000

More place value

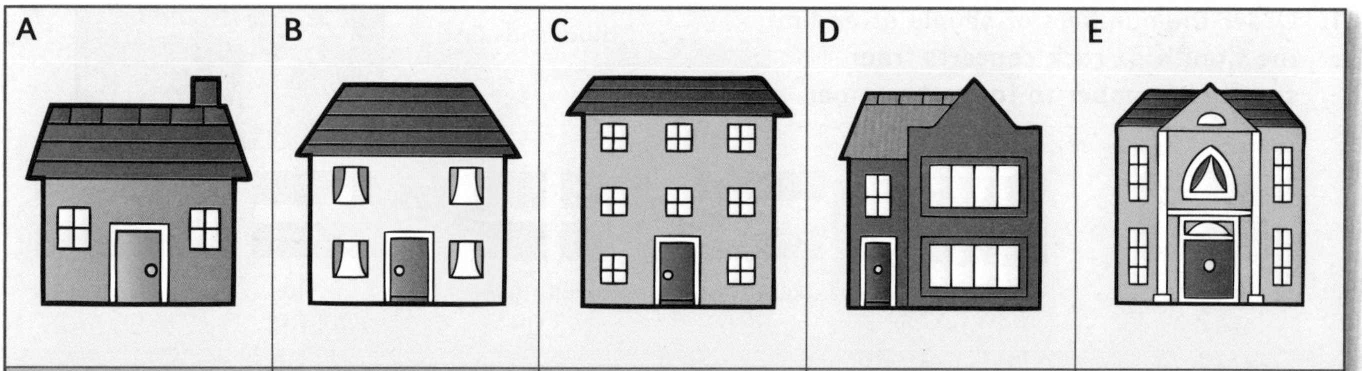

A	B	C	D	E
€98,264	€82,946	€98,462	€69,862	€98,642

1. (a) Order the properties from the most expensive to the least expensive.
   (b) Write the digit in (i) the hundreds place in House **E**; (ii) the ten thousands place in House **C**.
   (c) In House **B**, if the 2 were changed to a 7, by how much would the value increase?
   (d) In House **D**, if the 8 were changed to a 6, by how much would the value decrease?
   (e) House **A** was sold for €10,000 less than the advertised price. What was the selling price?

Ancient Chinese rod numerals

The ancient Chinese placed **red** rods on a counting board to represent numbers.

A blank space was left for zero as they had no symbol for it.

Tens and thousands were represented by horizontal lines. Numbers greater than 5 had a vertical line representing 5 above the horizontal lines.

Units and hundreds were represented by vertical lines. Numbers greater than 5 had a horizontal line representing 5 above the vertical lines.

Counting board

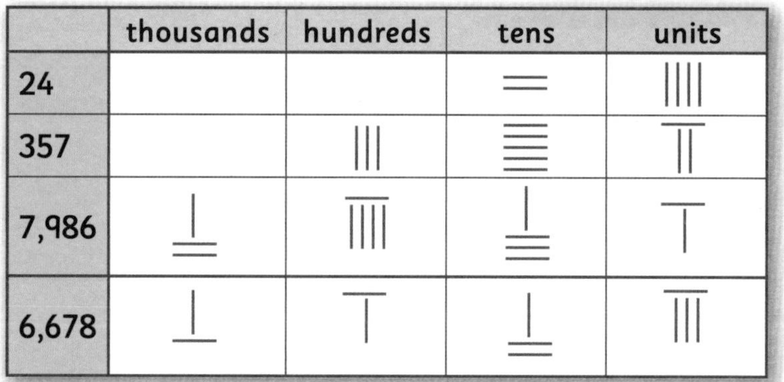

2. Write each number shown.

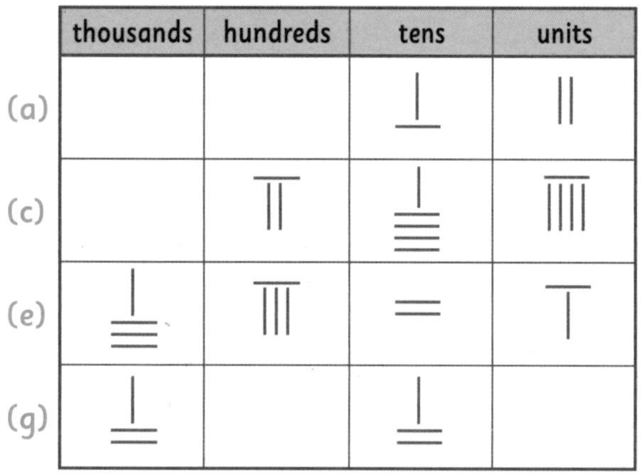

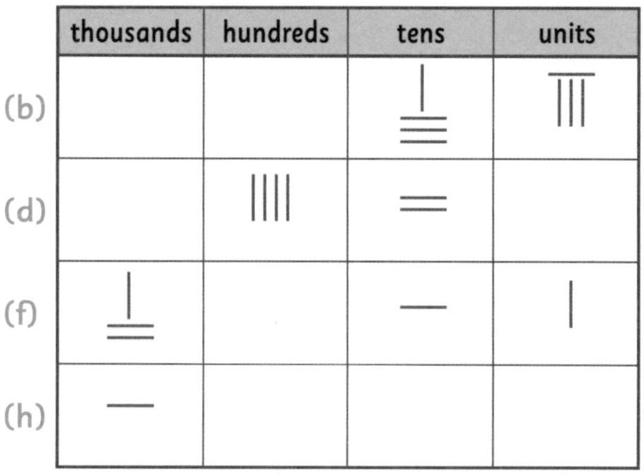

3. Write these numerals on a Chinese counting board. Remember to write the rod numerals in red.
(a) 64 (b) 97 (c) 46 (d) 295 (e) 804 (f) 530 (g) 3,281 (h) 7,093 (i) 4,601

Chapter 3: Addition strategies

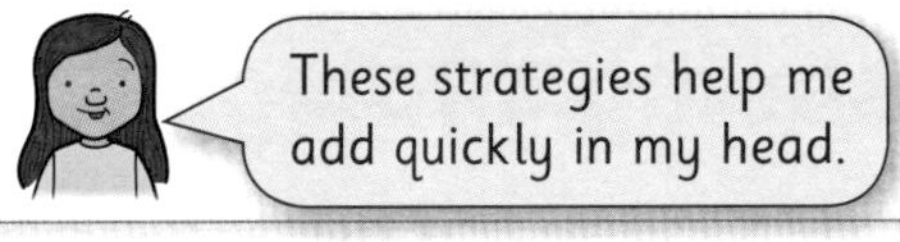

These strategies help me add quickly in my head.

Strategy A:

3,425 + 5,173 = ☆

Step 1: Add the units. → 5 + 3 →

Step 2: Add the tens. → 20 + 70 →

Step 3: Add the hundreds. → 400 + 100 →

Step 4: Add the thousands. → 3,000 + 5,000 →

th	h	t	u
			8
		9	0
	5	0	0
8	0	0	0
8	5	9	8

3,425 + 5,173 = 8,598

1. Now practise Strategy A by doing these.

(a) 1,234 + 3,462
(b) 2,438 + 5,251
(c) 4,237 + 2,642
(d) 3,341 + 5,438
(e) 6,273 + 2,516
(f) 8,245 + 1,634

Strategy B:

3,425 + 5,173 = ☆

Break up the second number into thousands, hundreds, tens and units.

Step 1: 3,425 + 5,000 + 100 + 70 + 3

Step 2: 3,425 + 5,000 = 8,425

Step 3: 8,425 + 100 = 8,525

Step 4: 8,525 + 70 = 8,595

Step 5: 8,595 + 3 = 8,598 → 3,425 + 5,173 = 8,598

I keep the first number in my head and I break the second number into thousands, hundreds, tens and units.

2. Now do these using Strategy B.

(a) 2,356 + 7,422
(b) 8,412 + 1,365
(c) 3,334 + 5,263
(d) 4,241 + 3,518
(e) 6,326 + 3,454
(f) 5,206 + 3,042

3. Solve the following using either Strategy A or B.

(a)

There were 6,243 cars in the red car park at the airport and 2,531 cars in the blue car park. What was the total number of cars? ________

(b) A car sales company sold 3,564 cars in January and 2,433 cars in February. How many cars were sold in total over the two months? ________

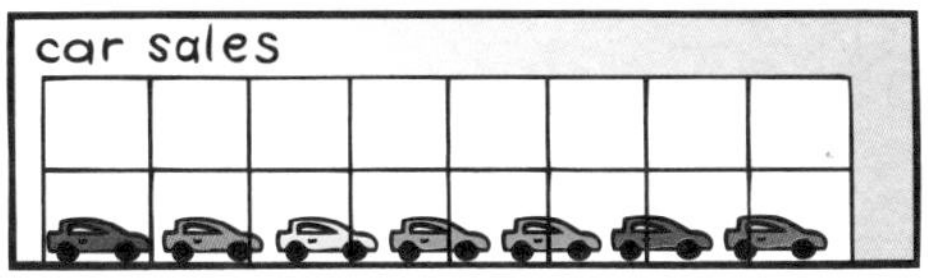

(c)

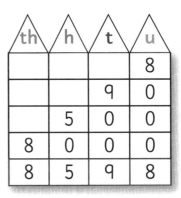

A hardware store sold 5,681 tins of paint in June and 3,260 tins of paint in July. How many tins of paint were sold altogether over the two months? ________

STRAND **Number** **STRAND UNIT/ELEMENT** *Operations*

LANGUAGE *Mental strategy, add, addition, subtract, subtraction, difference, take away, minus, break up, round, rounding, nearest, thousand, estimate, match, fewer, more, sum, zero, grid/table*

Clustering strategy

We use this strategy when a group of numbers cluster around a common number.

A Fashion show attendances:

Mon	Tues	Wed	Thurs
611	623	599	630

All of the numbers are close to 600.
There are 4 numbers.
The total is about 4 × 600 or 2,400.

B Motor show attendances:

Mon	Tues	Wed	Thurs	Fri
1,885	2,641	1,938	2,214	2,000

All of the numbers are close to 2,000.
There are 5 numbers.
The total is about 5 x 2,000 or 10,000.

1. (a) Use the clustering strategy to estimate the answers to the following problems.
(b) Then calculate the correct answers.

Remember to compare the answer to the estimate.

(i) Find the total rainfall for the six months.

Monthly rainfall totals in Castlebar

October	November	December	January	February	March
338mm	369mm	412mm	435mm	389mm	341mm

(ii) Find the total number of bikes sold over the four seasons. Use the clustering strategy to estimate first.

The number of bikes sold on eBay

spring	summer	autumn	winter
6,295	6,473	6,132	5,903

Special numbers strategy

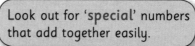

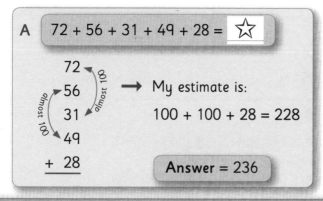

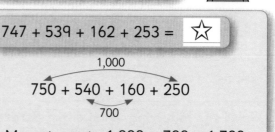

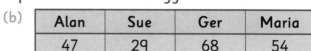

Look out for 'special' numbers that add together easily.

A 72 + 56 + 31 + 49 + 28 = ☆

72
56
31
49
+ 28

(72 + 31: almost 100; 56 + 49: almost 100)

→ My estimate is:
100 + 100 + 28 = 228

Answer = 236

B 747 + 539 + 162 + 253 = ☆

750 + 540 + 160 + 250

(750 + 250: 1,000; 540 + 160: 700)

→ My estimate is: 1,000 + 700 = 1,700

Answer = 1,701

2. Practise the special numbers strategy first before working out the exact answer.

(a) 64 + 41 + 22 + 76
(b) 234 + 228 + 374 + 768
(c) 381 + 518 + 441 + 258
(d) 2,224 + 1,489 + 5,516 + 1,746

3. Find the sum of the ages of these people. Use the special numbers strategy to estimate first.

(a)

Mark	Adam	Michelle	Nina
18	33	41	78

(b)

Alan	Sue	Ger	Maria
47	29	68	54

Mental strategy – Rounding to the nearest 10, 100, 1,000

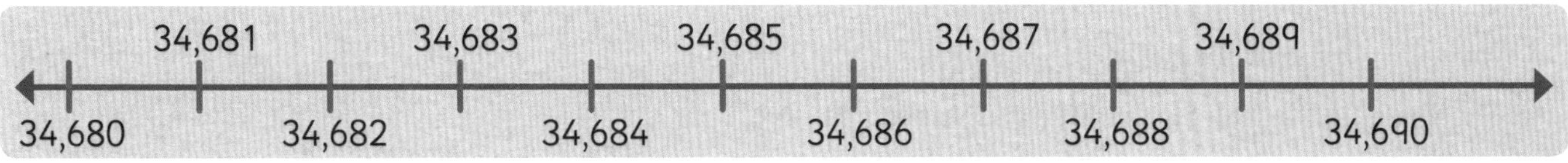

Rounding to the nearest 10:

(i) Box the tens digit. → 3 4, 6 [8] 3

(ii) Look right next door at the units. → 3 4, 6 [8] (3)

(iii) Round up if it's 5 or more, round down if it's 4 or less. → 3 4, 6 8 0

Rounding to the nearest 100:

(i) Box the hundreds digit. → 3 4, [6] 8 3

(ii) Look right next door. → 3 4, [6] (8) 3

(iii) Round up if it's 5 or more, round down if it's 4 or less. → 3 4, 7 0 0

Rounding to the nearest 1,000:

(i) Box the thousands digit. → 3 [4], 6 8 3

(ii) Look right next door. → 3 [4], (6) 8 3

(iii) Round up if it's 5 or more, round down if it's 4 or less. → 3 5, 0 0 0

1. Round these numbers to the nearest 10, 100 and 1,000.

	Number	Nearest 10	Nearest 100	Nearest 1,000
(a)	371			
(b)	586			
(c)	2,495			
(d)	6,812			
(e)	8,981			
(f)	9,134			

	Number	Nearest 10	Nearest 100	Nearest 1,000
(g)	11,499			
(h)	19,687			
(i)	26,581			
(j)	47,237			
(k)	61,755			
(l)	85,108			

2. Round the capacity of each of these stadia in Ireland.

	Stadium	Capacity	Nearest 10	Nearest 100	Nearest 1,000
(a)	Páirc Uí Chaoimh	43,551			
(b)	Fitzgerald Stadium	43,188			
(c)	Dr Hyde Park	18,895			
(d)	Pearse Stadium	26,197			
(e)	Cusack Park	14,864			
(f)	Markievicz Park	18,558			
(g)	Tallaght Stadium	5,947			
(h)	Croke Park	82,293			
(i)	Aviva Stadium	51,699			

Note: These are not the exact capacities.

Chapter 4: Addition and subtraction

Do the following. Match the answers to the correct letters. Write the words to complete the poem.

a = 2,607
b = 3,432
c = 3,991
d = 7,698
e = 5,532
g = 8,661
h = 4,978
i = 3,545
k = 2,657
l = 7,464
m = 5,485
n = 44
o = 1,019
p = 4,823
r = 3,964
s = 2,218
t = 3,705
u = 3,983
w = 876

My Teacher Ate My Homework

My teacher ate my homework
which I thought was rather A__________.
He sniffed at it and B__________
with an approving sort of nod.

He took a little C__________,
it's unusual, but true –
then had a somewhat larger bite
and gave a thoughtful D__________.

I think he must have liked it,
for he really went to E__________.
He gobbled it with gusto,
and he wolfed the whole thing down.

He licked off all his fingers,
gave a F__________, and said,
"You G__________".
I guess that's how they grade you
when you're in a H__________ class.

Kenn Nesbitt

A

673 + 346 = ____ ☐	3,427 + 4,271 = ____ ☐	3,460 + 4,238 = 7,698 d

B

648 + (322 + 1,248) = ____ ☐
(1,274 + 3,642) + 569 = ____ ☐
(693 + 384) + 2,468 = ____ ☐
2,453 + (3,716 + 1,295) = ____ ☐
(1,639 + 47) + 3,846 = ____ ☐
5,064 + (93 + 2,541) = ____ ☐

C

83 − 39 = ____ ☐	4,286 − 741 = ____ ☐	6,348 − 2,916 = ____ ☐
8,642 − 5,210 = ____ ☐	8,652 − 1,188 = ____ ☐	7,511 − 1,979 = ____ ☐

D

(6,481 – 2,126) – 364 = ____ ☐
5,277 + 325 – 624 = ____ ☐
(9,822 – 168) – 4,122 = ____ ☐
(1,024 – 56) – 92 = ____ ☐

E

(5,234 + 1,685) – 3,214 = ____ ☐
(3,569 + 3,641) – 6,191 = ____ ☐
(3,528 + 163) – 2,815 = ____ ☐
(6,821 – 3,799) – 2,978 = ____ ☐

F

(6,588 – 2,498) – 658 = ____ ☐
(3,261 + 5,412) – 4,690 = ____ ☐
(6,581 – 2,965) + 348 = ____ ☐
(1,366 + 2,578) + 879 = ____ ☐

G

(3,258 + 2,661) – 1,096 = ____ ☐
(657 – 96) + 2,046 = ____ ☐
(6,541 – 1,877) – 2,446 = ____ ☐
(2,153 + 3,860) – 3,795 = ____ ☐

H

Find the sum of 368 + 742 + 1,034 + 1,847. ____ ☐
Find the sum of 564 and 455. ____ ☐
Find the difference between 6,421 and 5,402. ____ ☐
How much less than 5,021 is 2,364? ____ ☐
What must be added to 398 to give 3,943? ____ ☐
How much greater is 1,038 than 994? ____ ☐
From the sum of 2,351 and 6,842, take 532. ____ ☐

STRAND Number **STRAND UNIT/ELEMENT** *Operations – Addition, Subtraction*
LANGUAGE *Add, subtract, addition, subtraction, greater/less than, plus, minus, take away, match, correct letters/answers, regroup, rename, amounts, auction, strategy, zero (0), units, tens, hundreds, thousands, opposite, statistics*

Addition to 99,999

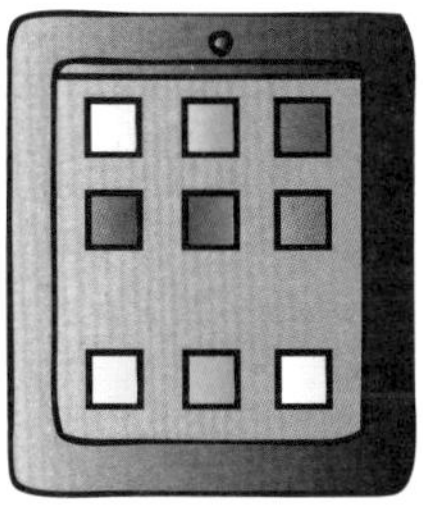

A tablet computer company sold 24,763 tablets last year and 36,598 this year. What is the total number of tablets sold over the two years?

24,763 + 36,598 = ☆

Estimate: 25,000 + 37,000 = 62,000

START

Step 1
Add the units:
3 + 8 = 11
Regroup the units as 1 ten + 1 unit. Write the 1 ten in the tens house.

Step 2
Add the tens:
6 + 9 + 1 = 16
Regroup 16 tens as 1 hundred and 6 tens.
Write the 1 hundred in the hundreds house.

Step 3
Add the hundreds:
7 + 5 + 1 = 13
Regroup the 13 hundreds as 1 thousand and 3 hundreds. Write the 1 thousand in the thousands house.

Step 4
Add the thousands:
4 + 6 + 1 = 11
Regroup the 11 thousands as 1 ten thousand + 1 thousand.
Write the 1 ten thousand in the ten thousands house.

Step 5
Add the ten thousands:
2 + 3 + 1 = 6

	tth	th	h	t	u
	2	4	7	6	3
+	3 ₁	6 ₁	5 ₁	9 ₁	8
	6	1	3	6	1

24,763 + 36,598 = 61,361

1. (a) 17,382 + 29,647 (b) 35,169 + 29,647 (c) 46,902 + 28,639 (d) 29,604 + 35,809 (e) 62,891 + 27,046

2. (a) 13,618 + 24,319 + 7,602 (b) 34,083 + 27,631 + 26,843 (c) 47,548 + 13,781 + 24,612 (d) 23,681 + 21,232 + 31,445 (e) 34,620 + 22,738 + 13,276

3. The following paintings were sold at an art auction for the amounts shown:

The Fiddler €46,206

The Joker €88,123

Man V €4,672

Angel €12,835

Quick Start €689

Colours €35,132

(a) Find the total cost of The Fiddler and Colours. €________

(b) Find the total cost of Man V, Angel and The Fiddler. €________

(c) Find the sum of the sale amounts of Colours, The Fiddler and Quick Start. €________

(d) Which two paintings together cost exactly €92,795? ________

(e) Which three paintings together cost €52,639? ________

(f) How much would you spend if you bought Angel, Man V, Colours and Quick Start? €________

Mental strategies – Subtraction

Strategy A:
Break up the second number.

(a) 348 – 36 = ☆

348 – 30 – 6
(348 – 30) – 6
318 – 6 = 312

(b) 564 – 321 = ☆

564 – 300 – 20 – 1
(564 – 300) – 20 – 1
(264 – 20) – 1
244 – 1 = 243

These strategies help me subtract easily and quickly in my head!

1. Now practise Strategy A by doing these mentally.

(a) 154 – 23	(b) 476 – 143	(c) 687 – 235	(d) 947 – 425
(e) 776 – 345	(f) 864 – 343	(g) 999 – 333	(h) 666 – 444

Strategy B:
Count up like a shopkeeper. Start with the smaller number and count up.

(a) 176 – 49 = ☆

49 to 50 → 1
50 to 100 → 50
100 to 170 → 70
170 to 176 → + 6
Answer 127

(b) 638 – 264 = ☆

264 to 270 → 6
270 to 300 → 30
300 to 600 → 300
600 to 638 → + 38
Answer 374

(c) 945 – 387 = ☆

387 to 390 → 3
390 to 400 → 10
400 to 900 → 500
900 to 945 → + 45
Answer 558

2. Now practise Strategy B by doing these mentally.

(a) 256 – 39	(b) 481 – 63	(c) 246 – 123	(d) 812 – 37
(e) 742 – 368	(f) 912 – 265	(g) 673 – 246	(h) 503 – 29

Strategy C:
Make the second number into groups of ten.

(a)

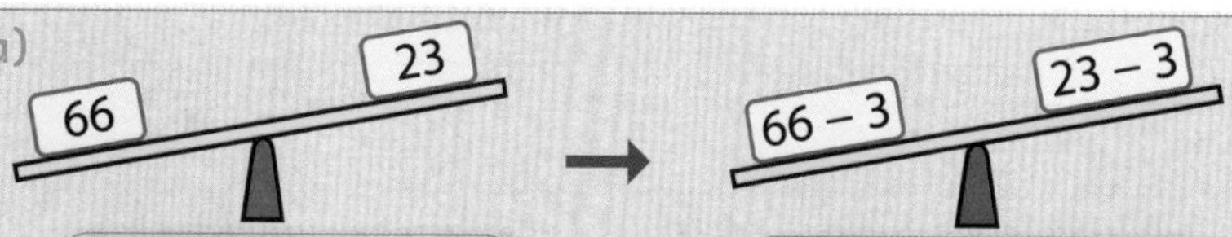

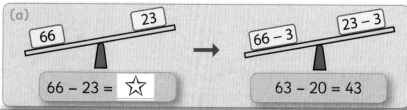

66 – 23 = ☆ 63 – 20 = 43

(b) 91 – 38 = ☆

(91 + 2) – (38 + 2) = ☆
93 – 40 = 53

3. Now practise Strategy C by doing these mentally.

(a) 46 – 18 (b) 68 – 31 (c) 75 – 42 (d) 57 – 22 (e) 88 – 59

4. Solve these problems using one of the strategies above.

(a) Ciara and Úna went rock climbing. Ciara climbed 258m and Úna climbed 33m. Find the difference between the two heights reached. ________ m

(b)

Denis swam 325 metres and Mary swam 212 metres. How many fewer metres did Mary swim? ________ m

Subtraction

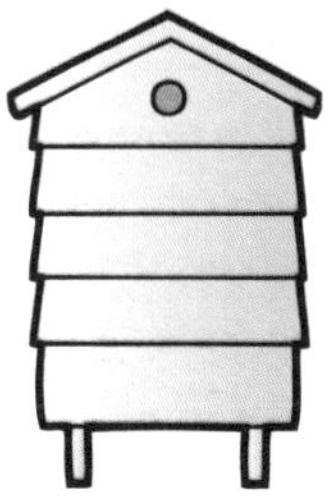

There are 42,516 worker bees and 23,729 drones in a beehive.
How many fewer drones are there than worker bees?

42,516 – 23,729 = ☆

Estimate: 43,000 – 24,000 = 19,000

Step 1
Rename 1 ten as 10 units.
Subtract the units:
16 – 9 = 7 units

Step 2
Rename 1 hundred as 10 tens.
Subtract the tens:
10 – 2 = 8 tens

Step 3
Rename 1 thousand as 10 hundreds.
Subtract the hundreds:
14 – 7 = 7 hundreds

Step 4
Rename 1 ten thousand as 10 thousands.
Subtract the thousands:
11 – 3 = 8 thousands

Step 5
Subtract the ten thousands:
3 – 2 = 1 ten thousand

	tth	th	h	t	u
	3	①1	①4	①0	①6
	~~4~~	~~2~~	~~5~~	~~1~~	~~6~~
–	2	3	7	2	9
	1	8	7	8	7

42,516 – 23,729 = 18,787

START

1. Subtract. Estimate first! You may use your calculator to check the answers.

(a) 68,594 – 23,182

(b) 69,581 – 36,293

(c) 81,346 – 45,687

(d) 74,126 – 56,824

(e) 56,318 – 18,859

2. (a) 53,286 – 17,538 (b) 65,119 – 27,325 (c) 71,223 – 6,547

(d) 39,116 – 462 (e) 92,615 – 27,409 (f) 43,651 – 24,362

3. This table shows the number of fish caught by a fish company over five months.

Month	Number of fish
Jan	8,762
Feb	29,560
Mar	33,765
Apr	68,912
May	52,680

(a) What is the difference between the number of fish caught in February and in April? ______

(b) How many fewer fish were caught in January than in May? ______

(c) Find the difference between the number of fish caught in April and May. ______

(d) How many fish must be added to the number caught in March to have the same number as were caught in May? ______

(e) What is the difference between the number of fish caught in May and the sum of the fish caught in January and March? ______

Challenge

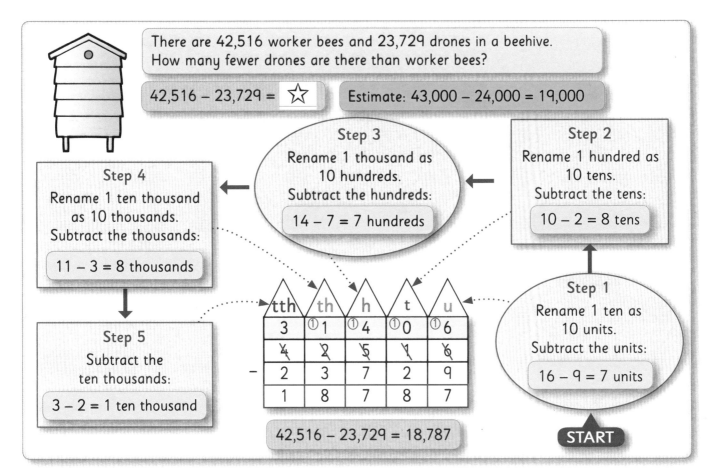

Subtract the total number of fish caught in May and January from the total number of fish caught in April and February. ______

Subtraction – Overcoming the zeros

Tina wants to raise €50,000 for her favourite charity. She raised €17,682 in an adventure race. How much has she still to raise?

€50,000 – €17,682 = ☆

Estimate: €50,000 – €18,000 = €32,000

Step 1
Rename 1 ten thousand as 10 thousands:
4tth + 10th + 0h + 0t + 0u

Step 2
Rename 1 thousand as 10 hundreds:
4tth + 9th + 10h + 0t + 0u

Step 3
Rename 1 hundred as 10 tens:
4tth + 9th + 9h + 10t + 0u

Step 4
Rename 1 ten as 10 units:
4tth + 9th + 9h + 9t + 10u

Step 5
Now I can subtract!

	tth	th	h	t	u
	4	9 10	9 10	9 10	10
€	~~5~~	~~0~~	~~0~~	~~0~~	~~0~~
– €	1	7	6	8	2
	3	2	3	1	8

Short way

```
  4 9  9 9 1
  5 0, 0 0 0
– 1 7, 6 8 2
  3 2, 3 1 8
```

1. This table represents the population of 'precious' towns. Complete it. Estimate first!

Town	Diamond	Ruby	Sapphire	Emerald	Topaz
Total population	20,000	40,000	50,000	90,000	70,000
Males	8,543	23,386			34,697
Females			29,215	41,364	

Subtraction is the opposite of addition! When we subtract, we can always check by adding the answer to the number we subtracted to find the top line!

	tth	th	h	t	u
	7	4	2	5	2
–	4	5	7	8	9
	2	8	4	6	3

Adding these two numbers gives us the top number.

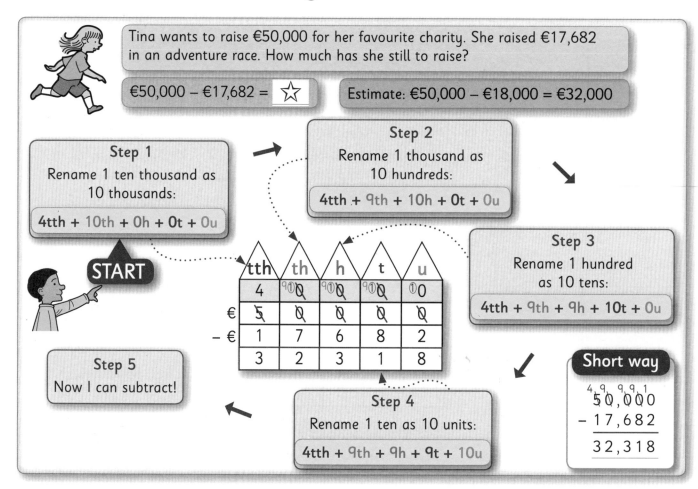

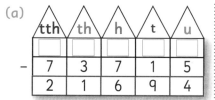

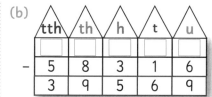

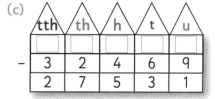

2. Now work out the missing top line in each of these.

(a)

	tth	th	h	t	u
	☐	☐	☐	☐	☐
–	7	3	7	1	5
	2	1	6	9	4

(b)

	tth	th	h	t	u
	☐	☐	☐	☐	☐
–	5	8	3	1	6
	3	9	5	6	9

(c)

	tth	th	h	t	u
	☐	☐	☐	☐	☐
–	3	2	4	6	9
	2	7	5	3	1

Use your calculator to check if your answers are correct.

Challenge

There were 81,000 football fans at the Kerry v Dublin All-Ireland final in Croke Park. 43,216 were Dublin supporters. 7,428 were neutral. How many Kerry supporters were at the All-Ireland final? ______

People and society – Central Statistics Office

Study this table and answer the questions below.

Number of marriages, births and deaths

Year	Number of marriages	Number of births	Number of deaths
1950	16,018	63,565	37,741
1970	20,778	64,382	33,686
1990	17,838	53,044	31,370
2010	20,594	75,174	27,961

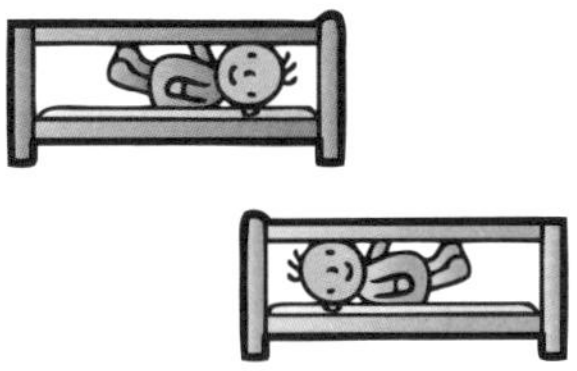

1. Which year had the greatest number of marriages?
2. Which year had the fewest number of births?
3. Which year had the most deaths?
4. Put the years in order starting with the one with the most amount of (a) deaths; (b) births.
5. Put the years in order starting with the one with the least amount of (a) marriages; (b) deaths.
6. Round the number of marriages for each year to the nearest ten.
7. Round the number of births for each year to the nearest thousand.
8. Round the number of deaths for each year to the nearest hundred.
9. Find the difference between the number of births and the number of deaths in 1950.
10. Find the total sum of marriages for the four years.
11. What must be added to the number of deaths in 2010 to equal the number of births?
12. How many fewer deaths were there than births in 1970?
13. What is the difference between the most number of marriages and the least number of marriages shown in the table?
14. What is the difference between the total number of marriages for 1950 and 1970 together, and the total for 1990 and 2010 together?
15. Add the difference between the number of births in 1950 and 1970 to the difference between the number of deaths in the same years.
16. Add the sum of marriages and births to the number of deaths in 1990.
17. If 31,678 boys were born in 1970, how many girls were born that year?
18. If 18,963 females died in 1950, how many males died that year?

Challenge Subtract the total number of marriages in 1950, 1970 and 1990 from the number of births in 2010. ______

Chapter 5: Data 1 – Averages

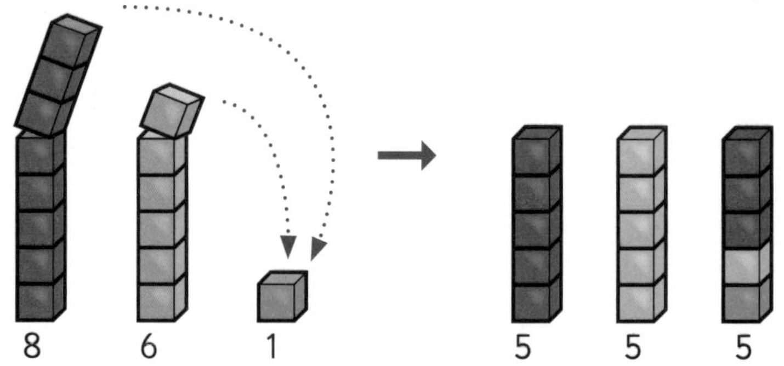

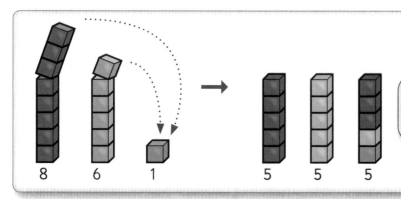

The average of 1, 6 and 8 is 5. We found the average by making the three stacks of cubes into equal stacks of five cubes.

Calculating averages

Calculate the average pocket money of these four children:

Step 1: Find the total value of money:

€3 + €6 + €4 + €7 = €20

Step 2: Divide the total by the number of children:

€20 ÷ 4 = €5

→ The average pocket money is €5.

1. Answer true or false.

(a) Each of the four children gets weekly pocket money of €5. ___________

(b) Two children get more than the average pocket money each week. ___________

(c) Two children get exactly the average pocket money each week. ___________

(d) We can say that all the children get **about** €5 pocket money a week. ___________

2. This bar chart shows how many books Cara read over a few months.

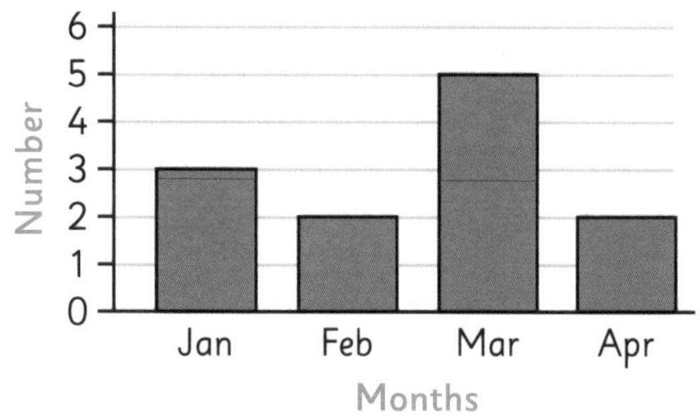

(a) How many books did she read in March?

(b) How many books did she read altogether?

(c) How many months are represented on the chart?

(d) What is the average number of books read per month?

(e) In which month did she read more than the average number of books?

(f) In which months did she read less than the average number of books?

3. What is the average age of each group?

(a)

(b)

(c)

Challenge 1

What is the average cost of a book? € ___________

Challenge 2

The average of four numbers is 6. What is the total of the four numbers? ___________

STRAND **Data** STRAND UNIT/ELEMENT *Representing and interpreting data*

LANGUAGE *Average, total, divide, true, false, about, represented, altogether, above/below, estimate, most/least, middle, identical*

Averages

The average lies somewhere around the middle!

1. The children in a karate class were weighed at the beginning of a training session.

Tom	Hannah	Rose	Leo	Cian	Alex	Lily	Ryan

41kg	40kg	35kg	46kg	42kg	39kg	40kg	37kg

(a) How many children are there in the karate class?

(b) Which child weighed the (i) most; (ii) least?

(c) What do you think the average weight is? (Estimate!)

(d) Calculate the average weight.

(e) Which two children weigh exactly the average weight?

(f) Name the children who are (i) above; (ii) below the average weight.

2. Olivia and her family ate dinner at Ben's Bistro. Each family member was asked to give the restaurant a score out of 10 to rate their meals. Here are their scores:

Olivia	8	Clara	5
Dad	6	Daisy	7
Robbie	7	Mam	9

(a) Who was (i) most; (ii) least satisfied with their meal?

(b) Estimate the average score given.

(c) Calculate the average score given.

(d) Who gave (i) an average; (ii) an above average; (iii) a below average score?

Discuss possible reasons for the family giving such different scores.

3. Calculate the average amount of money spent daily by each child over the three days.

(a) **Fiona**

Fri	Sat	Sun
€3·40	€6·25	€4·75

(b) **Max**

Fri	Sat	Sun
€6·90	€4·80	€6·30

(c) **Steve**

Fri	Sat	Sun
€4·10	€5·80	€5·70

4. Calculate the average daily temperature in each city over the week.

	City	M	T	W	T	F	S	S
(a)	Cork	17°C	16°C	21°C	19°C	16°C	18°C	19°C
(b)	New York	24°C	27°C	28°C	28°C	25°C	22°C	28°C
(c)	Reykjavík	9°C	11°C	14°C	8°C	10°C	13°C	12°C
(d)	Beijing	31°C	34°C	29°C	33°C	34°C	30°C	33°C
(e)	Madrid	22°C	28°C	26°C	23°C	29°C	31°C	30°C

More averages

1. What is the average number of letters in each group of names?

(a)

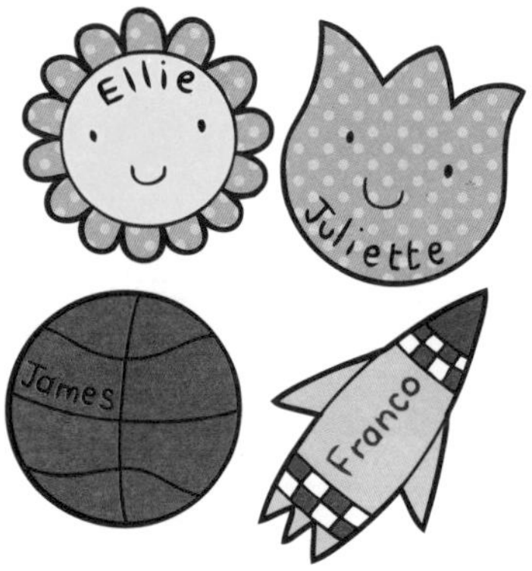

(b)

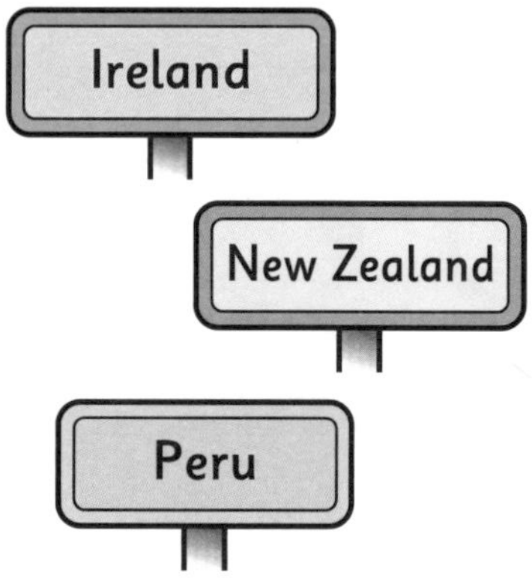

(c)

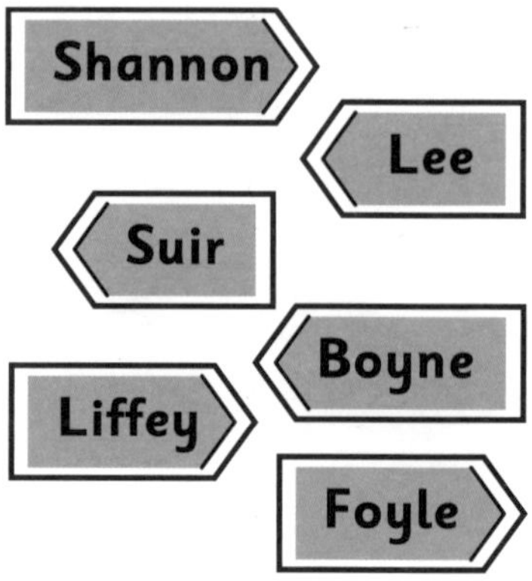

2. Use your calculator to find the average of each of the following groups.

(a) 349 | 483 (b) 6m 25cm | 7m 43cm | 5m 7cm (c) €3,264 | €4,039 | €480

(d) 3·42kg | 6·39kg | 5·25kg (e) 1,372 | 2,463 | 899 | 1,708 | 1,698

3. (a) The average of three numbers is 8. What is the sum of the three numbers? ______

(b) The average of five numbers is 11. What is the sum of the five numbers? ______

(c) The average of eight numbers is 25. What is the sum of the eight numbers? ______

4. (a) The average of these four numbers is 7. What is the missing number?

8 | 5 | ☐ | 7

(b) The average of these five numbers is 11. What is the missing number?

13 | ☐ | 6 | 12 | 10

(c) The average of these three numbers is 24. What is the missing number?

☐ | 31 | 21

(d) The average of these six numbers is 30. What is the missing number?

28 | 42 | 25 | 29 | 27 | ☐

(e) The average of four numbers is 15. Two of the numbers are identical, what are they?

☐ | 12 | 14 | ☐

(f) The average of five numbers is 23. The missing numbers are identical, what are they?

☐ | 16 | ☐ | ☐ | 21

Challenge 1

The average of four numbers was 16. When one number was removed, the average of the remaining three numbers was 14. What number was removed? ______

Challenge 2

The top three goal scorers on the school soccer panel scored an average of seven goals. The remaining 12 players scored an average of two goals.

(a) How many goals were scored in total? ______

(b) What was the average number of goals scored by the whole panel? ______

Chapter 6: Data 2 – Charts and graphs

1. Study the chart. Choose the correct answer to make each sentence true. Write.

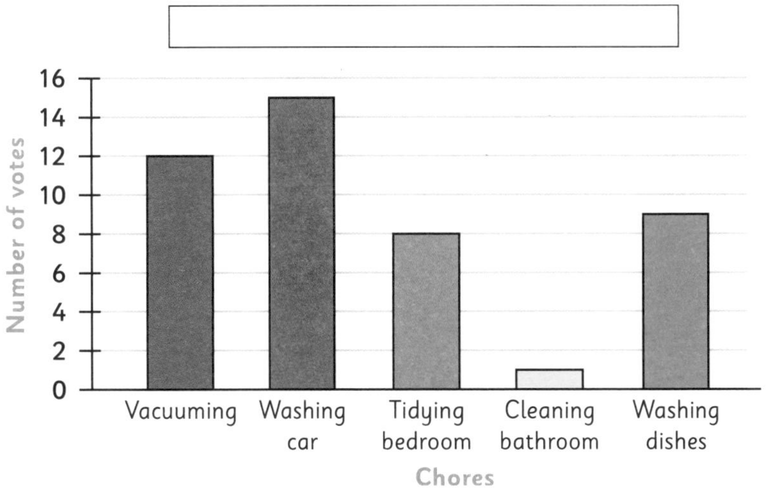

(a) This is a bar-line graph, bar chart, pictogram, pie chart.

(b) The title of the chart is Chores, Favourite chores, Number of votes.

(c) The bars on the chart are vertical, horizontal.

(d) The scale of the chart is 1 : 1, 1 : 2, 1 : 5, 1 : 10, 1 : 100.

2. Answer these questions about the bar chart above.

(a) Which chore was (i) most popular; (ii) least popular? (i) ____________; (ii) ____________

(b) How many children prefer washing a car to washing dishes? ________

(c) How many children altogether voted in the survey? ________

(d) How many options did the children have to choose from in the survey? ________

(e) What was the average number of votes given to each chore? ________

(f) How many votes more than the average did vacuuming get? ________

3. The children in Brookline Athletic Club were asked to vote for their favourite athletic activity. The table below shows the results. Represent this data on a bar-line graph.

Activity	Votes
sprinting	25
hurdling	15
long jump	20
relay	30
high jump	25

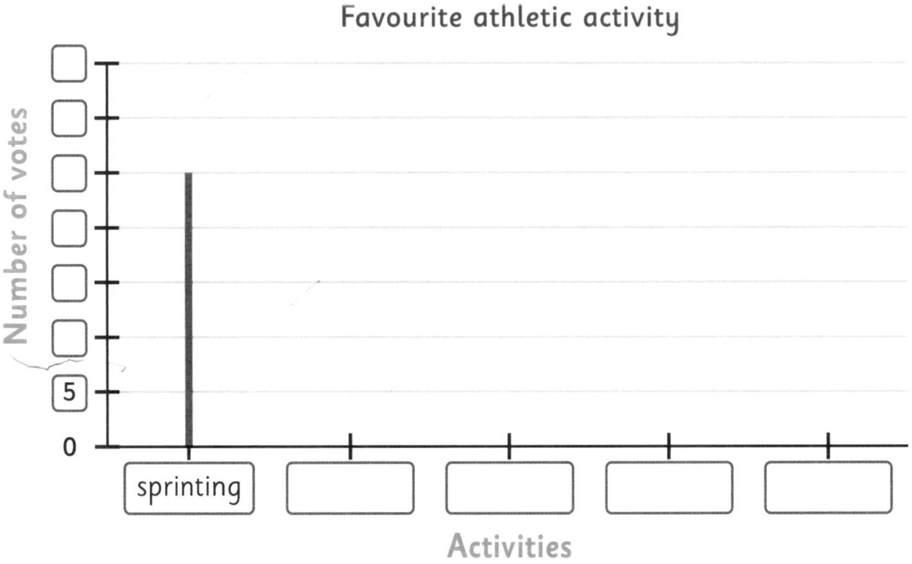

Data – Pictograms and tallies

1. **Last Monday, Ms Duffy asked the children in her class to keep a record of the number of hours they slept that night. Here are the results they gave on Tuesday morning.**

10	11	12	9	10	9	12	8	9	10	11	10	9	10	12	10	11
8	7	10	10	9	11	11	10	10	12	10	11	10	10	10	8	10

(a) Represent the data on the tally sheet.

(b) Which time was recorded most often?

(c) What was the total number of hours spent sleeping by all the children?

(d) What was the average number of hours spent sleeping by the children on Monday night?

(e) Represent the above information on a bar chart.

(f) If three children were absent on Tuesday, how many children are in the class?

Time spent sleeping		
7 hours		
8 hours		
9 hours	卌	5
10 hours		
11 hours		
12 hours		

2. **All the 5th Class children in Blackwater Primary School were asked to name their shoe size. This pictogram shows the results.**

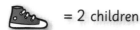

 = 2 children

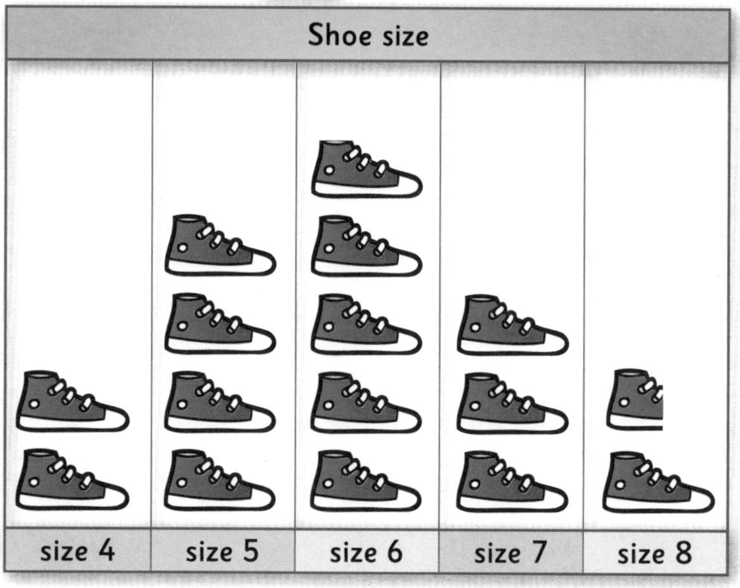

(a) Which shoe size is (i) most common; (ii) least common?

(b) How many children wear size 8 shoes?

(c) How many children took part in the survey?

(d) Represent the results on a tally sheet.

(e) Represent the results on a bar-line graph.

(f) If the average shoe size of five friends is size 7, calculate the missing shoe size.

7	8	5		9

Challenge

Find out the shoe sizes worn by the children in your class.

(a) Represent this information on a tally sheet.

(b) Represent this data on a bar-line graph.

Data – Multiple bar charts

1. **This is a multiple bar chart. It shows the number of baby boys and girls born in North Valley Hospital each day last weekend (including Friday).**

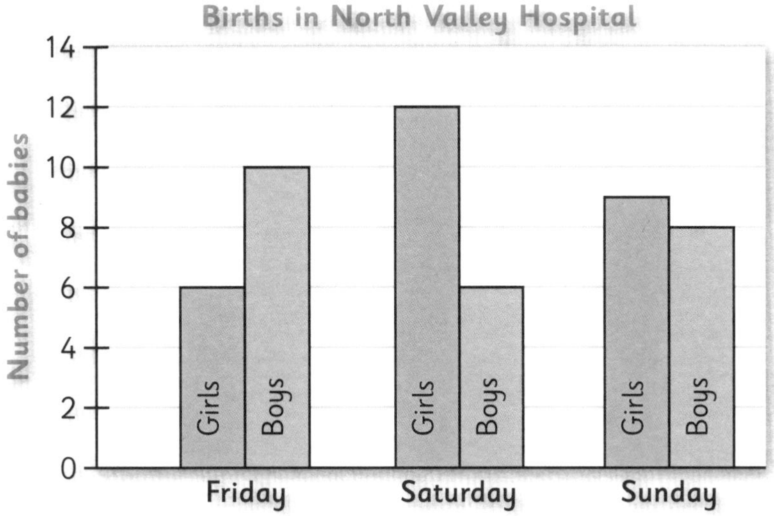

(a) Represent the data on this results table.

Day	Girls	Boys	Total
Fri	6		
Sat			
Sun			

(b) How many (i) girls; (ii) boys were born on Friday?

(c) What was the average number of babies born on Friday?

(d) How many (i) girls; (ii) boys were born over the whole weekend?

(e) How many babies in total were born over the weekend?

(f) On average, how many babies were born in the hospital each day over the weekend?

---

2. **Joe was asked to sell raffle tickets for his local club. The tally below shows his ticket sales over two weeks.**

Ticket sales			
Week 1		Week 2	
Mon	卌 III	Mon	卌 卌 II
Tues	卌 IIII	Tues	卌 II
Wed	卌 卌 I	Wed	卌
Thur	卌	Thur	III
Fri	卌 卌 II	Fri	卌 III

(a) Draw and complete this multiple bar chart in your copybook, showing Joe's ticket sales over the two weeks.

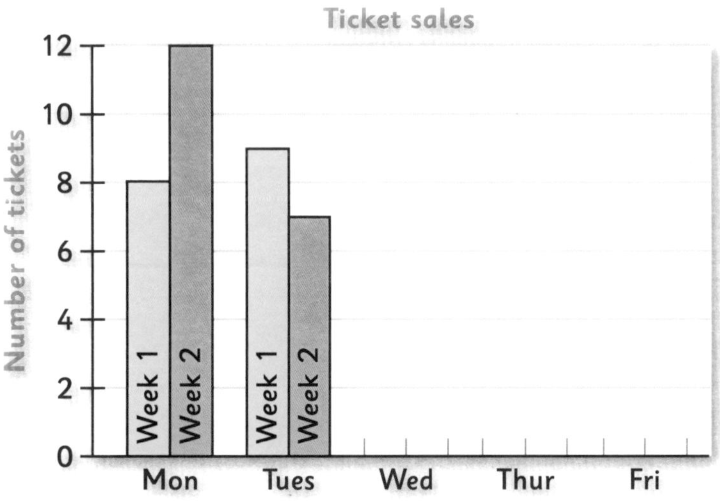

(b) How many tickets did Joe sell in (i) week 1; (ii) week 2?

(c) What was the daily average number of tickets sold in week 1?

(d) What was the average number of tickets sold on (i) Mondays; (ii) Thursdays?

(e) What was Joe's total ticket sales over the two weeks?

(f) What was the average daily number of tickets sold over the two weeks?

Data – More multiple bar charts

1. Jack and Rosie were asked to keep a record of how long they spent doing homework each evening for four days. The data collected is shown on the results table below.

	Jack	Rosie
Monday	40 mins	30 mins
Tuesday	70 mins	40 mins
Wednesday	55 mins	65 mins
Thursday	35 mins	25 mins

(a) Represent the data on a multiple bar chart.

(b) How long did Jack spend on homework altogether in (i) minutes; (ii) hours and minutes?

(c) What was the average time Jack spent on homework over the four evenings?

(d) How long did Rosie spend on homework altogether in (i) minutes; (ii) hours and minutes?

(e) What was the average time spent by Rosie on homework over the four evenings?

2. Serena and Will kept track of the amount of time they spent at tennis practice over four weeks. The pictogram below shows the data they collected.

◯ = 2 hours

	Tennis practice	
	Serena	Will
Week 1	◯◯◯	◯◯◯◯
Week 2	◯◯◯◯◖	◯◯◯◯◖
Week 3	◯◯◯◯◖	◯◯◖
Week 4	◯◯◯◯◯◯	◯◯◯◯◯

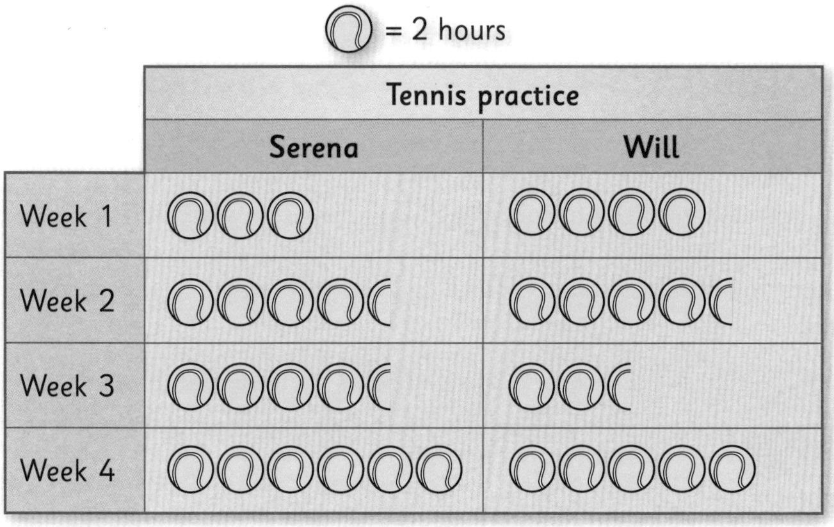

(a) Write the data onto a results table (see the table in question 1 above for guidance).

(b) Represent the data on a multiple bar chart.

(c) What was the weekly average time spent on tennis practice by Serena?

(d) What was the weekly average time spent on tennis practice by Will?

3. Barry's Burger Bar sells beefburgers and turkey burgers. The tally below shows the sales for both types of burger over four days.

	BURGER SALES	
	Beefburgers	Turkey burgers
Thursday	卌 卌 卌 I	卌 卌
Friday	卌 卌 III	卌 卌 I
Saturday	卌 卌 卌 卌 I	卌 卌 卌 II
Sunday	卌 卌 卌 III	卌 卌 IIII

(a) Represent the data on a multiple bar chart.

(b) What was the average number of burgers sold on Friday?

(c) What was the average number of turkey burgers sold over the four days?

(d) What was the total number of burgers sold over the four days?

(e) What was the average number of burgers sold over the four days?

A quick look back 2

LOOK BACK

1. Ring the digit that is in the hundreds place:

   6 6, 6 6 6

2. Write the number that is 2,000 greater than 63,587. ________

3. Make the largest number possible using all five digits:

   3 7 4 1 2 ________

4. Make the smallest number possible using all five digits:

   5 4 8 9 1 ________

5. Round 7,168 to the nearest (a) ten and (b) hundred.

   (a) ________ (b) ________

6. Gaelic Park has a capacity of 13,594. Round this to the nearest thousand.

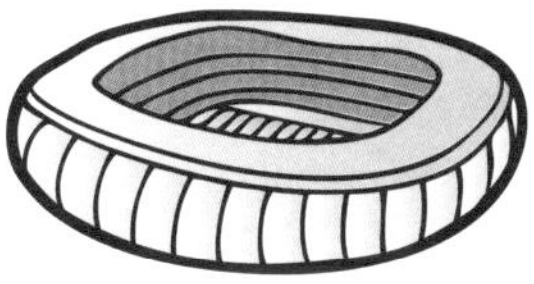

   ____

7. 

   The owner of a thoroughbred colt expected to get €74,500 for him. She sold him for €63,000. This was

   € ________ less than expected.

8. 645 – 329 = ________

9. Peter wrote down the number 573 instead of 357. What was the difference between what he wrote and the correct number?

   ____

10. 

   What is the average of these three amounts of money?

   € ________

11. The average of three numbers is 30. Two of the numbers are 25 and 45.

   The third number is ________ .

12. There are 3,508 males and 3,460 females living in Kilcarrig. How many people live there in total?

   ____

13. Write the number that is 5 less than 60,000. ________

14. Write the number that is 8 more than 39,995. ________

15. The temperature in Cork at 2pm on three consecutive days one summer was 27°C, 29°C and 25°C. What was the average temperature over the three days?

   ________ °C

16. Use the mental strategy of making the second number into 10s only to do this.

   89 – 27 = ☆

   Subtract 7 from each number first.

   (89 – 7) = ________ (27 – 7) = ________

   Answer: ________

17. Use the shopkeeper method to find what is left from €9·00 when I spend €4·70. € ________

18. What must be added to 89,990 to make 90,000? ________

19. The average cost of four items is €12. Three of the items cost €11, €14 and €16. What is the cost of the fourth item?

   € ________

20. Use a mental strategy to complete this:

   492 – 63 = ________

Chapter 7: Multiplication 1

Complete the following. Check your answers using your calculator.

1. (a) 342 × 2 = ______ (b) 453 × 3 = ______ (c) 137 × 5 = ______ (d) 274 × 4 = ______

2. (a) 617 × 5 = ______ (b) 528 × 6 = ______ (c) 736 × 7 = ______ (d) 925 × 8 = ______

3. (a) 58 × 10 = ______ (b) 60 × 10 = ______ (c) 70 × 10 = ______ (d) 49 × 10 = ______

4. (a) 125 × 10 = ______ (b) 246 × 10 = ______ (c) 380 × 10 = ______ (d) 472 × 10 = ______

5. (a) 15 × 20 = ______ (b) 32 × 30 = ______ (c) 134 × 20 = ______ (d) 270 × 30 = ______

When we multiply by 10, we move each digit one place to the left.

27 × 10 = ☆

	th	h	t	u
			2	7
×			1	0
		2	7	0

27 × 10 = 270

270 × 10 = 2,700

	th	h	t	u
		2	7	0
×			1	0
	2	7	0	0

Now try these.

6. (a) 43 × 10 = ______ (b) 76 × 10 = ______ (c) 84 × 10 = ______ (d) 89 × 10 = ______

7. (a) 123 × 10 = ______ (b) 247 × 10 = ______ (c) 356 × 10 = ______ (d) 573 × 10 = ______

8. (a) 1,372 × 10 = ______ (b) 3,578 × 10 = ______ (c) 4,579 × 10 = ______ (d) 6,879 × 10 = ______

A 36 × 20 = ☆

h	t	u
	3	6
3	6	0

36 × 10 = 360
360 × 2 = 720

36 × 20 = 720

B 238 × 30 = ☆

th	h	t	u
	2	3	8
2	3	8	0

238 × 10 = 2,380
2,380 × 3 = 7,140

238 × 30 = 7,140

Now try these using the strategy above.

9. (a) 27 × 20 = ______ (b) 48 × 20 = ______ (c) 73 × 20 = ______ (d) 34 × 30 = ______

10. (a) 135 × 20 = ______ (b) 167 × 20 = ______ (c) 309 × 30 = ______ (d) 512 × 40 = ______

11. (a) 265 × 40 = ______ (b) 316 × 30 = ______ (c) 427 × 50 = ______ (d) 251 × 60 = ______

Maths Fact On average, 650 people are mauled or killed each year by big wild cats. How many people, on average, have been mauled or killed by big cats over the past 30 years? ______

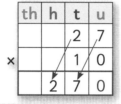

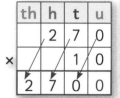

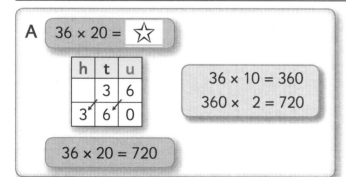

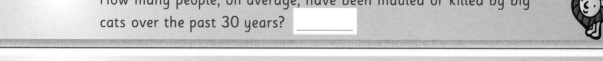

Challenge Using a strategy, solve these:

(a) 24 × 100 = ______ (b) 38 × 100 = ______ (c) 26 × 200 = ______ (d) 35 × 300 = ______

STRAND Number **STRAND UNIT/ELEMENT** *Operations*

LANGUAGE *Multiply, calculator, estimate, solve, strategy, addition/multiplication, sentence, long multiplication, multiples, thousands, hundreds, tens, units, money, euro, cent*

Multiplication – Big numbers

A farmer in Kerry has 328 sheep. A farmer in Australia has 14 times this number of sheep. How many sheep has the Australian farmer?

328 × 14 = ☆

Estimate: 300 × 10 = 3,000

Method A: You could add 328 + 328 + 328… 14 times. Is this a good method?

Method B:

You could multiply in groups and add the answers.

→ 328 × 5 = 1,640
328 × 5 = 1,640
328 × 4 = 1,312
328 × 14 = 4,592

Method C:

You could multiply by 10 and add this to 4 times the number.

→ 328 × 10 = 3,280
328 × 4 = 1,312
328 × 14 = 4,592

1. Use Method B above to solve these.

(a) Make 267 fourteen times bigger.
(b) Make 438 sixteen times bigger.
(c) Make 518 seventeen times bigger.
(d) Make 869 eighteen times bigger.

2. Use Method C above to solve these.

(a) Make 337 thirteen times bigger.
(b) Make 472 fifteen times bigger.
(c) Make 574 sixteen times bigger.
(d) Make 685 nineteen times bigger.

A container holds 528 crates of apples.
How many crates will 46 such containers hold?

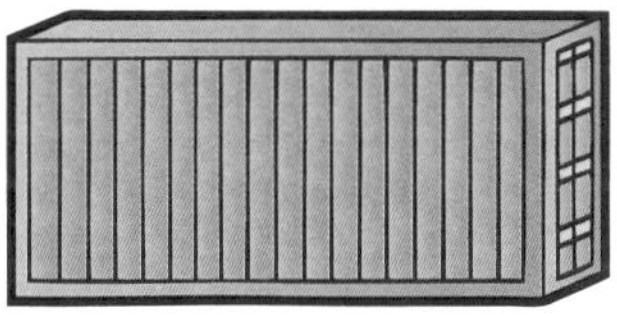

528 × 46 = ☆

Estimate: 500 × 50 = 25,000

A: Multiples method

528 × 10 = 5,280
528 × 10 = 5,280
528 × 10 = 5,280
528 × 10 = 5,280
528 × 6 = 3,168
528 × 46 = 24,288

B: Long multiplication method

	tth	th	h	t	u
			5	2	8
			×	4	6
6 times 528 →		3	1	6	8
+ 40 times 528 → +	2	1	1	2	0
46 times 528 →	2	4	2	8	8

Find how many crates each of these containers can hold. Use both methods. Estimate first!

3. (a) 346 × 34 (b) 274 × 28 (c) 318 × 35 (d) 472 × 53 (e) 369 × 44

4. (a) 472 × 47 (b) 538 × 57 (c) 481 × 65 (d) 592 × 64 (e) 398 × 67

5. (a) 289 × 76 (b) 683 × 96 (c) 539 × 94 (d) 507 × 87 (e) 978 × 79

Check your answers by using a calculator!

Maths Fact A leopard can carry up to 120kg of prey. What total weight of prey can be carried by a pack of 47 such leopards? ______ kg

Multiplication – Bigger numbers

City Bus Fleet reported that each of their 36 buses carried a total of 2,472 passengers over a week. What was the total number of passengers carried by City Bus Fleet?

2,472 × 36 = ☆

Estimate: 2,000 × 40 = 80,000

A: Multiples method

2,472 × 10 =	24,720
2,472 × 10 =	24,720
2,472 × 10 =	24,720
2,472 × 6 =	14,832
2,472 × 36 =	88,992

B: Long multiplication method

		tth	th	h	t	u
			2	4	7	2
				×	3	6
6 times 2,472 →		1	4	8	3	2
+ 30 times 2,472 →	+	7	4	1	6	0
36 times 2,472 →		8	8	9	9	2

1. **Help City Bus Fleet work out total passenger numbers for these buses. Use both methods. Estimate first!**

   (a) 2,453 × 17 (b) 3,274 × 26 (c) 2,459 × 37 (d) 4,157 × 18 (e) 2,894 × 23
   (f) 1,825 × 27 (g) 4,751 × 15 (h) 2,177 × 28 (i) 3,978 × 22 (j) 5,314 × 17

2. **Calculate the next set of figures for City Bus Fleet using the long multiplication method. Don't forget to estimate. Check your answers using your calculator.**

   (a) 2,164 × 37 (b) 2,574 × 29 (c) 3,358 × 19 (d) 1,073 × 38 (e) 5,324 × 14
   (f) 2,358 × 27 (g) 1,969 × 43 (h) 3,207 × 29 (i) 2,688 × 31 (j) 4,216 × 22

Use long multiplication to solve these. Estimate first!

3. Mount Kilimanjaro in Tanzania, Africa is 5,895 metres above sea level. What was the total number of metres climbed by 16 climbers who reached the top? ________ m

4. 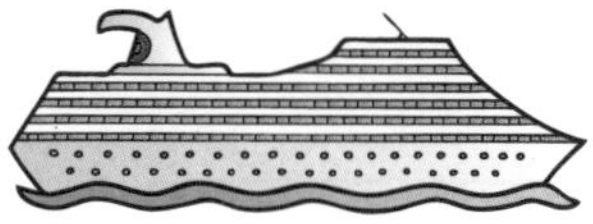

   6,318 passengers can be carried on the cruise ship *Allure of the Sea*. How many passengers were carried during 12 full voyages of the cruise ship? ________

5. A newsagent sells 1,427 newspapers every week. How many newspapers will the newsagent sell in a year? ________

Maths Fact 1

To reach Poenari Castle in Romania, you have to climb 1,480 steps. If a guide climbed these steps each day during the month of October, how many steps would she have climbed? ________

Maths Fact 2

The Gotthard Tunnel in Switzerland is 57km long. What is the total distance travelled through the tunnel by 45 trains, travelling one way? ________ km

Multiplication – Using decimals

Find the total cost of nine pairs of shorts for the school basketball team if each pair costs €14·95.

€14·95 × 9 = ☆

Estimate: €15 × 10 = €150

A: Multiples method

€14·95 × 4 = €59·80

€14·95 × 4 = €59·80

€14·95 × 1 = €14·95

€14·95 × 9 = €134·55

B: Multiplication method

€14·95 × 9 ⟶

€14·95
× 9
€134·55

1. Use both methods to solve these. Don't forget to estimate!

(a) €12·35 × 9 (b) €15·45 × 7 (c) €18·17 × 6 (d) €23·67 × 7 (e) €72·85 × 5

(f) €32·58 × 8 (g) €47·69 × 9 (h) €63·54 × 8 (i) €82·16 × 7 (j) €96·34 × 6

2. A basketball team wants to buy new singlets. They are priced differently for each colour. Use the multiplication method to calculate the cost for the following quantities:

(a)

× 7
€ ______

(b)

× 8
€ ______

(c)

× 9
€ ______

(d)

× 8
€ ______

(e)

× 9
€ ______

(f)

× 7
€ ______

3. 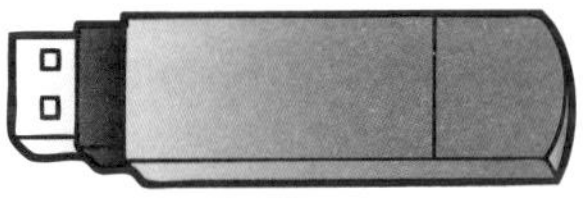

A memory stick for a laptop costs €15·47.
How much would eight memory sticks cost? € ______

4. Bracelets are on sale at a Craft Fair for €23·85 each. How much will the stall-holder take in if she sells seven on Saturday and six on Sunday? € ______

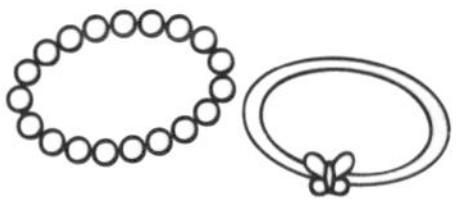

5. 

A sports bag costs €37·68.
How much would six sports bags cost? € ______

6. There are 17·5g of sugar in each 100g of a yoghurt dessert.
How many grammes of sugar are there in eight such desserts? ______ g

7. A garden fence post is 97·8cm tall. If nine posts were placed in a line end to end, how long would the line be in:

(a) centimetres ______; (b) metres ______?

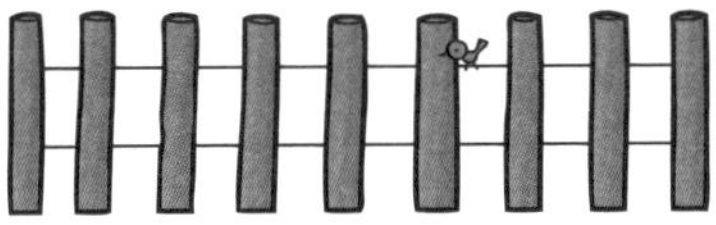

Maths Fact There are 29·5 days from one full moon to the next. This is called the lunar cycle. How many days will pass during nine lunar cycles? ______

Challenge Tim jumped 4·36m in the long jump.
How far would he jump in total with seven such jumps? ______ m

Multiplication – Bigger decimal numbers

A size 32 hurley costs €19·75.
How much would 23 of these hurleys cost?

€19·75 × 23 = ☆ | Estimate: €20 × 20 = €400

A: Multiples method

€19·75 × 10 = €197·50
€19·75 × 10 = €197·50
€19·75 × 3 = €59·25
€19·75 × 23 = €454·25

B: Long multiplication method

	€19·75
	× 23
€19·75 × 3 →	€59·25
€19·75 × 20 →	€395·00
	€454·25

You must have two digits after the decimal point in money questions.

1. Do these using the long multiplication method. Estimate first.

(a) €23·56 × 18	(b) €41·67 × 27	(c) €68·85 × 48	(d) €74·39 × 32
(e) €34·62 × 36	(f) €58·17 × 49	(g) €93·29 × 52	(h) €87·35 × 73
(i) €134·57 × 26	(j) €229·37 × 56	(k) €304·69 × 38	(l) €672·54 × 65

2. Paula paid €2·75 for a bran muffin.
How much would two dozen muffins cost? € ______

3. 

A bicycle helmet costs €32·79.
How much would it cost to purchase 26 helmets? € ______

4. The County Council bought 47 lengths of fencing, each length measuring 3·68m.
What was the total length of fencing bought? ______ m

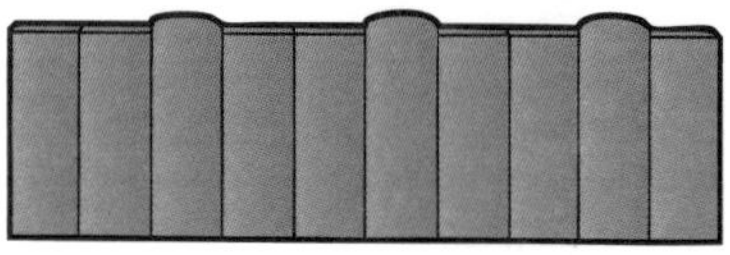

5. 

Sarah is saving €12·75 each week.
How much will she have saved after a year? € ______

6. A logistics company has a fleet of 38 trucks.
Each truck can carry 16·58 tonnes of cargo.
What is the total capacity of the fleet? ______ tonnes

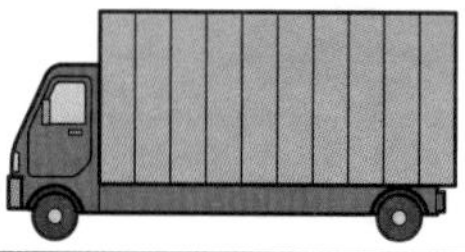

7. 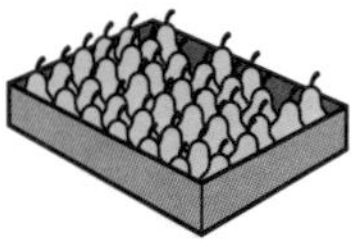

A box of pears costs €14·76.
Find the cost of: (a) 16 boxes € ______ (b) 24 boxes € ______ (c) 39 boxes € ______ (d) 48 boxes. € ______

Challenge One day, a restaurant sold 47 bowls of soup costing €4·75 per bowl and 63 cups of coffee costing €2·87 per cup. How much did the restaurant receive in total for the soup and the coffee that day? € ______

Maths Fact 

91·5 metres of tubing carries water around the underwear of an astronaut on a spacewalk to keep him/her cool. What length of tubing would be needed by 26 astronauts on a spacewalk? ______ metres

Chapter 8: Lines and angles

An **angle** is made when two straight lines meet.

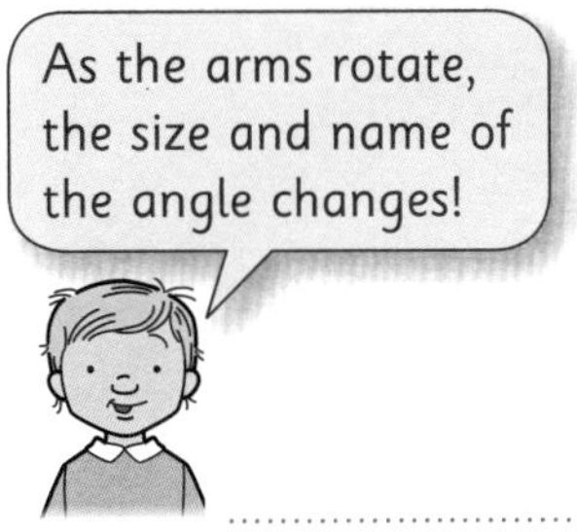

As the arms rotate, the size and name of the angle changes!

no angle

acute angle

right angle

obtuse angle

straight angle

reflex angle

full rotation

1. What type of angle is made in each of these pictures as shown in red?

(a)

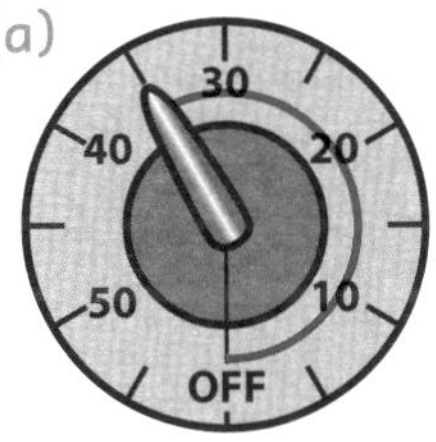

(b)

(c)

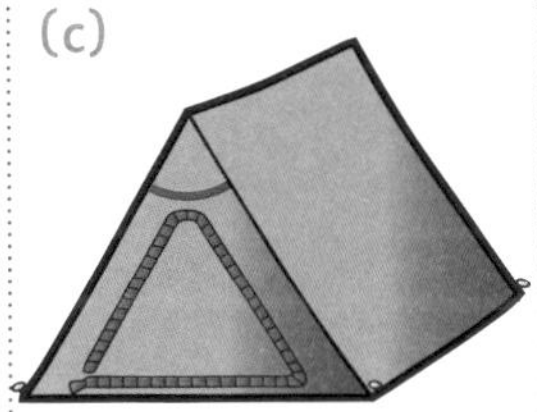

(d)

(e)

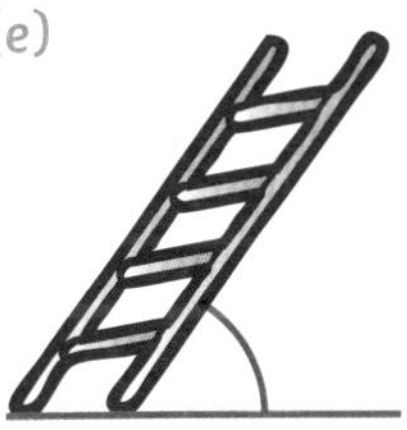

(f)

(g)

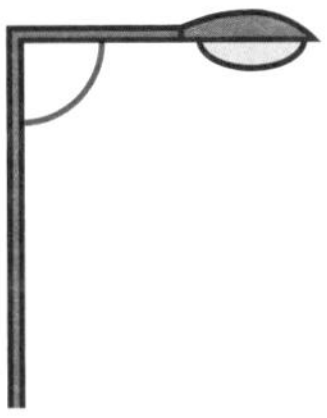

(h)

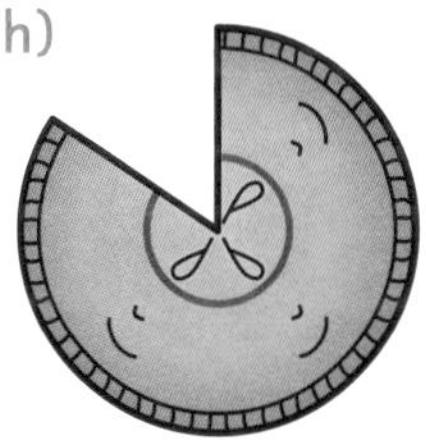

(i)

(j)

2. Name the angle shown by the (i) blue arc and the (ii) orange arc.

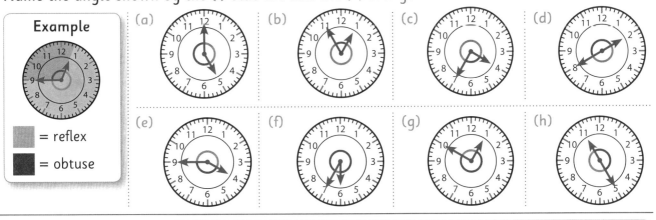

Example

= reflex

= obtuse

(a)

(b)

(c)

(d)

(e)

(f)

(g)

(h)

Challenge

List all the pairs of numbers on the clock face that make right angles when joined to the centre point.

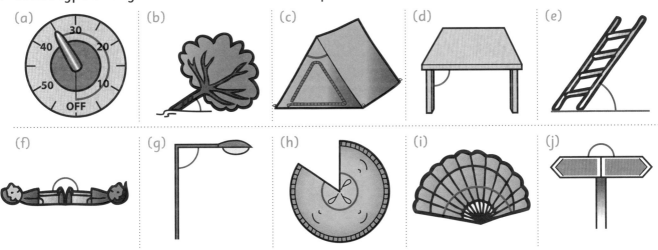

STRAND **Shape and space** **STRAND UNIT/ELEMENT** *Lines and angles*

LANGUAGE *Angle, space, straight lines, acute, right, obtuse, straight, reflex, rotate, rotation, protractor, measure, inside, outside, degrees*

Lines and angles – The protractor

We use a **protractor** to measure and construct angles.

- It has two scales.
- The outside scale reads from left to right.
- The inside scale reads from right to left.
- Angles are measured in degrees (e.g. 60°).

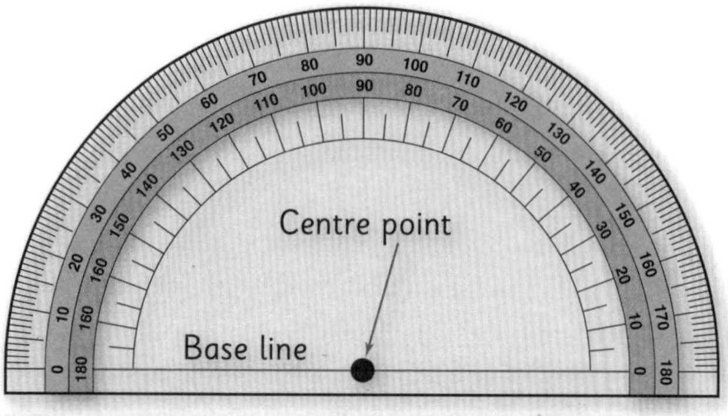

1. (a) What 2-D shape is a protractor?

(b) How many degrees are marked on a protractor?

(c) How many degrees are in a straight angle?

(d) How many degrees are in a right angle?

(e) How many degrees are in a full circle?

(f) How many degrees are in $\frac{1}{8}$ of a full circle?

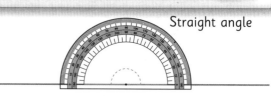

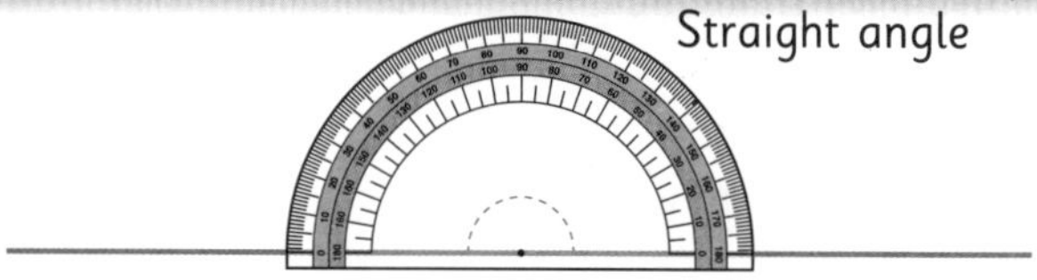

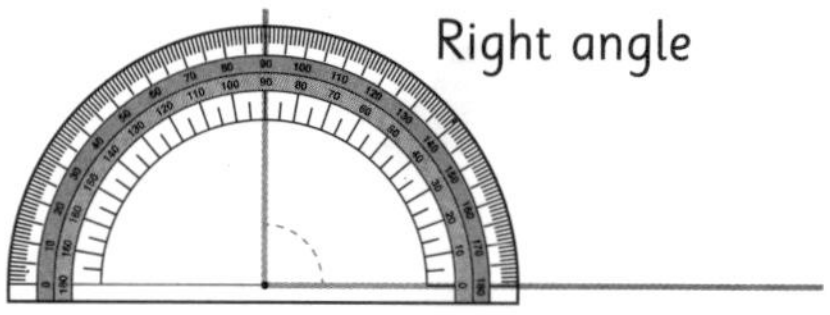

Measuring angles

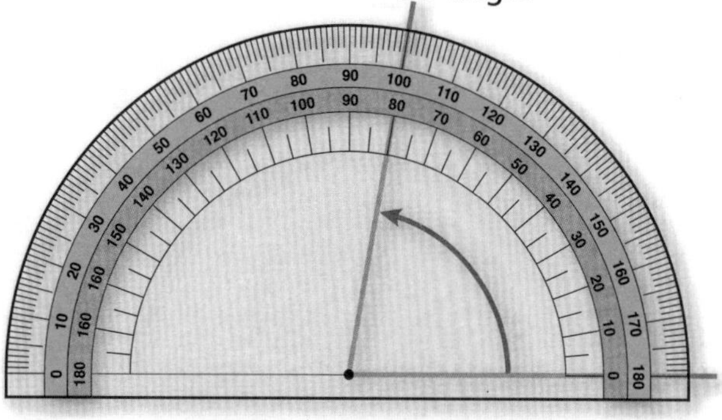

Step 1 Place the centre point of the protractor on the vertex (point) of the angle.

Step 2 Place the base line of the protractor on one arm (line) of the angle.

Step 3 Count the degrees, starting at zero, until you reach the other arm. (All arms can be made longer, using a ruler and pencil, if necessary.)

We used the **inside scale** to measure this angle!

Estimate whether the angle is < or > a right angle.

2. **Use the inside scale of your protractor to measure these angles.**

(a)

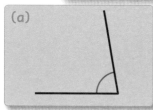

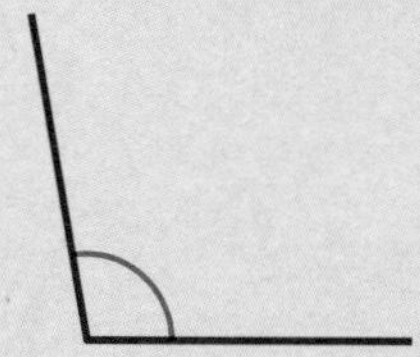

(b)

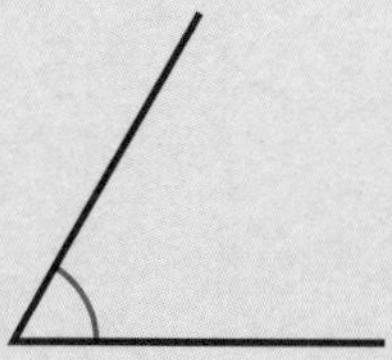

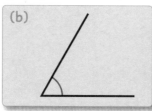

(c)

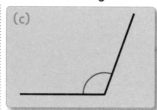

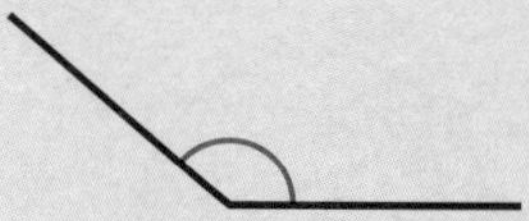

(d)

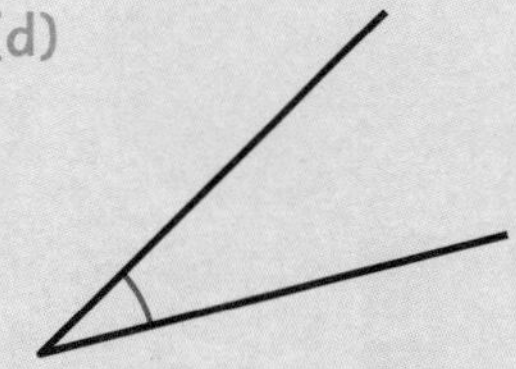

3. **Use the outside scale of your protractor to measure these angles.**

(a)

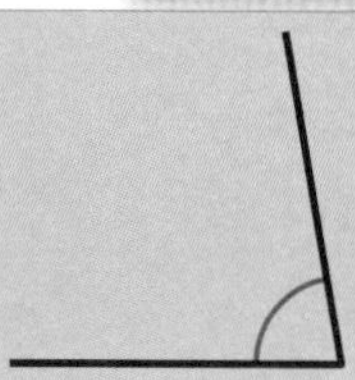

(b)

(c)

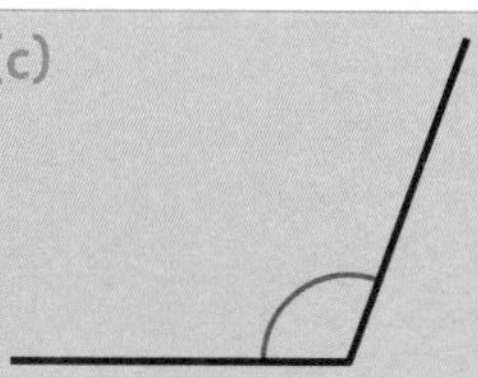

(d)

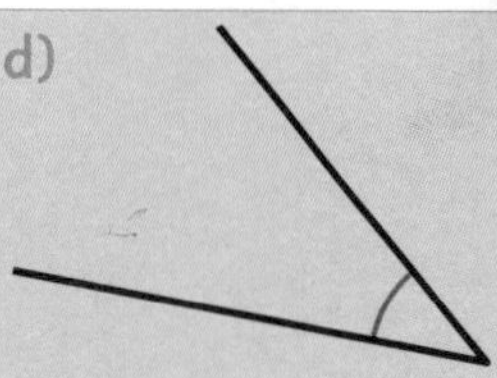

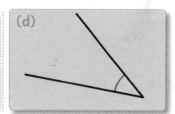

4. **Use either scale to measure these angles.**

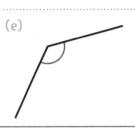

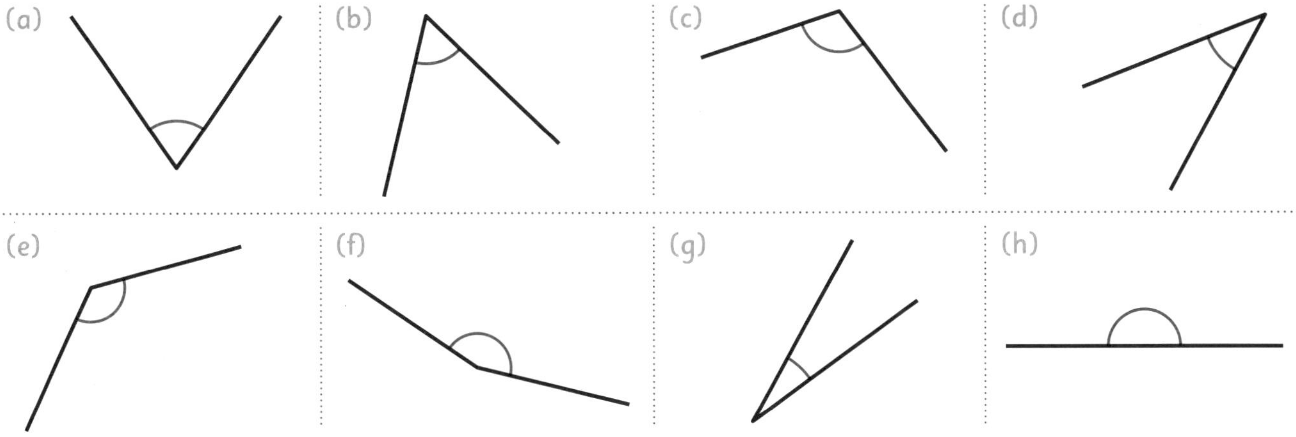

5. **Measure the angles in each 2-D shape.**

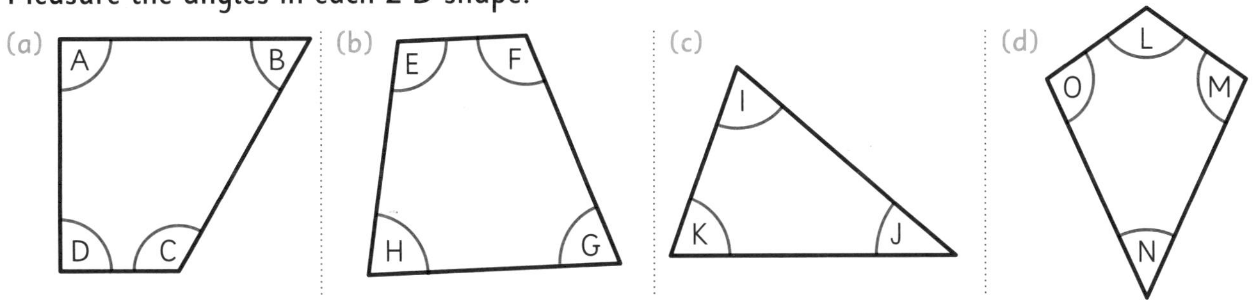

Drawing angles: Draw a 70° angle.

Step 1:

Draw the line AB.

Step 2:

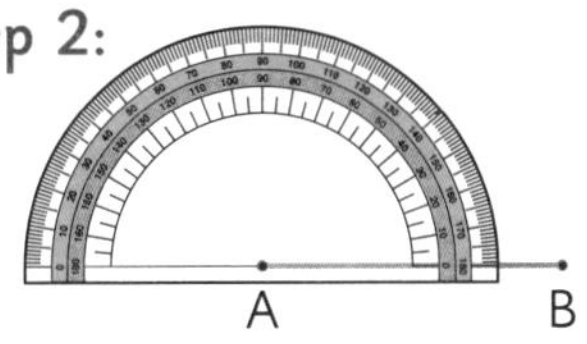

Place centre point on A.

Step 3:

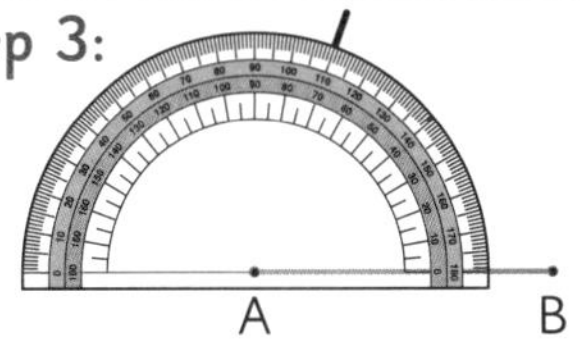

Count up from 0° to 70°.
Make a mark at 70°.

Step 4:

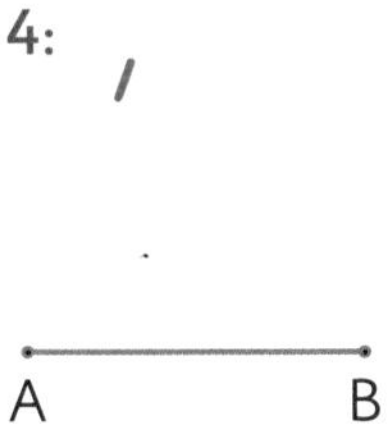

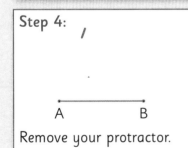

Remove your protractor.

Step 5:

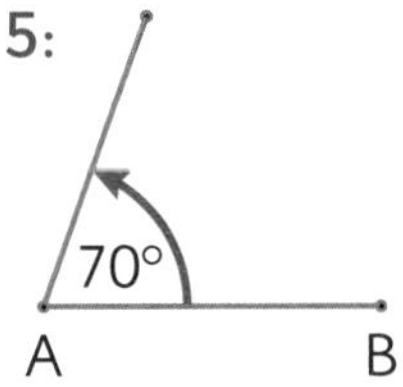

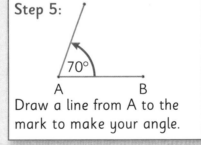

Draw a line from A to the mark to make your angle.

You could have started at **B** and used the outside scale.

6. **Use your protractor to draw the following angles, using the inside or outside scale.**

(a) 40°	(b) 70°	(c) 55°	(d) 85°	(e) 10°	(f) 45°	(g) 60°
(h) 100°	(i) 145°	(j) 180°	(k) 160°	(l) 105°	(m) 130°	(n) 175°

Challenge 1

Measure this reflex angle. ______

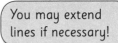

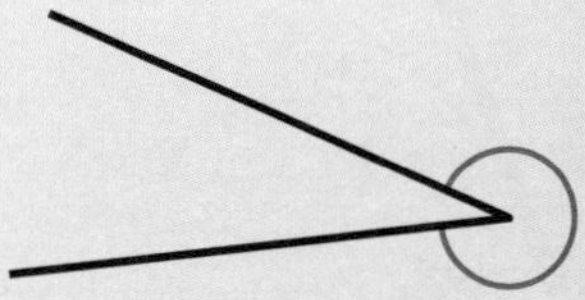

Challenge 2

Draw a reflex angle that measures 280°.

180
−125
055 ✓

Lines and angles

How many degrees are there in total in the angles of a triangle?

If you cut out the three angles of any triangle, you will be able to form them into a straight angle – just like a jigsaw puzzle!

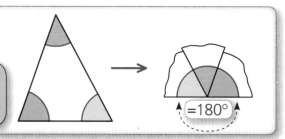

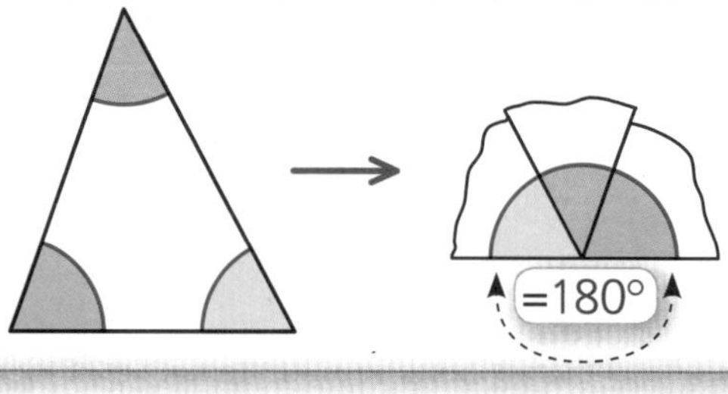

Without using a protractor:

(i) **Calculate the measure of each unknown angle and**

(ii) **say whether the angle is acute, right, obtuse, straight or reflex.**

1. (a)

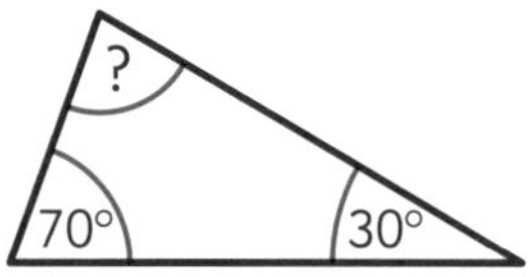

(b)

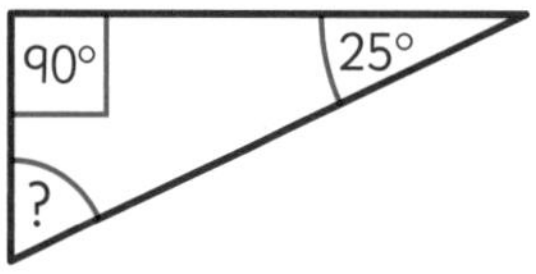

(c)

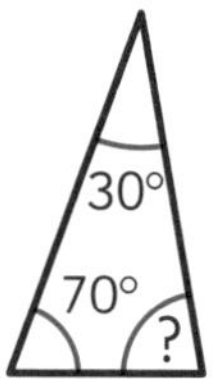

(d)

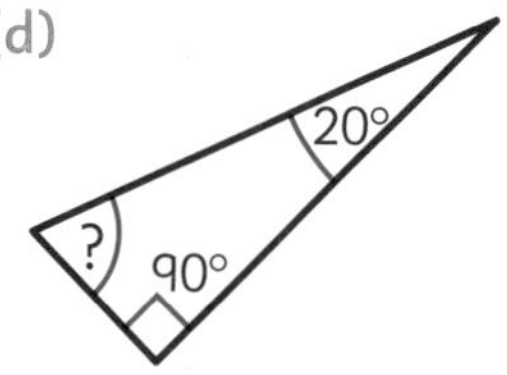

(e)

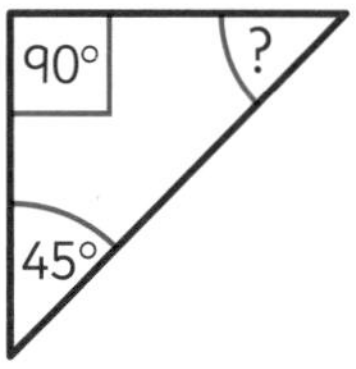

(f)

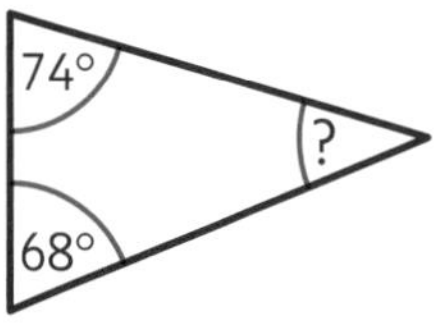

(g)

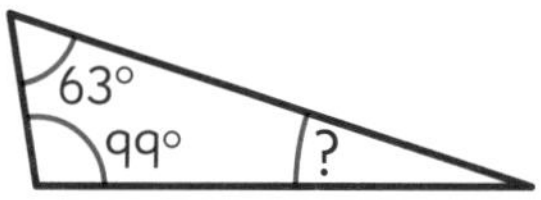

(h)

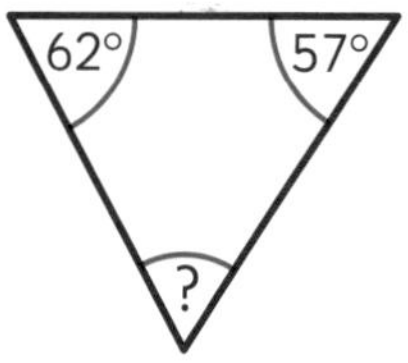

2. Calculate the unknown angles, without using a protractor.

(a)

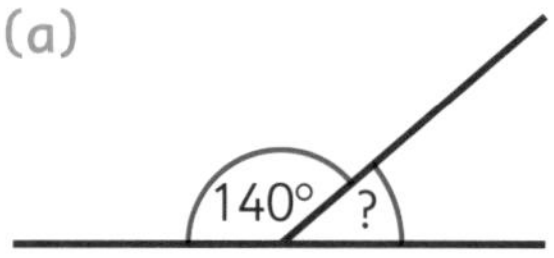

(b)

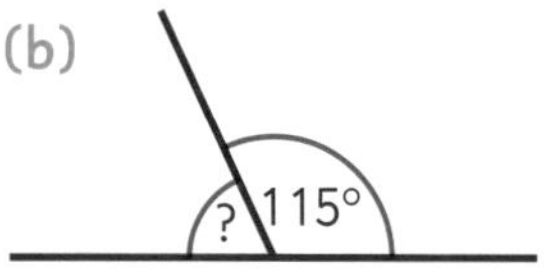

(c)

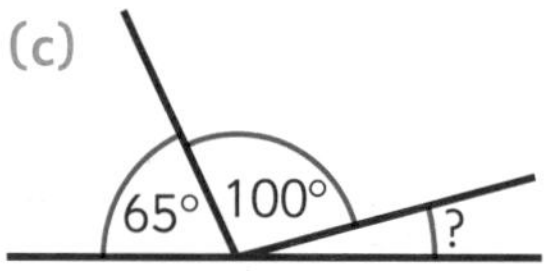

(d)

3.

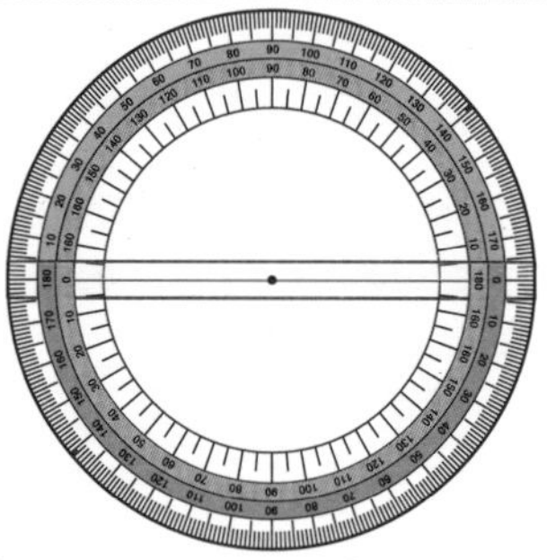

Two protractors form a circle, so a circle has 360°.

(a)

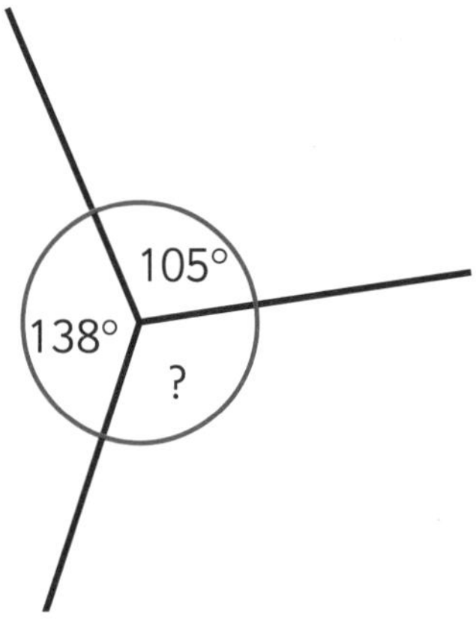

(b)

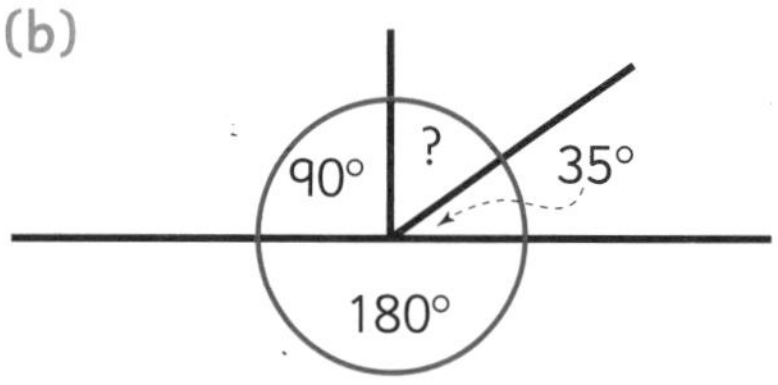

(c)

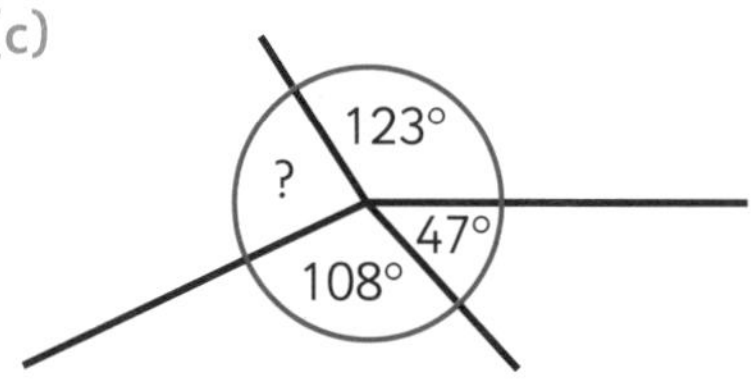

4.

(a)

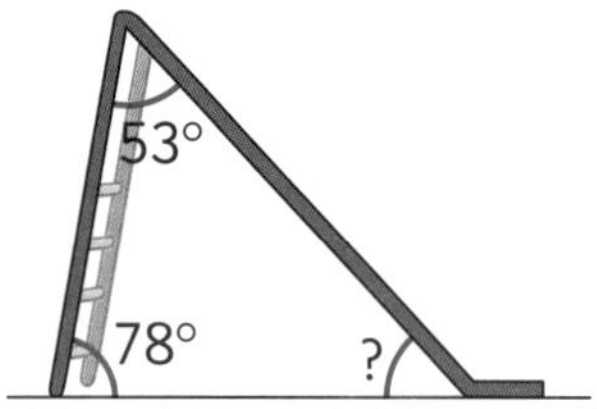

(b)

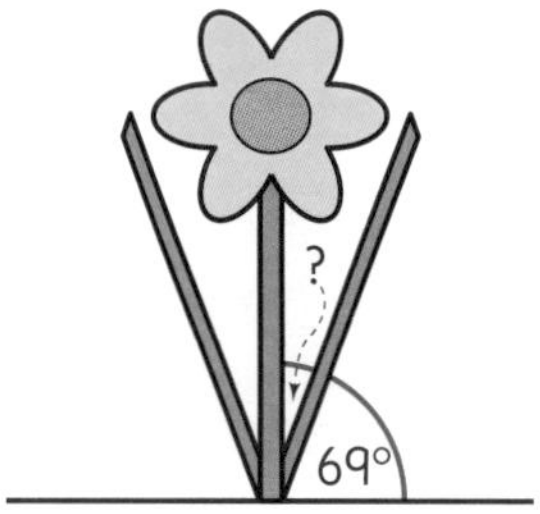

(c)

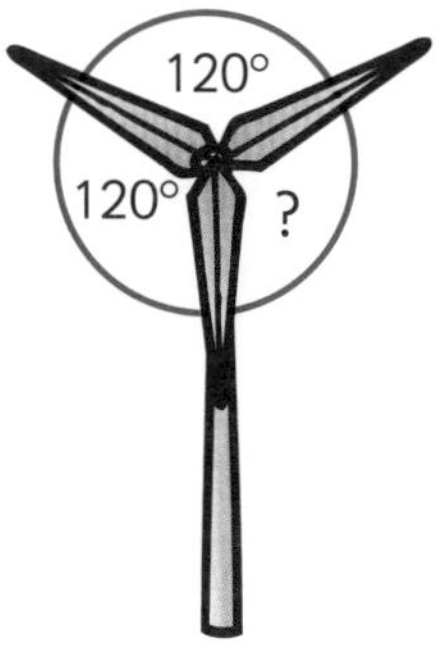

(d)

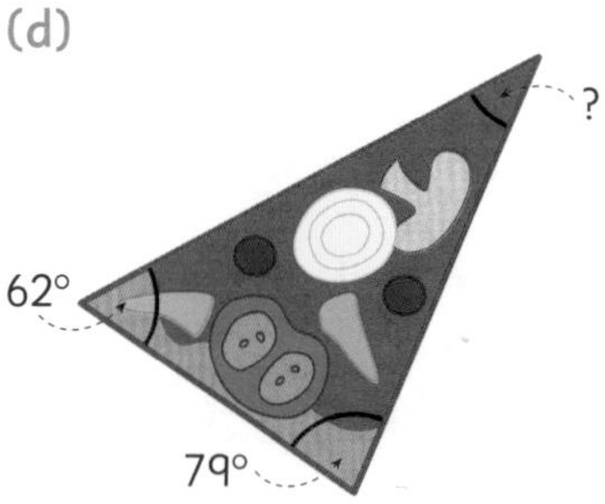

Chapter 9: Division 1

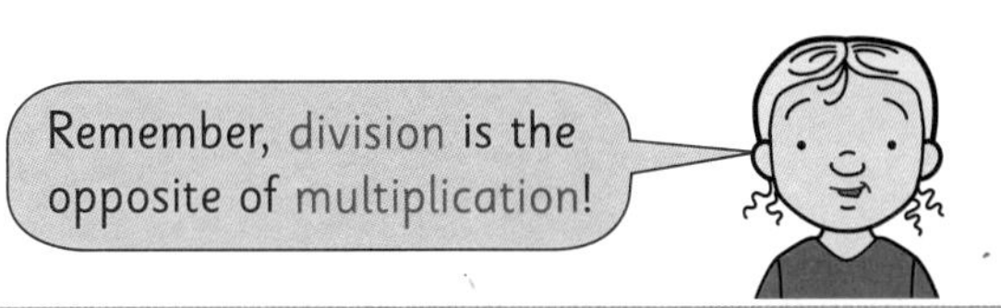
Remember, division is the opposite of multiplication!

Complete these multiplication and division tables.

1.

	21	÷	3	=	7	so	7	×	3	=	21
(a)	45	÷	5	=	9	so	___	×	5	=	45
(b)	24	÷	6	=	___	so	___	×	___	=	___
(c)	24	÷	___	=	12	so	___	×	___	=	___
(d)	56	÷	___	=	8	so	___	×	___	=	___
(e)	___	÷	___	=	___	so	9	×	___	=	36

2.

	40	÷	5	=	8	so	8	×	5	=	40
(a)	36	÷	___	=	6	so	___	×	___	=	___
(b)	28	÷	7	=	___	so	___	×	___	=	___
(c)	___	÷	___	=	___	so	10	×	___	=	60
(d)	63	÷	___	=	7	so	___	×	___	=	___
(e)	___	÷	___	=	___	so	8	×	9	=	___

Here are five ways to do division. Complete.

3. (a) 49 ÷ 7 = ___ (b) 21 ÷ 7 = ___ (c) 64 ÷ 8 = ___ (d) 27 ÷ 9 = ___ (e) 75 ÷ 8 = ___ R___

4. (a) $\frac{25}{3}$ = ___ R___ (b) $\frac{19}{3}$ = ___ R___ (c) $\frac{56}{8}$ = ___ (d) $\frac{32}{4}$ = ___ (e) $\frac{39}{6}$ = ___ R___

5. (a) $\frac{1}{2}$ of 18 = ___ (b) $\frac{1}{3}$ of 33 = ___ (c) $\frac{1}{7}$ of 42 = ___ (d) $\frac{1}{5}$ of 60 = ___ (e) $\frac{1}{9}$ of 81 = ___

6. (a) 3)15 ___ (b) 7)29 ___ R___ (c) 6)54 ___ (d) 7)50 ___ R___ (e) 9)54 ___

7. (a) 2)29 ___ R___ (b) 4)49 ___ R___ (c) 6)72 ___ (d) 7)38 ___ R___ (e) 8)72 ___

These questions are a little more challenging!

8. (a) 465 ÷ 3 = ___ (b) 564 ÷ 4 = ___ (c) 536 ÷ 2 = ___ (d) 636 ÷ 4 = ___ (e) 375 ÷ 5 = ___

9. (a) 833 ÷ 7 = ___ (b) 762 ÷ 6 = ___ (c) 472 ÷ 4 = ___ (d) 944 ÷ 8 = ___ (e) 657 ÷ 9 = ___

These will have remainders:

10. (a) 643 ÷ 4 = ___ R___ (b) 368 ÷ 5 = ___ R___ (c) 701 ÷ 3 = ___ R___ (d) 856 ÷ 7 = ___ R___

11. (a) 967 ÷ 7 = ___ R___ (b) 833 ÷ 6 = ___ R___ (c) 907 ÷ 6 = ___ R___ (d) 971 ÷ 8 = ___ R___

12. There are six classes of equal size in a school of 174 pupils. How many pupils are there in each class? ___

Maths Fact

A meerkat colony has up to 90 entrances into its burrow! If the entrances to the burrow were shared equally among six meerkats, how many entrances were there for each meerkat? ___

Dividing by 10 and by 100

Remember: When we **multiply** by **10**, we move all digits **one** place to the **left**.
To **divide**, we do the reverse. We move all digits **one** place to the **right**.

A

h	t	u	
	5	0	× 10
5	0	0	= 500

h	t	u	$\frac{1}{10}$	
5	0	0		÷ 10
	5	0	·0	= 50

B

h	t	u	$\frac{1}{10}$	
3	8	0		÷ 10
	3	8	·0	= 38

C

h	t	u	$\frac{1}{10}$	
2	7	5		÷ 10
	2	7	·5	= 27·5

1. **Make each of these numbers 10 times smaller.**

(a)

h	t	u	$\frac{1}{10}$
	8	0	

(b)

h	t	u	$\frac{1}{10}$
1	7	0	

(c)

h	t	u	$\frac{1}{10}$
	2	9	

(d)

h	t	u	$\frac{1}{10}$
4	5	6	

(e)

h	t	u	$\frac{1}{10}$
3	0	4	

Divide each of these numbers by 10.

Place a decimal point after the units digit and move all digits **one** place to the right.

2. (a) 700 = ______ (b) 430 = ______ (c) 300 = ______ (d) 260 = ______ (e) 800 = ______

3. (a) 49 = ______ (b) 127 = ______ (c) 86 = ______ (d) 90 = ______ (e) 324 = ______

4. (a) 578 = ______ (b) 508 = ______ (c) 114 = ______ (d) 41 = ______ (e) 410 = ______

When **multiplying** by **100**, we move all digits **two** places to the **left**.
When **dividing** by **100**, we move all digits **two** places to the **right**.

A

th	h	t	u	
		4	9	× 100
	4	9	0	
4	9	0	0	

th	h	t	u	$\frac{1}{10}$	
4	9	0	0		÷ 100
	4	9	0	·0	
		4	9	·0	

B

th	h	t	u	$\frac{1}{10}$	
5	8	6	0		÷ 100
	5	8	6	·0	
		5	8	·6	

Divide each of these numbers by 100.

Place a decimal point after the units digit and move all digits **two** places to the right.

5. (a) 600 = ______ (b) 710 = ______ (c) 200 = ______ (d) 350 = ______ (e) 460 = ______

6. (a) 4,000 = ______ (b) 1,630 = ______ (c) 7,040 = ______ (d) 3,080 = ______ (e) 8,000 = ______

7. Pat scored a total of 180 points in a game of ten-pin bowling. Amazingly, he got the same score in each of his 10 rounds. What was his score in each round? ______

8. 

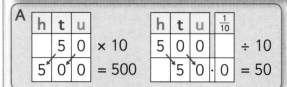

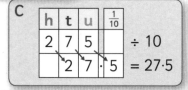

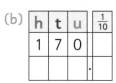

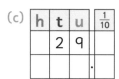

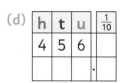

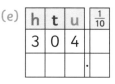

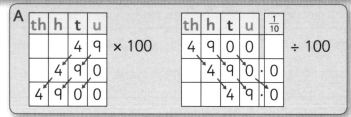

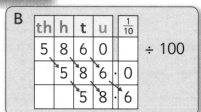

One hundred winners shared a lotto prize of €970 equally.
How much did each winner receive? € ______

Maths Fact At a circus, the Great Throwdini threw 76 knives around a human body in one minute. How many knives should he throw in 15 seconds, throwing at a steady rate? ______

Repeated subtraction

A A delivery driver delivers 35 cases of apples to each store. He has 140 cases altogether. How many stores will he deliver to?

$$\begin{array}{r} 140 \\ -\ 35 \\ \hline 105 \\ -\ 35 \\ \hline 70 \\ -\ 35 \\ \hline 35 \\ -\ 35 \\ \hline 0 \end{array}$$

You can take 35 from 140 four times!

140 ÷ 35 = 4

B Another delivery driver has 38 cases of apples to deliver to each store. He has 160 cases altogether. How many stores will he deliver to and how many cases will be left over?

$$\begin{array}{r} 160 \\ -\ 38 \\ \hline 122 \\ -\ 38 \\ \hline 84 \\ -\ 38 \\ \hline 46 \\ -\ 38 \\ \hline 8 \end{array}$$

You can take 38 from 160 four times!

160 ÷ 38 = 4R8

1. Use the repeated subtraction method when doing these.

(a) 150 ÷ 25 = ____ (b) 108 ÷ 27 = ____ (c) 115 ÷ 23 = ____ (d) 230 ÷ 46 = ____

(e) 228 ÷ 38 = ____ (f) 256 ÷ 64 = ____ (g) 432 ÷ 72 = ____ (h) 415 ÷ 83 = ____

2. Now try these. All the answers will have remainders.

(a) 107 ÷ 19 = ____ (b) 176 ÷ 36 = ____ (c) 278 ÷ 53 = ____ (d) 229 ÷ 43 = ____

(e) 224 ÷ 43 = ____ (f) 279 ÷ 54 = ____ (g) 468 ÷ 76 = ____ (h) 377 ÷ 57 = ____

Use the **repeated subtraction** method to solve the following problems.

3. A punnet holds 38 strawberries. How many punnets can be filled from a basket holding 304 strawberries? ____

4. A school library has 490 books.

(a) How many shelves each holding 78 books will be needed to display them? ____

(b) How many books will be left over? ____

5.

The manager of a shoe shop spent €469 on pairs of shoes costing €67 per pair. How many pairs of shoes did she buy? ____

6. A carpenter was making extension ladders and had a stock of 170 rungs. Each ladder required 22 rungs.

(a) How many ladders did he make? ____

(b) How many rungs were left over? ____

7. An art dealer went to an auction with €380 to spend.
She bought as many pictures as she could costing €77 each.

(a) How many pictures did she buy? ____ (b) How much money had she left over? €____

8.

There are 48 balloons in each packet.
How many packets can be made from a box of 336 balloons? ____

Maths Fact

The world's largest rodent is the South American capybara. It can reach a weight of 66kg. A zoo scales holding a group of capybaras shows 396kg. How many capybaras each weighing 66kg are on the scales? ____

Long division – Small numbers

A How many coaches each holding 12 passengers are needed to bring 48 people to a football match?

We can take 12 from 48 four times and there are no people left over.

48 ÷ 12 = 4

$$\begin{array}{r} 48 \\ -\ 12 \\ \hline 36 \\ -\ 12 \\ \hline 24 \\ -\ 12 \\ \hline 12 \\ -\ 12 \\ \hline 0 \end{array}$$

B How many coaches each holding 12 passengers are needed to bring 55 people to the same football match and how many passengers are left over?

Again, we can take 12 from 55 four times but there are 7 people left over.

55 ÷ 12 = 4R7

$$\begin{array}{r} 55 \\ -\ 12 \\ \hline 43 \\ -\ 12 \\ \hline 31 \\ -\ 12 \\ \hline 19 \\ -\ 12 \\ \hline 7 \end{array}$$

1. Do these using the **repeated subtraction** method.

(a) 36 ÷ 12 = ____	(b) 60 ÷ 12 = ____	(c) 80 ÷ 20 = ____	(d) 60 ÷ 15 = ____
(e) 58 ÷ 12 = ____	(f) 69 ÷ 12 = ____	(g) 96 ÷ 20 = ____	(h) 63 ÷ 15 = ____
(i) 90 ÷ 15 = ____	(j) 100 ÷ 20 = ____	(k) 100 ÷ 25 = ____	(l) 130 ÷ 25 = ____

How many bags of 15 apples can we make from 70 apples?

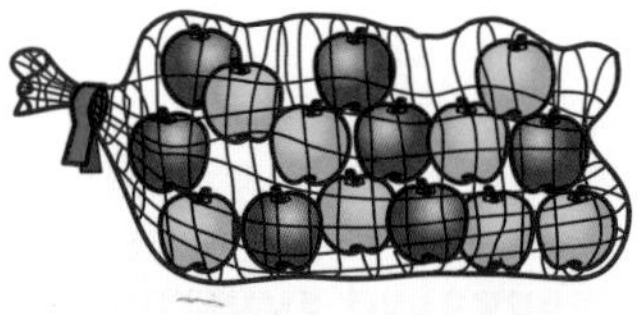

C Multiples method

$$\begin{array}{r} 70 \\ -\ 60 \\ \hline 10 \end{array}$$

60 ⟵ (15 × 4)

10 ⟵ left over

70 ÷ 15 = 4R10

D Long division method

$$\begin{array}{r} 4 \\ 15\overline{)70} \\ -\ 60 \\ \hline 10 \end{array}$$

60 ⟵ (15 × 4)

10 ⟵ left over

70 ÷ 15 = 4R10

I multiply 15 by 4 to get 60. I then subtract 60 from 70 to get the remainder.

2. Use the **multiples** method when doing the following.

(a) 75 ÷ 30 = ____	(b) 58 ÷ 15 = ____	(c) 68 ÷ 15 = ____	(d) 76 ÷ 20 = ____
(e) 86 ÷ 30 = ____	(f) 95 ÷ 20 = ____	(g) 78 ÷ 15 = ____	(h) 123 ÷ 20 = ____

3. Use the **long division** method when doing the following.

(a) 86 ÷ 12 = ____	(b) 93 ÷ 30 = ____	(c) 78 ÷ 12 = ____	(d) 96 ÷ 25 = ____
(e) 112 ÷ 20 = ____	(f) 136 ÷ 30 = ____	(g) 143 ÷ 25 = ____	(h) 167 ÷ 20 = ____

4. Make 79 children into teams of 15. How many children will be left over? ____

5.

(a) How many bags of 20 pears can be filled from a box of 124 pears? ____
(b) How many pears will be left over? ____

Maths Fact A hummingbird beats its wings up to 78 times every second to keep itself in the air. How many wingbeats should a hummingbird make in $\frac{1}{6}$ of a second at that rate? ____

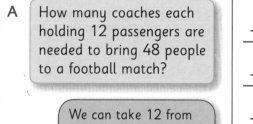

Bigger numbers using repeated subtraction

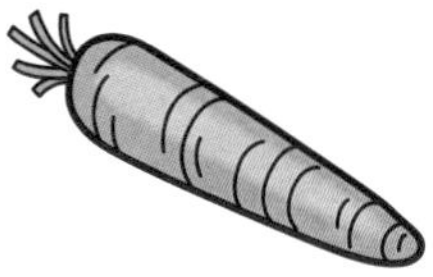

How many rows of 19 carrots can a farmer sow using 510 plants?

510 ÷ 19 = ☆ Estimate: 500 ÷ 20 = 25

The repeated subtraction method using two groups of 10 first followed by a group of six.

	510
19 × 10 →	− 190
	320
19 × 10 →	− 190
	130
19 × 6 →	− 114
	16 **left**

510 ÷ 19 = 26R16

→

10 rows = 190
10 rows = 190
6 rows = 114
26 rows = 494

510 − 494 = 16 **left over**

Use the **repeated subtraction** method, using groups of 10 first, to do the following. Use a calculator to check your answers. (Multiply and add the remainder.)

1. (a) 798 ÷ 21	(b) 513 ÷ 25	(c) 685 ÷ 27	(d) 461 ÷ 26	(e) 612 ÷ 24
2. (a) 845 ÷ 33	(b) 952 ÷ 34	(c) 972 ÷ 36	(d) 696 ÷ 37	(e) 798 ÷ 38
3. (a) 782 ÷ 46	(b) 994 ÷ 45	(c) 836 ÷ 54	(d) 967 ÷ 63	(e) 958 ÷ 72
4. (a) 987 ÷ 60	(b) 802 ÷ 48	(c) 984 ÷ 24	(d) 988 ÷ 75	(e) 854 ÷ 57

Now use the same method to solve these problems. Check your answers using a calculator.

5. 

A concert promoter took in €812 by selling tickets for a show. How many tickets were sold if they cost €29 each? ______

6. An office block lift carried 612 people over 36 trips with the lift full each trip. How many people fit in the full lift? ______

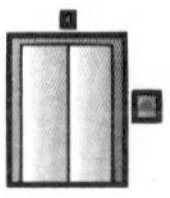

7. A leaflet printer has 800 leaflets to distribute. He has 17 distributors and wants them all to have the same amount. (a) How many leaflets will each distributor get? ______
(b) How many leaflets will be left over? ______

8. 

A gardener has 900 daffodil bulbs. He wants to plant them in groups of 24. (a) How many groups will be planted? ______
(b) How many bulbs will be left over? ______

9. A coach can carry 28 passengers. How many coaches are needed to take 448 people to a camogie match? ______

Maths Fact In a group of 23 people, at least two should have the same birthday. There are 368 people at a film. How many of these people should have the same birthday? ______

Factors and rounding

Sometimes we can use **factors** to make division easier.

A 768 ÷ 6 = ☆ (6 = 2 × 3)

2) 7¹6²8
3) 38²4
= 128

The divisor 6 can be made into factors 2 and 3.

B 945 ÷ 15 = ☆ (15 = 5 × 3)

5) 9⁴4⁴5
3) 189
= 63

The divisor 15 can be made into factors 5 and 3.

1. Now try these using this method of splitting divisors into two factors.

(a) 904 ÷ 8: (8 = 4 × ___)
) 904
) ____
____

(b) 972 ÷ 9: (9 = ___ × 3)
) 972
) ____
____

(c) 852 ÷ 6: (6 = ___ × ___)
) 852
) ____
____

(d) 486 ÷ 18: (18 = ___ × ___)
) 486
) ____
____

(e) 735 ÷ 15: (15 = ___ × ___)
) 735
) ____
____

(f) 924 ÷ 21: (21 = ___ × ___)
) 924
) ____
____

Estimating accurately is an important skill for division.
It is best to **round** both numbers to the nearest **ten**.

A 269 ÷ 32 = ☆
→ 270 ÷ 30
→ 27 tens ÷ 3 tens
→ 27 ÷ 3
= 9

B 493 ÷ 17 = ☆
→ 500 ÷ 20
→ 50 tens ÷ 2 tens
→ 50 ÷ 2
= 25

C 898 ÷ 28 = ☆
→ 900 ÷ 30
→ 90 tens ÷ 3 tens
→ 90 ÷ 3
= 30

Round both numbers to the nearest ten to help you estimate the answers to the following.

	(a)	(b)	(c)	(d)	(e)
2.	(a) 388 ÷ 22	(b) 423 ÷ 31	(c) 197 ÷ 43	(d) 251 ÷ 19	(e) 416 ÷ 32
3.	(a) 267 ÷ 49	(b) 512 ÷ 18	(c) 338 ÷ 27	(d) 176 ÷ 13	(e) 571 ÷ 48
4.	(a) 639 ÷ 52	(b) 747 ÷ 47	(c) 608 ÷ 31	(d) 564 ÷ 78	(e) 829 ÷ 62
5.	(a) 887 ÷ 68	(b) 403 ÷ 26	(c) 947 ÷ 53	(d) 845 ÷ 62	(e) 716 ÷ 39

Maths Fact Having 15 feathers per cm^2 makes emperor penguins the most feathery of all birds. How many cm^2 of an emperor penguin's body would be covered by 180 feathers? ____ cm^2

The long division method

How many boxes each holding 32 bananas can be packed from 558 bananas?

558 ÷ 32 = ☆

Estimate: 600 ÷ 30 = 20 boxes

```
     17
32 ) 558     ← Divide 32 into the 55 tens first. It goes in 1 time.
   - 32↓     ← Subtract 1 group of 32 from the 55 tens.
   ----
     238     ← Bring down the 8 units and divide 32 into 238.
   - 224     ← Subtract 7 groups of 32 from 238 to find the remainder.
   ----
      14     ← Remainder.
```

558 ÷ 32 = 17 R 14

1. Let's try these. Complete the work started.

```
(a)      2       (b)      1       (c)      3       (d)      3       (e)      2
   27 ) 653         38 ) 495         19 ) 596         24 ) 870         33 ) 819
      - 54↓            - 38↓            - 57↓            - 72↓            - 66↓
        11 _             11 _              2 _             15 _             15 _
      - ___            - ___            - ___            - ___            - ___
      _ R _            _ R _            _ R _            _ R _            _ R _
```

Have a go at these using the long division method. Estimate first. Check using your calculator.

2.	(a) 239 ÷ 19	(b) 416 ÷ 27	(c) 371 ÷ 34	(d) 522 ÷ 48	(e) 618 ÷ 39
3.	(a) 407 ÷ 27	(b) 634 ÷ 31	(c) 725 ÷ 46	(d) 827 ÷ 58	(e) 516 ÷ 43
4.	(a) 846 ÷ 56	(b) 739 ÷ 62	(c) 592 ÷ 45	(d) 805 ÷ 22	(e) 628 ÷ 51
5.	(a) 370 ÷ 28	(b) 608 ÷ 47	(c) 924 ÷ 63	(d) 751 ÷ 45	(e) 508 ÷ 48

6. A car transporter delivered 216 cars over 24 trips. How many cars were carried on each trip if it carried the same number each time? ______

7. 

Divide a box of 500 crayons equally among a class of 28 children.

(a) How many will each child get? ______ (b) How many will be left over? ______

Maths Fact

There are 33 vertebrae in the human body. How many humans would it take to have a total of 528 vertebrae? ______

Challenge

A railway carriage holds 44 passengers. How many carriages will be needed to take 952 people to a concert? (Be careful!) ______

Chapter 10: Money

1. Here are all the euro coins and notes. Fill in the missing amounts.

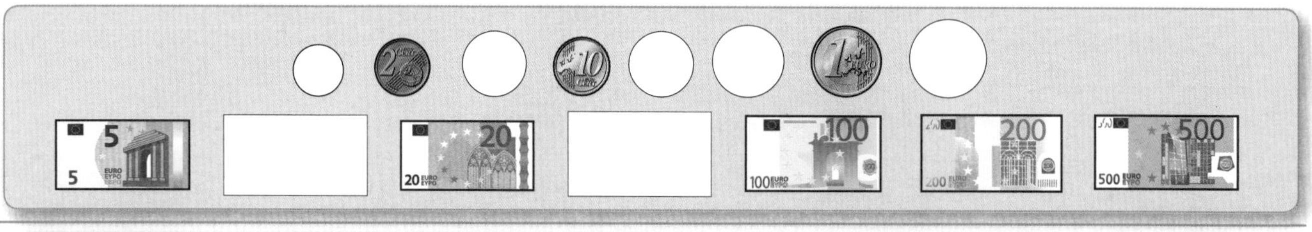

2. (a) Using as few notes and coins as possible, write the amounts needed to buy the following:
   (i) Tablet (ii) Flatscreen TV (iii) Headphones (iv) Smartphone (v) Laptop

   (b) One day, the shopkeeper sold one of each item to five customers. Each customer paid with a €500 note. How much change did each customer get? (Count in your head to get the change.)
   (i) Tablet € ________ (ii) Flatscreen TV € ________ (iii) Headphones € ________
   (iv) Smartphone € ________ (v) Laptop € ________

   (c) What would be the total cost if a customer bought all five items? € ________

   (d) A school bought six 🎧. What was the total cost? € ________

   (e) The shopkeeper sold five smartphones one day.
   How much money was taken in on smartphones that day? € ________

   (f) What would be the total cost of three televisions and two laptops? € ________

3. Rounding and estimating

			Estimate:	Actual cost:
(a)	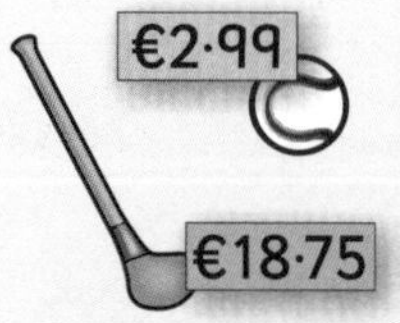 €2·99 €18·75	How much for five of each item?	5 × €3 + 5 × €20 ________	€2·99 × 5: €18·75 × 5: + ________
(b)	 FLOUR 5kg €4·79	A baker wants 100kg of flour. How much will it cost?	20 × €5 = ________	
(c)	 21 sharpeners cost €8·40	How much does one sharpener cost?		
(d)	 €6·00 GOLF BALLS	A golfer has €54. How many golf balls can she buy?		
(e)	 €9·64	A teacher bought a book for each of the 32 children in his class. How much did he pay?		

STRAND **Measures** STRAND UNIT/ELEMENT *Money*
LANGUAGE *Money, coins, notes, euro, cent, round, estimate, prices, cost, comparing, save, value, shop bills, receipt, budget, quiz*

Money – Comparing prices

1. **Cinema prices**
Adult: €12·10
Child: €6·99

How much for two adults and five children?

Estimate:

Actual cost:

2. What is the sale price of the television if the pre-sale price was €509·56?

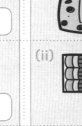

Estimate:

Actual cost:

3. Comparing prices – which is better value? Find the cost of one first.

(a) (i)

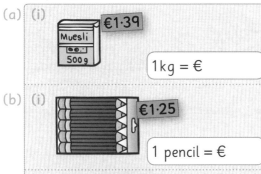

1kg = €

(ii)

1kg = €

Better value

(b) (i)
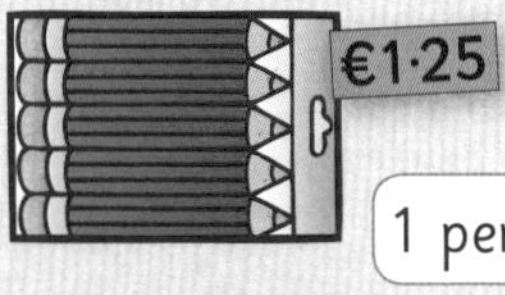

1 pencil = €

(ii)
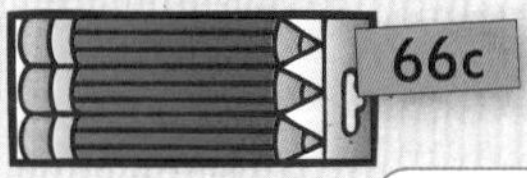

1 pencil = €

Better value

(c) (i)

1 orange = €

(ii)

1 orange = €

Better value

(d) (i)

Buy one, get one free!
1kg rice = €

(ii)

1kg rice = €

Better value

(e) (i)
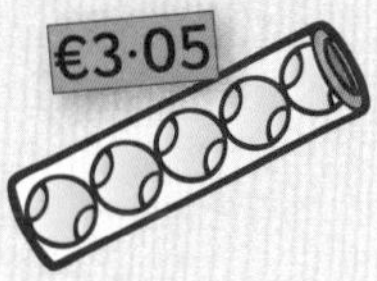

1 ball = €

(ii)
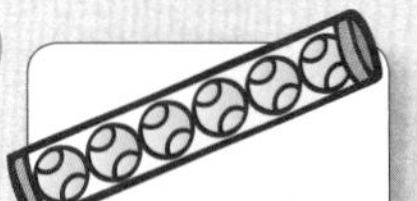
Was **€8·40**.
Now $\frac{1}{2}$ price.
1 ball = €

Better value

4. Compare the prices of each pair of items. How much do you save?

(a) (i)

(ii)

2l of the cheaper milk would save you €________, so
10l of the cheaper milk would save you €________.

(b) (i)

(ii)

The cheaper chicken wings are €________ cheaper per wing. If you wanted 30 for a barbecue, you would save €________.

(c) (i)

(ii)

4 plants **€2·04**
plus 2 free!

A lettuce plant in the cheaper box saves you €________.
Buying 48 of the better value plants would save you €________.

Value for money

1. Station 1
Diesel €1·52 per litre

How much money would a taxi driver save if she bought 40 litres of diesel at the better value petrol station? €______

Station 2
Diesel €1·65 per litre
Buy 9 litres, get 1 free!

2. **Apple Juice**

(a) Find the cost per litre of each carton.

(b) If you bought 6 litres of the most expensive apple juice, how much more would it cost you than the same amount of the cheapest juice?

3. What change did Carmel get from €50 when she bought six chickens at €4·79 each? €______

4. **Saving money for a purpose! Complete the following.**

(a) Mary saves €5 each week. How long will it take her to save enough to buy the tennis racquet? ______ weeks

(b) How much will Fred need to save per week if he wants to be able to buy a concert ticket in nine weeks? €______

(c)

Sasha has decided to cycle to work instead of drive to work.
She was spending €1·85 each day while using her car.
How much would she save in a year? (She works a five-day week.) €______

(d) Dan spent €14·50 on a pizza every Friday. He started cooking his own dinner to save money. His dinner now costs him €4·90. How much will he save in a year? €______

(e)

Oliver gave up drinking a can of cola each day.
How much did he save in a year? (not a leap year) €______

5. **How much do they cost?** (i) **Estimate the cost of each of these.** (ii) **Then find the actual cost.**

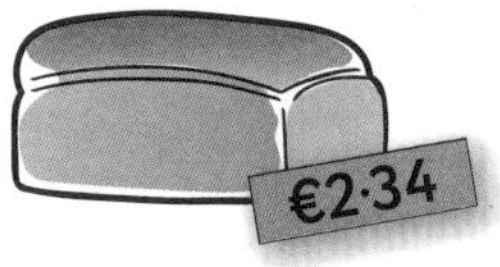

		Estimate	Actual cost
(a)	6 loaves of bread		
(b)	7 cartons of eggs		
(c)	9 bunches of bananas		
(d)	8 chickens		
(e)	12l of petrol		

Challenge A hotel charges €79·50 per person per night. It has an offer of €67·25 per person per night for a three-night stay. How much would two adults staying for three nights save by taking the three-night offer? €______

Shop bills

1. (a) Estimate the total shopping bill by rounding the cost of each item to the nearest euro.
   (b) Use your calculator to help you find the total cost of the bill.
   (c) Tina handed in €50 to buy all the items. How much change did she get? € ______
   (d) What is the price of one tin of sweetcorn? € ______
   (e) How much does one tube of toothpaste cost? € ______
   (f) How much would $3\frac{1}{2}$kg of sausages cost? € ______
   (g) Which costs more and by how much – 8 litres of orange juice or 150 tea bags?
   ______ by € ______

Mega Save Bill:

ORANGE JUICE 2L	€2·14
50 TEA BAGS	€3·50
$\frac{1}{2}$ KG SAUSAGES	€3·42
3 TINS OF SWEETCORN	€4·35
1 KG MUESLI	€3·17
1 BAG APPLES	€1·99
3 TUBES TOOTHPASTE	€9·18
2 TOOTHBRUSHES	€6·26
1 BAG OF CARROTS	€2·47
10 ONIONS	€2·60

Going shopping

2. **Find the total for each of these bills.**

(a) **Jack**
2 jerseys: €
2 rugby balls: €
1 goggles: €
Total: €

(b) **Maeve**
1 hurley: €
3 sliotars: €
2 goggles: €
Total: €

(c) **Emma**
1 surfboard: €
1 goggles: €
3 tennis balls: €
Total: €

(d) **Brian**
2 racquets: €
10 tennis balls: €
3 jerseys: €
Total: €

(e) **Deirdre**
3 jerseys: €
2 goggles: €
4 racquets: €
Total: €

(f) **Paul**
2 surfboards: €
2 hurleys: €
3 goggles: €
Total: €

(g) **Alan**
3 rugby balls: €
4 sliotars: €
5 tennis balls: €
Total: €

(h) **Sue**
8 tennis balls: €
5 racquets: €
4 jerseys: €
Total: €

3. 
During a sale, Jim bought three items costing €29·65, €47·99 and €19·45. What change had he from €100? € ______

4. How much less than €200 is the sum of €35·95, €63·92 and €28·19? € ______

Challenge The average cost of four items is €16·35. One of the items costs €23·25. Find the average cost of the other three items. € ______

Money – Family holiday

1. Mam, Dad and their three children are planning a holiday to Portugal.

(a) Which is the best value airline for the family?

(i) ☐ **Go Flights**
€120 each way per person.

(ii) ☐ **Sun Airline**
€235 return per person plus €10 booking fee per person.

(iii) ☐ **First Fliers**
€360 return per person. Children half price!

(iv) ☐ **Atlantic Air**
€275 return per person. Spend over €1,000 and get €200 off.

(b) Select the best value accommodation for seven nights for the family.

(i) ☐ **SEA VIEW HOTEL**
Family deal! €147 per night.

(ii) ☐ **Waves Hotel**
€30 per person per night.

(iii) ☐ **Apartment Hotel**
Special offer – one week for €1,000 (7 nights).

(c) The family is bringing €875 for their food for the week.
What is their daily food allowance? €________

(d) Which is the better bike hire deal for three days?

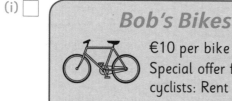

(i) ☐ **Bob's Bikes**

€10 per bike per day.
Special offer for all cyclists: Rent two days, get one extra day free.

(ii) ☐ **Seaside Cycles**

Group deal (max. 6 people):
Total of €40 per day.

(e) The family took the better deal on all offers, including bikes.

(i) How much did the holiday, including food, cost altogether? €________

(ii) How much did they save overall by choosing the best value offers instead of the most expensive? €________

You may use your calculator for this!

2. A group of six young adults went to a music festival and spent one night in a tent.

Cost of tickets:
€75 per ticket

Six-person tent:
€252 + space rental €60

Three-person tent:
€150 + space rental €42 per tent

(a) What was the total cost of the tickets and a six-person tent? €________

(b) What was the total cost of the tickets and two three-person tents? €________

(c) How much cheaper is it to rent a six-person tent instead of two three-person tents? €________

(d) What was the total spend per person, including tickets, using the cheaper option? €________

(e) How much did they save per person by taking the cheaper option? €________

Money problems

1.  Elaine earns €24·50 per hour. What was her total earnings for a week if she worked 38 hours? € ______

2. A hotel charges €96·50 per person per night including breakfast.
What was the total hotel charge for two adults who spent five nights at the hotel? € ______

3. Share €267 between Pat and Martha, giving Martha twice as much as Pat. Martha got € ______.

4.  A car can travel 25km on one litre of diesel. What is the cost of the diesel for a 275km journey if diesel costs €1·68 per litre? € ______

5. **What's their pay?**

(a) **Funtown Fair**
Rollercoaster:
Open 9 to 5.

Barry gets paid €10 per hour. He worked from Mon to Fri.

(b) **Bumper Cars**
Open 10 to 6.

Jerry worked Fri, Sat and Sun at €9 per hour.

(c) **Popcorn Stand**
€2 per box.

Enda gets €5 per hour plus half of the popcorn sales. He worked for 9 hours and sold 32 boxes of popcorn.

(d) **Carousel**
Open 9 to 6, seven days a week.

Ciara earns €8 per hour and $1\frac{1}{2}$ times that on Sun. She worked Wed to Mon.

(e) **Waltzer**
Open 9 to 6 each day.

Jenny gets paid €7 per hour and double that on Sun. She worked from Fri to Tues.

(f) **Ring-Toss**
€3 per game.

Natalie has a choice of €10 per hour or $\frac{1}{2}$ of sales. She worked 35 hours and sold 400 games. Which offer would have been the better choice?

6. **Money quiz**

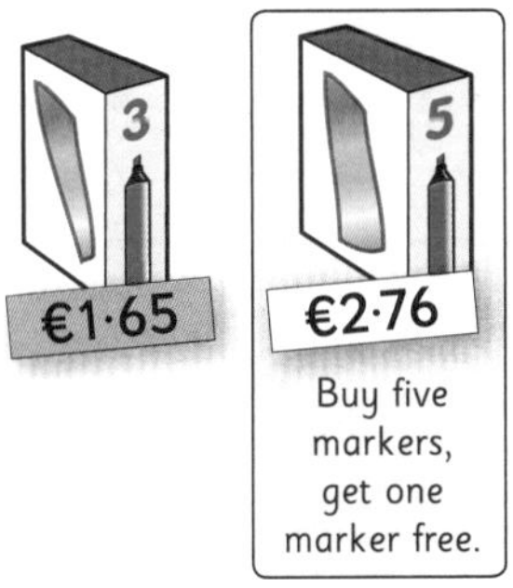

(a) What is the total cost of 16 apples at 35c each? € ______

(b) What would you save by buying 30 of the better value markers? € ______

(c) 

Jim has saved €156.
He still needs € ______ to buy the skateboard.

(d) What change would you get from €20 if you spent €10·50 on a match ticket and €4·25 on a programme? € ______

(e) Liz worked from 06:00 to 12:00 Monday to Friday.
How much did she earn per week if she was paid €32·50 per hour? € ______

Challenge Peter got €11·72 change from €20 when he bought six tennis balls.
Pam got €4·56 change from €10 when she bought four tennis balls.

(a) Who got the better value? ______

(b) How much would a person save if s/he bought 24 of the better value balls? € ______

A quick look back 3

LOOK BACK

1. 3,728 × 10 = ______

2. 600 × 50 = ______

3. €17·65 × 100 = € ______

4. Through how many degrees does the minute hand of a clock turn in one hour? ______

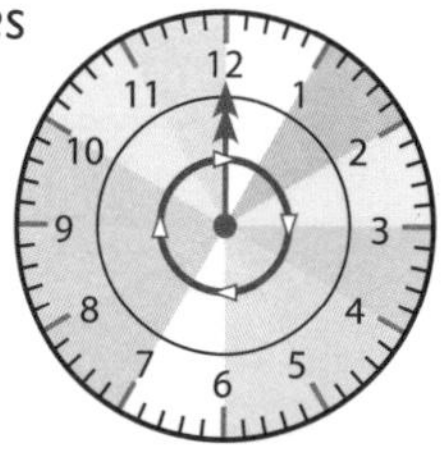

5. What type of angle is an 80° angle? ______

6. 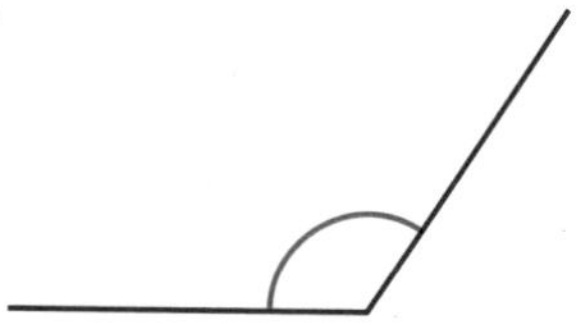

What do we call this type of angle?

______

7. This is an ______ angle.

8. 76 ÷ 8 = ______ R ______

9. 

How much would $3\frac{1}{2}$kg of muesli cost?

€ ______

10. A bunch of five bananas costs €1·90. What would eight such bunches of bananas cost?

€ ______

11. 80 ÷ 15 = ______ R ______

12. A melon costs €2·25.
How much would ten such melons cost?

€ ______

13. Which of the three boxes of plums can be packed into bags of five or six without leaving any plums leftover? ______

(a) (b) (c)

14. What is the total cost of 15 oranges at 28c each? € ______

15. Victor saved €0·35 by buying the larger box of eggs rather than two smaller boxes. How much would he save by buying 60 of the better value eggs? € ______

16. How many degrees altogether are there in two right angles? ______

17. 288 ÷ 5 = ☆

______ R ______

5) 2 8 8

18. If I divide 50 tens by 2 tens,
I get ______ .

19. 5,900 ÷ 100 = ______

20. Two of the angles in a triangle are 60° and 80°. How many degrees are there in the third angle? ______

Chapter 11: Fractions 1

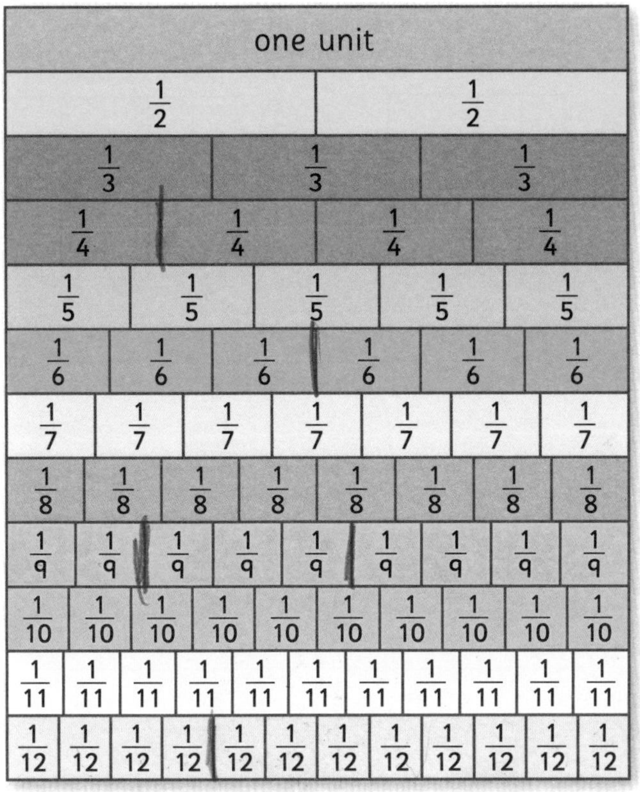

1. Write the missing numbers.

(a) $\frac{1}{2} = \frac{\square}{6}$ (b) $\frac{2}{10} = \frac{\square}{5}$ (c) $\frac{\square}{6} = \frac{2}{3}$

(d) $\frac{3}{12} = \frac{1}{\square}$ (e) $\frac{1}{\square} = \frac{5}{10}$ (f) $\frac{8}{12} = \frac{\square}{6}$

2. Which is bigger? Write >, = or <.

(a) $\frac{2}{3} \bigcirc \frac{5}{9}$ (b) $\frac{8}{12} \bigcirc \frac{2}{3}$ (c) $\frac{3}{10} \bigcirc \frac{2}{5}$

(d) $\frac{2}{7} \bigcirc \frac{3}{9}$ (e) $\frac{4}{5} \bigcirc \frac{8}{10}$ (f) $\frac{1}{2} \bigcirc \frac{6}{12}$

3. True ✓ or false ✗?

(a) $\frac{3}{5} = \frac{4}{10}$ ☐ (b) $\frac{2}{3} > \frac{7}{9}$ ☐ (c) $\frac{10}{12} < \frac{3}{4}$ ☐

(d) $\frac{3}{4} = \frac{8}{12}$ ☐ (e) $\frac{1}{5} > \frac{3}{10}$ ☐ (f) $\frac{4}{9} > \frac{1}{3}$ ☐

(g) $\frac{5}{9} < \frac{2}{3}$ ☐ (h) $\frac{11}{12} = \frac{5}{6}$ ☐ (i) $\frac{9}{12} > \frac{7}{8}$ ☐

4. Match each fraction to the correct coloured picture.

(a)
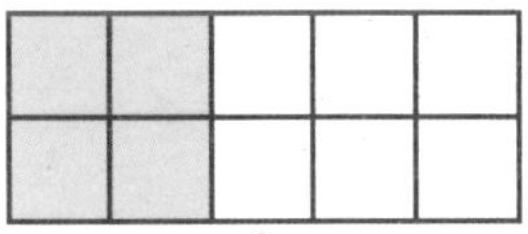

(b)
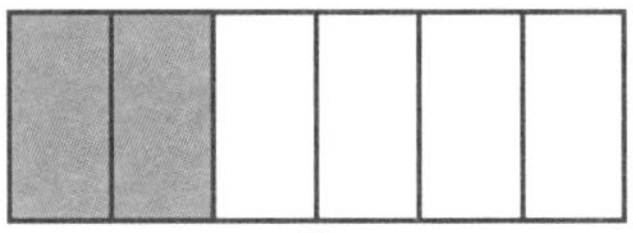

(c)
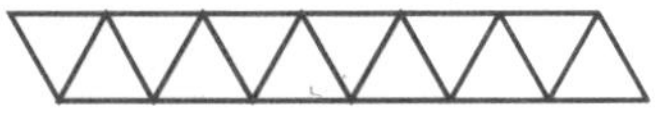

$\frac{1}{3}$ $\frac{2}{5}$ $\frac{3}{4}$ $\frac{2}{3}$ $\frac{1}{4}$ $\frac{1}{2}$

(d)
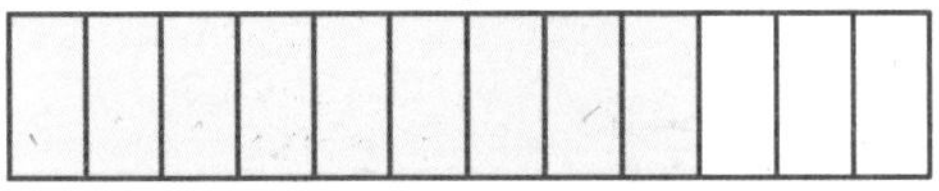

(e)
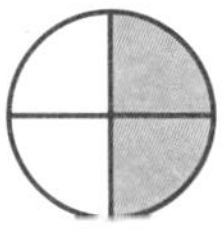

(f)
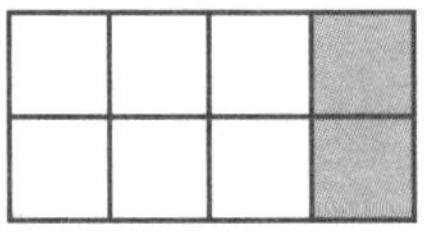

5. These blocks have to be built in order. Start with the **biggest** or they will topple over!

(a)
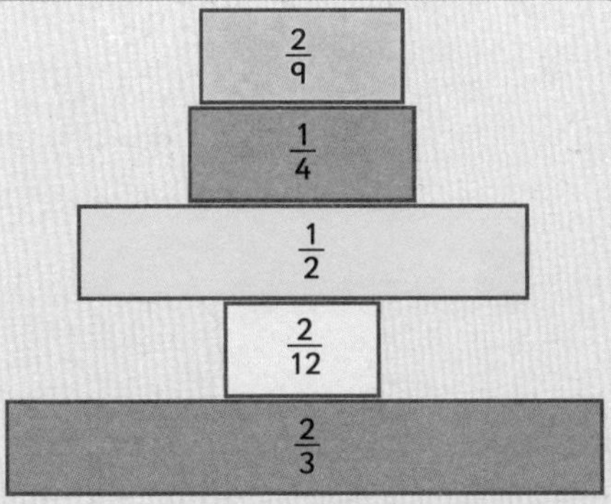

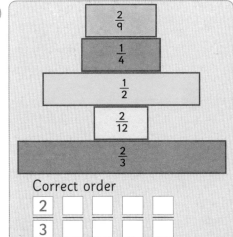

Correct order

$\frac{2}{3}$ ☐ ☐ ☐ ☐

(b) $\frac{2}{3}$, $\frac{2}{12}$, $\frac{2}{6}$, $\frac{3}{4}$, $\frac{1}{2}$

Correct order

☐ ☐ ☐ ☐ ☐

(c) $\frac{1}{5}$, $\frac{3}{10}$, $\frac{1}{2}$, $\frac{4}{5}$, $\frac{6}{10}$

Correct order

☐ ☐ ☐ ☐ ☐

(d) $\frac{5}{8}$, $\frac{3}{4}$, $\frac{1}{2}$, $\frac{5}{12}$, $\frac{1}{4}$

Correct order

☐ ☐ ☐ ☐ ☐

(e) $\frac{2}{9}$, $\frac{1}{4}$, $\frac{3}{6}$, $\frac{4}{12}$, $\frac{5}{9}$

Correct order

☐ ☐ ☐ ☐ ☐

STRAND Number **STRAND UNIT/ELEMENT** *Fractions*

LANGUAGE *Fraction wall, order, match, multiply, numerator, denominator, equivalent, amount, proper/improper, fractions, mixed numbers, number line, express, whole number, sale, original price*

Equivalence

1. **Julia tiled $\frac{1}{4}$ of each of these walls one morning. How many tiles did she put on each wall? Colour them.**

(a) 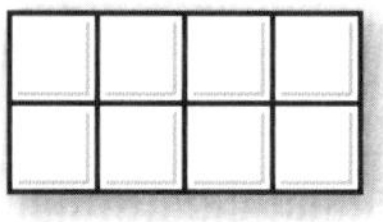

$\frac{1}{4}$ of 8 = ______

(b) 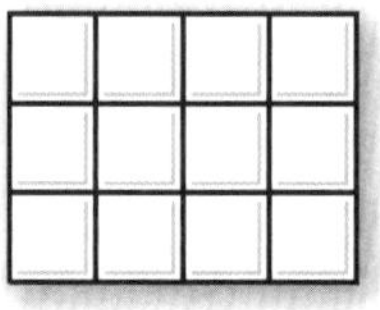

$\frac{1}{4}$ of ______ = ______

(c) 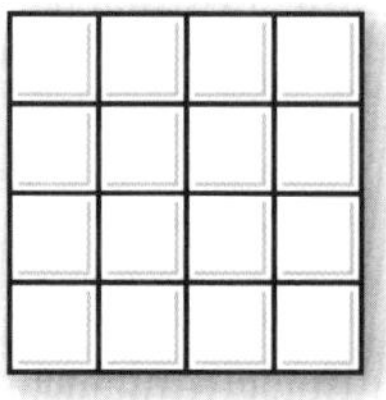

$\frac{1}{4}$ of ______ = ______

(d) 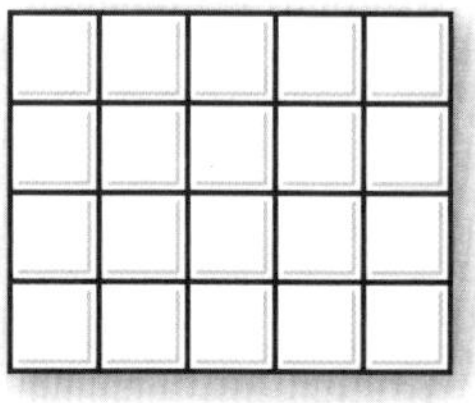

$\frac{1}{4}$ of ______ = ______

She tiled a further $\frac{1}{2}$ of each wall that afternoon.

(e) What fraction of each wall is now tiled? $\frac{\square}{\square}$

(f) How many tiles are now on each wall?

(i) ______ tiles (ii) ______ tiles (iii) ______ tiles (iv) ______ tiles

2. **Who is winning? These girls are running a 100m race.**

Jenny has $\frac{1}{2}$ of the race completed. Mary has $\frac{3}{5}$ completed and Holly has $\frac{3}{4}$ of the race completed. Jill has $\frac{1}{5}$ of the race still to complete while Sasha has $\frac{4}{10}$ of the race completed.

(a) Write how many metres each girl has run.

(b) Write each girl's name in the correct box above.

Numerators and denominators

$$\frac{\text{numerator}}{\text{denominator}} = \frac{\text{how many of the parts are used}}{\text{how many parts something is divided into}}$$

Example: $\frac{3}{4}$ = 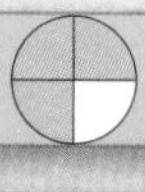

If you multiply the numerator and denominator of a fraction by the same number, it keeps the same value.

A

$\frac{1}{2} \times \frac{2}{2} = \frac{2}{4}$

This is because $\frac{2}{2}$ or $\frac{4}{4}$ or $\frac{8}{8}$ are equal to 1.

B

$\frac{2}{4} \times \frac{2}{2} = \frac{4}{8}$

3. **Complete these to make equivalent fractions.**

(a) $\frac{1}{2} \times \frac{3}{3} = \frac{\square}{\square}$ (b) $\frac{2}{5} \times \frac{2}{2} = \frac{\square}{\square}$ (c) $\frac{2}{3} \times \frac{\square}{\square} = \frac{10}{15}$ (d) $\frac{7}{8} \times \frac{\square}{\square} = \frac{21}{24}$ (e) $\frac{5}{12} \times \frac{\square}{\square} = \frac{\square}{36}$

More equivalence

1. Write three equivalent fractions for each of these coloured amounts.

(a) 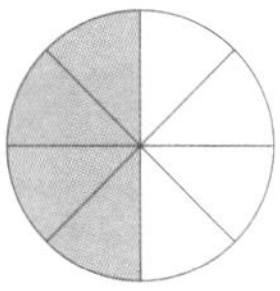

$\frac{\square}{2}$, $\frac{\square}{4}$, $\frac{\square}{8}$

(b) 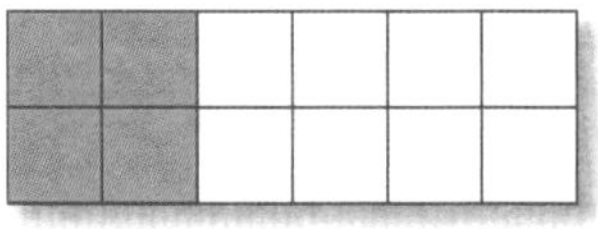

$\frac{\square}{3}$, $\frac{\square}{6}$, $\frac{\square}{12}$

(c) 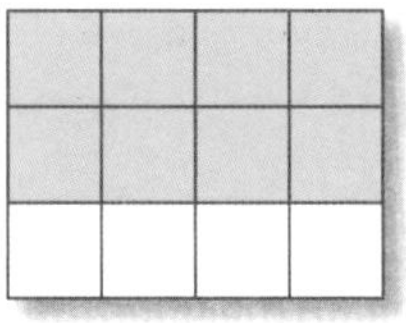

$\frac{2}{\square}$, $\frac{\square}{6}$, $\frac{\square}{12}$

(d) 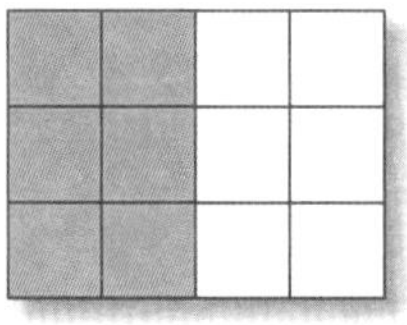

$\frac{1}{\square}$, $\frac{\square}{6}$, $\frac{\square}{12}$

I can also divide the numerator and denominator of a fraction by the same number without changing its value.

Example: $\frac{4}{8} \div \frac{4}{4} = \frac{1}{2}$ 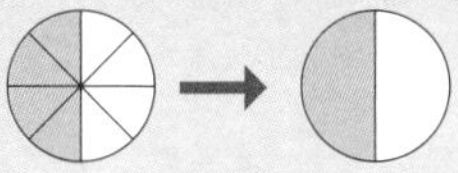

2. Write an equivalent fraction for each of these coloured amounts by dividing.

(a) 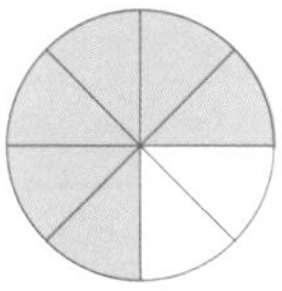

$\frac{6}{8} \div \frac{\square}{2} = \frac{\square}{4}$

(b) 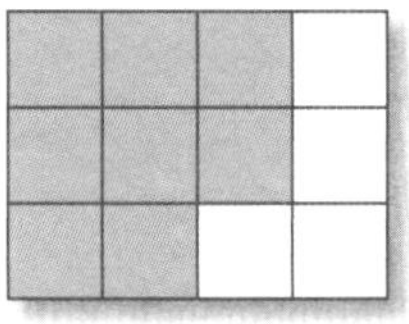

$\frac{8}{\square} \div \frac{4}{4} = \frac{\square}{3}$

(c) 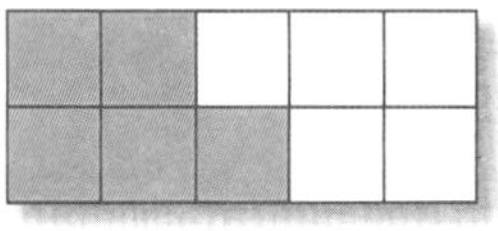

$\frac{\square}{10} \div \frac{\square}{\square} = \frac{1}{2}$

(d) 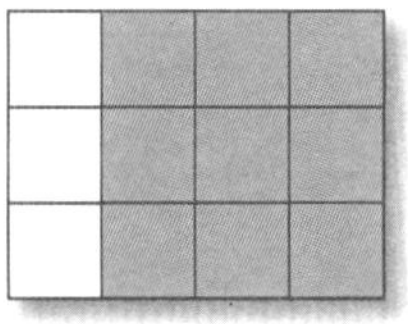

$\frac{\square}{12} \div \frac{3}{\square} = \frac{\square}{4}$

3. Complete these sentences to make equivalent fractions.

(a) $\frac{4}{6} \div \frac{2}{2} = \frac{\square}{\square}$

(b) $\frac{9}{12} \div \frac{\square}{\square} = \frac{3}{4}$

(c) $\frac{8}{12} \div \frac{\square}{\square} = \frac{2}{3}$

(d) $\frac{6}{9} \div \frac{\square}{\square} = \frac{2}{3}$

(e) $\frac{6}{12} \div \frac{\square}{\square} = \frac{1}{2}$

(f) $\frac{10}{20} \div \frac{10}{10} = \frac{\square}{\square}$

(g) $\frac{15}{25} \div \frac{5}{5} = \frac{\square}{\square}$

(h) $\frac{5}{20} \div \frac{\square}{\square} = \frac{\square}{4}$

4. (a) Peter had €18. He spent $\frac{8}{12}$ of it. How much did he spend? €________

(b) Pam spent $\frac{4}{6}$ of her €18. She spent €________.

(c) John had 24c. He spent $\frac{6}{9}$ of it. How much did he spend? €________

(d)  Jill had 36 marbles. She lost $\frac{4}{12}$ of them. She lost ________ marbles.

(e) There are 40 oranges in a box. $\frac{3}{12}$ of them are bad.

How may bad oranges are there? ________

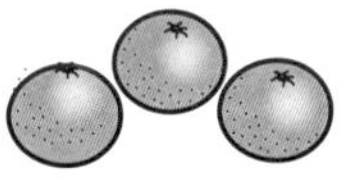

(f)  A tray can hold 20 eggs. $\frac{12}{16}$ of the tray is full. How many eggs are on the tray? ________

Challenge

(a) Joanne had €5 left when she bought the T-shirt. What fraction of her money did she spend on it? $\frac{\square}{\square}$

(b) Vera had €30. She bought the blouse. She spent $\frac{\square}{\square}$ of her money buying it.

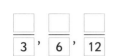

Improper fractions and mixed numbers

Proper fractions and improper fractions

$$\frac{\text{numerator}}{\text{denominator}} = \frac{\text{how many of the parts are used}}{\text{how many parts something is divided into}}$$

$= \frac{4}{5}$ 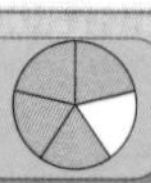

A In a proper fraction, the numerator is always less than the denominator.
Examples: $\frac{3}{5}$, $\frac{8}{9}$, $\frac{7}{12}$, $\frac{11}{12}$, $\frac{19}{20}$

B In an improper fraction, the numerator is always greater than the denominator.
Examples: $\frac{3}{2}$, $\frac{6}{5}$, $\frac{7}{4}$, $\frac{11}{8}$, $\frac{13}{9}$, $\frac{19}{12}$, $\frac{23}{20}$

1. Sort these fractions into groups of (a) proper fractions and (b) improper fractions.

$\frac{4}{5}$, $\frac{4}{3}$, $\frac{2}{3}$, $\frac{7}{9}$, $\frac{13}{12}$, $\frac{17}{10}$, $\frac{8}{9}$, $\frac{9}{8}$, $\frac{11}{12}$, $\frac{19}{20}$, $\frac{24}{20}$, $\frac{53}{50}$

Changing improper fractions to mixed numbers (units and proper fractions)

(i) 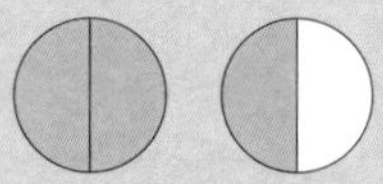
→ $\frac{3}{2} = 1\frac{1}{2}$

(ii) 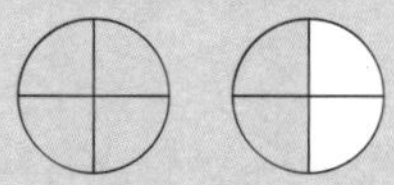
→ $\frac{6}{4} = 1\frac{2}{4} = 1\frac{1}{2}$

(iii) 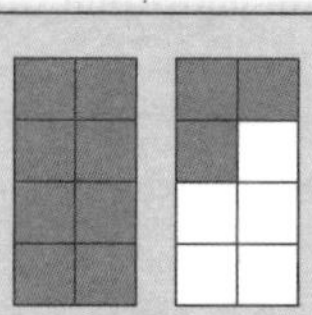
→ $\frac{11}{8} = 1\frac{3}{8}$

(iv) 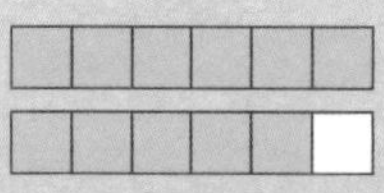
→ $\frac{11}{6} = 1\frac{5}{6}$

2. Write the missing improper fraction or mixed number.

(a) $\frac{4}{3}$ = ____ (b) $\frac{9}{5}$ = ____ (c) $1\frac{3}{4}$ = ____ (d) $\frac{12}{5}$ = ____ (e) $1\frac{7}{8}$ = ____ (f) $1\frac{5}{12}$ = ____

(g) $\frac{23}{12}$ = ____ (h) $1\frac{2}{9}$ = ____ (i) $2\frac{1}{4}$ = ____ (j) $2\frac{5}{6}$ = ____ (k) $\frac{27}{10}$ = ____ (l) $3\frac{4}{5}$ = ____

3. Find a match in the bottom row for each proper fraction, improper fraction or mixed number in the top row.

Top row: $\frac{3}{4}$, $1\frac{1}{2}$, $2\frac{1}{4}$, $2\frac{2}{4}$, $3\frac{1}{2}$, $\frac{13}{4}$

Bottom row: $\frac{9}{4}$, $2\frac{1}{2}$, $\frac{7}{2}$, $\frac{6}{8}$, $3\frac{1}{4}$, $\frac{3}{2}$

4. Fractions on the number line

(a) Write where $\frac{3}{2}$, $2\frac{1}{2}$, $\frac{7}{4}$, $\frac{2}{4}$, $1\frac{1}{4}$ and $\frac{4}{2}$ go on the number line.

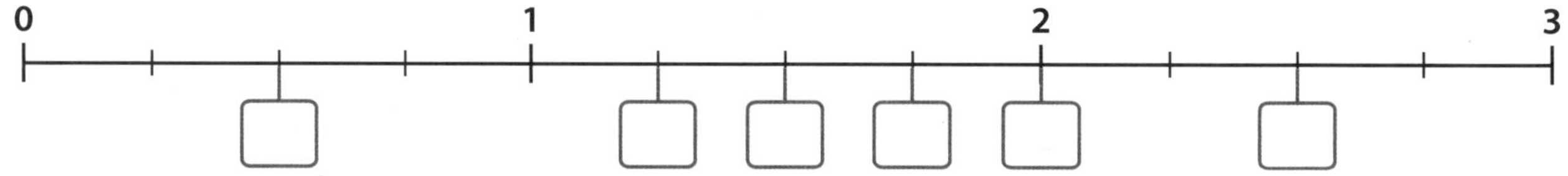

(b) Write where $\frac{7}{6}$, $1\frac{2}{3}$, $2\frac{2}{6}$, $\frac{3}{3}$, $2\frac{3}{3}$ and $1\frac{5}{6}$ go on the number line.

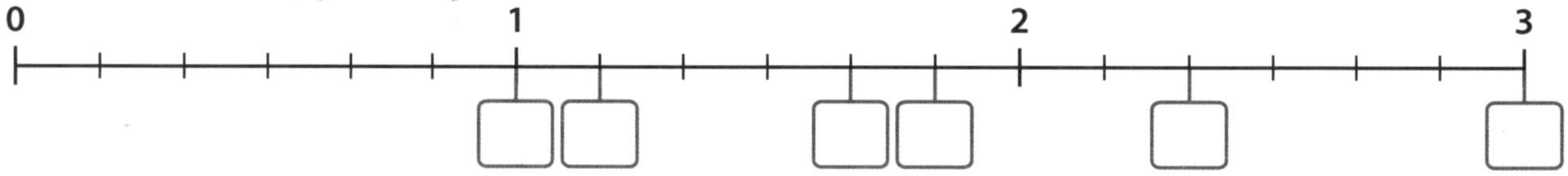

Fractions of whole numbers – Using fractions

Find $\frac{3}{5}$ of these candles.

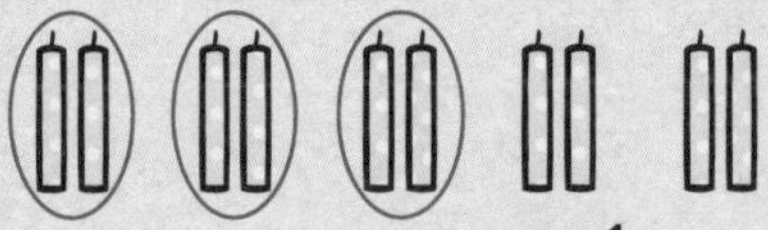

$\rightarrow$ $10 \div 5 = 2$ $\rightarrow$ $\frac{1}{5} = 2$

$\frac{5}{5}$ = 10 candles

$\frac{1}{5}$ = $5\overline{)10}$
2 candles

$\frac{3}{5}$ = $\times$ 3
6 candles

Quick way

$\frac{5}{5} = 10$

$\frac{1}{5} = 2$

$\frac{3}{5} = 6$

1.

(a)	(b)	(c)	(d)	(e)	(f)
Jim scored $\frac{3}{4}$ of 20 shots	Jack scored $\frac{5}{8}$ of 40 shots	Mary scored $\frac{5}{9}$ of 36 shots	Sasha scored $\frac{3}{5}$ of 50 shots	Emma scored $\frac{5}{6}$ of 30 shots	Tom scored $\frac{4}{7}$ of 56 shots
Score ☐	Score ☐	Score ☐	Score ☐	Score ☐	Score ☐

(g) Who scored the most? ________ (h) Who scored the least? ________

2. Correct Louisa's homework. ✓ or ✗

(a) $\frac{4}{5}$ of 40 = 35 ☐ (b) $\frac{2}{3}$ of 27 = 18 ☐ (c) $\frac{3}{8}$ of 48 = 18 ☐ (d) $\frac{1}{5}$ of 55 = 5 ☐

(e) $\frac{3}{12}$ of 24 = 6 ☐ (f) $\frac{5}{7}$ of 49 = 35 ☐ (g) $\frac{6}{11}$ of 33 = 18 ☐ (h) $\frac{4}{4}$ of 16 = 16 ☐

3.

These children have the following fractions of the price of the rugby ball. How much money has each child?

(a) John has $\frac{5}{6}$. (b) Liz has $\frac{3}{8}$. (c) Joe has $\frac{3}{4}$. (d) Ella has $\frac{7}{8}$. (e) Brian has $\frac{5}{12}$.

4. Fix the printer! The printer did not print the following numbers. Can you write them in their correct places?

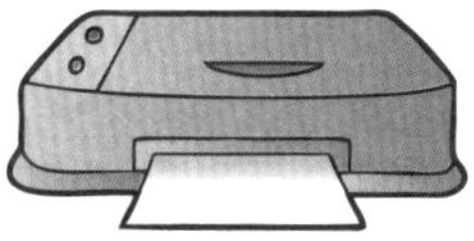

27 4 24 12 9 1 5 11

(a) $\frac{2}{3}$ of 18 = ___ (b) $\frac{2}{☐}$ of 10 = 4 (c) $\frac{7}{9}$ of ___ = 21 (d) $\frac{☐}{8}$ of 40 = 5

(e) $\frac{7}{12}$ of ___ = 14 (f) $\frac{☐}{8}$ of 40 = 20 (g) $\frac{3}{11}$ of 33 = ___ (h) $\frac{1}{☐}$ of 11 = 1

5. These are the answers to Sam's homework. They are jumbled up. Can you write them in the correct places?

35 36 27 15 40 21 63 88

(a) $\frac{3}{4}$ of 36 = ___ (b) $\frac{5}{9}$ of 63 = ___ (c) $\frac{7}{8}$ of 72 = ___ (d) $\frac{5}{12}$ of 36 = ___

(e) $\frac{5}{6}$ of 48 = ___ (f) $\frac{6}{7}$ of 42 = ___ (g) $\frac{11}{12}$ of 96 = ___ (h) $\frac{7}{20}$ of 60 = ___

Challenge

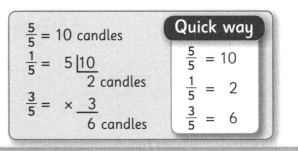

Dan spent $\frac{3}{4}$ of his money buying a hopper. Della spent half of her money buying one, while Peter spent $\frac{2}{3}$ of his money when he bought a hopper. Who had the most money at the beginning? ________

Expressing one number as a fraction of another

A

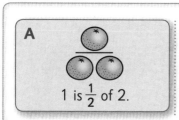

1 is $\frac{1}{2}$ of 2.

B

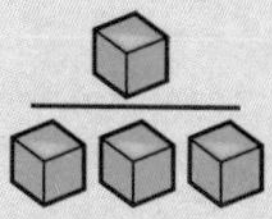

1 is $\frac{1}{3}$ of 3.

C

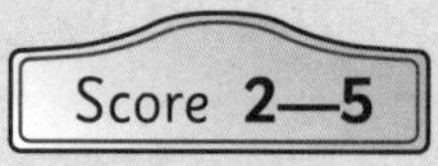

2 is $\frac{2}{5}$ of 5.

D

€5 is $\frac{1}{4}$ of €20.

1. Write a number sentence for each of these. Then simplify each fraction.

(a)

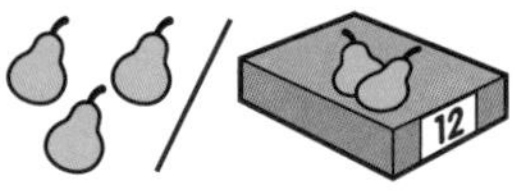

3 is $\frac{\square}{12}$ of 12

Simplified:

3 is $\frac{\square}{\square}$ of 12

(b)

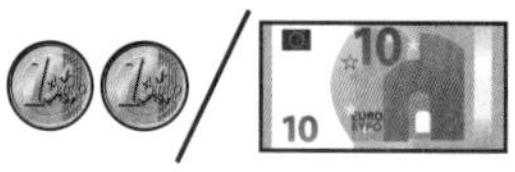

2 is $\frac{\square}{10}$ of ____

Simplified:

2 is $\frac{\square}{\square}$ of ____

(c)

____ is $\frac{\square}{10}$ of ____

Simplified:

____ is $\frac{\square}{\square}$ of ____

(d)

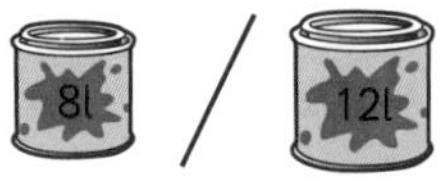

____ is $\frac{\square}{12}$ of ____

Simplified:

____ is $\frac{\square}{\square}$ of ____

2. Write a number sentence for each of these, then simplify it.

(a)

(b)

(c)

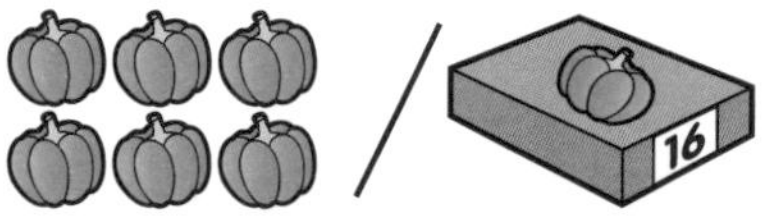

(d)

(e)

(f)

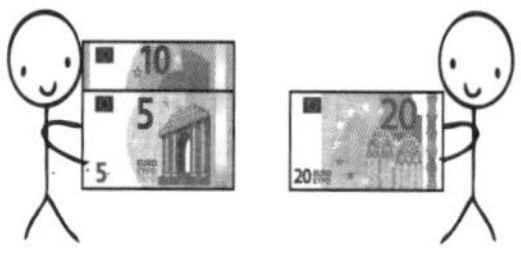

(g)

3. Study the following. Then answer the questions.

(a) What fraction of the children are girls?

(b) What fraction of the boys have schoolbags?

(c) What fraction of the girls have long hair?

(d) What fraction of the children have blonde hair?

(e) $\frac{\square}{\square}$ of the children are wearing runners.

(f) ____ children are wearing shoes and of those $\frac{\square}{\square}$ are boys.

(g) What fraction of the children are wearing shorts?

(h) $\frac{\square}{\square}$ of those wearing shorts have grey shorts.

(i) What fraction of the children with black hair have long black hair?

(j) What fraction of the girls are wearing a skirt?

(k) What fraction of the children are wearing a skirt?

(l) Make up two more questions for your partner to answer.

Finding the whole number

A

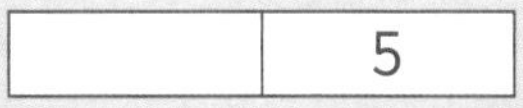

If $\frac{1}{2}$ of a number is 5, then $\frac{2}{2} = 10$.

Whole number = 10

B

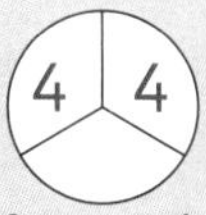

If $\frac{2}{3}$ of a number = 8,

then $\frac{1}{3} = 4$ and $\frac{3}{3} = 12$.

C

If $\frac{4}{5}$ of a number = 12,

then $\frac{1}{5} = 3$ and $\frac{5}{5} = 15$.

1. Complete these.

(a)

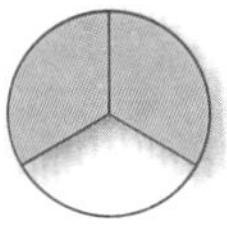

$\frac{2}{3} = 10$

$\frac{1}{3} =$ ____

$\frac{3}{3} =$ ____

(b)

$\frac{3}{4} = 18$

$\frac{1}{4} =$ ____

$\frac{4}{4} =$ ____

(c)

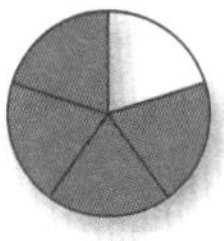

$\frac{4}{5} = 16$

$\frac{1}{5} =$ ____

$\frac{5}{5} =$ ____

(d)

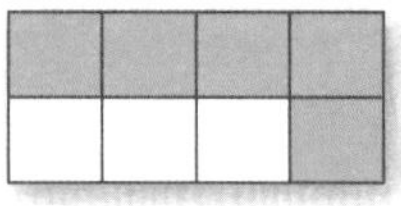

$\frac{5}{8} = 15$

$\frac{1}{8} =$ ____

$\frac{8}{8} =$ ____

(e)

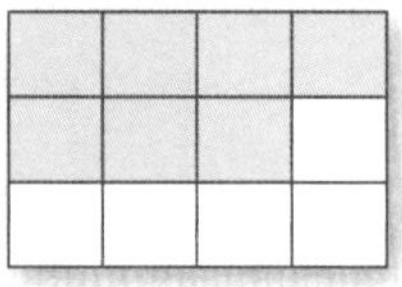

$\frac{7}{12} = 35$

$\frac{1}{12} =$ ____

$\frac{12}{12} =$ ____

2. Eight children are doing different jigsaws. How many pieces altogether are there in each puzzle?

(a) Jack: $\frac{1}{5}$ done

____ pieces

(b) Jim: $\frac{2}{3}$ done

____ pieces

(c) Jenny: $\frac{4}{9}$ done

____ pieces

(d) Jane: $\frac{3}{8}$ done

____ pieces

(e) Ellie: $\frac{2}{11}$ done

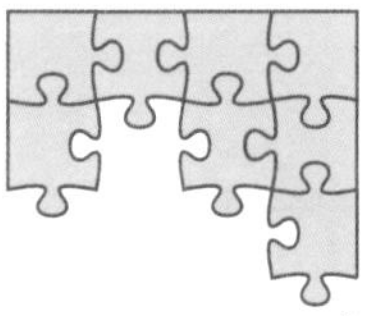

____ pieces

(f) Ava: $\frac{4}{7}$ done

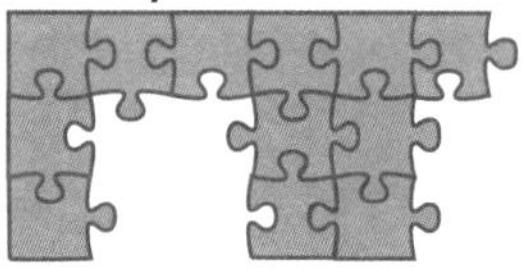

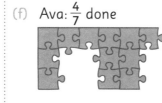

____ pieces

(g) Emmie: $\frac{2}{5}$ done

____ pieces

(h) Luke: $\frac{3}{10}$ done

____ pieces

3. Everything in the sports shop is on sale. What were the original prices?

(a)

$\frac{2}{3}$ of original price

Original price:

€ ____

(b)

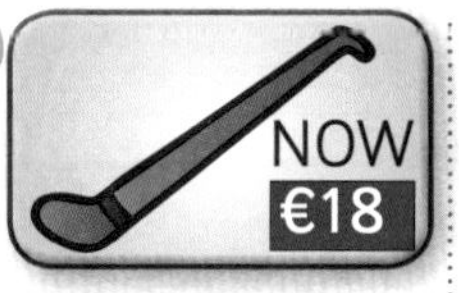

$\frac{2}{5}$ of original price

Original price:

€ ____

(c)

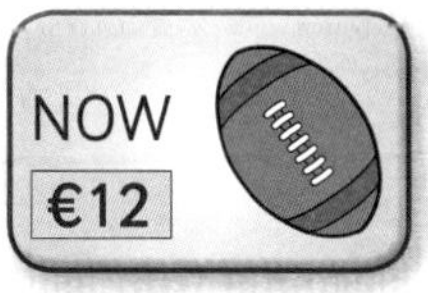

$\frac{3}{4}$ of original price

Original price:

€ ____

(d)

$\frac{5}{9}$ of original price

Original price:

€ ____

(e)

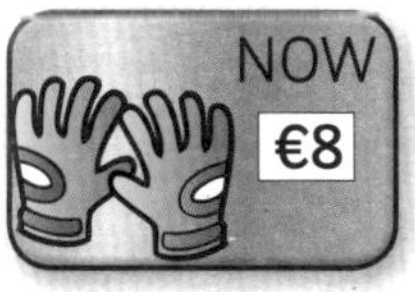

$\frac{4}{7}$ of original price

Original price:

€ ____

4. Joe spent $\frac{3}{4}$ of his money buying football boots for €36.
How much money had he at first? € ____

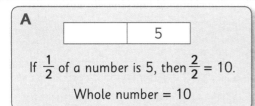

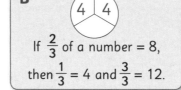

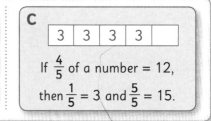

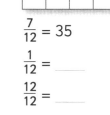

Challenge $\frac{3}{5}$ of the members of a club totals 90. (a) How many are there in the club altogether? ____ (b) What is $\frac{7}{10}$ of the members? ____

Chapter 12: 2-D shapes

1. Complete this grid. Use the word box to help you.

isosceles triangle   octagon   semi-circle   rhombus   pentagon   equilateral triangle

	Shape	Name	Number of sides	Pairs of parallel lines	Types of angle	Is it symmetrical?
(a)		equilateral triangle				
(b)	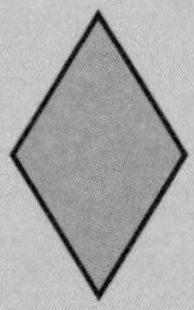				Two acute Two obtuse	
(c)	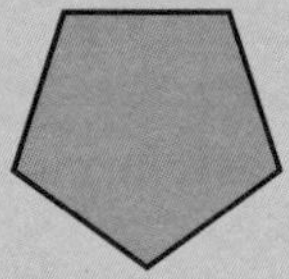					
(d)	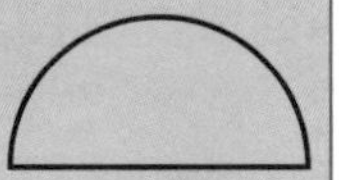			0		
(e)	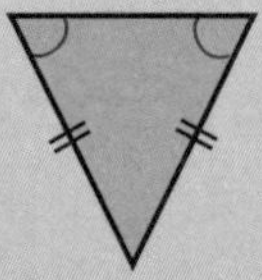					✓
(f)	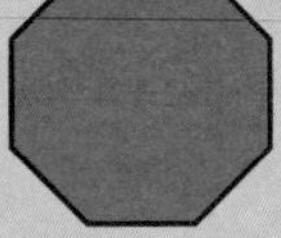		8			

A **polygon** is a 2-D shape with three or more straight sides.

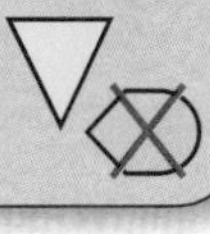

2. List the shapes from Question 1 that are polygons.

All polygons have straight sides. The sides and angles of **regular** polygons are all equal. All other polygons are **irregular**.

3. List the above shapes that are (a) **regular** polygons and (b) **irregular** polygons.

4. List all the 2-D shapes visible on these flags.

(a) 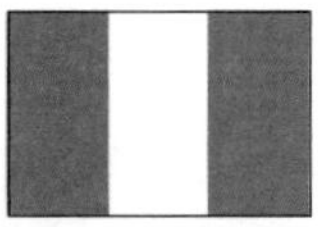
Ireland

(b) 
Jamaica

(c) 
Japan

(d) 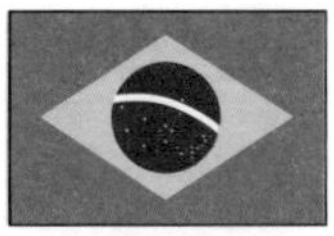
Brazil

(e) 
Greenland

STRAND **Shape and space**   **STRAND UNIT/ELEMENT** *2-D shapes*
LANGUAGE *Parallel lines, angles, pentagon, semi-circle, octagon, triangles, quadrilaterals, square, rhombus, rectangle, parallelogram, trapezium, regular, irregular, polygon, pentominoes, tessellation, tangrams*

Triangles

Types of triangle:

A equilateral

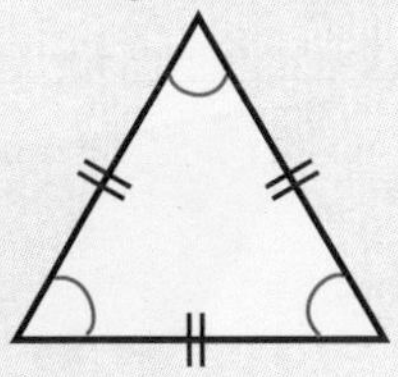

- All sides equal
- All angles equal

B isosceles

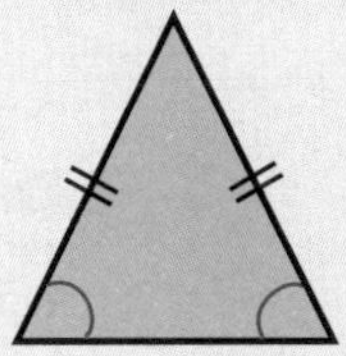

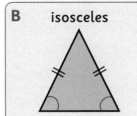

- Two sides equal
- Two angles equal

C scalene

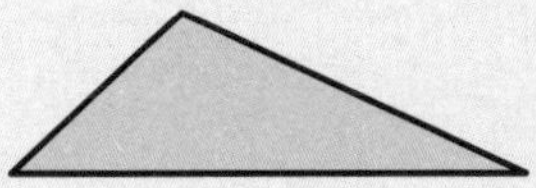

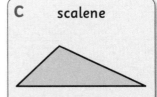

- No sides equal
- No angles equal

D right angled

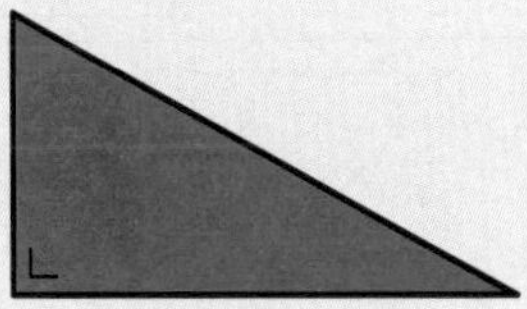

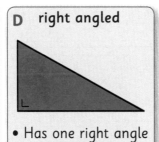

- Has one right angle

Remember: The three angles of a triangle always add up to 180°. They make a straight angle!

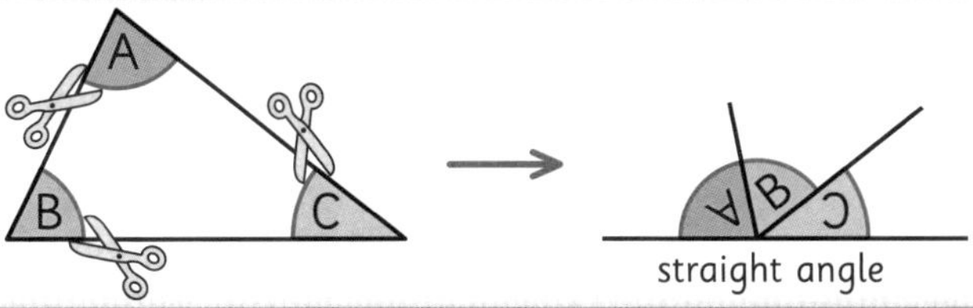

1. **Without using your protractor, calculate the measure of the unknown angle(s) in each triangle.**

(a)

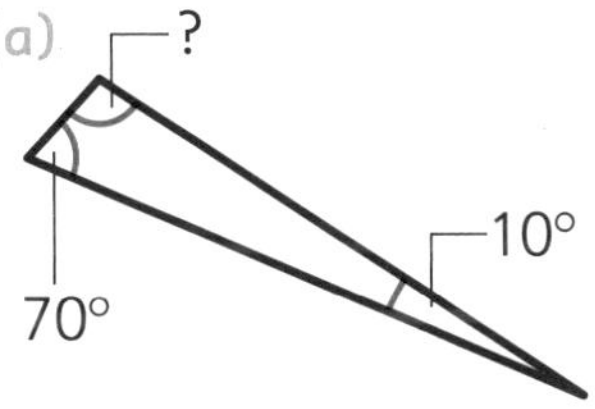

(b)

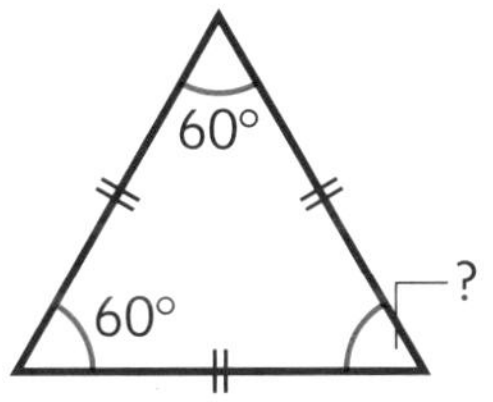

(c)

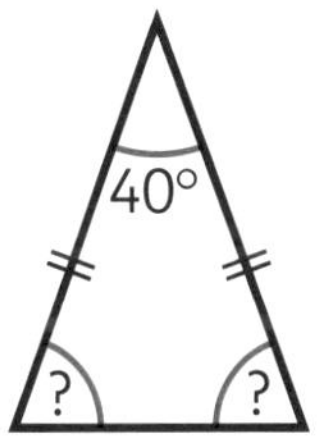

(d)

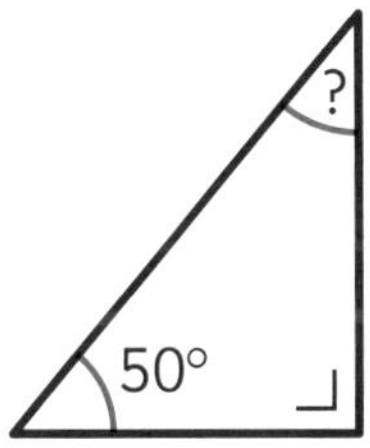

2. **Measure the (i) sides of each triangle, (ii) angles of each triangle and (iii) name the triangle. Use your protractor.**

Example:

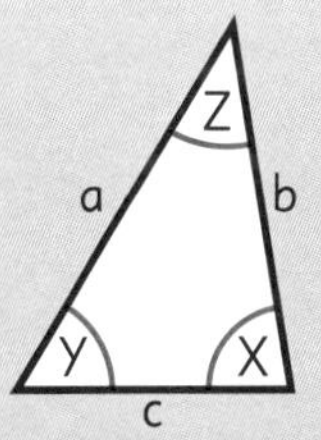

(i)	a = 3cm	b = $2\frac{1}{2}$cm	c = 2cm
(ii)	X = 80°	Y = 60°	Z = 40°
(iii)	scalene		

(a)

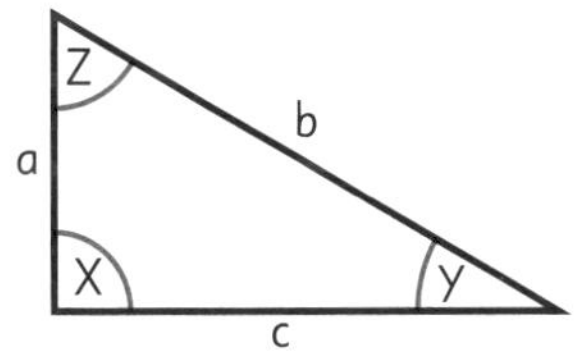

(b)

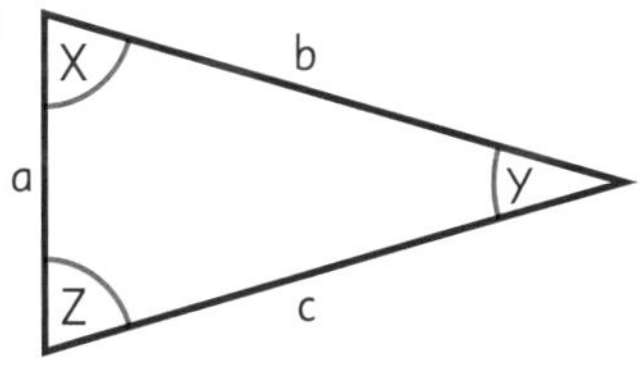

(c)

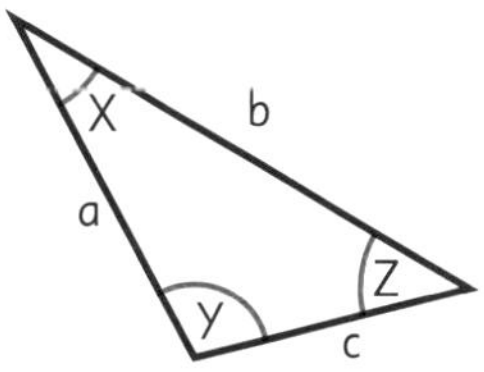

(d)

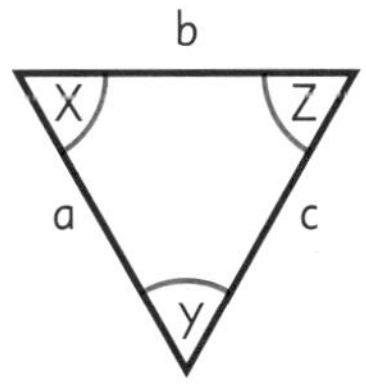

3.

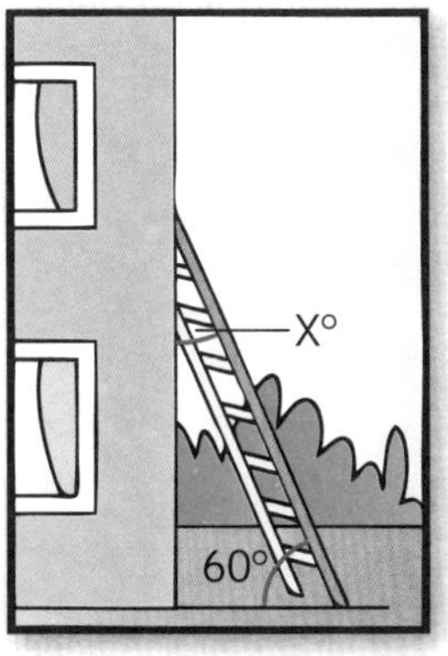

Jane propped a ladder against the wall so she could paint the top of the house. The ladder makes an angle of 60° with the ground. What is the measure of angle X? ______

4. The park is shaped like an isosceles triangle. The perimeter is 710m. The shortest side is 170m.

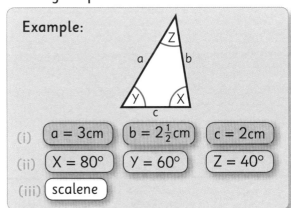

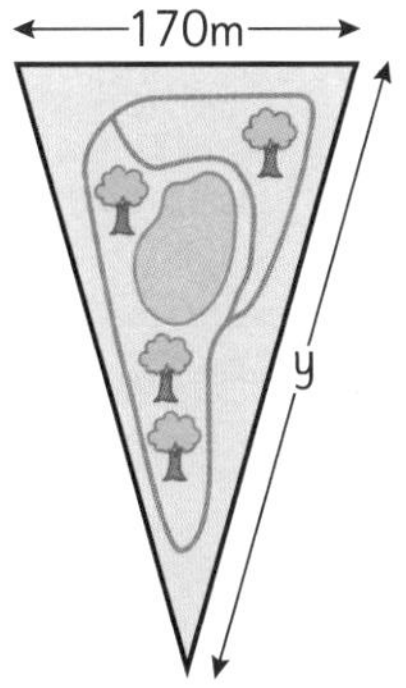

(a) What is the length of side Y? ______ m

(b) Jane ran around the perimeter of the park six times. How many km did she run? ______ km

Quadrilaterals

A **quadrilateral** is a 2-D shape with four straight sides.

A **regular** quadrilateral has all equal sides and equal angles. All other quadrilaterals are **irregular**.

1.

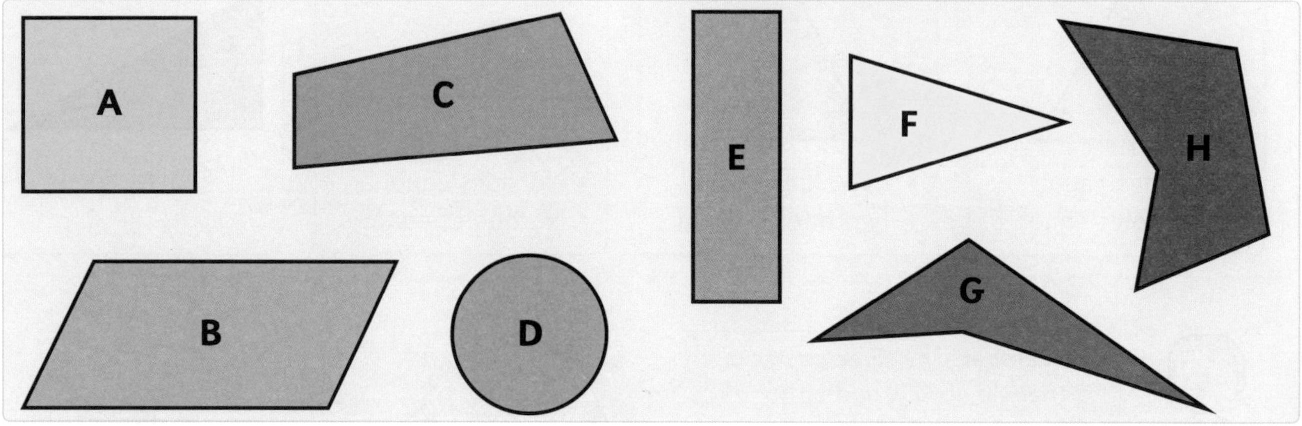

(a) Which of the above shapes are **not** quadrilaterals?

(b) Name the quadrilaterals in the above collection of 2-D shapes.

(c) Name the only **regular** quadrilateral that is in the collection.

---

2. **Answer the questions below about these five quadrilaterals.**

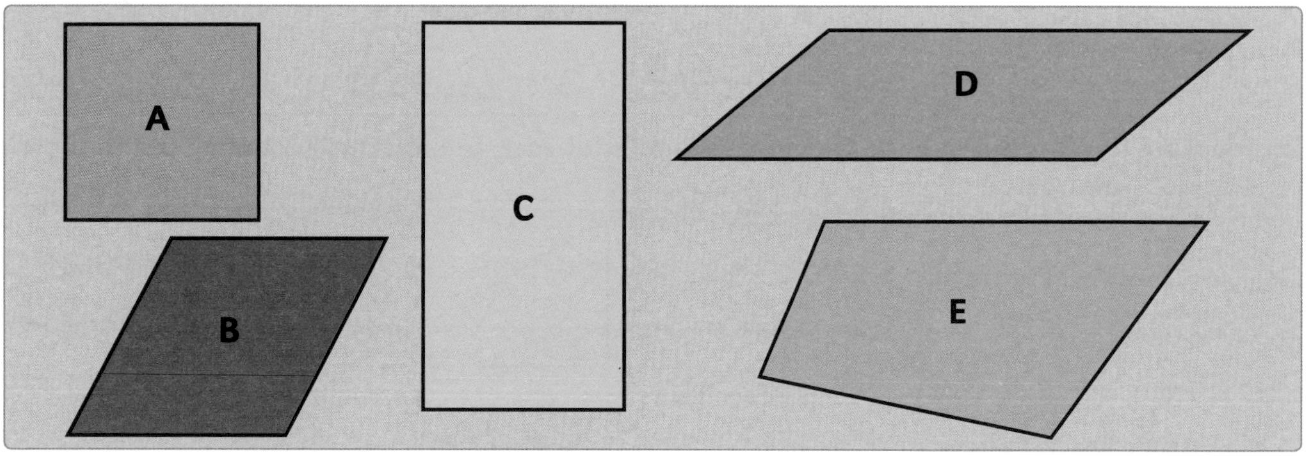

(a) List the shapes that have four straight sides.

(b) Which two shapes have four right angles?

(c) Which two shapes have four equal sides?

(d) Which shape does not have pairs of parallel sides?

(e) The opposite sides of which shapes are equal?

(f) Which shape looks like a square pushed out of shape?

(g) List the shapes that have two acute and two obtuse angles.

(h) How many parallelograms are there? List them.

(i) Draw examples of each quadrilateral in your copy.

rectangle
square
parallelogram
rhombus
irregular quadrilateral

A **rectangle** has four straight sides and four right angles.

Challenge

(a) Is a square a rectangle?

(b) Is a rectangle a square?

More quadrilaterals – The trapezium

A trapezium is a special quadrilateral. It has:

- four straight sides
- one pair of parallel sides.

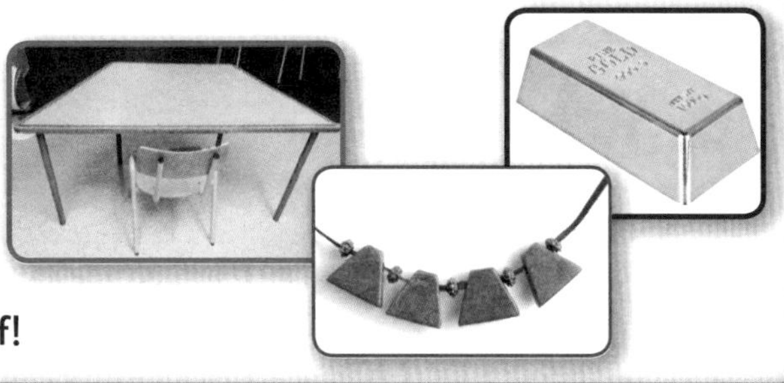

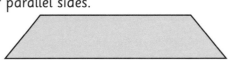

A trapezium looks like a triangle with a piece cut off!

1. (a) Trace these trapezia into your copy. Complete the triangle for each, as in the example.

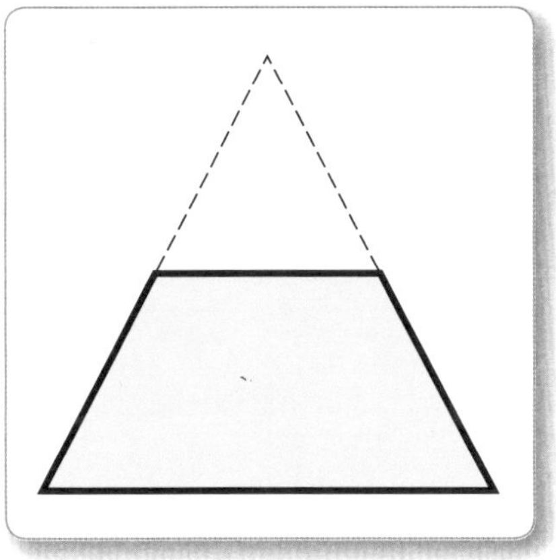

(i)

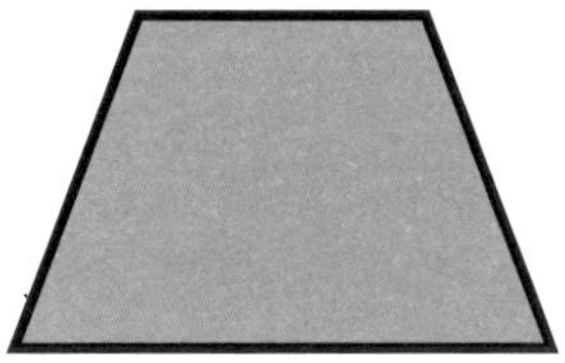

(ii)

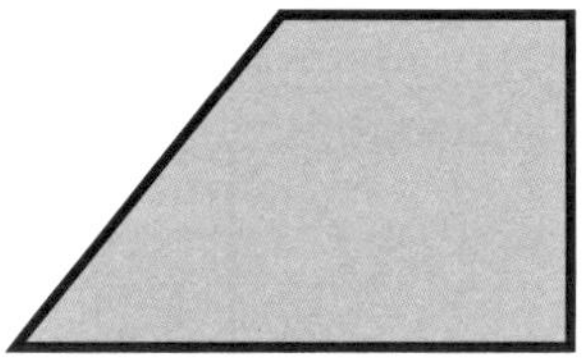

(iii)

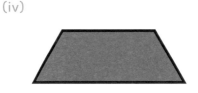

(iv)

(b) What types of triangles do the trapezia in (i), (ii), (iii) and (iv) make when completed?

(c) Which trapezia are symmetrical?

2.

(a) Draw this trapezium on squared paper.

(b) Complete the shape by using the green line as the line of symmetry.

(c) What 2-D shape have you now?

3. Draw this pattern into your copy three times.

Mark out a
(a) small;
(b) medium-sized
and
(c) large trapezium.

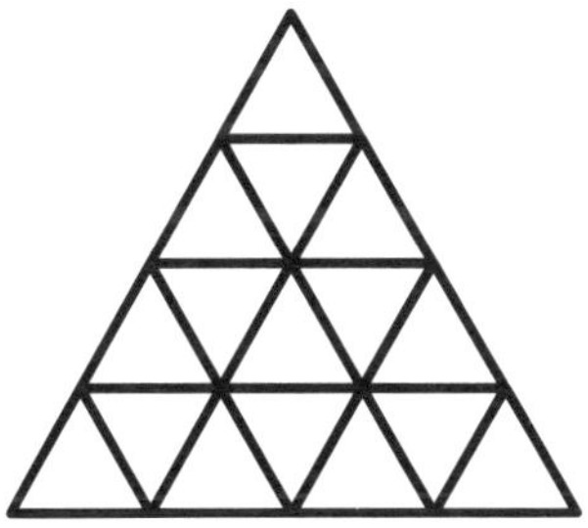

4.

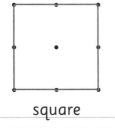

Using the nine-dot pattern below, we can make lots of different quadrilaterals.

(a) Draw the following quadrilaterals in your copy.

(b) Label each quadrilateral.

(c) Draw five more of your own.

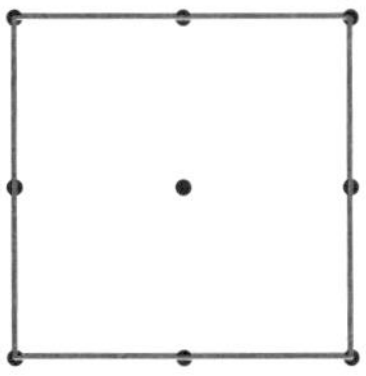

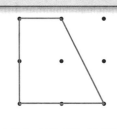

square

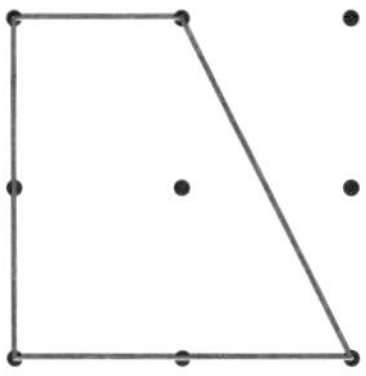

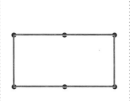

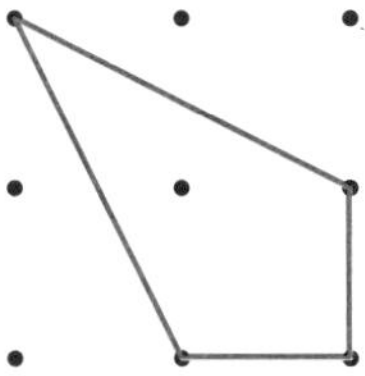

Challenge The three angles of a triangle add up to 180°.
What do the four angles of a quadrilateral add up to? ______

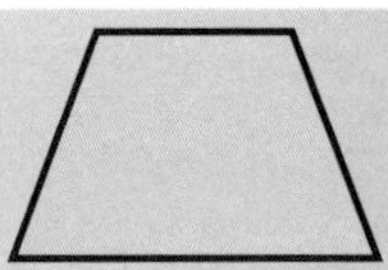

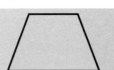

2-D shapes – Symmetry

Pentominoes are shapes made by joining five squares together.

There are 12 pentominoes in total.

Instructions:

Draw each pentomino into your copy or onto squared paper.

(i) Write whether each pentomino is symmetrical or not symmetrical. If it is symmetrical, draw in the line(s) of symmetry.

(ii) Each pentomino represents a letter from the alphabet. Write which letter you think each pentomino represents. Some are more obvious than others! (Hint: You might have to rotate them.)

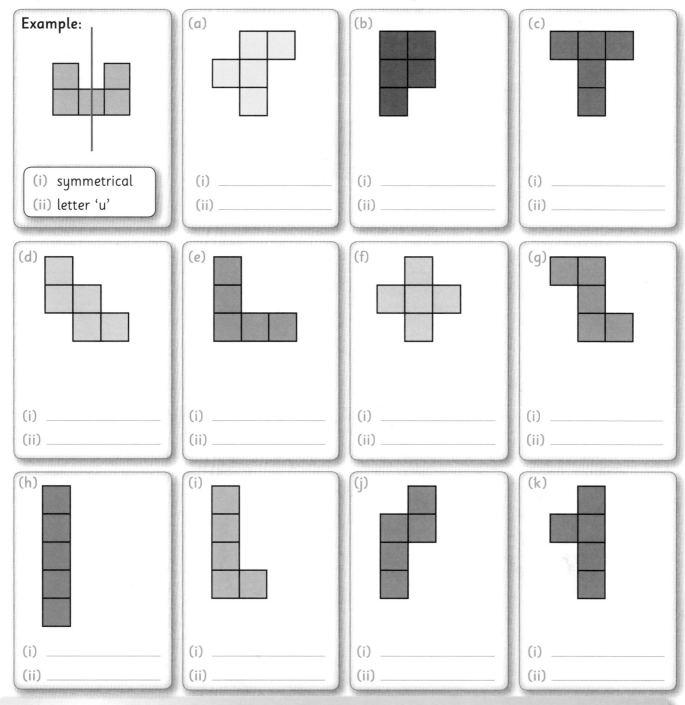

Example:

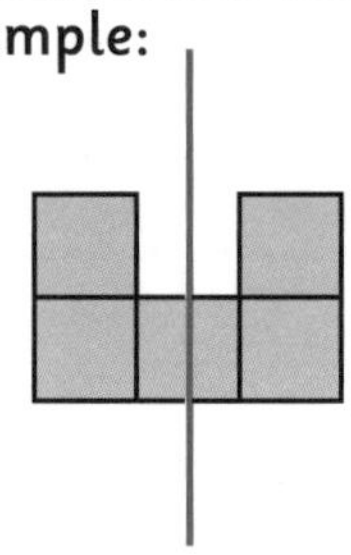

(i) symmetrical
(ii) letter 'u'

(a)

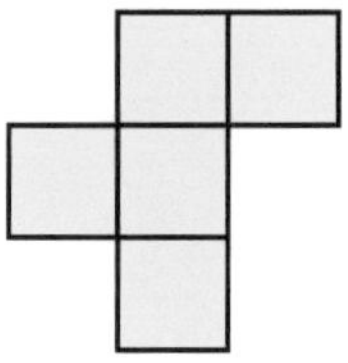

(i) ____________
(ii) ____________

(b)

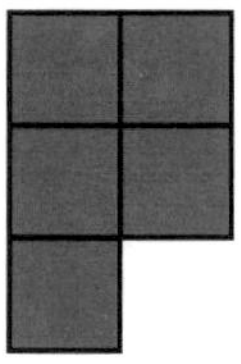

(i) ____________
(ii) ____________

(c)

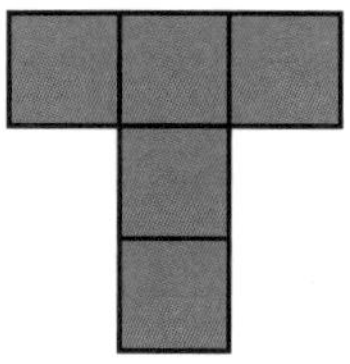

(i) ____________
(ii) ____________

(d)

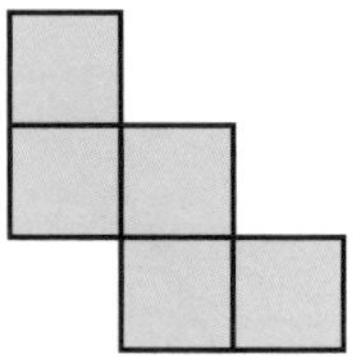

(i) ____________
(ii) ____________

(e)

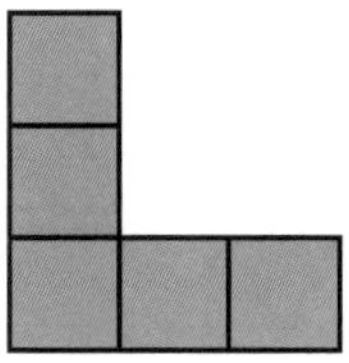

(i) ____________
(ii) ____________

(f)

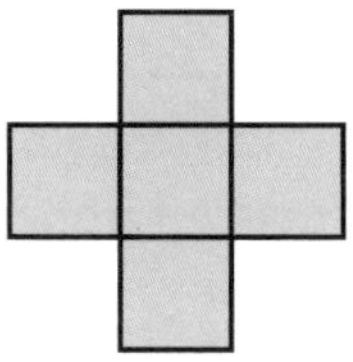

(i) ____________
(ii) ____________

(g)

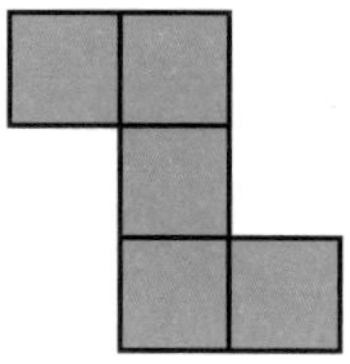

(i) ____________
(ii) ____________

(h)

(i) ____________
(ii) ____________

(i)

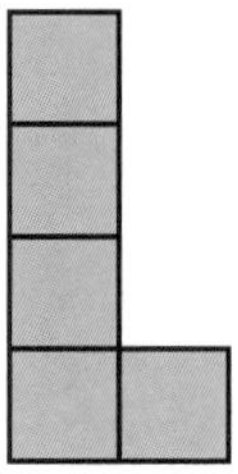

(i) ____________
(ii) ____________

(j)

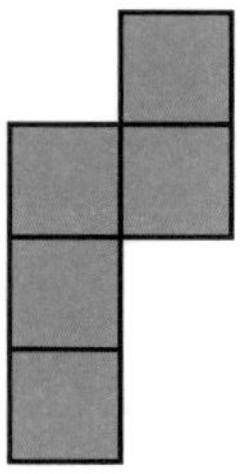

(i) ____________
(ii) ____________

(k)

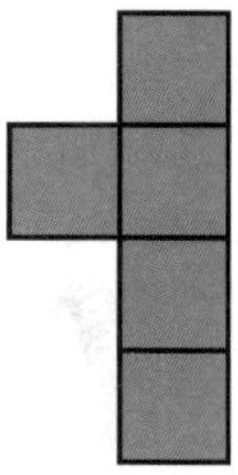

(i) ____________
(ii) ____________

Challenge A tetromino is made by joining four squares together. There are only five different tetrominoes in total. Draw them in your copy using squared paper.

2-D shapes – More symmetry

1. Imagine that these pentominoes are half of symmetrical shapes. Use squared paper to complete each full shape. Pay careful attention to the line of symmetry!

(a)
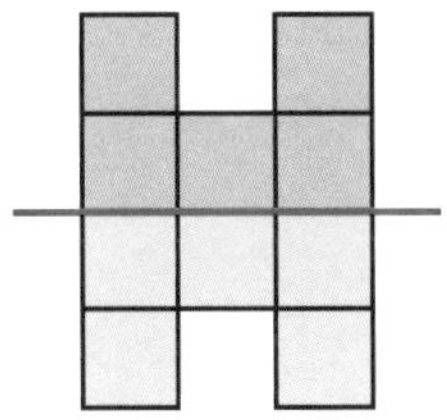
(b)
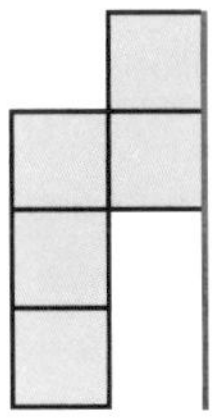
(c)
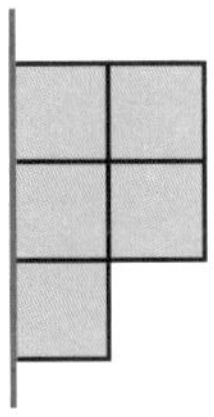
(d)
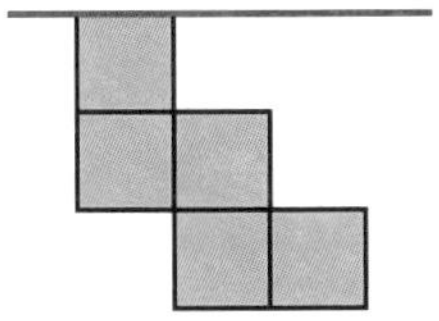
(e)
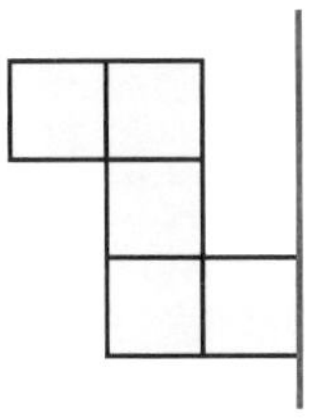
(f)
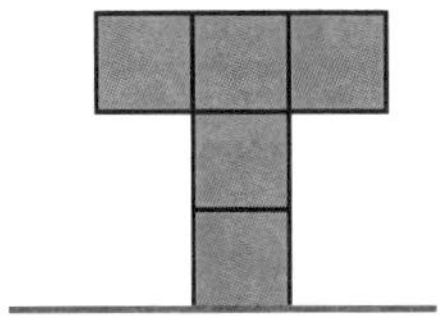
(g)
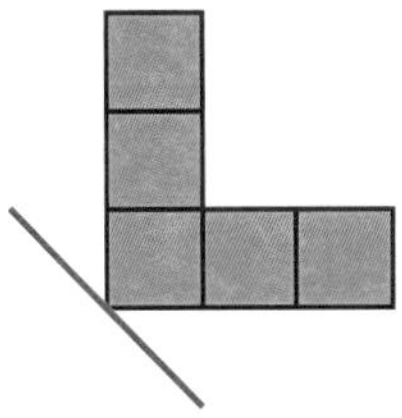
(h)
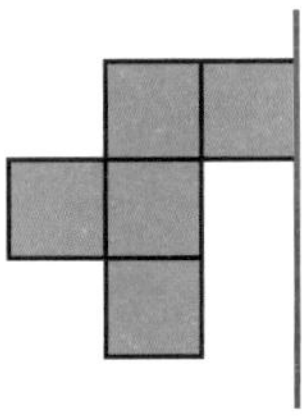

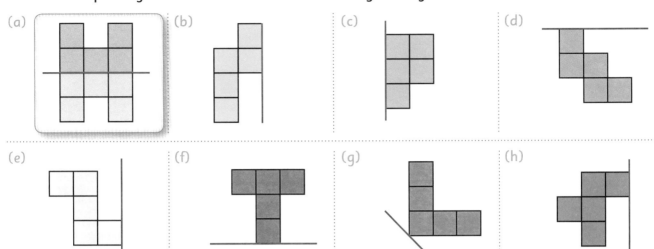

2. Copy or trace these 2-D shapes into your copy. Draw in **all** the lines of symmetry.

(a)
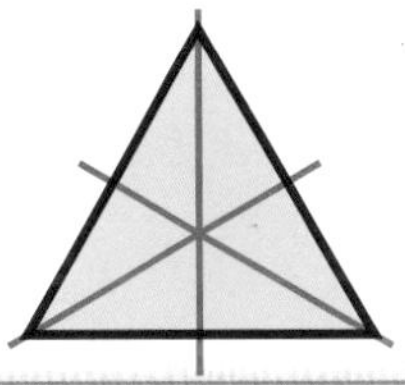
(b)

(c)

(d)
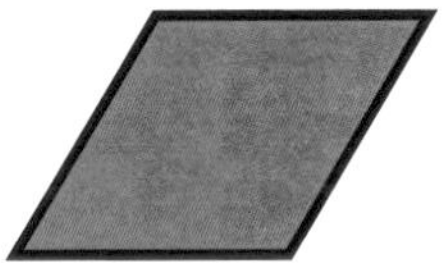
(e)

(f)
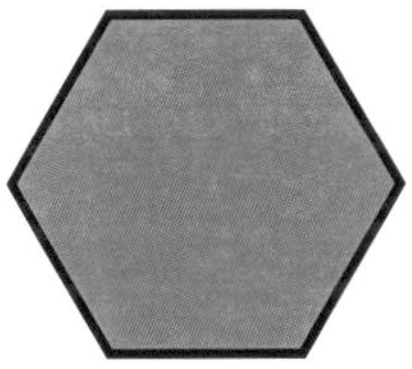
(g)
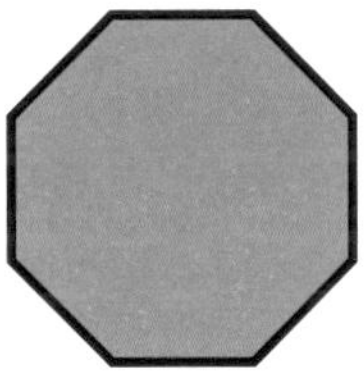

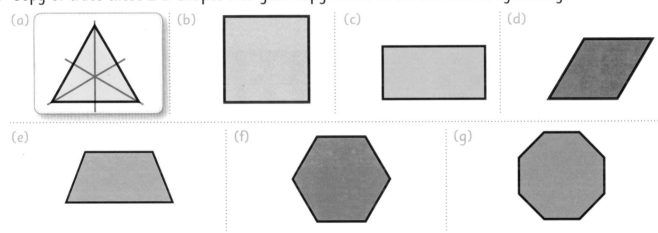

3. Complete this grid. The shapes in Question 2 may be of help to you!

		Lines of symmetry			
	Shape	**Vertical**	**Horizontal**	**Diagonal**	**Total**
(a)	Equilateral triangle	1	0	2	3
(b)	Square				
(c)	Rectangle				
(d)	Rhombus				
(e)	Trapezium				
(f)	Regular hexagon				
(g)	Regular octagon				

Tessellating shapes

Tessellating shapes fit together without leaving any gaps.

Regular tessellation is when shapes fit together on their own.

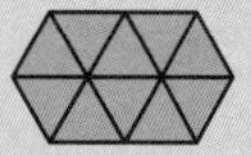

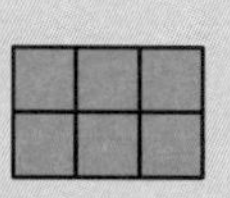

Some shapes tessellate when combined with others. This is called **combined tessellation**.

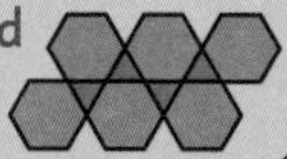

1. Look at the following floor tiles. (i) **Write the name(s) of the tessellating shapes.** (ii) **Write if it is a** regular **or a** combined **tessellation.**

(a)

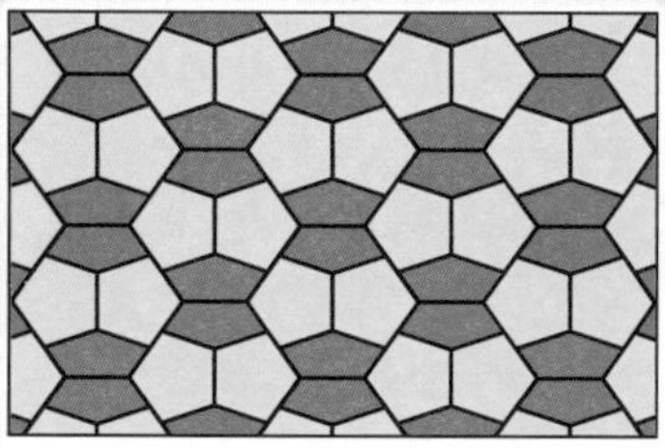

(i) pentagons

(ii) combined tessellation

(b)

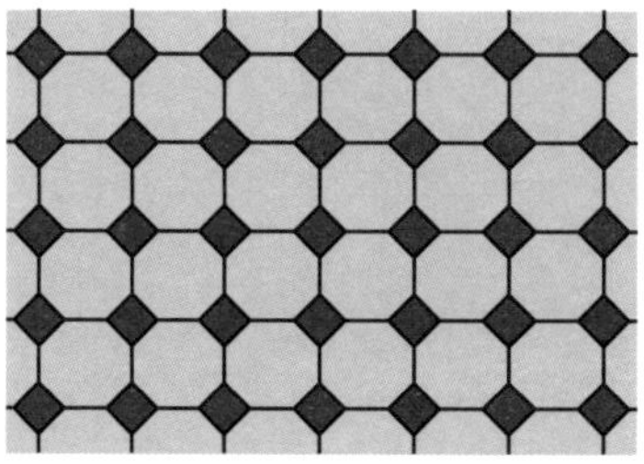

(i) __________

(ii) __________

(c)

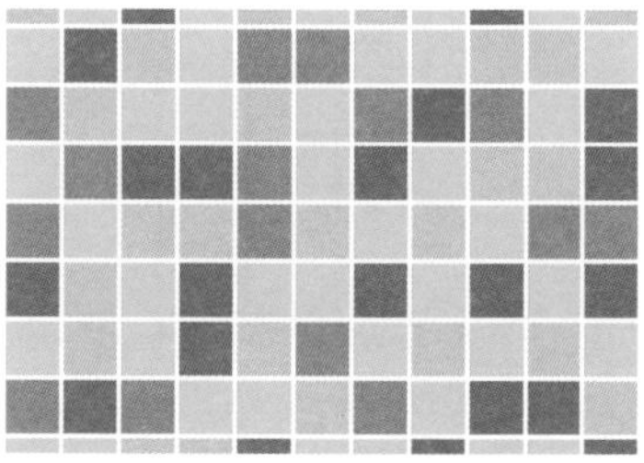

(i) __________

(ii) __________

(d)

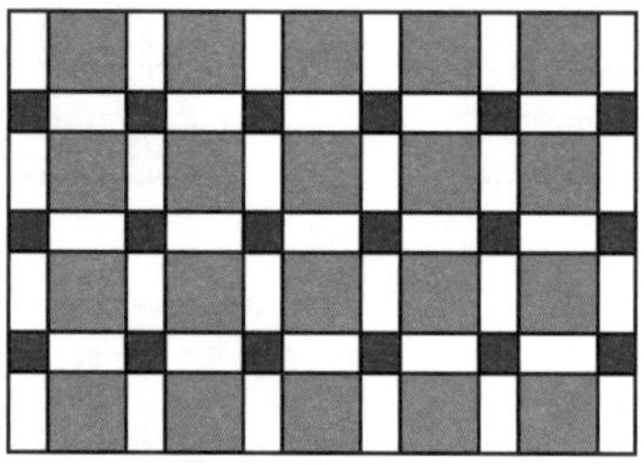

(i) __________

(ii) __________

(e)

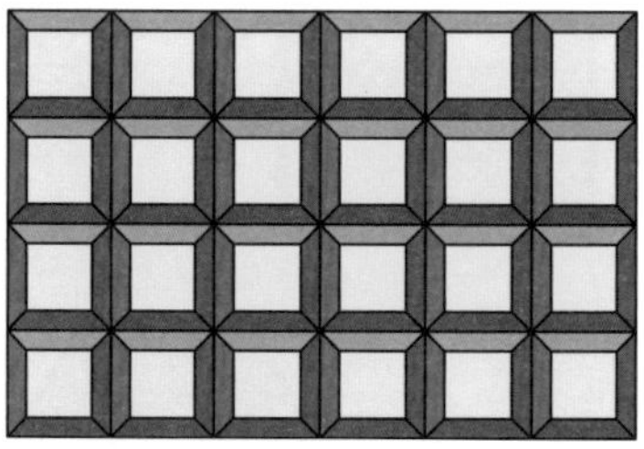

(i) __________

(ii) __________

(f)

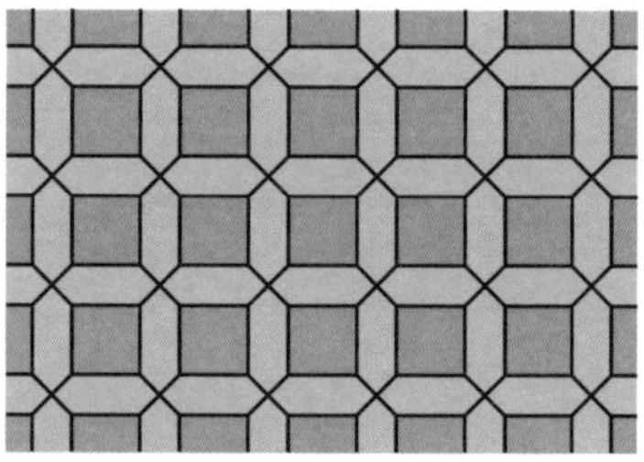

(i) __________

(ii) __________

2. Draw these patterns in your copy and expand them.

(a)

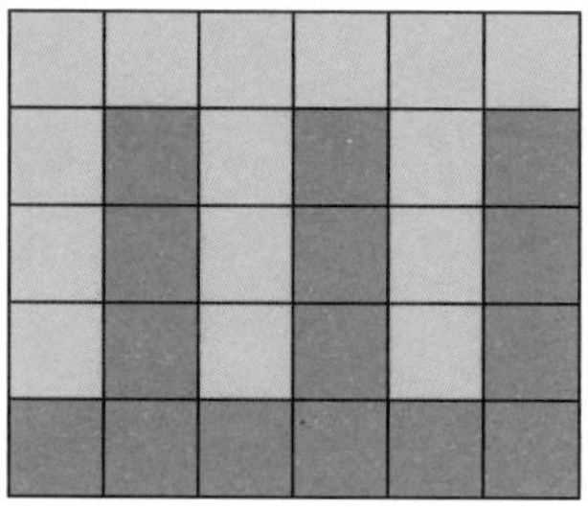

(b)

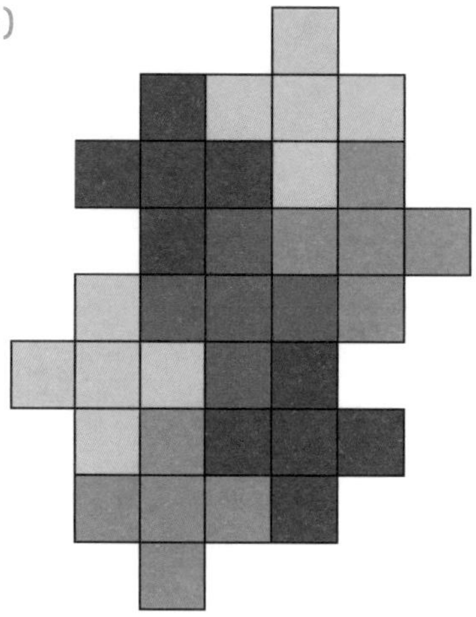

(c)

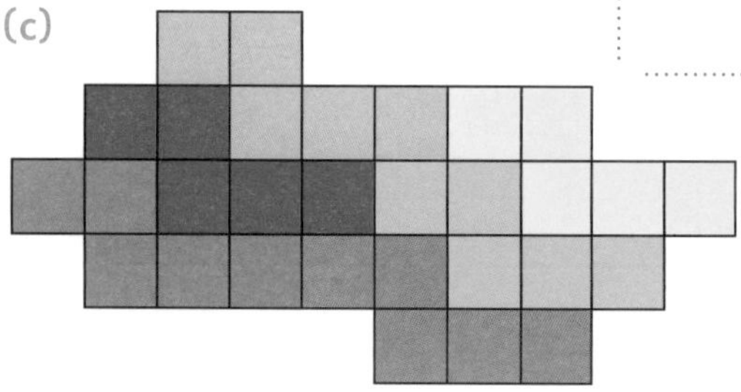

3. All the pentominoes can be combined to make this picture of an ostrich. Make your own pentomino ostrich.

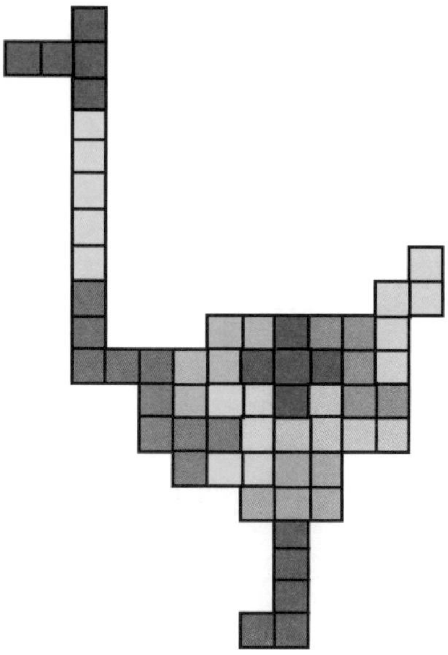

2-D shapes – Tangrams

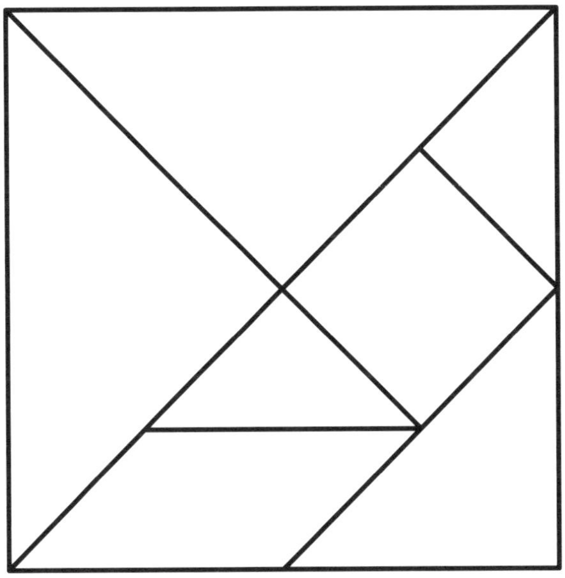

The tangram is an ancient Chinese puzzle. It is made up of seven pieces. Each piece is called a tan. The purpose of the puzzle is to make different shapes using all of the pieces.

1. Fill in the blanks.

The seven tans include:

(a) ____ large triangles;

(b) ____ medium-sized triangle;

(c) ____ small triangles;

(d) ____ square;

(e) one ____________________.

2. Make your own tangram out of cardboard. Cut out the seven tans (pieces). Use the tans to make examples of tessellating patterns (regular or combined) in your copybook.

3. Your tangram can be formed perfectly into other quadrilaterals. Use all seven tans to make the following shapes. The first two tans have been placed for you, but you might prefer to start with different tans.

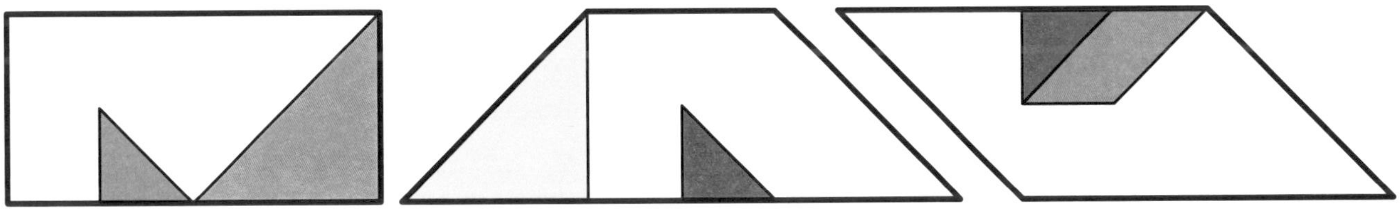

4. Construct the following interesting shapes using all seven tans.

(a)

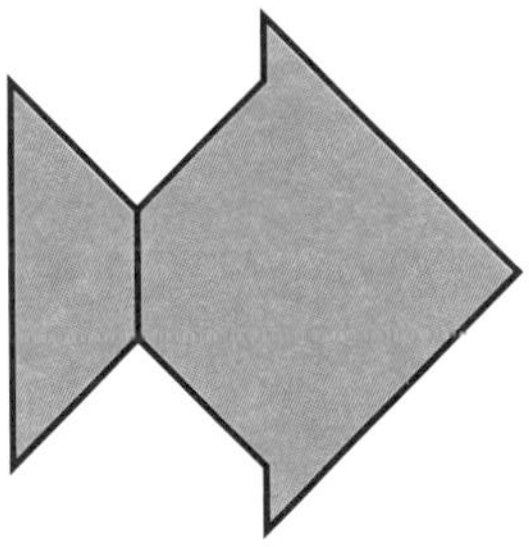

fish

(b)

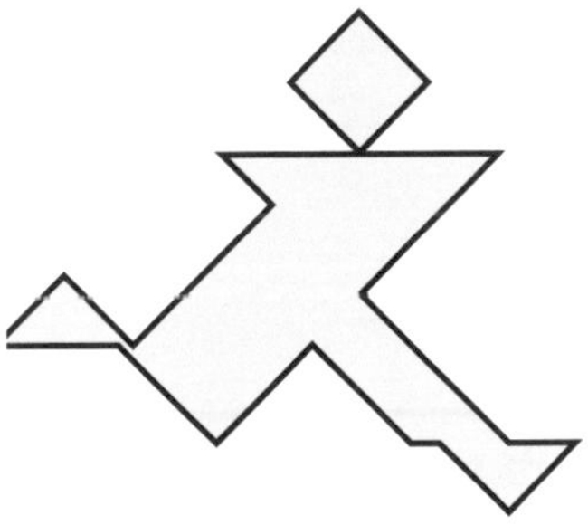

runner

(c)

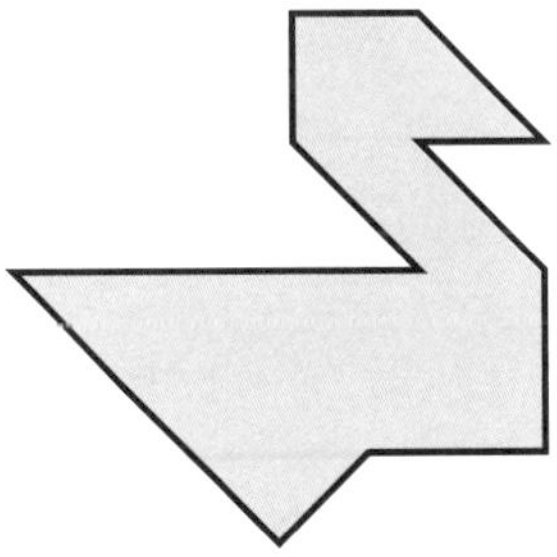

swan

(d)

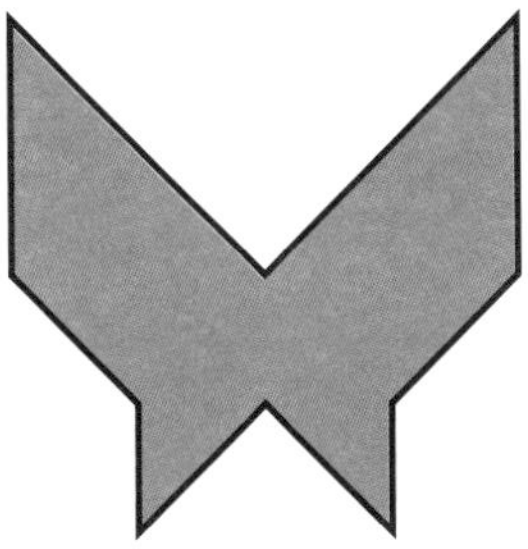

butterfly

(e)

house

(f)

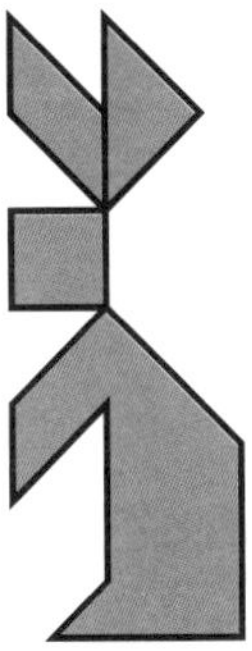

rabbit

Chapter 13: Fractions 2

Adding fractions

A baker sold $\frac{2}{6}$ of a carrot cake in the morning and $\frac{3}{6}$ of it in the afternoon. What fraction of the cake did she sell altogether?

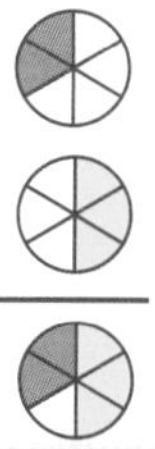

$$\begin{array}{r} \frac{2}{6} \\ + \frac{3}{6} \\ \hline \frac{5}{6} \end{array}$$

1. **Add.**

(a) $\frac{1}{4} + \frac{2}{4}$ = ____

(b) $\frac{2}{12} + \frac{3}{12}$ = ____

(c) $\frac{4}{9} + \frac{7}{9}$ = ____

(d) $\frac{6}{11} + \frac{2}{11}$ = ____

(e) $\frac{2}{7} + \frac{6}{7}$ = ____

(f) $\frac{8}{12} + \frac{3}{12}$ = ____

Adding fractions and mixed numbers (simplify the answer to units and fractions)

A $\frac{3}{4}$ of this frisbee is coloured. →

$\frac{3}{4}$ of this frisbee is coloured. →

How much is coloured altogether?

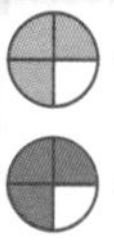

$$\begin{array}{r} \frac{3}{4} \\ + \frac{3}{4} \\ \hline \frac{6}{4} \\ \hline 1\frac{2}{4} \\ \hline 1\frac{1}{2} \end{array}$$

B Ava drank $2\frac{2}{3}$ l of water during a marathon and $1\frac{2}{3}$ l afterwards. How much water did she drink altogether?

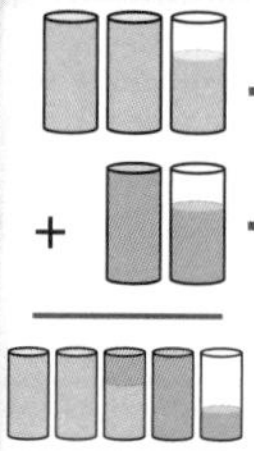

$$\begin{array}{r} 2\frac{2}{3} \\ + 1\frac{2}{3} \\ \hline 3\frac{4}{3} \\ \hline 4\frac{1}{3} \end{array}$$

2. **Do these. Use the pictures to help you. Write the answers as mixed numbers and then simplify.**

(a) 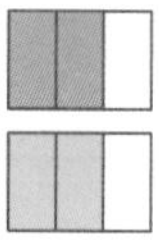 $\frac{2}{3} + \frac{2}{3}$ = ____ → ____

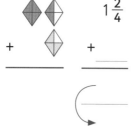

(b) 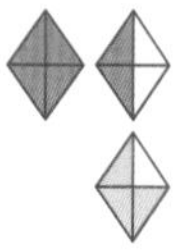 $1\frac{2}{4}$ + ____ = ____ → ____

(c) 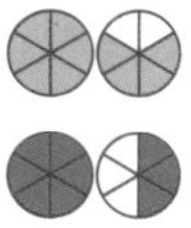 ____ + $1\frac{3}{6}$ = ____ → ____

(d) 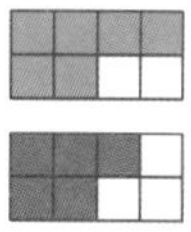 ____ + ____ = ____ → ____

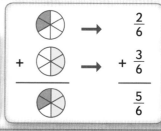

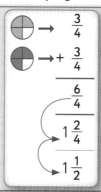

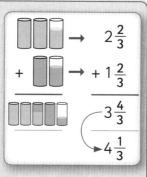

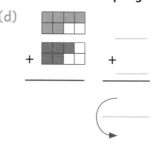

3. **Add these fractions. Simplify where possible to a mixed or whole number.**

(a) $\frac{5}{8} + \frac{4}{8}$ = ____ → ____

(b) $2\frac{1}{2} + 3\frac{1}{2}$ = ____ → ____

(c) $1\frac{3}{4} + 3\frac{2}{4}$ = ____ → ____

(d) $1\frac{8}{12} + \frac{5}{12}$ = ____ → ____

(e) $2\frac{9}{11} + 5\frac{8}{11}$ = ____ → ____

(f) $7\frac{5}{7} + 3\frac{3}{7}$ = ____ → ____

(g) $6\frac{4}{10} + 3\frac{9}{10}$ = ____ → ____

Challenge A wall is $2\frac{4}{6}$m long. Another wall is $3\frac{3}{6}$m long. What is the total length of the two walls? ____ m Simplified: ____ m

STRAND **Number** STRAND UNIT/ELEMENT *Fractions*

LANGUAGE *Adding, mixed numbers, amount, simplify, different denominations, puzzles, rename, subtracting, multiplication*

Different denominators – Mixed numbers

1. Check Jack's homework. ✓ or ✗

(a) $1\frac{4}{5} + \frac{2}{5} = 1\frac{6}{5} \rightarrow 2\frac{1}{5}$ ☐

(b) $1\frac{3}{4} + 2\frac{2}{4} = 3\frac{5}{4} \rightarrow 3\frac{1}{4}$ ☐

(c) $1\frac{9}{12} + \frac{3}{12} = 1\frac{12}{12} \rightarrow 2$ ☐

(d) $2\frac{3}{5} + 4\frac{4}{5} = 6\frac{7}{5} \rightarrow 7\frac{2}{5}$ ☐

(e) $2\frac{2}{3} + 4\frac{2}{3} = 6\frac{4}{3} \rightarrow 7\frac{4}{3}$ ☐

What if the fractions have different denominators?

Jamie painted $\frac{1}{3}$ of a wall and Gemma painted $\frac{1}{6}$ of it. What fraction of the wall did they paint altogether?

We can't <u>add</u> fractions that have different denominators. We must change them to the same denominator.

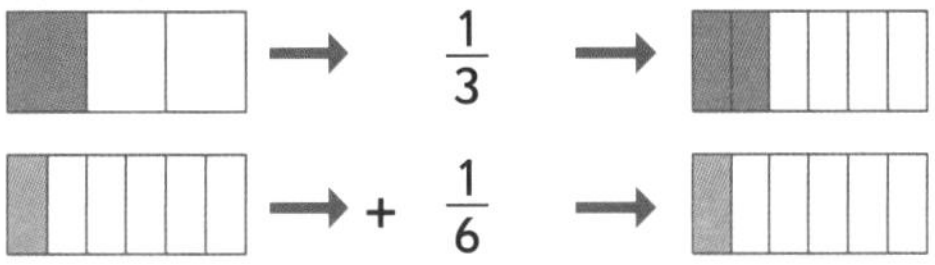

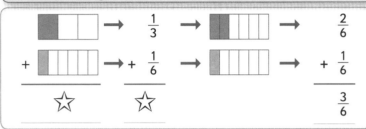

$\frac{1}{3} \rightarrow \frac{2}{6}$

$+\frac{1}{6} \rightarrow +\frac{1}{6}$

☆ ☆ $\frac{3}{6}$

2. (a) Brian filled $\frac{1}{2}$ of a glass with water and $\frac{1}{4}$ of it with juice. What fraction of the glass was full?

$\frac{1}{2} \rightarrow \frac{2}{4}$

$+\frac{1}{4} \rightarrow +\frac{1}{4}$

☆ ☆

(b) June ran $1\frac{1}{2}$ km during a match. Sue ran $2\frac{3}{8}$ km. How far did they run altogether?

$1\frac{1}{2} \rightarrow 1\frac{4}{8}$

$+2\frac{3}{8} \rightarrow +2\frac{3}{8}$

☆

3. Now do these.

(a) $\frac{1}{4} \rightarrow \frac{2}{8}$; $+\frac{3}{8} \rightarrow +\frac{3}{8}$ ☆

(b) $\frac{2}{5} \rightarrow \frac{4}{10}$; $+\frac{3}{10} \rightarrow +$ ☆

(c) $2\frac{1}{3} \rightarrow 2\frac{2}{6}$; $+3\frac{1}{6} \rightarrow +$ ☆

(d) $5\frac{4}{9} \rightarrow$; $+2\frac{1}{3} \rightarrow +$ ☆

4. **Fraction puzzle**

Dave spent $\frac{1}{2}$ of his money on a scarf and $\frac{3}{8}$ of it on a tie. What fraction of his money did he spend?

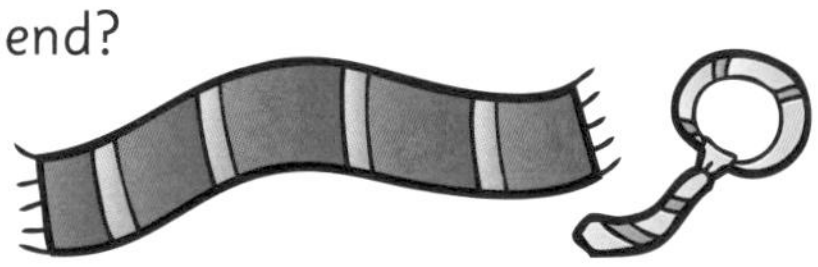

☐ →

+ ☐ → +

☆

5. Add and rename the answer as a mixed number.

(a)

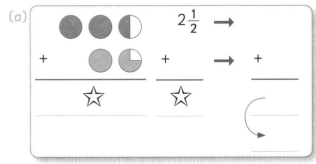

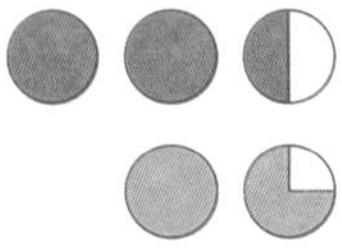

$2\frac{1}{2} \rightarrow$

$+ \quad\quad \rightarrow +$

☆ ☆

(b)

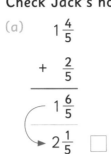

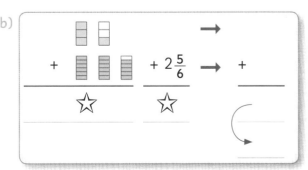

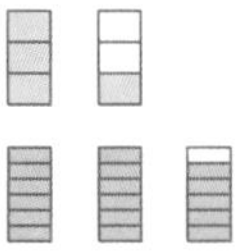

→

$+2\frac{5}{6} \rightarrow +$

☆ ☆

Fractions 2 – Addition and subtraction

1. Add and rename the answer as a **mixed number**.

(a) $3\frac{4}{5} \rightarrow$; $+\ 2\frac{9}{10} \rightarrow +$; ☆

(b) $7\frac{11}{12} \rightarrow$; $+\ 2\frac{1}{2} \rightarrow +$; ☆

(c) $3\frac{5}{9} \rightarrow$; $+\ 4\frac{2}{3} \rightarrow +$; ☆

(d) $6\frac{1}{4} \rightarrow$; $+\ 5\frac{11}{12} \rightarrow +$; ☆

2. (a) Paul has $3\frac{1}{2}$ boxes of crayons. Pearl has $4\frac{7}{8}$ boxes. How many boxes have they altogether?

$3\frac{1}{2} \rightarrow$; $+\ 4\frac{7}{8} \rightarrow +$; ☆

(b) Joe ate $2\frac{5}{6}$ oranges. Jill ate $1\frac{7}{12}$ oranges. How many oranges did they eat between them?

$2\frac{5}{6} \rightarrow$; $+\ 1\frac{7}{12} \rightarrow +$; ☆

Subtracting fractions with the same denominators

A An ice cube tray was full. Zoe took $\frac{3}{8}$ of the cubes. What fraction of the cubes was left?

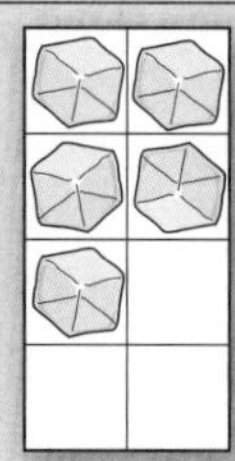

$\frac{8}{8} - \frac{3}{8} = \frac{5}{8}$

B A technician spent $\frac{5}{6}$ of an hour in a house to repair a fridge. He spent $\frac{1}{6}$ of an hour chatting. What fraction of the hour did he spend repairing the fridge?

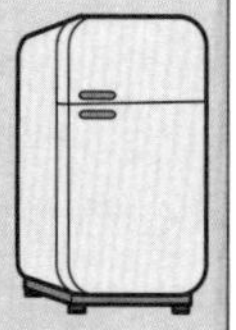

$\frac{5}{6} - \frac{1}{6} = \frac{4}{6}$

3. Complete these subtraction questions.

(a) $\frac{3}{4} - \frac{1}{4}$

(b) $\frac{10}{10} - \frac{4}{10}$

(c) $\frac{5}{7} - \frac{2}{7}$

(d) $\frac{7}{8} - \frac{5}{8}$

(e) $\frac{11}{12} - \frac{5}{12}$

(f) $\frac{7}{9} - \frac{2}{9}$

Subtracting fractions with different denominators

A There was $\frac{7}{10}$ of an apple tart left on a table. Paul ate $\frac{2}{5}$ of the apple tart. What fraction of the apple tart was still left?

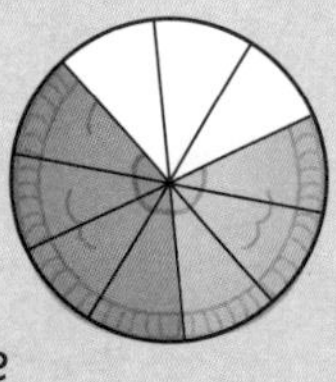

$\frac{7}{10} \rightarrow \frac{7}{10}$

$-\ \frac{2}{5} \rightarrow -\ \frac{4}{10}$

☆ $\frac{3}{10}$

B

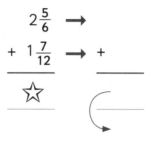

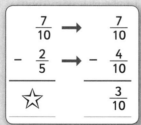

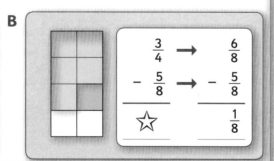

$\frac{3}{4} \rightarrow \frac{6}{8}$

$-\ \frac{5}{8} \rightarrow -\ \frac{5}{8}$

☆ $\frac{1}{8}$

4. Now have a go at these.

(a) $\frac{3}{4} - \frac{1}{2}$

(b) $\frac{7}{8} - \frac{3}{4}$

(c) $\frac{9}{10} - \frac{3}{5}$

(d) $\frac{11}{12} - \frac{5}{6}$

(e) $\frac{4}{5} - \frac{7}{10}$

(f) $\frac{8}{9} - \frac{2}{3}$

Subtraction of mixed numbers; Renaming; + and −

A

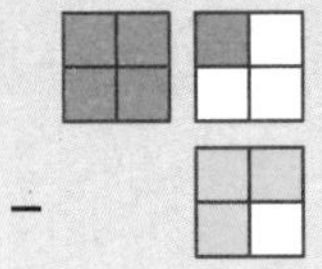

$1\frac{1}{4} - \frac{3}{4} = ☆$ → $\frac{5}{4} - \frac{3}{4} = \frac{2}{4}$

B

There were $1\frac{1}{3}$ trays of lasagne. The lady sold $\frac{2}{3}$ of a tray. What fraction of a tray of lasagne was left?

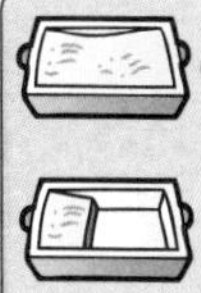

$1\frac{1}{3} - \frac{2}{3} = ☆$ → $\frac{4}{3} - \frac{2}{3} = \frac{2}{3}$

1. Now complete these. Don't forget to rename a unit as fractions.

(a) $2\frac{5}{12} - 1\frac{9}{12} = ☆$ → $1\frac{17}{12} - \_\_\_$

(b) $2\frac{3}{11} - \frac{7}{11} = ☆$ → $1\frac{14}{11} - \_\_\_$

(c) $4\frac{3}{8} - 1\frac{7}{8} = ☆$ → $3\frac{11}{8} - \_\_\_$

(d) $6\frac{1}{6} - 3\frac{5}{6} = ☆$ → $\_\_\_ - \_\_\_$

2. Subtracting **fractions** and **mixed numbers** that have different denominators.

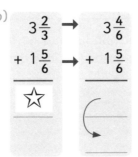

(a)

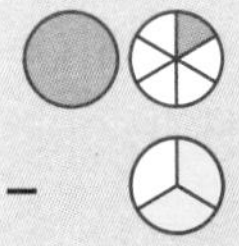

☆ → $1\frac{1}{6} - \frac{2}{3} = ☆$ → $\frac{7}{6} - \frac{4}{6}$

(b)

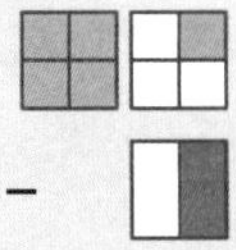

☆ → $1\frac{1}{4} - \frac{1}{2} = ☆$ → $\frac{5}{4} - \_\_\_$

(c)

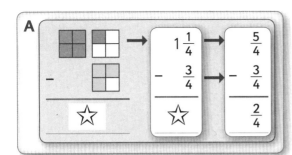

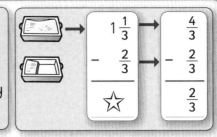

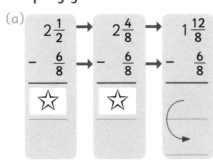

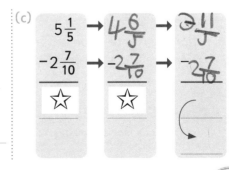

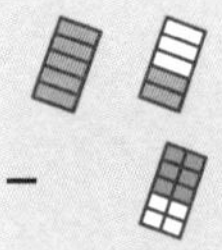

☆ → $1\frac{2}{5} - \_\_\_ = ☆$ → $\_\_\_ - \_\_\_$

3. Now do these.

(a) $2\frac{7}{8} - 1\frac{1}{4}$

(b) $3\frac{4}{5} - 1\frac{3}{10}$

(c) $5\frac{11}{12} - 2\frac{1}{6}$

(d) $6\frac{2}{3} - 3\frac{5}{12}$

(e) $9\frac{7}{10} - 4\frac{2}{5}$

(f) $8\frac{4}{5} - 3\frac{9}{10}$

4. Write these fractions using a common denominator. You will also have to **rename a unit**.

(a) $4\frac{1}{12} - 2\frac{5}{6} = ☆$ → $\_\_\_ - \_\_\_$

(b) $3\frac{1}{5} - 2\frac{9}{10} = ☆$ → $\_\_\_ - \_\_\_$

(c) $4\frac{2}{3} - 1\frac{11}{12} = ☆$ → $\_\_\_ - \_\_\_$

(d) $1\frac{1}{2} - \frac{7}{8} = ☆$ → $\_\_\_ - \_\_\_$

5. **Simplify** your answers to these **addition** and **subtraction** questions.

(a) $2\frac{1}{2} - \frac{6}{8} = ☆$ → $2\frac{4}{8} - \frac{6}{8} = ☆$ → $1\frac{12}{8} - \frac{6}{8}$ = ___ → ___

(b) $3\frac{2}{3} + 1\frac{5}{6} = ☆$ → $3\frac{4}{6} + 1\frac{5}{6}$ = ___ → ___ or ___

(c) $5\frac{1}{5} - 2\frac{7}{10} = ☆$ → $4\frac{6}{5} - 2\frac{7}{10} = ☆$ → $3\frac{11}{5} - 2\frac{7}{10}$ = ___ → ___

Multiplying fractions

A

Jerry spends $\frac{1}{2}$ an hour each day reading. How many hours does he spend reading in a week?

Multiplication method:

Remember: $\frac{7}{1} = 7$

$7 \times \frac{1}{2} \rightarrow \frac{7}{1} \times \frac{1}{2} \rightarrow \frac{7}{2} = 3\frac{1}{2}$

B

A baker sells $\frac{3}{4}$ of a carrot cake each hour. How much would she sell in two hours?

+ method

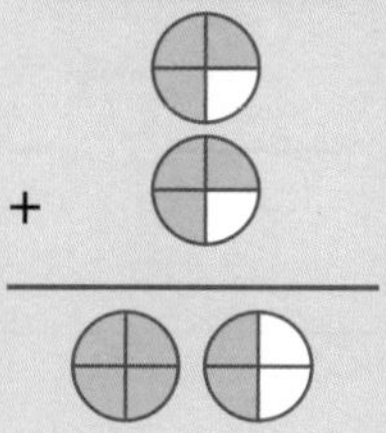

$1\frac{2}{4} = 1\frac{1}{2}$

× method

$\frac{3}{4} \times \frac{2}{1} = \frac{6}{4}$

$\rightarrow 1\frac{2}{4}$

$= 1\frac{1}{2}$

1. Use the multiplication method when doing these.

(a) 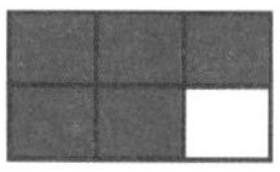 $\times 3 \rightarrow \frac{5}{6} \times \frac{3}{1} \rightarrow \frac{15}{6} \rightarrow \frac{5}{\square} =$ ______

(b) 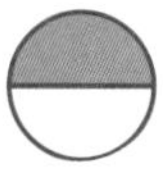 $\times 4 \rightarrow \frac{1}{2} \times$

(c) 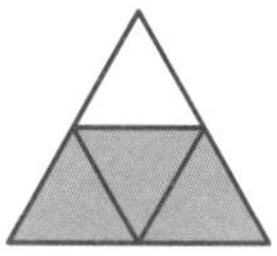 $\times 5 \rightarrow$

(d) 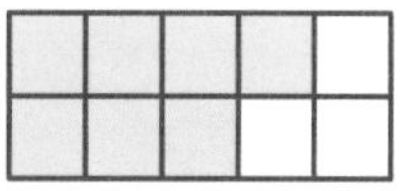 $\times 3 \rightarrow$

(e) 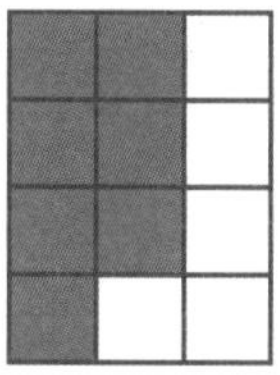 $\times 4 \rightarrow$

(f) 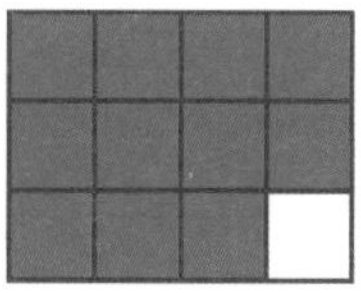 $\times 6 \rightarrow$

2. True ✓ or false ✗?

(a) $\frac{1}{4} \times \frac{4}{1} \rightarrow \frac{4}{4} = 1$ ☐

(b) $\frac{3}{8} \times 2 \rightarrow \frac{6}{8} = \frac{3}{4}$ ☐

(c) $\frac{1}{2} \times 7 = 7\frac{1}{2}$ ☐

(d) $\frac{5}{6} \times 3 \rightarrow \frac{15}{6} \rightarrow \frac{5}{2} = 2\frac{1}{2}$ ☐

(e) $\frac{2}{3} \times 7 \rightarrow \frac{14}{3} = 3\frac{2}{3}$ ☐

(f) $\frac{4}{9} \times 8 = 3\frac{5}{9}$ ☐

3. Multiply and simplify.

(a) $\frac{2}{3} \times 8 =$ ______ (b) $\frac{3}{7} \times 7 =$ ______ (c) $\frac{3}{4} \times 9 =$ ______ (d) $\frac{7}{8} \times 6 =$ ______ (e) $\frac{2}{9} \times 3 =$ ______

4. Mary swam $\frac{7}{8}$ of a kilometre each morning before work.
How far in total did she swim from Monday to Friday? ______ km

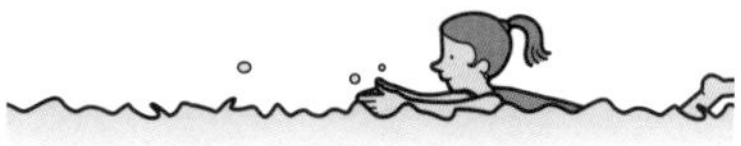

5. 

The forester planted $\frac{7}{10}$ of a bundle of oak plants each hour.
How many bundles did he plant in eight hours? ______

6. Dad used $\frac{5}{8}$ of a loaf of bread each day making lunches for his children.
How many loaves would he need to make lunches for five days? ______

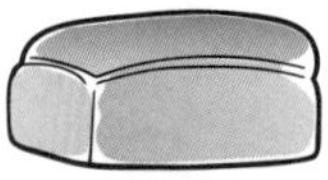

Challenge Zeta ate $\frac{7}{12}$ of a healthy snack bar each afternoon.
How many healthy bars did she eat in six days? ______

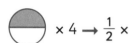

Fractions 2 – Check what you have learned!

1. **Match each question to the correct answer.**

(a) Ciara spends $\frac{5}{12}$ of her 24-hour day asleep. How many hours per day does she sleep? •

(b) James gets €10 pocket money each week. If he saved $\frac{1}{2}$ of it for four weeks, how many euro did he save? •

(c) How many litres of water did Tim drink if he drank $1\frac{5}{12}$ l during a 5km run and $\frac{3}{4}$ of a litre afterwards? •

(d) Write $\frac{20}{6}$ as a mixed number in its simplest form. •

(e)  A baker had $1\frac{5}{6}$ of his cakes left at the end of the day. If he had baked five cakes, how many cakes did he sell? •

• 20

• $3\frac{1}{3}$

• $3\frac{1}{6}$

• 10

• $2\frac{1}{6}$

2. **Arrange these fractions in order starting with the biggest.**

(a) $\frac{3}{6}, \frac{2}{12}, \frac{1}{3}, \frac{5}{12}, \frac{1}{4}$ (b) $\frac{2}{5}, \frac{3}{10}, \frac{1}{2}, \frac{4}{5}, \frac{7}{10}$ (c) $\frac{7}{12}, \frac{5}{10}, \frac{2}{3}, \frac{3}{4}, \frac{5}{6}$

3. **Complete to make these fractions equivalent.**

(a) $\frac{2}{3} \times \frac{5}{5} = \frac{\square}{\square}$ (b) $\frac{3}{4} \times \frac{\square}{4} = \frac{\square}{\square}$ (c) $\frac{5}{6} \times \frac{\square}{\square} = \frac{\square}{30}$ (d) $\frac{5}{9} \times \frac{\square}{\square} = \frac{\square}{54}$ (e) $\frac{7}{12} \times \frac{\square}{\square} = \frac{\square}{48}$

4. (a) $\frac{6}{10} \div \frac{\square}{2} = \frac{\square}{5}$ (b) $\frac{9}{12} \div \frac{\square}{\square} = \frac{3}{4}$ (c) $\frac{8}{12} \div \frac{\square}{4} = \frac{\square}{\square}$ (d) $\frac{6}{8} \div \frac{2}{\square} = \frac{\square}{\square}$ (e) $\frac{3}{6} \div \frac{\square}{3} = \frac{\square}{\square}$

5. **Fill in the missing improper fraction or mixed number.**

(a) $1\frac{7}{11}$ = ____ (b) $6\frac{5}{7}$ = ____ (c) $\frac{47}{8}$ = ____ (d) $4\frac{8}{9}$ = ____ (e) $\frac{65}{12}$ = ____

6. (a) $\frac{3}{8}$ of a number is 12. whole number = ____

(b) $\frac{5}{9}$ of a number is 35. whole number = ____

(c) $\frac{11}{12}$ of a number is 55. whole number = ____

7. (a) Add $2\frac{3}{8}$ oranges and $2\frac{3}{4}$ oranges. ____

(b) How much less is $2\frac{7}{10}$ than $4\frac{2}{5}$? ____

(c) What must I add to $3\frac{5}{8}$ to make $6\frac{1}{2}$? ____

8. A family ate $\frac{5}{12}$ of a melon each day. How many melons did they eat in a week? ____ 

9. Sarah ran $\frac{7}{8}$ km each day. How many kilometres did she run in nine days? ____ km

10.  Paul ate $2\frac{2}{5}$ apples. Orla ate $1\frac{7}{10}$ apples. How many apples did they eat altogether? ____

Challenge Paul ran $3\frac{1}{3}$ km. Sandra ran $2\frac{3}{4}$ km and Sue ran $4\frac{7}{12}$ km.

(a) How many km did Sandra and Sue run altogether? ____ km

(b) How much further did Sue run than Paul? ____ km

A quick look back 4

LOOK BACK

1. What must be added to €2·65 to make €5?

€ ______

2. A butternut squash costs €1·80. How much would five of them cost?

€ ______

3. The average of three numbers is 32. Two of the numbers are 30 and 40.

What is the third number? ______

4. Make 368 a hundred times bigger.

26,800

5. 

A school has 279 pupils. They are divided equally among nine classes. How many pupils are in each class?

______

6. What fraction of this shape is coloured?

$\frac{\square}{\square} = \frac{\square}{\square}$

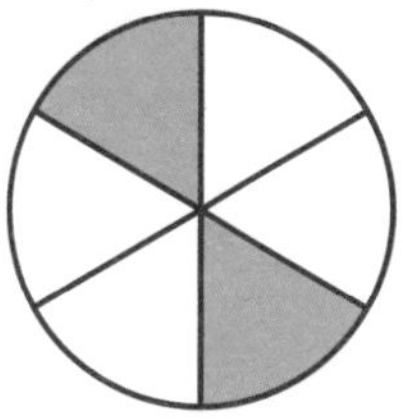

7. Ring the fraction that has the same value as $\frac{3}{4}$:

$\frac{2}{3}$ $\frac{5}{8}$ $\frac{5}{6}$ $\frac{9}{12}$ $\frac{6}{10}$

8. $\frac{1}{2} + \frac{3}{8} = \frac{\square}{\square}$

9. Through how many degrees does the minute hand of a clock turn in 30 minutes?

______

10. Subtract 3,500 from 47,836.

______

11. 

Ricky has $\frac{3}{4}$ of a one kilometre race completed. How many metres has he still to run?

______ m

12. Write the missing denominator.

$\frac{3}{4} \times \frac{6}{\square} = \frac{18}{24}$

13. Write $2\frac{5}{8}$ as an improper fraction. $\frac{\square}{\square}$

14. Is this shape symmetrical?

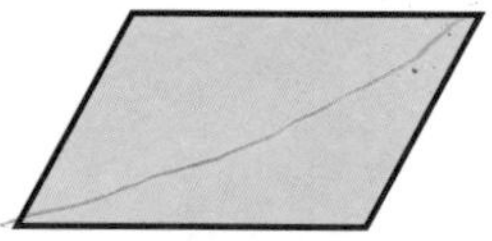

☐ yes ☐ no

15. 

A regular pentagon has ______ lines of symmetry.

16. Is a shape like this good for tessellating?

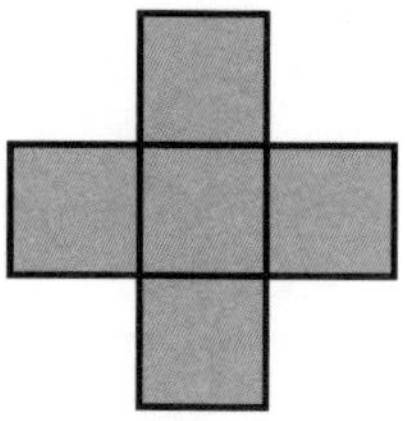

☐ yes ☐ no

17. Alan spent $\frac{5}{9}$ of his money. Penny spent $\frac{2}{3}$ of her money. Who spent the greater fraction of their money?

______

18. A family ate $\frac{7}{12}$ of a vegetable pie each day. How many pies did they eat in seven days? ______

19. Write the missing number.

$\frac{35}{40} \div \frac{\square}{5} = \frac{7}{8}$

20. $\frac{7}{12} \times \frac{5}{2} = \frac{\square}{\square} = 1\frac{\square}{\square}$

Chapter 14: Decimals

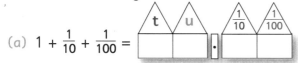

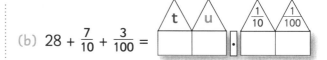

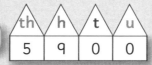

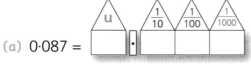

A **decimal** is a **fraction** of a unit. Decimals are really **decimal fractions** because they are parts of a unit. **A** 0·1 means no units and $\frac{1}{10}$ of a unit and **B** 0·07 means 0 units + $\frac{7}{100}$ of a unit.

1. Write the following in the decimal houses.

(a) $1 + \frac{1}{10} + \frac{1}{100} =$

t	u	·	$\frac{1}{10}$	$\frac{1}{100}$
		·		

(b) $28 + \frac{7}{10} + \frac{3}{100} =$

t	u	·	$\frac{1}{10}$	$\frac{1}{100}$
		·		

2. Write the following as whole numbers, **tenths** and **hundredths**.

(a)

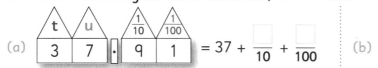

t	u	·	$\frac{1}{10}$	$\frac{1}{100}$
3	7	·	9	1

$= 37 + \frac{\square}{10} + \frac{\square}{100}$

(b)

u	·	$\frac{1}{10}$	$\frac{1}{100}$
6	·	7	9

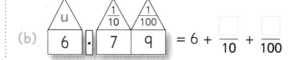

$= 6 + \frac{\square}{10} + \frac{\square}{100}$

A A quick way to divide a number by 10 is to move each digit **one place** to the right →.

Example: 280 ÷ 10 = 28

h	t	u
2	8	0

÷ 10 →

h	t	u
	2	8

B To divide a number by 100, move each digit **two places** to the right →.

Example: 5,900 ÷ 100 = 59

th	h	t	u
5	9	0	0

÷ 100 →

th	h	t	u
		5	9

C To divide a number by 1,000, move each digit **three places** to the right →. 16,000 ÷ 1,000 = 16

Changing fractions to decimals

Remember: $\frac{1}{10}$ is one part of a unit that has been divided into ten equal parts.

A (a bar divided into ten equal parts, one shaded) → $\frac{1}{10}$ → 1·0 ÷ 10 = 0·1

B $\frac{7}{10}$ → 7·0 ÷ 10 = 0·7 **C** $\frac{19}{100}$ → 19·0 ÷ 100 = 0·19 **D** $\frac{47}{1000}$ → 47·0 ÷ 1,000 = 0·047

3. Write these fractions as decimal fractions.

(a) $\frac{9}{10}$ (b) $\frac{23}{100}$ (c) $\frac{3}{10}$ (d) $\frac{437}{1000}$ (e) $\frac{7}{10}$ (f) $\frac{35}{1000}$ (g) $\frac{70}{100}$ (h) $\frac{100}{1000}$

4. Check to see if these answers are correct. ✓ or ✗

(a) $\frac{6}{1000} = 0·06$ ☐ (b) $\frac{45}{100} = 0·045$ ☐ (c) $\frac{8}{10} = 0·8$ ☐ (d) $\frac{9}{100} = 0·9$ ☐

(e) $\frac{7}{1000} = 0·007$ ☐ (f) $\frac{312}{1000} = 0·312$ ☐ (g) $\frac{40}{100} = 0·40$ ☐ (h) $\frac{17}{1000} = 0·017$ ☐

5. Write these decimal numbers in the unit and decimal houses.

(a) 0·087 =

u	·	$\frac{1}{10}$	$\frac{1}{100}$	$\frac{1}{1000}$
	·			

(b) $1 + \frac{3}{10} + \frac{7}{100} + \frac{9}{1000} =$

u	·	$\frac{1}{10}$	$\frac{1}{100}$	$\frac{1}{1000}$
	·			

Decimals – Tenths, hundredths and thousandths

A full block  represents one unit. 

The red section of each block shows the fraction or decimal fraction of that block.

A

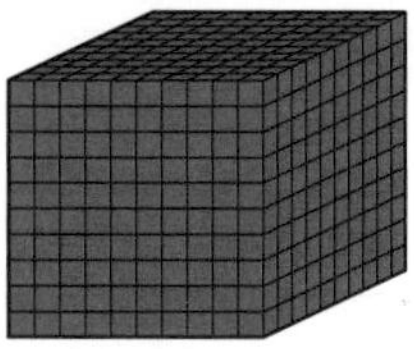

$\frac{1}{1}$ or 1·0

B

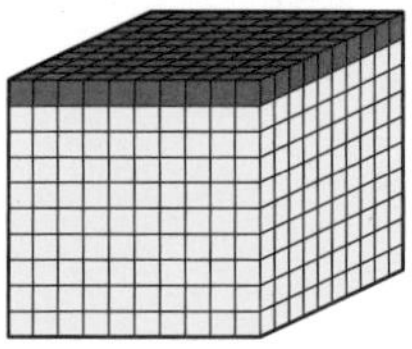

$\frac{1}{10}$ or 0·1

C

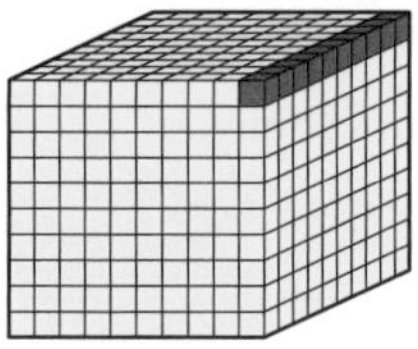

$\frac{1}{100}$ or 0·01

D

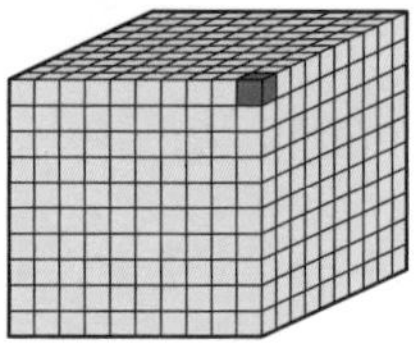

$\frac{1}{1000}$ or 0·001

1. Write the correct (i) **fraction** and (ii) **decimal fraction** of a full block each of these represent.

(a)

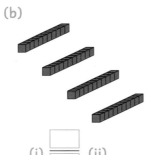

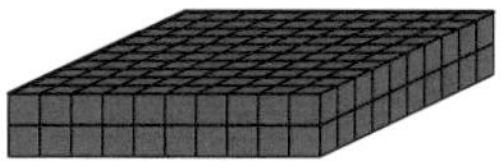

(i) $\frac{\square}{\square}$ (ii) ______

(b)

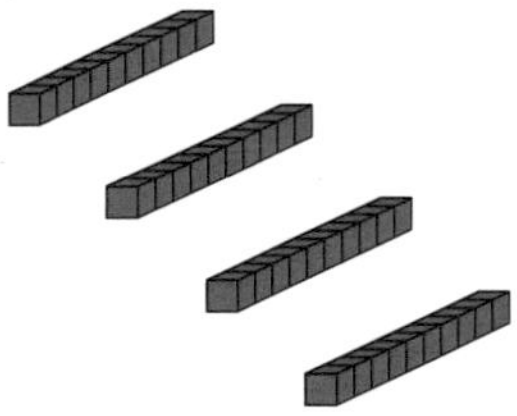

(i) $\frac{\square}{\square}$ (ii) ______

(c)

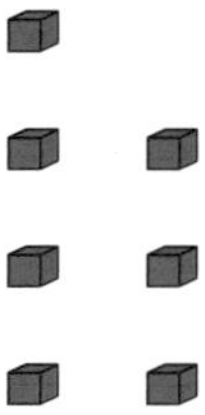

(i) $\frac{\square}{\square}$ (ii) ______

(d)

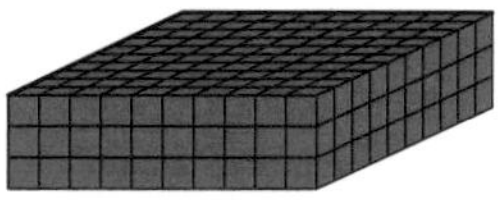

(i) $\frac{\square}{\square}$ (ii) ______

Equivalent tenths, hundredths, thousandths

thousandths

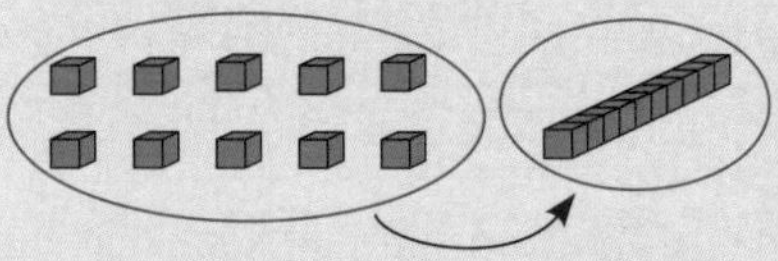

$\frac{10}{1000} = \frac{1}{100} = 0{\cdot}01$

hundredths

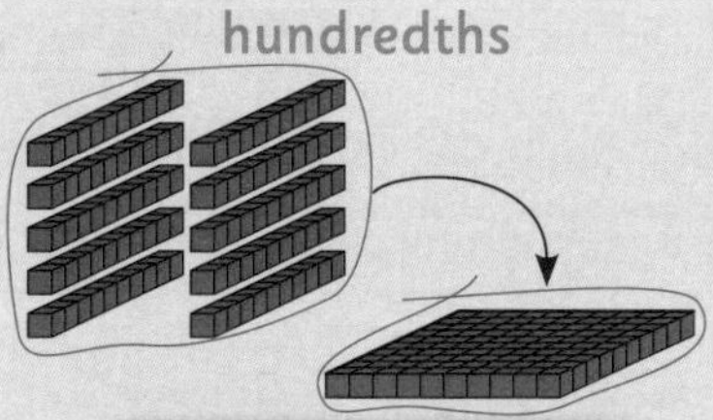

$\frac{10}{100} = \frac{1}{10} = 0{\cdot}1$

tenths

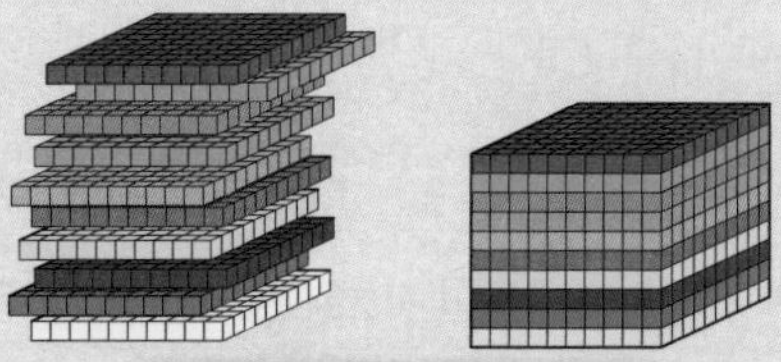

$\frac{10}{10} = 1 = 1{\cdot}0$

2. Draw the following fractions using as few blocks as possible. 
Then write them in decimal form. (Make them using actual blocks, if available.)

(a) $\frac{12}{1000}$ = 0·012

(b) $\frac{43}{1000}$ = ______

(c) $\frac{9}{100}$ = ______

(d) $\frac{12}{100}$ = ______

(e) $\frac{7}{10}$ = ______

(f) $\frac{34}{100}$ = ______

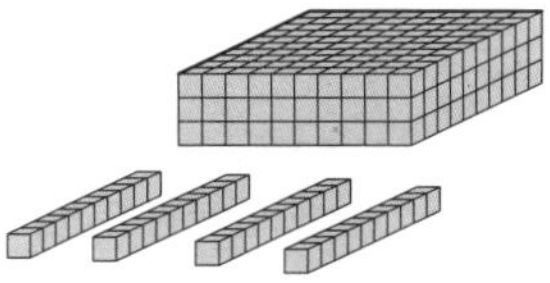

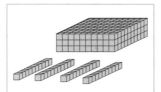

(g) $\frac{9}{10}$ = ______

(h) $\frac{243}{1000}$ = ______

Decimals – Problem-solving

1. Fill in the fractions and match each to the correct decimal fraction.

(a) 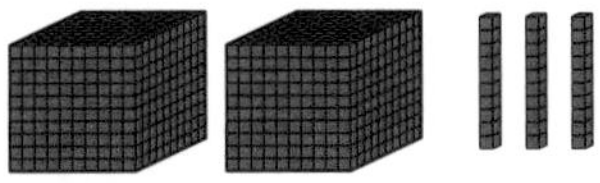 $= 2\frac{\square}{\square}$ •

(b) 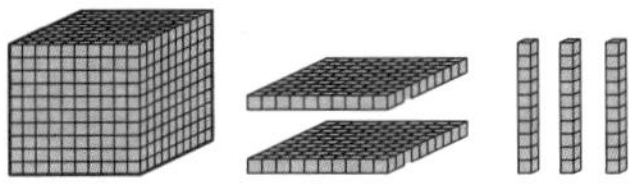 $= 1\frac{\square}{\square}$ •

(c) 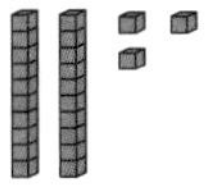 $= \frac{\square}{\square}$ •

(d) 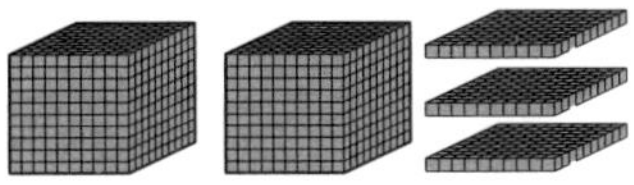 $= 2\frac{\square}{\square}$ •

(e) 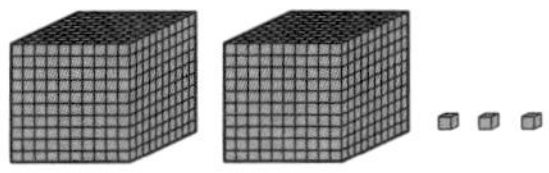 $= 2\frac{\square}{\square}$ •

(f) 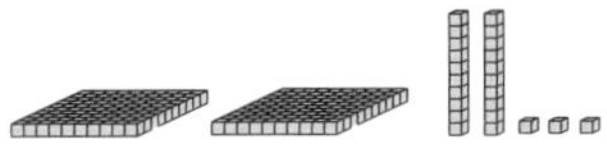 $= \frac{\square}{\square}$ •

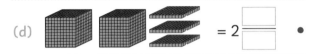

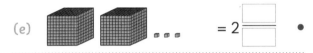

• 2·3

• 0·023

• 1·23

• 2·03

• 0·223

• 2·003

2. Write these mixed numbers as decimal numbers.

(a) $1\frac{1}{10}$ = ______ (b) $3\frac{5}{100}$ = ______ (c) $9\frac{9}{1000}$ = ______ (d) $4\frac{23}{100}$ = ______

(e) $10\frac{239}{1000}$ = ______ (f) $6\frac{47}{1000}$ = ______ (g) $1\frac{111}{1000}$ = ______ (h) $5\frac{900}{1000}$ = ______

3. Write the correct symbol (<, = or >) in each oval ◯.

(a) $3\frac{3}{10}$ ◯ 3·03 (b) $6\frac{6}{1000}$ ◯ 6·06 (c) $4\frac{44}{100}$ ◯ 4·44 (d) $7\frac{62}{1000}$ ◯ 7·620

(e) $\frac{7}{100}$ ◯ 0·07 (f) $8\frac{89}{1000}$ ◯ 8·089 (g) $2\frac{2}{10}$ ◯ 0·22 (h) $\frac{66}{1000}$ ◯ 0·66

4. SPORTS DAY!

The following children took part in a long jump competition.
Mark their jumps on the number line with the capital letter of each name.

(a) **K**evin jumped $\frac{7}{10}$m. (b) **M**ary jumped $1\frac{3}{10}$m. (c) **C**ara jumped $2\frac{1}{10}$m.

(d) **J**ohn jumped $\frac{2}{10}$m. (e) **A**idan jumped $1\frac{70}{100}$m. (f) **S**ue jumped $2\frac{40}{100}$m.

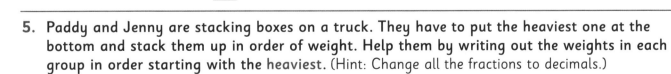

5. Paddy and Jenny are stacking boxes on a truck. They have to put the heaviest one at the bottom and stack them up in order of weight. Help them by writing out the weights in each group in order starting with the heaviest. (Hint: Change all the fractions to decimals.)

(a) $1\frac{1}{10}$kg, 1·0kg, 1·001kg

(b) 0·7kg, $\frac{77}{100}$kg, 0·077kg

(c) 4·04kg, $4\frac{44}{100}$kg, $4\frac{1}{10}$kg

(d) $3\frac{3}{10}$kg, $3\frac{3}{1000}$kg, 3·333kg

(e) 5·5kg, $\frac{5}{10}$kg, $\frac{55}{1000}$kg

(f) $22\frac{22}{100}$kg, $22\frac{2}{10}$kg, 22·222kg

Changing decimals to fractions

Use place value to change a decimal to a fraction

u	.	$\frac{1}{10}$	$\frac{1}{100}$	$\frac{1}{1000}$		
0	.	4			= tenths	$\frac{4}{10}$
0	.	2	3		= hundredths	$\frac{23}{100}$
0	.	7	0	6	= thousandths	$\frac{706}{1000}$

u	.	$\frac{1}{10}$	$\frac{1}{100}$	$\frac{1}{1000}$	
3	.	7			$= 3\frac{7}{10}$
5	.	4	8		$= 5\frac{48}{100}$
9	.	0	4	7	$= 9\frac{47}{1000}$

1. Work out the fraction part only for each of these.

(a) 0·9 = $\frac{\square}{\square}$　(b) 0·47 = $\frac{\square}{\square}$　(c) 0·245 = $\frac{\square}{\square}$　(d) 0·91 = $\frac{\square}{\square}$　(e) 0·007 = $\frac{\square}{\square}$

(f) 3·067 = 3 $\frac{\square}{\square}$　(g) 1·002 = 1 $\frac{\square}{\square}$　(h) 8·602 = 8 $\frac{\square}{\square}$　(i) 8·08 = 8 $\frac{\square}{\square}$　(j) 5·1 = 5 $\frac{\square}{\square}$

Simplifying fractions

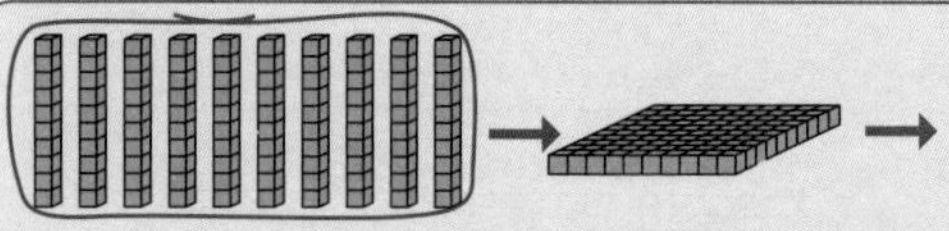

$\frac{10}{100} = \frac{1}{10}$ (zeros crossed off)

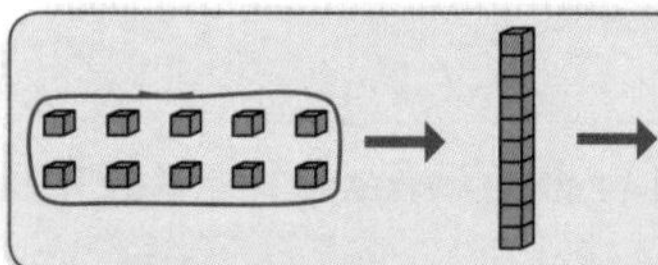

$\frac{10}{1000} = \frac{1}{100}$ (zeros crossed off)

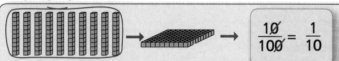

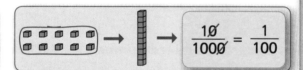

If there is a 0 at the end of both numbers, we can divide both by ten and cross the zeros off.

2. Write these decimal fractions as units and fractions, and then simplify.

(a) 2·020 = 2 $\frac{20}{1000}$ = 2 $\frac{2}{\square}$　(b) 3·800 = 3 $\frac{\square}{\square}$ = 3 $\frac{\square}{\square}$　(c) 5·450 = 5 $\frac{\square}{\square}$ = 5 $\frac{\square}{\square}$

(d) 8·880 = 8 $\frac{\square}{\square}$ = 8 $\frac{\square}{\square}$　(e) 6·090 = 6 $\frac{\square}{\square}$ = 6 $\frac{\square}{\square}$　(f) 4·700 = 4 $\frac{\square}{\square}$ = 4 $\frac{\square}{\square}$

3. Decimals on a bar chart

These children are investigating how far they cycle to school. Change their fractions to decimals and colour them on the chart.

Maggie: $1\frac{3}{10}$ km　Danny: $3\frac{60}{100}$ km

Fred: $2\frac{400}{1000}$ km　Conor: $1\frac{40}{100}$ km

Carlos: $1\frac{90}{100}$ km

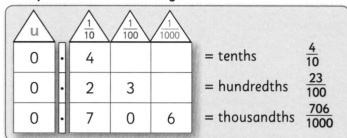

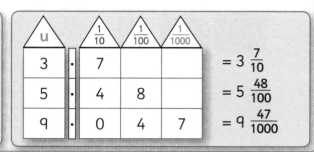

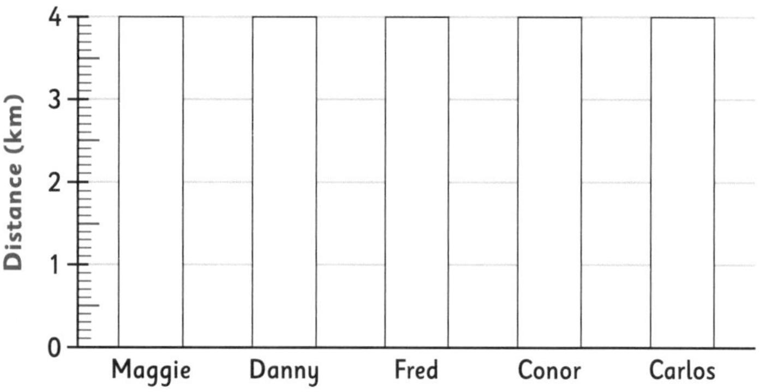

4. Work out the equivalent fraction for each of the following decimal fractions.

(a) 6·250 = 6 $\frac{\square}{\square}$　(b) 2·07 = 2 $\frac{\square}{\square}$　(c) 9·045 = 9 $\frac{\square}{\square}$　(d) 7·71 = 7 $\frac{\square}{\square}$

(e) 4·009 = 4 $\frac{\square}{\square}$　(f) 8·003 = 8 $\frac{\square}{\square}$　(g) 1·111 = 1 $\frac{\square}{\square}$　(h) 8·065 = 8 $\frac{\square}{\square}$

(i) 3·475 = 3 $\frac{\square}{\square}$　(j) 6·307 = 6 $\frac{\square}{\square}$　(k) 9·980 = 9 $\frac{\square}{\square}$　(l) 7·006 = 7 $\frac{\square}{\square}$

Changing fractions to decimals

We can use division to change any fraction to a decimal

We know that $\frac{4}{10} \rightarrow 4 \div 10 = 0{\cdot}4$.

A $\frac{1}{2} \rightarrow 1 \div 2 = 2\overline{)1{\cdot}0}$ = 0·5 (Add in a **zero** when necessary.)

B $\frac{3}{4} \rightarrow 4\overline{)3{\cdot}00}$ = 0·75

C $\frac{7}{8} \rightarrow 8\overline{)7{\cdot}000}$ = 0·875

1. Change these to **decimals** using division.

(a) $\frac{1}{4}$ = ______ (b) $\frac{1}{5}$ = ______ (c) $\frac{3}{5}$ = ______ (d) $\frac{2}{4}$ = ______ (e) $\frac{17}{20}$ = ______

(f) $\frac{1}{20}$ = ______ (g) $\frac{7}{10}$ = ______ (h) $\frac{13}{20}$ = ______ (i) $\frac{99}{100}$ = ______ (j) $\frac{3}{25}$ = ______

Changing fractions to decimals using equivalent tenths and hundredths

If the **denominator** is a **factor** of 10 or 100, we can change it to an equivalent fraction.

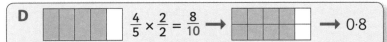

D 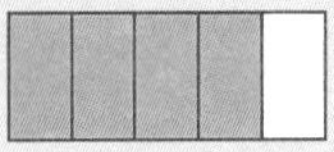 $\frac{4}{5} \times \frac{2}{2} = \frac{8}{10} \rightarrow$ 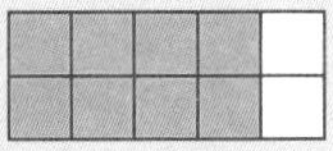 $\rightarrow 0{\cdot}8$

E $\frac{1}{4} \times \frac{25}{25} \rightarrow \frac{25}{100} = 0{\cdot}25$

2. Find the equivalent **tenth** or **hundredth** to help you change these to decimals.

(a) $\frac{1}{5} \times \frac{\square}{2} = \frac{\square}{10}$ = 0·______ (b) $\frac{9}{20} \times \frac{\square}{\square} = \frac{\square}{100}$ = 0·______ (c) $\frac{6}{25} \times \frac{\square}{\square} = \frac{\square}{100}$ = 0·______

(d) $\frac{1}{2} \times \frac{\square}{\square} = \frac{\square}{\square}$ = ______ (e) $\frac{3}{4} \times \frac{\square}{\square} = \frac{\square}{\square}$ = ______ (f) $\frac{4}{5} \times \frac{\square}{\square} = \frac{\square}{\square}$ = ______

(g) $\frac{1}{20} \times \frac{\square}{\square} = \frac{\square}{\square}$ = ______ (h) $\frac{10}{25} \times \frac{\square}{\square} = \frac{\square}{\square}$ = ______ (i) $\frac{11}{20} \times \frac{\square}{\square} = \frac{\square}{\square}$ = ______

3. Hailey wants to make some smoothies. The ingredients in the recipe are measured in fractions but her jug only measures in decimals. Change the fractions below to decimals to help her. Then find the total liquid in each smoothie.

(a) **Tropical:** $\frac{1}{5}$ l pineapple juice, $\frac{3}{10}$ l papaya juice, $\frac{40}{100}$ l coconut milk, $\frac{2}{10}$ l ice cubes

(b) **Summer Fruits:** $\frac{1}{2}$ l strawberry juice, $\frac{4}{10}$ l raspberry juice, $\frac{1}{4}$ l ice cubes, $\frac{2}{10}$ l natural yogurt

(c) **Autumn Harvest:** $\frac{3}{4}$ l apple juice, $\frac{2}{5}$ l blackcurrant juice, $\frac{150}{1000}$ l yogurt, $\frac{1}{5}$ l of ice cubes

(d) **Citrus Sunshine:** $\frac{35}{100}$ l orange juice, $\frac{3}{20}$ l lemon juice, $\frac{4}{25}$ l lime juice, $\frac{200}{1000}$ l grapefruit juice

Challenge Roy had three parcels that weighed $2\frac{7}{10}$kg, $1\frac{4}{5}$kg and $3\frac{3}{4}$kg.

(a) Change to decimals to find the total weight of the three parcels. ______ kg

(b) How much less than $9\frac{1}{2}$kg do they weigh? ______ kg

Adding and subtracting decimals

Always remember **place value** when adding or subtracting decimals. €0·90 is not the same as €0·09 and 0·8kg is a lot heavier than 0·008kg!

Adding decimals: 4 + 1·09 + 0·007 = ☆

```
   4·000
   1·090
 + 0·007
   -----
   5·097
```

Add extra zeros to help you.

Subtracting decimals: 3 − 1·038 = ☆

```
  ²3·0⁹¹0⁹¹0¹0
 − 1·038
   -----
   1·962
```

Always keep decimal points straight under each other!

1. Now try these.

(a) 1·05 + 4 + 0·009 (b) 7·6 − 2·325 (c) 0·007 + 0·39 + 6

(d) 5 − 0·05 (e) 10·059 + 3·921 + 0·09 (f) 0·09 − 0·003

2. Change these fractions to decimals and add or subtract.

(a) $3\frac{43}{100} - \frac{529}{1000}$ (b) $\frac{7}{20} + \frac{3}{4}$ (c) $6 + 3\frac{2}{5} + 4\frac{1}{2}$

(d) $3\frac{10}{25} - 2\frac{9}{10}$ (e) $3 + \frac{9}{1000} + 4\frac{8}{100}$ (f) $4 + \frac{17}{1000} + 2\frac{9}{100}$

3. Work out these problems using decimals.

(a) How much did the shopping cost in total?

(b) Find the total weight of these children.

(c) What distance did Cathy swim this week?

Monday	Tuesday	Wednesday
1·05km	$1\frac{1}{5}$km	1·009km

(d) How far is the library from Conor's house?

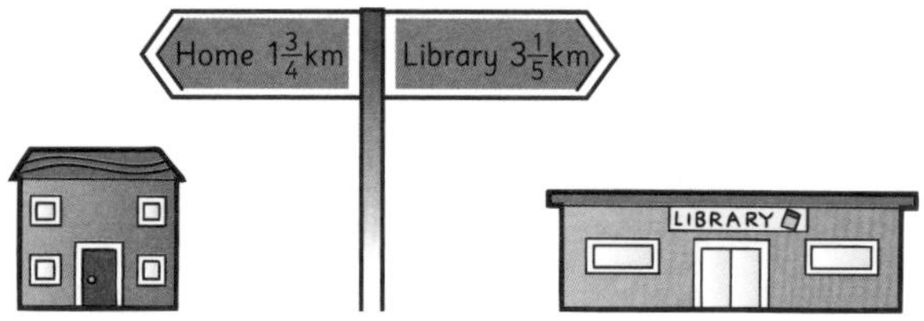

(e) A newborn cheetah cub weighs $\frac{1}{4}$kg, while a tiger cub weighs $1\frac{1}{5}$kg. How much heavier is the tiger cub?

(f) An Ironman Triathlon is made up of a $3\frac{86}{100}$km swim, $180\frac{1}{4}$km cycle and a 42·2km marathon. What is the total distance?

(g) There are 4·589 million people living in Ireland. 1·27 million live in Dublin. How many of these people do not live in Dublin?

(h) An adult drinks on average $2\frac{1}{2}$ litres of water per day. A child drinks 1·75 litres of water on average per day. How much less does a child drink than an adult?

Challenge Morgan cycled $6\frac{3}{4}$km on Monday, $7\frac{2}{5}$km on Wednesday and $8\frac{65}{100}$km on Friday. How far did he cycle in total? (Answer in decimal form). ________ km

Chapter 15: Multiplication 2

Remember: When we multiply by 10, we move **all** the digits **one** place to the **left** (←).
It is the same with decimals.

A 49 × 10 = ☆

th	h	t	u	
		4	9	
	4	9	0	(← × 10)

49 × 10 = 490

B 15·3 × 10 = ☆

th	h	t	u		$\frac{1}{10}$	
		1	5	·	3	
	1	5	3	·	0	(← × 10)

15·3 × 10 = 153·0

C 6·28 × 10 = ☆

h	t	u		$\frac{1}{10}$	$\frac{1}{100}$	
		6	·	2	8	
	6	2	·	8	0	(← × 10)

6·28 × 10 = 62·80

1. Complete the following table by multiplying each number by 10 and the answer by 10.

	h	t	u		$\frac{1}{10}$	$\frac{1}{100}$	$\frac{1}{1000}$	(× 10)	th	h	t	u		$\frac{1}{10}$	$\frac{1}{100}$	(× 10)	th	h	t	u		$\frac{1}{10}$	$\frac{1}{100}$
(a)		7	2	·	4			(× 10)		7	2	4	·	0		(× 10)	7	2	4	0	·	0	
(b)			3	·	1			(× 10)			3	1	·	0		(× 10)		3	1	0	·	0	
(c)		5	6	·	8			(× 10)					·			(× 10)					·		
(d)			8	·	4			(× 10)					·			(× 10)					·		
(e)			2	·	9	5		(× 10)					·			(× 10)					·		
(f)		4	1	·	0	6		(× 10)					·			(× 10)					·		
(g)			2	·	7	8	3	(× 10)			2	7	·	8	3	(× 10)					·		
(h)			0	·	9			(× 10)					·			(× 10)					·		
(i)		1	5	·	4	0	7	(× 10)					·			(× 10)					·		
(j)			6	·	0	0	4	(× 10)					·			(× 10)					·		
(k)			0	·	3	7		(× 10)					·			(× 10)					·		

2. Groups of 25 soldiers were lining up for parade. If there were 10 groups in all, what was the total number of soldiers on parade? ________

3.  A paintbrush costs €15·38. What will an artist pay if he buys 10 paintbrushes? €________

4. Each railway wagon carries 6·25 tonnes of freight. What is the total weight carried by 10 such railway wagons? ________ tonnes

5. 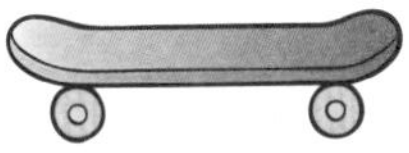 A skateboard costs €42·76.
What is the cost of 10 such skateboards? €________

6. A barrel holds 82·3 litres of water. How many litres would: (a) 10 such barrels hold? ________ (b) 100 such barrels hold? ________ (c) 1,000 such barrels hold? ________

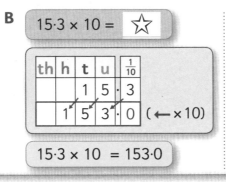

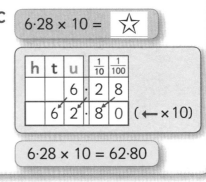

Maths Fact The world's tallest tree is a redwood in California. It measures 115·66m in height. What would be the total height of 10 such redwood trees? ________ m

Multiplying decimals

The first article sold on eBay was a laser printer. It sold for $14·83 (US dollars). How much would: (a) 6 and (b) 34 such laser printers be sold for?

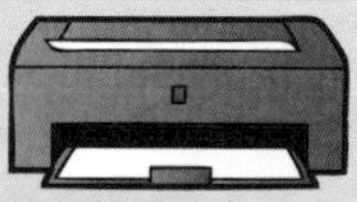

A $14·83 × 6 = ☆

Estimate: $15 × 6 = $90

Dollars can be multiplied the same way as euro and cent.


```
  $14·83
 ×     6
  $88·98
```

B $14·83 × 34 = ☆

Estimate: $15 × 30 = $450

```
                          $14·83
                        ×     34
$14·83 ×  4 ⟶              59·32
$14·83 × 30 ⟶           + 444·90
$14·83 × 34 ⟶            $504·22
```

Short way

```
  $14·83
 ×    34
   59·32
 + 444·90
 $504·22
```

1. Try these the short way. Remember to estimate. Check your answers using a calculator.

(a) $12·76 × 8	(b) $18·34 × 5	(c) $14·29 × 7	(d) $17·53 × 9
(e) €43·69 × 4	(f) €61·92 × 7	(g) €83·55 × 6	(h) €94·64 × 8
(i) €6·72 × 24	(j) €5·78 × 36	(k) €9·26 × 57	(l) €8·17 × 78
(m) 35·37 × 48	(n) 52·89 × 57	(o) 76·31 × 84	(p) 96·64 × 69
(q) 71·86 × 50	(r) 30·72 × 89	(s) 87·08 × 67	(t) 65·65 × 79

2. A workman painted lines each 2·17m long in a car park. How many metres did he paint if he painted 36 lines? ______ metres

3.  A dog kennel costs €29·95. How much would 28 kennels cost? € ______

4. A small cement mixer produces 135·78 litres of cement mix called mortar. How many litres of mortar can nine such cement mixers produce? ______ l

5.  A water butt can hold 96·34 litres of rainwater. How much water would 37 such water butts hold? ______ l

6. A marathon runner runs 78·73km each week while training. How many kilometres will she run in 28 weeks? ______ km

7. A hotel sells rooms at different rates. What will its total take be if it sells eight rooms at €53·78 each and 27 rooms at €76·29 each? € ______

8. 12 seats on a flight to London were bought for €69·95 each. Nine seats were bought for €117·56 each. What was the total cost of the seats? € ______

9. Tara runs 2·45km to the bus stop each day. How far will she run in 24 days? ______ km

Maths Fact

The smallest car on sale in the world at present is the Peel P50. It weighs 59kg and is 1·37m long. Find the total length of 47 Peel P50 cars placed bumper to bumper. ______ m

Multiplying big numbers

A Greek soldier called Pheidippides ran 42·195km from Marathon to Athens to bring news of the victory in the Battle of Marathon in 490BC. What distance would an athlete cover in three of these marathon runs?

42·195 × 3 = ☆

Estimate: 40 × 3 = 120km

A Repeated addition method

$$\begin{array}{r} 42{\cdot}195\text{km} \\ 42{\cdot}195\text{km} \\ +\ 42{\cdot}195\text{km} \\ \hline 126{\cdot}585\text{km} \end{array}$$

B Multiplication method

h	t	u	$\frac{1}{10}$	$\frac{1}{100}$	$\frac{1}{1000}$	
	4	2·	1	9	5	km
				×	3	
1	2	6·	5	8	5	km

1. Use the repeated addition and multiplication methods to do these. Estimate first!

(a) 7·276 × 3 (b) 15·378 × 4 (c) 4·926 × 5 (d) 13·182 × 6
(e) 36·629 × 5 (f) 8·023 × 6 (g) 27·241 × 3 (h) 9·668 × 4
(i) 45·536 × 4 (j) 6·647 × 5 (k) 8·594 × 7 (l) 7·863 × 9

2. Do these using the multiplication method. Estimate first!

(a) 3·529 × 7 (b) 18·416 × 6 (c) 7·653 × 8 (d) 21·957 × 7
(e) 6·073 × 9 (f) 34·508 × 8 (g) 28·729 × 6 (h) 5·008 × 9
(i) 7·318 × 6 (j) 45·525 × 7 (k) 53·478 × 8 (l) 72·695 × 9

3. 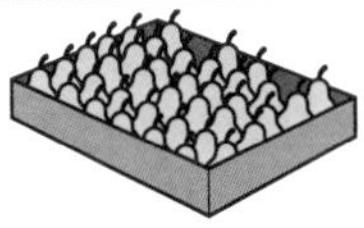

A box of pears weighs 28·749kg.
What is the total weight of seven boxes of pears? ________ kg

4. The distance around one circuit of a Formula 1 race track is 8·638km.
How far would a car travel if it did nine circuits of the track? ________ km

5. 

A car weighs 976·84kg. A lorry weighs seven times this amount.
What is the weight of the lorry? ________ kg

6. A foam fire extinguisher holds 6·228 litres in the medium size and 8·936 litres in the large size. What is the total amount of foam in six of the medium size and nine of the large size? ________ litres

7. A forest walk is 3·498km. What was the total distance travelled by nine children who completed the walk? ________ km

8. 

In a mini-triathlon, the competitors had to swim 0·76km, cycle $8\frac{4}{8}$ km and run $10\frac{78}{1000}$ km. What distance in total did eight competitors complete in the mini-triathlon? ________ km

Maths Fact 3·75 million litres of water is the minimum required to fill an Olympic-sized 50m swimming pool. What would be the minimum amount of water required to fill eight such Olympic-sized pools (in millions of litres)? ________

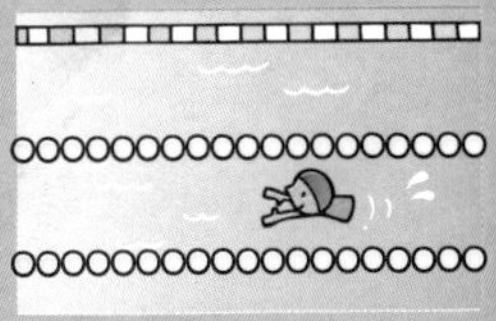

Multiplying bigger numbers

The highest mountain in Europe is Mount Elbrus in Russia. It is a dormant volcano and stands 5·642km above sea level. Find the total distance travelled by 48 mountaineers who climbed Mount Elbrus.

5·642km × 48 = ☆

Estimate: 6 × 50 = 300km

A Multiples method

5·642 × 10 = 56·420km
5·642 × 10 = 56·420km
5·642 × 10 = 56·420km
5·642 × 10 = 56·420km
5·642 × 8 = 45·136km
5·642 × 48 = 270·816km

B Long multiplication method

	h	t	u	·	$\frac{1}{10}$	$\frac{1}{100}$	$\frac{1}{1000}$	
			5	·	6	4	2	km
					×	4	8	
5·642 × 8 →		4	5	·	1	3	6	
5·642 × 40 → +	2	2	5	·	6	8	0	
5·642 × 48 →	2	7	0	·	8	1	6	km

1. Do these using the long multiplication method. Estimate first!

(a) 4·715 × 14 (b) 2·565 × 23 (c) 5·824 × 35 (d) 3·629 × 45 (e) 4·476 × 53
(f) 3·691 × 47 (g) 4·368 × 39 (h) 1·877 × 76 (i) 5·392 × 84 (j) 3·986 × 74

2. Use the long multiplication method to do these. (Use a calculator to check the answers.)

(a) 3·356 × 17 (b) 2·742 × 36 (c) 1·709 × 4 (d) 4·519 × 24 (e) 1·886 × 57
(f) 6·297 × 47 (g) 1·093 × 58 (h) 3·774 × 68 (i) 5·008 × 96 (j) 2·998 × 76

3. Rory visited the Cash & Carry Store and bought the following quantities of items.

(a)

€3·67 each × 15
Cost: €______

(b)
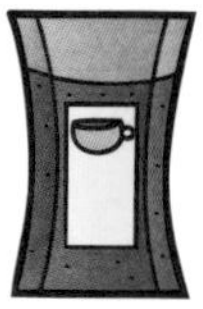
€4·73 each × 36
Cost: €______

(c)

€5·68 × 19
Cost: €______

(d)
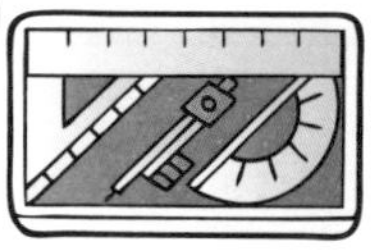
€1·59 × 27
Cost: €______

(e)

€18·36 × 29
Cost: €______

(f) What was the total cost of Rory's purchases at the Cash & Carry Store? €______

4. A roll of electrical cable has 2·075km of cable.
What is the total length of cable on 39 such rolls? ______ km

5.

A watering can holds 9·783l of water. A bath tub can hold 29 times that amount of water. How much water can the bath tub hold? ______ l

6. A path in Roscommon is 5·987km long. A girl walked this path each day for the month of July.
How far did she walk in total? ______ km

Maths Fact

Mt Everest, the world's highest mountain, is 8·848km above sea level. Find the total height reached by an aeroplane that flew at the exact height of Mt Everest on each of 37 flights. ______ km

Multiplication 2 – Mountain fun

Ready for some more multiplication mountaineering?

Start at the bottom and work to the top to climb the seven highest peaks in Ireland. Each peak gets a little higher – and the questions get a little harder.

FINISH

7. (a) 17·83 × 37 = ____ (b) 69·79 × 48 = ____ (c) 51·28 × 56 = ____ (d) 36·35 × 79 = ____ (e) 44·76 × 93 = ____

Stay in MacGillicuddy's Reeks to climb Carrauntoohil, 1,038m high.

6. (a) €24·95 × 16 = € ____ (b) €36·52 × 37 = € ____ (c) 58·17 m × 29 = ____ m (d) 60·34 × 59 = ____ (e) €53·08 × 47 = € ____

Nearly at the top, so tackle Beenkeragh at 1,010m.

5. (a) €6·83 × 7 = € ____ (b) €5·79 × 8 = € ____ (c) €3·40 × 7 = € ____ (d) €13·27 × 6 = € ____ (e) €35·82 × 9 = € ____ (f) €52·08 × 8 = € ____

First peak over 1,000m is Caher Mountain at 1,001m.

4. (a) 3,562 × 18 = ____ (b) 2,877 × 25 = ____ (c) 2,168 × 37 = ____ (d) 5,254 × 13 = ____ (e) 1,708 × 26 = ____ (f) 1,065 × 78 = ____

Knocknapeasta is next up at 988m.

3. (a) 257 × 36 = ____ (b) 469 × 47 = ____ (c) 594 × 85 = ____ (d) 786 × 94 = ____ (e) 380 × 26 = ____ (f) 606 × 78 = ____

Move on to Kerry and Mount Brandon at 953m.

2. (a) 74 × 100 = ____ (b) 90 × 100 = ____ (c) 527 × 100 = ____ (d) 704 × 100 = ____ (e) 6·3 × 100 = ____ (f) 14·9 × 100 = ____ (g) 23·26 × 100 = ____

You are now going to climb Lugnaquilla at 925m.

1. (a) 38 × 10 = ____ (b) 65 × 20 = ____ (c) 127 × 10 = ____ (d) 307 × 10 = ____ (e) 814 × 30 = ____ (f) 2,918 × 10 = ____ (g) 605 × 60 = ____

Climb Galtymore Mountain at 919m. **START**

Chapter 16: Division 2

Let's revise our **division methods**. Complete the following. Some answers will have remainders.

	(a)	(b)	(c)	(d)	(e)
1.	$\frac{427}{5}$	$\frac{336}{7}$	$\frac{558}{6}$	$\frac{930}{4}$	$\frac{763}{8}$
2.	711 ÷ 6	803 ÷ 9	665 ÷ 4	510 ÷ 7	899 ÷ 8
3.	7)835	6)917	5)508	8)713	9)884
4.	6)759	8)906	7)708	5)898	9)857

Use the **long division method** to do these. Estimate first! These questions have remainders.

	(a)	(b)	(c)	(d)	(e)
5.	636 ÷ 29	850 ÷ 19	822 ÷ 23	914 ÷ 38	877 ÷ 34
6.	17)421	19)605	49)872	28)983	52)927
7.	918 ÷ 44	898 ÷ 39	960 ÷ 56	923 ÷ 29	976 ÷ 64

When estimating with **decimals**, it is best to **round** to the nearest **whole number**:

(a) 0·7 ⟶ 1 (b) 0·62 ⟶ 1 (c) 7·3 ⟶ 7 (d) 4·5 ⟶ 5 (e) 16·4 ⟶ 16

Round these decimals to the nearest whole number.

	(a)	(b)	(c)	(d)	(e)	(f)
8.	0·9	0·65	4·3	6·5	9·7	14·4
9.	21·8	59·3	36·21	58·37	131·62	719·51

A carpenter cut 19·6m of wood into four equal pieces. How long was each piece?

19·6 ÷ 4 = ☆

Estimate: 20 ÷ 4 = 5

A Short division method

4)19·³6m
4·9m

B Long division method

4·9m
4)19·³6m

Hot tip!
Put in the decimal point before dividing!

Try these using the **long division method**.

Estimate first by rounding.

	(a)	(b)	(c)	(d)	(e)
10.	22·8 ÷ 6	21·5 ÷ 5	18·8 ÷ 4	23·1 ÷ 3	52·5 ÷ 7
11.	26·04 ÷ 6	26·75 ÷ 5	32·52 ÷ 4	24·81 ÷ 3	46·02 ÷ 6
12.	7·74 ÷ 9	9·45 ÷ 7	31·98 ÷ 6	29·76 ÷ 8	30·52 ÷ 7

Maths Fact The temperature in Death Valley, California, once reached 56·7°C. What is a typical Irish summer temperature if it is $\frac{1}{3}$ of the above temperature in Death Valley? ______ °C

STRAND Number **STRAND UNIT/ELEMENT** *Operations*
LANGUAGE *Divide, estimate, long/short division, remainder, nearest, calculator, better value, share, equals, kilogrammes, metres*

Long division of decimals

The school lights were left on over 19 days during the school holidays and the meter reading was 55·1 units. What was the average number of electricity units used each day?

55·1 ÷ 19 = ☆ Estimate: 60 ÷ 20 = 3

Remember: Put in the decimal point first!

```
      2·9
19 ) 55·1    ← Divide 19 into 55 first. It goes in 2 times. (19 × 2 = 38)
   – 38↓     ← Subtract 2 groups of 19 (38) from 55 to find the remainder.
     171     ← Bring down the 1. Divide 19 into 171. (19 × 9 = 171)
   – 171     ← Subtract 9 groups of 19 (171) from 171 to find the remainder.
       0     ← Remainder.
```

55·1 ÷ 19 = 2·9 units of electricity

1. Have a go at completing these. Estimate first.

(a)
```
      1·
23 ) 39·1
   – 23↓
     16_
   – __
```

(b)
```
      1·
37 ) 59·2
   – 37↓
     22_
   – __
```

(c)
```
      3·
18 ) 68·4
   – 54↓
     14_
   – __
```

(d)
```
       8·
53 ) 450·5
   – 424↓
      26_
   – __
```

Now try these. You may check your answers using a calculator.

	(a)	(b)	(c)	(d)	(e)
2.	40·8 ÷ 24	73·1 ÷ 17	91·2 ÷ 16	94·5 ÷ 27	88·5 ÷ 15
3.	96·2 ÷ 37	114·4 ÷ 26	136·5 ÷ 39	243·6 ÷ 58	64·4 ÷ 23
4.	43) 120·8	55) 203·5	29) 49·3	58) 40·6	63) 100·8
5.	128·8 ÷ 46	100·8 ÷ 28	194·4 ÷ 72	373·5 ÷ 83	60·8 ÷ 76

6. A car used 43 litres of fuel to travel 253·7km.
How many km did it travel for each litre of fuel used? ______ km

7. Share 82·8 litres of water equally among 36 runners in a race.
How much water will each runner get? ______ litres

8. How many times can I withdraw 28 litres from a tank that holds 75·6 litres? ______

Maths Fact

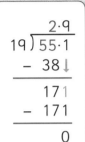

37·8°C is the temperature needed to melt lanolin, a waxy substance in sheep's wool. It is used as an ingredient in chewing gum! Divide the melting temperature of lanolin: (a) by 6 and (b) by 9. (a) ______ °C (b) ______ °C

More decimal places

Tony can buy (a) seven hurley grips for €27·93 or (b) 16 hurley grips for €59·04. Help Tony decide which is better value for his team.

€27·93 ÷ 7 = ☆ Estimate: €28 ÷ 7 = €4 €59·04 ÷ 16 = ☆ Estimate: €60 ÷ 15 = €4

A Short division method

$$7\overline{)€27·\overset{6}{9}\overset{6}{3}}$$
$$€3·99$$

Each grip will cost €3·99.

Which option is better value, **A** or **B**?

B Long division method

```
        €3·69
16 ) €59·04
    − 48↓
      110
    −  96↓
      144
    −  144
        0
```

Each grip will cost €3·69.

Working with money will require answers to two decimal places. Try these. Estimate first.

1. (a) €14·82 ÷ 6 (b) €23·94 ÷ 9 (c) €24·57 ÷ 7 (d) €26·40 ÷ 5 (e) €63·52 ÷ 8

2. (a) €24·18 ÷ 13 (b) €24·65 ÷ 17 (c) €42·66 ÷ 18 (d) €94·08 ÷ 24 (e) €98·91 ÷ 21

3. (a) $42\overline{)€91·56}$ (b) $28\overline{)€66·36}$ (c) $37\overline{)€97·31}$ (d) $19\overline{)€92·53}$ (e) $54\overline{)€74·52}$

4. (a) €35·28 ÷ 28 (b) €55·44 ÷ 33 (c) €94·08 ÷ 48 (d) €90·48 ÷ 26 (e) €99·18 ÷ 57

Sometimes we can get an answer that is less than one unit!

€4·14 ÷ 23 = ☆

Estimate: 400c ÷ 20 = 20c

Share €4·14 equally among 23 children.

```
      €0·18
23 ) €4·14
   − 23↓
     184
   − 184
       0
```

Hot tip!
Always write a zero in the units place before the decimal point if the answer is less than one unit.

Check your answer by multiplying €0·18 × 23 = €4·14.

Now try these. You may use a calculator to check your answers.

5. (a)
```
         0·1
35 ) 5·95
   − 35↓
      24
   −
```
(b) $49\overline{)6·86}$ (c) $28\overline{)6·44}$ (d) $37\overline{)16·65}$

(e) $45\overline{)27·9}$ (f) $66\overline{)34·98}$ (g) $58\overline{)20·3}$

(h) $72\overline{)17·28}$ (i) $76\overline{)12·92}$ (j) $83\overline{)21·58}$

Maths Fact

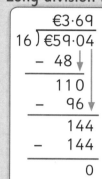

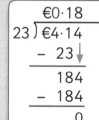

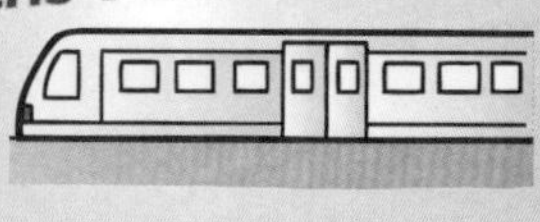

The world's shortest underground metro is in Haifa, Israel. It is just 1·8km long. The system has six stations. What would be the distance between each station if they were set equally apart? _____ km

Division 2 – Problem-solving

1. Jane spent €80·85 filling her car with 55 litres of diesel fuel. What price did she pay per litre? €______

2.  A baker sold 37 apple tarts for a total of €88·06. What was the sale price of each tart? €______

3. A gardener mixed 19 containers of weedkiller, each holding an equal amount. She had a total of 16·34 litres of weedkiller. What quantity of weedkiller was in each container? ______l

4. Edel added 6·29 and 9·69. She divided the total by 47. What answer did she get? ______

5. Sammy subtracted 24·31 from 122·73. He then divided the result by 38. What answer did he get? ______

6. Divide 62·7 by 10. Now divide your answer by 10. ______

7.  A teacher went to a bookstore to buy scrapbooks. She had €20 and bought 14 scrapbooks. She got €9·36 change. What was the cost of each scrapbook? €______

8. Jack multiplied two numbers and got 29·07 as his answer. One of the numbers was 57. What was the other number? ______

9. A lorry travelled 520·8km on 24 litres of diesel fuel. How far did it travel per litre of fuel? ______km

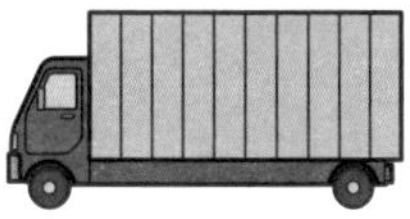

10.  A coil of rope measuring 99·56m was cut into 19 equal pieces. How long was each piece? ______m

11. A piece of wood 33·15m long was cut into 17 poles of equal length. How long was each pole? ______m

12.  The potatoes in a container weigh 90·25kg. The potatoes are packed equally into 19 bags. What weight of potatoes is in each bag? ______kg

13. A farmer received €2,506 for 28 sheep. If each sheep was sold for the same price, what was the selling price per sheep? €______

14. Sofia spent €34·20 buying 38 pencils. How much was each pencil? €______

Maths Fact

110·4kg of pure gold was used to make the coffin of the Egyptian pharaoh Tutankhamun. If 15 slaves carried an equal amount of the gold to make the coffin, what weight did each slave carry? ______kg

Do I multiply or divide?

Solve the following real-life problems.

1.  It takes 3m of cloth to make a dress. How many dresses can be made from 27m of cloth? ________

2. There are eight apples in a box. How many apples are there in:
(a) six such boxes? ________
(b) 12 such boxes? ________

3. A coach can carry 17 people. How many coaches are needed to carry 153 people? ________
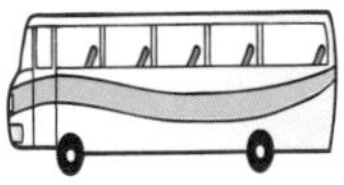

4. 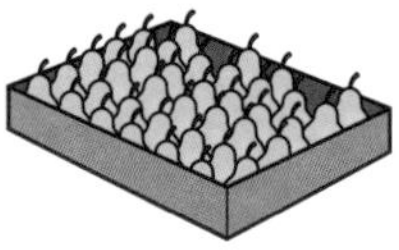 Each box holds 38 pears. How many pears would 27 such boxes hold? ________

5. Ciara runs 2·455km each evening for 27 evenings. How far does she run altogether? ________ km

6.  A tank of water holds 24·3 litres. How many buckets, each holding nine litres, can be filled from the tank? ________

7. A concert ticket costs €48·75. What is the cost of eight tickets? €________
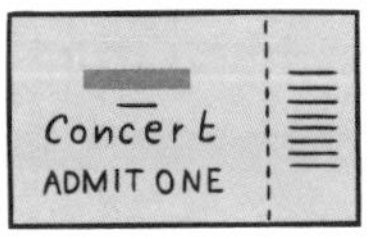

8.  A book costs €17·28. How much would 32 books cost? €________

9. There were 288 guests at a wedding. If the guests sat at tables of 12, how many tables were needed? ________

10.  Pete cycled 35·68km each day while training for a race. How far did he cycle in the month of June? ________ km

11. A car can travel 49km on 1 litre of diesel fuel. How far should it travel on 34l of diesel? ________ km

12. A firm made €8,256 selling hurleys. If each hurley cost €32, how many hurleys did the firm sell? ________

13. There were 384 people at the cinema. If each person paid €15 for a ticket, how much money did the cinema take in? €________

14. 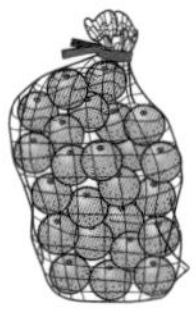 Oranges are packed into bags of 24. How many bags can be packed from a container of 2,088 oranges? ________

15. A roll of rope measuring 91·76m was cut into 37 strips. What was the length of each strip? ________ m
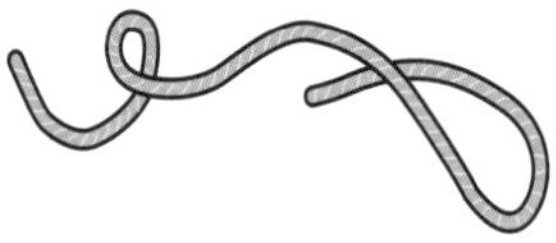

16. 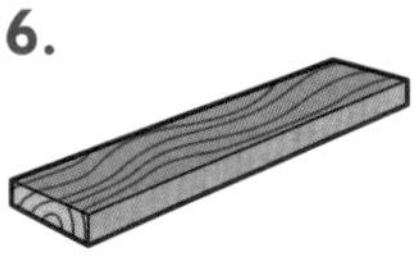 A piece of wood is 3·46m long. What would be the total length of 35 such pieces of wood placed end to end? ________ m

17. Teacher shared 1,512 marbles equally among 36 children. How many marbles did each child get? ________
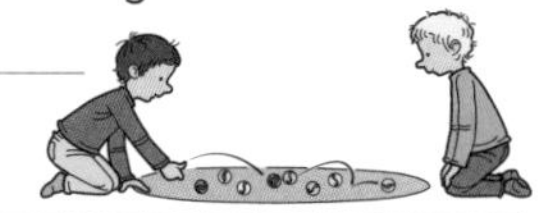

18.  Sam got €15·56 change from €50 when she bought 28 rolls of ribbon. How much did each roll cost? €________

19.  An athlete runs 18·67km each day while training for a marathon. How far will he run in 38 days? ________ km

20. A rugby ball costs €32·76. What change will a club get from €800 when it buys 19 balls? €________

Chapter 17: Calculator fun

1. Enter [7][7][3][8] in the calculator. Turn the calculator upside down to read the word BELL. Work out the following problems using a calculator. Turn the answers upside down. Read the words. Write each word in the correct place to complete the crossword.

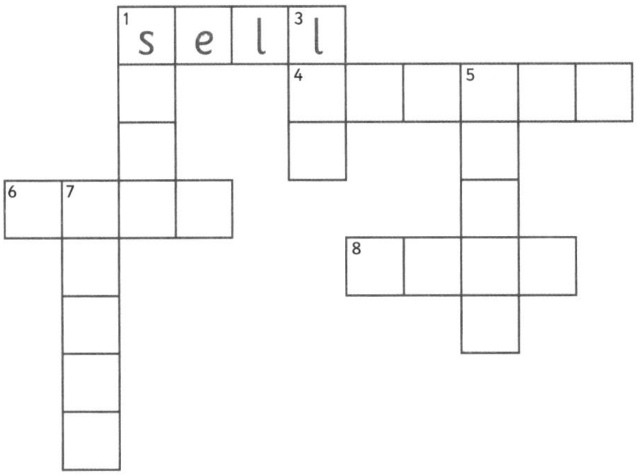

Across:	Clue:
1. (88 × 88) – 9	opposite to buy
4. (500 × 1,000) + 761	houses made of snow
6. (40 × 100) – 295	type of fish
8. (55 × 100) + 8	person in charge

Down:	Clue:
1. 7th + 1h + 0t + 5u	earth
3. (6,893 – 5,241) – 1,435	girl's name
5. (40,000 – 5,000) + 380	very overweight
7. (81 × 98) + 23,832	boy's name

2. Match each number on the pirate's ship to the correct multiplier to help the six pirates reach the treasure. (Use a calculator.)

The [5] key on Uzzy's calculator is broken.
However, he can still work out the answer to 35 + 85 by:

(a) **Keying in:** [3][4][+][1][+][8][4][+][1][=] or

(b) **Keying in:** [3][8][–][3][+][8][8][–][3][=]

Can you find another way of doing it?

3. **Help Uzzy calculate the answers to these on his broken calculator.**

(a) 85 + 59	(b) 356 + 542	(c) 850 – 35	(d) 542 – 153
(e) 3,500 – 1,285	(f) 27,350 – 6,500	(g) 55,000 – 5	(h) 5,533 – 55

Challenge It took Neil Armstrong and his crew 3 days and 3 hours to get to the moon in 1969.

(a) How many hours did it take? ______ (b) How many minutes is that? ______

(c) How many seconds is that? ______

Learning through the calculator 1

Explore these patterns on the calculator. Predict what questions 1(g) and 2(g) should be.

1.
(a) [1] [×] [9] [+] [2] = ______
(b) 12 × 9 + 3 = ______
(c) 123 × 9 + 4 = ______
(d) 1,234 × 9 + 5 = ______
(e) 12,345 × 9 + 6 = ______
(f) 123,456 × 9 + 7 = ______
(g) ______ = ______

2.
(a) [9] [×] [9] [+] [7] = ______
(b) 98 × 9 + 6 = ______
(c) 987 × 9 + 5 = ______
(d) 9,876 × 9 + 4 = ______
(e) 98,765 × 9 + 3 = ______
(f) 987,654 × 9 + 2 = ______
(g) ______ = ______

3. Write the correct symbol (+, −, × or ÷) to finish these number sentences.

(26 (×) 37) (−) 15 = 947

(a) (346 ◯ 97) ◯ 51 = 300
(b) (16 ◯ 39) ◯ 24 = 600
(c) (12,435 ◯ 2,645) ◯ 1,166 = 8,624
(d) (17,000 ◯ 2,593) ◯ 3,690 = 10,717
(e) (99 ◯ 3) ◯ 100 = 3,300
(f) (18 ◯ 3) ◯ 512 = 566
(g) (20,000 ◯ 3,651) ◯ 42 = 16,391
(h) (365 ◯ 5) ◯ 3 = 70

4. Write the missing digits.

(a)
```
  2 □
+ □ 4
-----
  6 9
```

(b)
```
  6 7
− □ □
-----
  2 3
```

(c)
```
  5, 4 3 6
+ □ □ □ □
---------
  7, 3 7 9
```

(d)
```
  2, □ 3 6
+ 4, 5 □ □
----------
  7, 1 4 8
```

(e)
```
  2 3 □
  ×   6
-------
1, 4 1 6
```

(f)
```
6)□ 7 □
   2 9
```

(g)
```
  5 2 6
− □ □ □
-------
  2 7 3
```

(h)
```
  5 □ 7
  ×   □
-------
1, 5 8 1
```

Challenge 1

Mo Farah won the men's 10,000 metres at the 2013 World Championships in Moscow. It took him 27 minutes and 21·71 seconds. How many seconds is that altogether? ______

Challenge 2

One newspaper is 1cm thick.

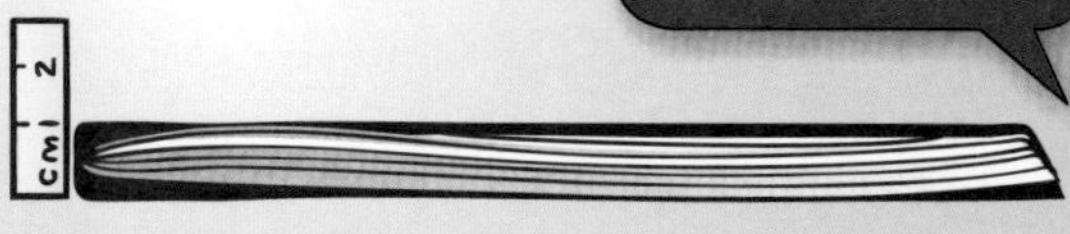

cm
1
2

How many newspapers does it take to make a pile:

(a) 10cm high? ______
(b) 1 metre high? ______
(c) 1 kilometre high? ______

Learning through the calculator 2

1. Change the underlined digit to zero in one step.

> 78,894 – 90 = ☆   78,8$\underline{9}$4 → press [7] [8] [8] [9] [4] [–] [9] [0] [=]
>
> 78,804 will appear on the screen.

(a) 2$\underline{7}$6	(b) 85$\underline{9}$	(c) $\underline{1}$,378	(d) 2,$\underline{4}$96
(e) $\underline{3}$,816	(f) 25,$\underline{2}$46	(g) 34,83$\underline{1}$	(h) $\underline{9}$7,624
(i) 66,6$\underline{6}$6	(j) 6$\underline{6}$,666	(k) $\underline{6}$6,666	(l) 66,$\underline{6}$66

2. Write down the keys you press from the given lists to reach the target numbers. Use the fewest number of keys possible. You may press the numbers in any order.

	Keys	Target number	Fewest keys possible	Number of keys
(a)	3, 5, +, ×, =	34	[5] [×] [5] [+] [3] [+] [3] [+] [3] [=]	10
(b)	4, 6, +, =	22		
(c)	8, 4, ×, +, =	116		
(d)	6, 3, ×, +, =	66		
(e)	18, 4, –, ×, =	180		

3. Use your calculator to complete these. Then select which numbers the answer falls between.

(a) 8 × 9 •	• 1,500 – 1,600	(i) 6 × 15 •	• 400 – 500
(b) 11 × 25 •	• 6,000 – 7,000	(j) 14 × 29 •	• 700 – 800
(c) 156 × 3 •	• 9,000 – 9,999	(k) 197 × 6 •	• 1,000 – 1,100
(d) 269 × 17 •	• 200 – 300	(l) 411 × 4 •	• 1,600 – 1,700
(e) 36 × 43 •	• 70 – 80	(m) 259 × 3 •	• 1,400 – 1,600
(f) 64 × 78 •	• 5,000 – 6,000	(n) 19 × 56 •	• 1,100 – 1,200
(g) 348 × 28 •	• 400 – 500	(o) 1,253 × 7 •	• 80 – 100
(h) 1,246 × 5 •	• 4,000 – 5,000	(p) 38 × 41 •	• 8,000 – 9,000

Challenge

Electricity meter readings for four months:

January	April	August	November
26,382	29,388	18,975	38,756

(a) How many fewer units were used in January than in April? ______

(b) Find the sum of the units used in January and November. ______

(c) Find the difference between the number of units used in August and in November. ______

Puzzles

1. Complete these triangular puzzles. They all work the same way.

(a)

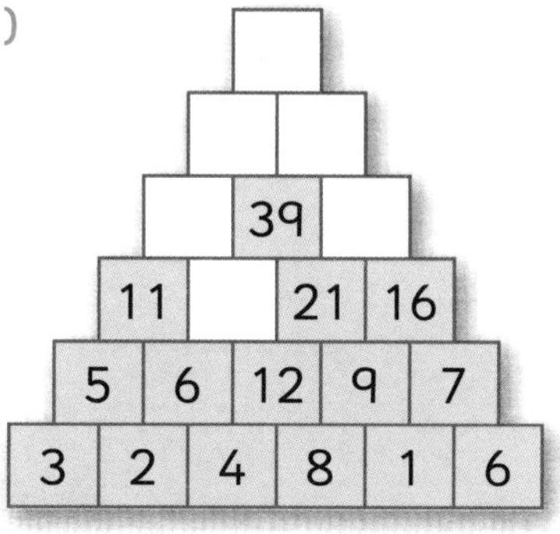

(b)

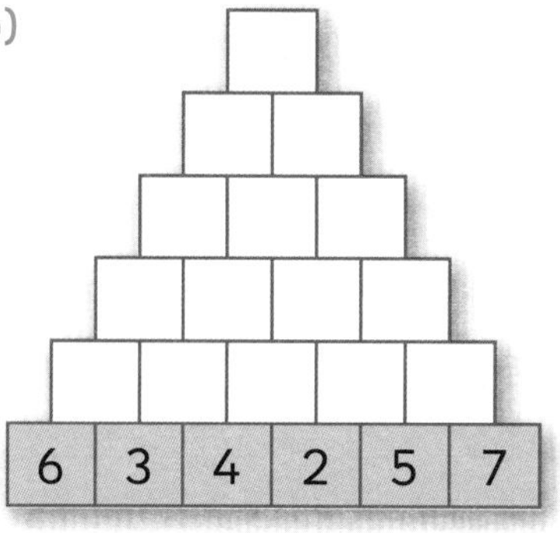

(c)

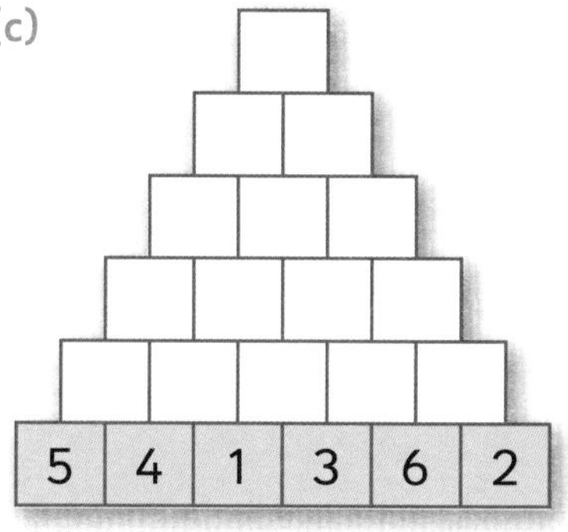

2. Complete these magic squares. First find the magic number.

(a)

16			13
	11	10	
	7	6	12
	14		1

(b)

17		4	14
6	12		9
10		7	
	15		2

(c)

	4	5	15
7		12	
	9		14
6		17	3

3. Study how this triangle is completed.

Step 1: $(5 + 1) \times 8 = 48$

Step 2: $(1 + 8) \times 5 = 45$

Step 3: $(8 + 5) \times 1 = 13$

Step 4: Work out how to find the number in the green triangle.

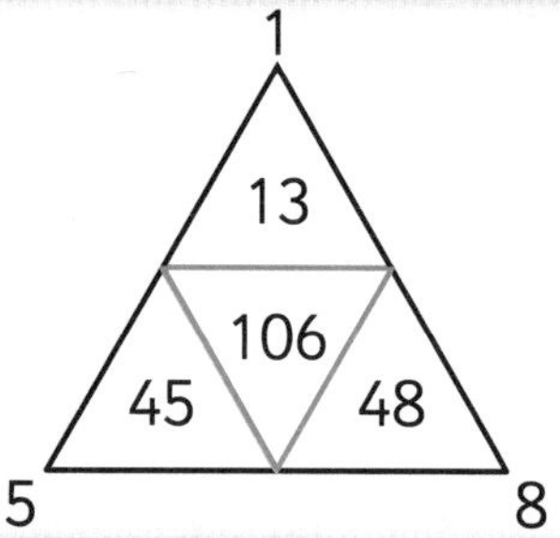

Now fill in the missing numbers in (a), (b), (c) and (d).

(a)

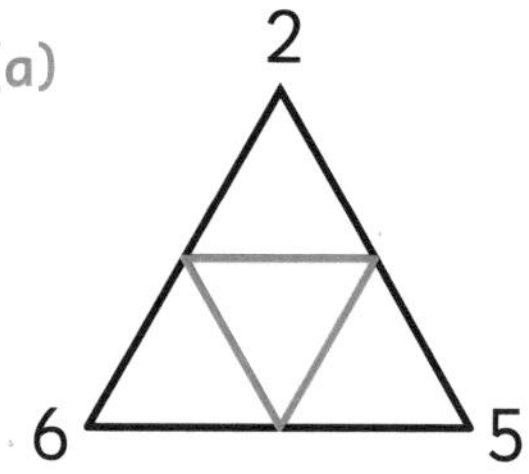

(b)

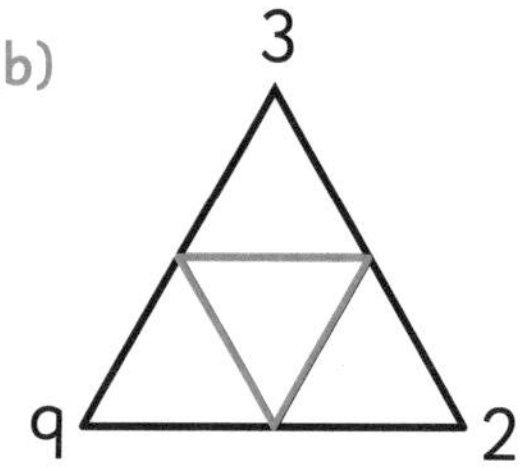

(c)

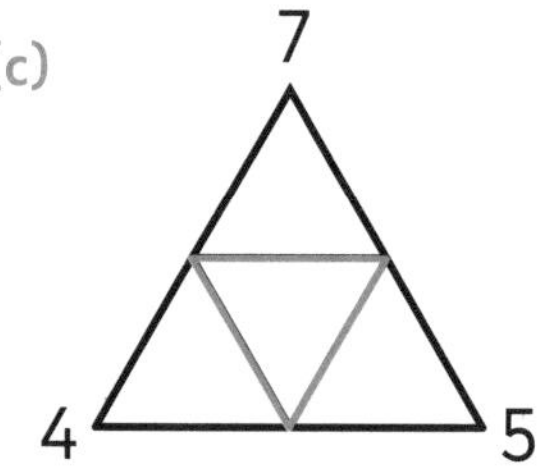

(d)

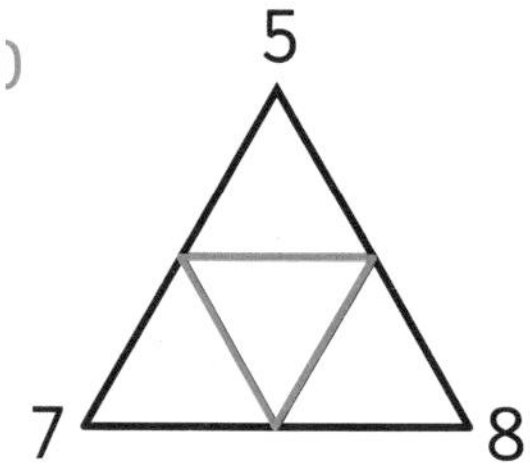

4. Complete these sudoku puzzles.

(a)

	1	9	6		4	5	7	2
	7		9	1				3
6		8	5		7		4	9
5	8		1		9		3	4
7		2		5	8	9	1	
	9	4		2	6	7	8	
	6	7	8		5		2	1
	4	1			3		5	
2		3	7	6		4		8

(b)

	5			1			9	4
4	9	7	6	3	8	5	1	2
3					5		6	
	1	9	8	4	3	2	5	
5		4	2	7		9		1
	8				9	4	7	
	7	2	3	8	1	6	4	5
		3	5	6			2	
1	6		9		4	7		8

A quick look back 5

LOOK BACK

1. Write $\frac{9}{100}$ in decimal form. ________

2. Write 0·093 in fraction form. $\frac{\square}{\square}$

3. Write in decimal form:

$3 + \frac{7}{10} + \frac{9}{100} + \frac{1}{1000}$. ________

4. Ring the digit that is in the hundreds place:

537·6

5. Ring the digit that is in the hundredths place:

65·437

6. Complete this shape using the red line as the line of symmetry.

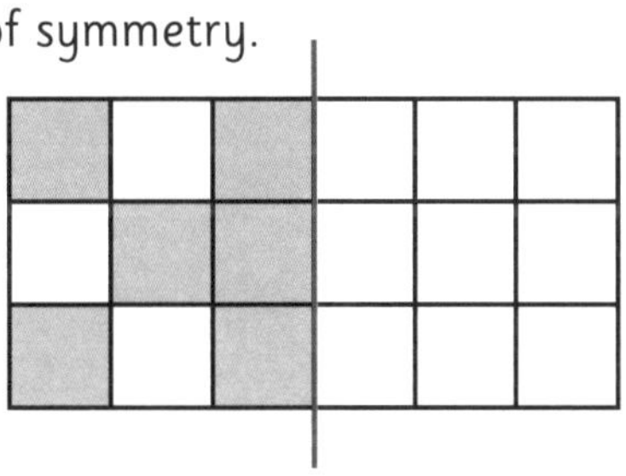

7. 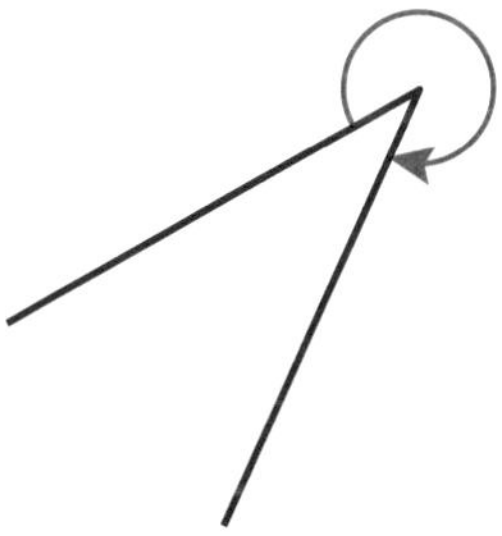

This is a ________ angle.

8. What is the total cost of 24 oranges at 25c each?

€ ________

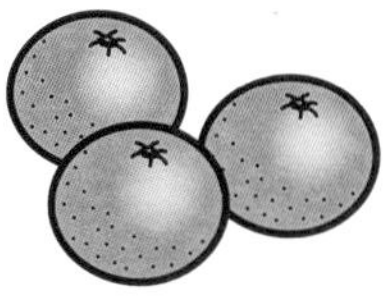

9. 

Seven pears cost €2·50. What would 35 pears cost? € ________

10. Write the following fraction in its lowest terms.

$\frac{54}{63} \div \frac{\square}{9} = \frac{\square}{\square}$

11. What is the sum of 2·3 and 5·374?

____

12. 16·38 × 100 = ________

13. A truck carries 100kg of sand. What weight of sand would 17 such trucks carry?

________ kg

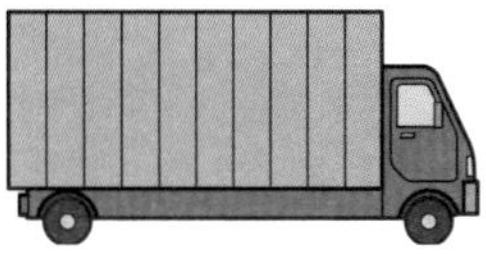

14. €12 × 7 × 100 = € ________

15. 

A fire extinguisher holds 6·012 litres of foam. Seven such fire extinguishers should hold

________ litres.

16. A jacket costs €32. How much would three boxes each containing 10 such jackets cost? € ________

17. 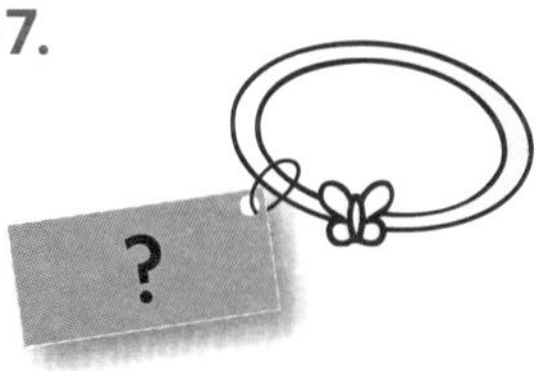

Pam spent $\frac{2}{3}$ of her €36 buying the bracelet. How much did the bracelet cost? € ________

18. Write the missing digits to find an equivalent fraction for $\frac{7}{12}$.

$\frac{7}{12} \times \frac{\square}{5} = \frac{\square}{\square}$

19. $\frac{3}{4}$ of a number is 24.

What is $\frac{3}{8}$ of the number? ________

20. $\frac{6}{7}$ of 42 is one of these numbers.

Ring the correct one.

30, 35, 34, 36, 38

Chapter 18: Length

Here are some metric units of length:

millimetres mm
centimetres cm

mm ×10 → cm ×100 → metre
mm ×1,000 → metre

10mm = 1cm
100cm = 1m
1,000mm = 1m

Did you know that it was a group of French scientists who worked out the metric system? They calculated the distance between the equator and the North Pole and ÷ by 10 million. They called this distance 1 metre.

1. We use millimetres (mm) to measure small lengths like those in the following pictures. Use a ruler to measure the length of each picture and write your answers in millimetres (mm).

(a)

Length: _____ mm

(b)

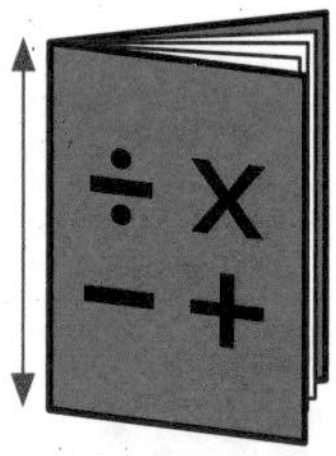

Length: _____ mm

(c)

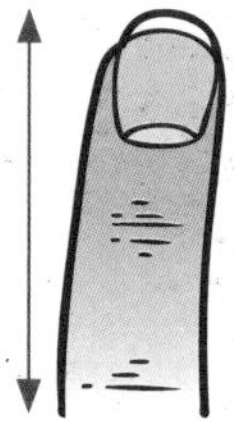

Length: _____ mm

(d)

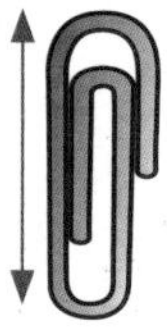

Length: _____ mm

(e)

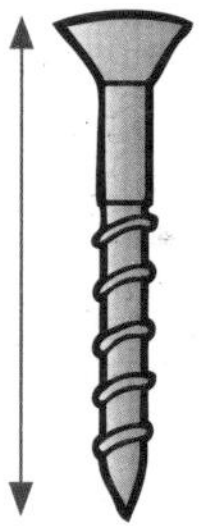

Length: _____ mm

2.

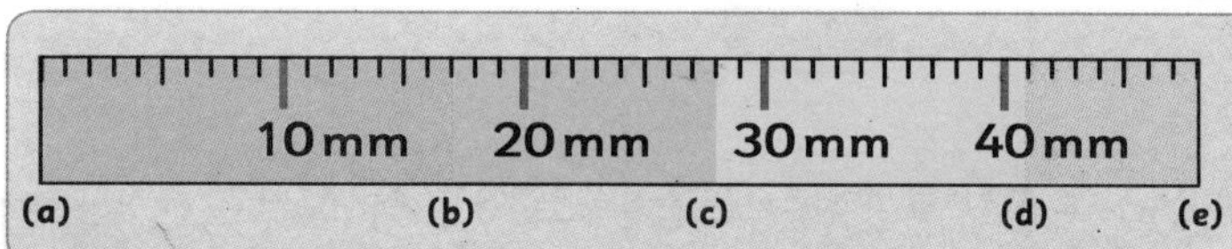

The distance on this line from (a) to (b) is 17mm. We can also write this as 1cm 7mm.

Record each of these lengths as mm and also as cm and mm.

(i) (a) to (c): _____ mm or _____ cm _____ mm.
(ii) (c) to (d): _____ mm or _____ cm _____ mm.
(iii) (e) to (c): _____ mm or _____ cm _____ mm.
(iv) (b) to (d): _____ mm or _____ cm _____ mm.
(v) (a) to (d): _____ mm or _____ cm _____ mm.
(vi) (e) to (b): _____ mm or _____ cm _____ mm.
(vii) (b) to (c): _____ mm or _____ cm _____ mm.
(viii) (d) to (e): _____ mm or _____ cm _____ mm.

3. Complete the following table by estimating in mm. Then measure in (i) mm and (ii) cm and mm.

		Estimate	Actual (mm)	Actual (cm and mm)
(a)	length of pen/pencil you are using			
(b)	width of your thumbnail			
(c)	this line: ______________________			
(d)	width of your lunch box			
(e)	length of the eraser you never need to use!			

Maths Fact A mining bee can dig its burrow 60cm deep.
Convert this measurement to mm. _____ mm

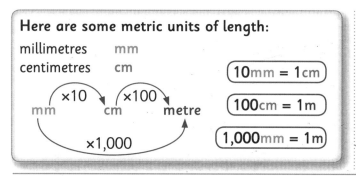

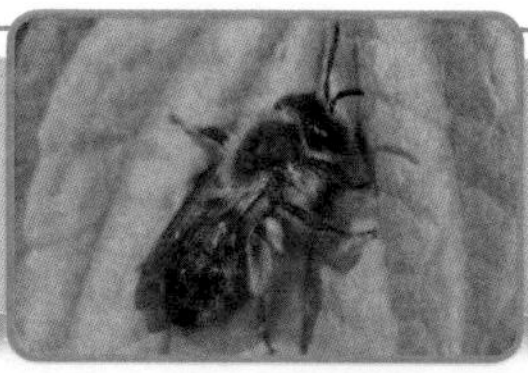

STRAND **Measures** **STRAND UNIT/ELEMENT** *Length*
LANGUAGE *Millimetres, centimetres, metre, kilometre, record, estimate, measure, add, subtract, decimal point, multiplication, divisions, problem, length, depth, perimeter, convert*

Length – Adding and subtracting

We know that 17mm = 1cm 7mm and 3cm 9mm = 39mm.

Complete this table.

1.	(a) 18mm = ___ cm ___ mm	(b) ___ mm = 2cm 7mm	(c) 11mm = ___ cm ___ mm
2.	(a) ___ mm = 1cm 5mm	(b) 36mm = ___ cm ___ mm	(c) ___ mm = 4cm 5mm
3.	(a) 51mm = ___ cm ___ mm	(b) 70mm = ___ cm ___ mm	(c) ___ mm = 6cm 2mm
4.	(a) ___ mm = 9cm	(b) 83mm = ___ cm ___ mm	(c) 49mm = ___ cm ___ mm
5.	(a) ___ mm = 7cm 6mm	(b) ___ mm = 3cm 3mm	(c) 57mm = ___ cm ___ mm

6. Write the following in fraction and decimal form.

29mm = $2\frac{9}{10}$ cm = 2·9cm	(a) 36mm = ___ = ___	(b) 54mm = ___ = ___
(c) ___ = $4\frac{7}{10}$ cm = ___	(d) ___ = $6\frac{3}{10}$ cm = ___	(e) ___ = $9\frac{1}{10}$ cm = ___
(f) ___ = ___ = 3·1cm	(g) ___ = ___ = 7·7cm	(h) ___ = ___ = 8·4cm
(i) ___ = ___ = 6·8cm	(j) ___ = ___ = 8·9cm	(k) ___ = ___ = 9·4cm

Adding and subtracting centimetres and millimetres

A

	cm	mm
	4	5
+	2_1	7
	7	2

→

	4 · 5	cm
+	2_1 · 7	cm
	7 · 2	cm

B

	cm	mm
	$^7\not{8}$	^{1}2
–	4	5
	3	7

→

	$^7\not{8}$ · ^{1}2	cm
–	4 · 5	cm
	3 · 7	cm

It's easy to add and subtract centimetres and millimetres.

7. Now try these.

(a) cm mm
  3 7
+ 1 4

(b)
  5 · 4 cm
+ 4 · 8 cm

(c) cm mm
  8 6
+ 15 6

(d)
  16 · 7 cm
+ 9 · 3 cm

(e) cm mm
  12 8
+ 9 7

(f)
  35 · 4 cm
+ 47 · 9 cm

8. (a) cm mm
  6 4
– 2 7

(b)
  5 · 6 cm
– 1 · 5 cm

(c) cm mm
  9 3
– 4 9

(d)
  31 · 6 cm
– 17 · 7 cm

(e) cm mm
  53 1
– 32 1

(f)
  20 · 7 cm
– 8 · 8 cm

9. How much longer is 56·3cm than 28·9cm? ________ cm

Maths Fact The biggest bee in the world is the Wallace's Giant Bee. Females can grow to 4cm in length. How many female Wallace's Giant Bees are needed to make a length of 60cm, if they stand end to end? ______

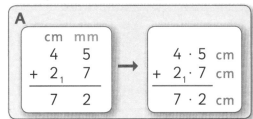

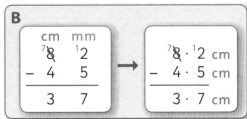

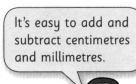

Length – Multiply and divide

Multiplying and dividing in the metric system is quite easy!

A

	cm	mm
	5	2
×	[1]	7
	36	4

or

$$\begin{array}{r} 5 \cdot 2 \text{ cm} \\ \times \quad 7 \\ \hline 36 \cdot 4 \text{ cm} \end{array}$$

(carried 1)

B

	cm	mm
4)	7	[3]6
	1	9

or

$$4\,)\,\overline{7 \cdot {}^{3}6\text{ cm}} = 1 \cdot 9\text{ cm}$$

Have a go at these.

1. (a) cm mm: 3 5 × 5 = ____
   (b) 9 · 4 cm × 6 = ____
   (c) cm mm: 7 6 × 8 = ____
   (d) 24 · 6 cm × 5 = ____
   (e) cm mm: 18 3 × 7 = ____
   (f) 41 · 8 cm × 9 = ____

2. (a) 9cm 6mm ÷ 4 (b) 8·1cm ÷ 3 (c) 37cm 1mm ÷ 7 (d) 30·4cm ÷ 8
   (e) 53cm 5mm ÷ 5 (f) 21cm 6mm ÷ 9 (g) 43·2cm ÷ 6 (h) 41cm 5mm ÷ 5
   (i) 59·4cm ÷ 9 (j) 65cm 6mm ÷ 8 (k) 93·6cm ÷ 4 (l) 86·1cm ÷ 7

3. A piece of wood is 220cm long. It is cut into 10 equal-sized pieces.
   What is the length of each piece in:
   (a) cm? ____ (b) mm? ____

4. 

   Georgia buys a length of ribbon 312cm long and cuts it into four equal pieces. What is the length of each piece in:
   (a) cm? ____ (b) mm? ____

5. An envelope is 15·8cm wide and 21·7cm long. Write these measurements as mm.
   (a) width: ____ mm (b) length: ____ mm

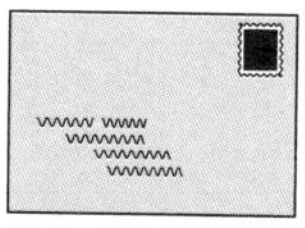

6. Ava's pet rabbit does a standing jump of 24cm 7mm.
   How far will it have jumped after nine such jumps? ____ cm

7. We divided the page of a scrapbook 32·4cm wide into three equal-sized columns.
   (a) What was the width of each column? ____ cm
   (b) If we divided the page into four equal columns, what width would each be? ____ cm

8. 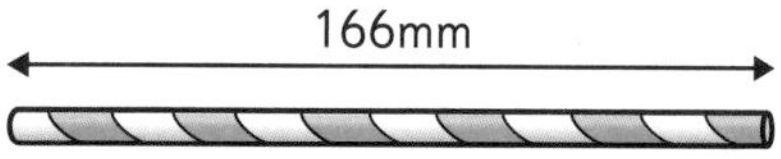

   What is the length in cm of seven such straws? ____ cm

Maths Fact Some types of bamboo plant can grow up to 91cm each day.
At this rate of growth, how tall should the bamboo grow in a fortnight? ____ cm

Challenge A piece of string 85·32cm long was cut into nine equal pieces.
How long was each piece? ____ cm

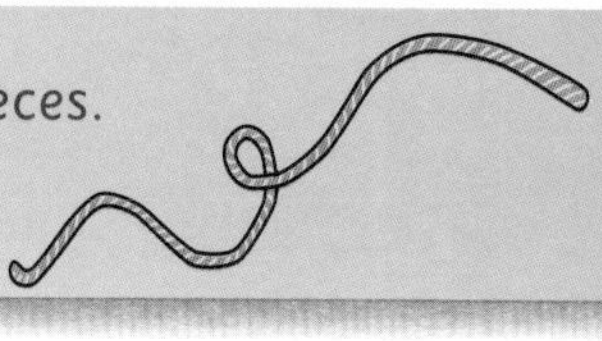

Length – Estimate and measure

It is important to use the **right measuring tool** when trying to measure a length or distance.

1. Complete the following table.

		Measuring tool	Estimate	Measure
(a)	height of classroom door			
(b)	thickness of *Busy at Maths 5*			
(c)	width of classroom whiteboard			
(d)	length of the playground			
(e)	width of a crayon			
(f)	length of your shoe			

2. Now that you are good at this, colour the best option from this list.

(a)	The length of an Olympic-sized swimming pool	50mm	250m	50m	500cm
(b)	The height of teacher's mug	10cm	12·5mm	10mm	22cm
(c)	The distance from your desk to school front door	3m	13m	23m	118m
(d)	The height of a typical family car	95cm	150mm	2·4m	1·5m
(e)	The length of a drawing pin	10mm	30mm	50mm	90mm
(f)	The height of the hurdles in a men's 110m track race	1·04m	6·6m	1·8m	2·7m

3. 

You grow 8mm every night when you are asleep. You shrink back to your original height during the day. If you didn't shrink, how many cm would you have grown during the months of April and May? ______ cm

4. Andrew has to buy enough wood to build four shelves for a store room. Each shelf must be 83·6cm long. How many cm of wood must he buy? ______ cm

5. Mum is tiling over the bathroom wash-hand basin. She needs to tile a length of 210cm. Each tile measures 70mm. How many tiles will she need to complete one row? ______

Maths Fact The fastest a sloth can move is 4·6 metres a minute. If the sloth 'runs' at top speed for 11 minutes, what distance will she have covered? ______ metres

Longer lengths

Remember:

1m = 100cm or 100cm = 1m	1cm = $\frac{1}{100}$ m = 0·01m	11cm = $\frac{11}{100}$ m = 0·11m
	10cm = $\frac{1}{10}$ m = 0·1m	29cm = $\frac{29}{100}$ m = 0·29m

1. Write as metres in fraction and decimal form.

(a) 3cm = $\frac{3}{100}$m = 0·03m
(b) 16cm = _____ = _____
(c) 7cm = _____ = _____
(d) 22cm = _____ = _____
(e) 49cm = _____ = _____
(f) 80cm = _____ = _____
(g) 154cm = _____ = _____
(h) 305cm = _____ = _____

2. Write as cm.

(a) 0·4m = 40cm
(b) 0·07m = _____
(c) 2·61m = _____
(d) 17·28m = _____
(e) 3·05m = _____

Do the following. Write the answers in decimal form.

3. (a) 734cm – 5m 65cm
(b) 11·26m – 338cm
(c) 218cm + 4·89m
(d) 4·76m + 285cm + 3m 17cm
(e) 2m 49cm + 6·76m + 38cm
(f) 57cm + 3m 68cm + 9·03m

4. (a) 459cm × 6
(b) 3·67m × 7
(c) 226cm × 9
(d) 8·43cm × 4
(e) 12·88m × 8
(f) 783cm × 6

5. (a) 14·1m ÷ 3
(b) 805cm ÷ 5
(c) 14·88m ÷ 6
(d) 680cm ÷ 8
(e) 469cm ÷ 7
(f) 4·14m ÷ 9

Remember:

1km = 1,000m or 1,000m = 1km	1m = $\frac{1}{1000}$ km = 0·001km	0·009km = $\frac{9}{1000}$ km = 9m
	11m = $\frac{11}{1000}$ km = 0·011km	0·076km = $\frac{76}{1000}$ km = 76m
	123m = $\frac{123}{1000}$ km = 0·123km	0·475km = $\frac{475}{1000}$ km = 475m

6. Write as kilometres in decimal form.

(a) 640m = _____
(b) 509m = _____
(c) 253m = _____
(d) 17m = _____
(e) 4m = _____

7. Write as metres.

(a) 5·173km = _____
(b) 2·403km = _____
(c) 7·290km = _____
(d) 3·006km = _____
(e) 0·352km = _____
(f) 0·207km = _____
(g) 5·8km = _____
(h) 0·006km = _____

8. (a) 5·67km × 4
(b) 3,174m x 6
(c) 2km 473m × 7
(d) 4·825km × 5
(e) 29·315km ÷ 5
(f) 6,104m ÷ 8
(g) 21·6km ÷ 6
(h) 11km 400m ÷ 4
(i) $7\frac{1}{2}$ km + 2,638m + 4km 517m
(j) 3km 68m + 6,277m + 2km 82m

Maths Fact

The length of a mature cycad pine cone is 90cm.
How many of these pine cones laid end to end are needed to cover a distance of 8·1 metres? _____

Length – Perimeter

Remember: Perimeter is the measure of the total length of the boundary of a shape.

Vince needs to put a fence around his garden. He must measure the perimeter. He does this by adding the four lengths.

6m + 4m + 3·75m + 4·2m = 17·95m

Perimeter = 17·95m

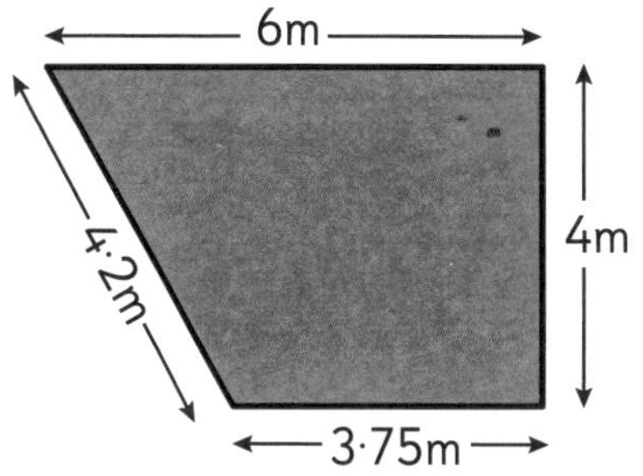

1. In the following shapes, the length of each square represents **1m**.
   Estimate first and then calculate the perimeter of each shape in **metres**.

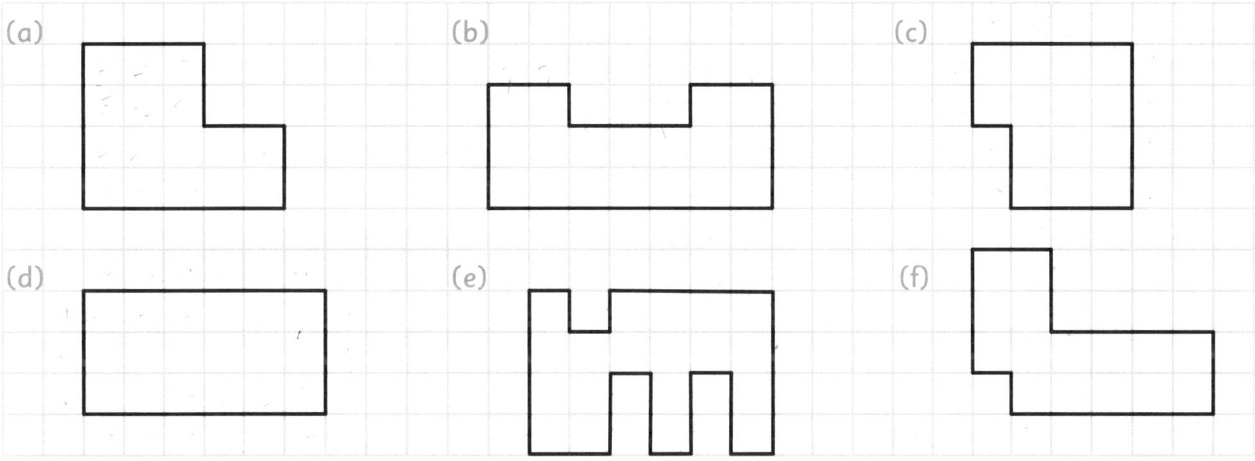

2. Elizabeth trains at the local sports field which is rectangular in shape. It is 75m wide and 112m long. If she runs around the perimeter of the field six times, how far does she run altogether? (a) ________ m (b) ________ km

3. A model train travels 27·76m while completing eight laps of the display track. What is the length of a single lap of the track? ________ m

4. Niall and Shane each took three jumps at a long jump sandpit. Niall jumped 2m 49cm, 263cm and 3·15m. Shane jumped 307cm, 2m 56cm and 258cm. Whose combined jumps were (a) longer and (b) by how many metres? (a) ________ (b) ________ m

5. The perimeter of a four-sided field is 238·5m. Three of the sides measure 67·34m, $78\frac{1}{4}$ m and $35\frac{77}{100}$ m. What is the length of the other side? ________ m

6. The perimeter of a rectangular stadium is 394·4m.
   The length of the stadium is 132·4m.
   Find the width of the stadium. ________ m

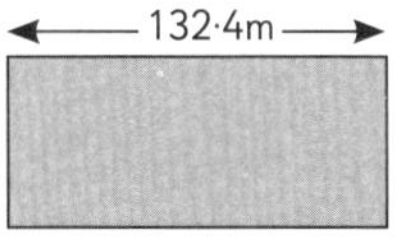

Maths Fact

It takes 100 years for a deep-sea clam to grow to just 8mm in length.
If it continued to grow at the same rate over a millennium (1,000 years), what length would the deep-sea clam be then? ________ mm

Lengthen your knowledge!

1. The fastest flying insect in the world is the dragonfly. It has a top speed of 58km per hour. How far would it travel at top speed in:

   (a) $\frac{1}{4}$ of an hour? ________ km; (b) 12 mins? ________ km; (c) 36 mins? ________ km

2. Phobos is the largest moon of Mars and its largest diameter measures 26km 800m. The diameter of the Earth's moon is 3,476km. What is the difference between the two diameters? ________ km ________ m

3. The length of the minute hand on London's famous Big Ben clock is 4·2m. Write this length as: (a) cm: ________ cm and (b) mm: ________ mm.

4. A cubit was a measurement used in ancient Egypt based on the length of an adult's arm from the elbow to the fingertips. 52·4cm was the length of Tom's cubit. What would be the length of nine such cubits? ________ cm

5. Some kinds of bamboo tree can grow up to 91cm each day. Calculate in metres how far these bamboo trees should grow during February in a leap year. ________ m

6. A fence pole is 118cm long. What is the total length in metres of eight such poles? ________ m

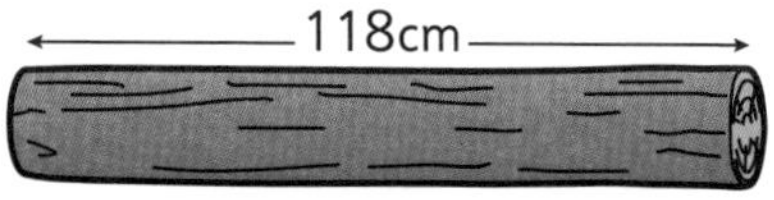

7. A girl is in training for a marathon. She runs the same distance each day. If she runs a total of 85·75km in a week, how far does she run each day? ________ km

8. **Here is a mixture of questions on length. Be careful with the signs!**

(a) 5·3km – 474m	(b) 12·6cm × 100	(c) 176cm + 3·5m + 86cm
(d) $5\frac{1}{2}$ km × 9	(e) 38km – 4,255m	(f) 3,071m – 2·99km
(g) 42·28km ÷ 8	(h) 27cm 3mm × 7	(i) $5\frac{3}{10}$ km × 6
(j) $4\frac{39}{100}$ km – 2,679m	(k) (6·26m + 577cm) – $3\frac{1}{4}$ m	(l) 6·543km ÷ 9
(m) (23mm + 4·8cm) × 6	(n) 54cm 8mm ÷ 8	(o) $8\frac{32}{1000}$ km + $6\frac{3}{4}$ km – $3\frac{7}{100}$ km
(p) ($7\frac{1}{2}$ km – $\frac{3}{4}$ km) + 82m	(q) $2\frac{57}{1000}$ km + (68cm × 7)	(r) $6\frac{572}{1000}$ km – $3\frac{79}{100}$ km + $5\frac{7}{8}$ km

Challenge Suzy ran $24\frac{2}{5}$km, Sarah ran $16\frac{3}{4}$km and Ruth ran $32\frac{539}{1000}$km.

(a) How far did the three girls run in total? ________ km

(b) What is the difference in kilometres between the longest and shortest distances run by the girls? ________ km

Maths Fact The Grand Canyon in Arizona is 446km long and up to 1,800 metres deep. What is the difference between the length and maximum depth of the Grand Canyon in:

(a) metres? ________ m (b) kilometres? ________ km

Chapter 19: Percentages 1

A **century** contains 100 years. There are 100 **cent** in a euro. Can you think of any other words with 'cent' in them?

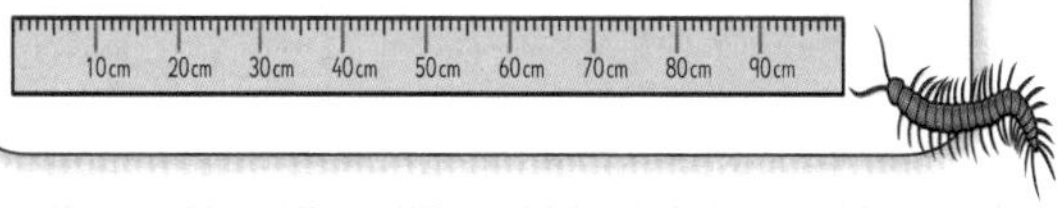

Per cent means per hundred **or** out of 100.
The symbol for per cent is **%** (for example, 45%).

1. Look at this hundred square and write the fraction and percentage of each coloured amount.

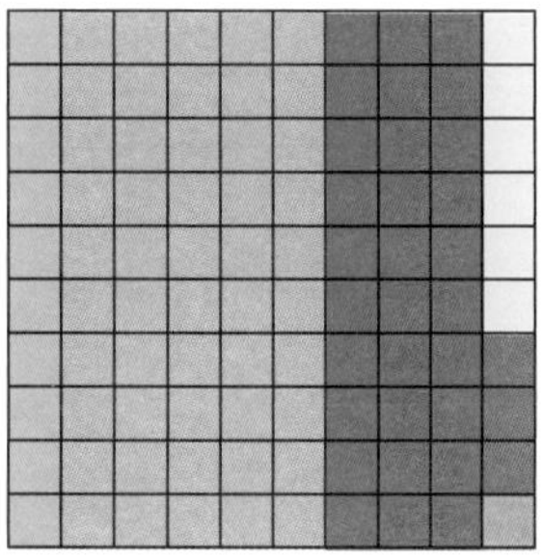

(a) green = $\frac{10}{100}$ = ____ %
(b) blue = ____ = ____ %
(c) red = ____ = ____ %
(d) yellow = ____ = ____ %
(e) purple = ____ = ____ %
(f) orange = ____ = ____ %
(g) What percentage more is coloured blue than yellow? ____ %

2. Change these hundredths to percentages (%).

(a) $\frac{9}{100}$ = ____
(b) $\frac{47}{100}$ = ____
(c) $\frac{1}{100}$ = ____
(d) $\frac{17}{100}$ = ____
(e) $\frac{50}{100}$ = ____
(f) $\frac{27}{100}$ = ____
(g) $\frac{100}{100}$ = ____
(h) $\frac{98}{100}$ = ____

Changing tenths to percentages (first change to hundredths)

Remember, $\frac{3}{10} \times \frac{10}{10} = \frac{30}{100}$ = 30%.

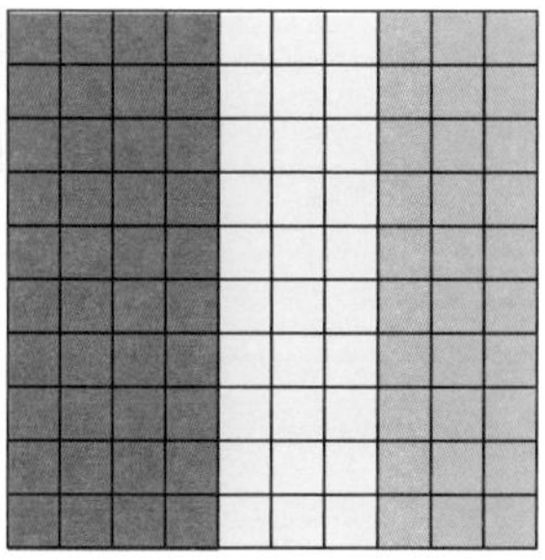

3. What percentage of this square is coloured...

(a) green? $\frac{2}{10} \rightarrow \frac{20}{100}$ = ____ %
(b) yellow? ____ → ____ = ____ %
(c) red? ____ → ____ = ____ %
(d) blue? ____ → ____ = ____ %

4. Write these fractions as percentages.

(a) $\frac{9}{100}$ = ____
(b) $\frac{5}{10}$ = ____
(c) $\frac{23}{100}$ = ____
(d) $\frac{7}{10}$ = ____
(e) $\frac{47}{100}$ = ____
(f) $\frac{80}{100}$ = ____
(g) $\frac{21}{100}$ = ____
(h) $\frac{10}{10}$ = ____
(i) $\frac{9}{10}$ = ____
(j) $\frac{99}{100}$ = ____

5. Put each of these groups in order, starting with the smallest amount in each case.

(a) 9%, $\frac{99}{100}$, $\frac{9}{10}$
(b) 43%, $\frac{42}{100}$, 34%
(c) $\frac{3}{10}$, 33%, $\frac{3}{100}$
(d) 50%, $\frac{55}{100}$, 5%
(e) 100%, $\frac{1}{100}$, 10%
(f) $\frac{8}{10}$, 8%, 88%
(g) $\frac{1}{10}$, $\frac{1}{100}$, 11%
(h) $\frac{2}{10}$, 22%, 2%

6. These children are watching the box sets they got for Christmas. What percentage have they still to watch if they have already viewed the following amounts?

(a) Lucy has watched $\frac{7}{10}$ of hers. ____ %
(b) Dara is $\frac{1}{2}$ way through his. ____ %
(c) Molly has viewed $\frac{34}{100}$ of hers. ____ %
(d) Mark is $\frac{4}{10}$ finished. ____ %
(e) Abbie watched $\frac{55}{100}$ of hers. ____ %
(f) Ethan has seen $\frac{80}{100}$ of his. ____ %

Percentages 1 – Other fractions

Changing fractions to hundredths and then to percentages.

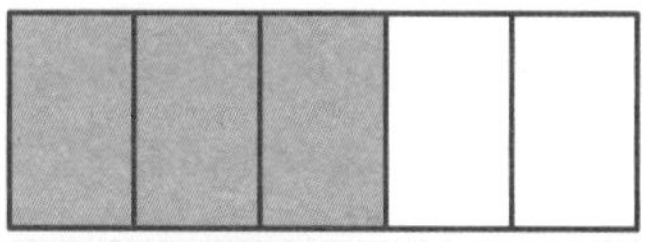

$\frac{3}{5} \times \frac{\square}{\square} = \frac{\square}{100}$ → $\frac{3}{5} \times \frac{20}{20}$ → $\frac{60}{100} = 60\%$

Remember: $\frac{20}{20} = 1$ unit.

1. What percentage of each of these shapes is coloured? Find the fraction first.

(a) 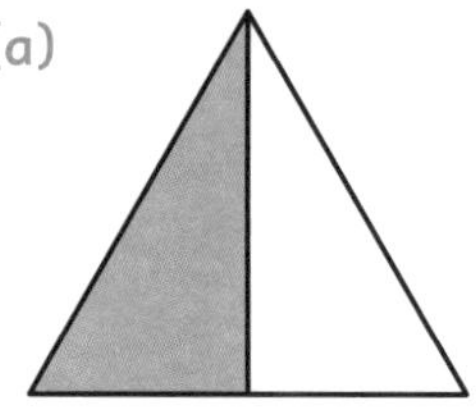

(b) 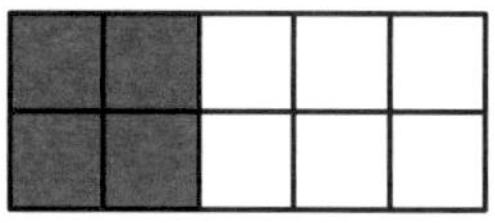

(c) 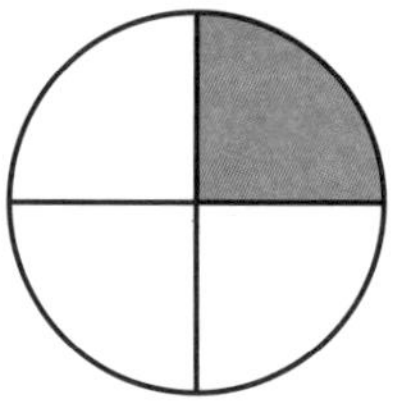

(d) 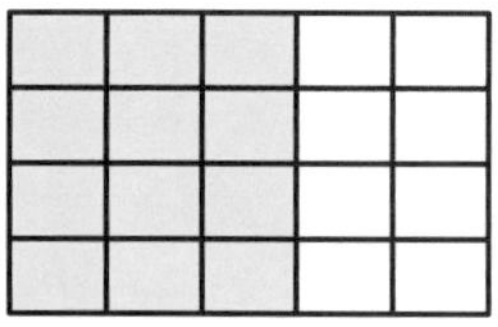

2. Now change these fractions to percentages.

(a) $\frac{4}{5}$ (b) $\frac{7}{20}$ (c) $\frac{2}{4}$ (d) $\frac{10}{25}$ (e) $\frac{7}{10}$ (f) $\frac{12}{25}$

3. Sarah just received her report card for her summer tests. Work out what percentage score she got in each subject.

(a) Maths = _____ % (b) Irish = _____ %

(c) English = _____ % (d) Science = _____ %

(e) History = _____ % (f) Geography = _____ %

(g) Music = _____ % (h) Art = _____ %

Summer test results

Name: Sarah

Maths:	$\frac{63}{100}$	Irish:	$\frac{29}{50}$
English:	$\frac{41}{50}$	Science:	$\frac{11}{20}$
History:	$\frac{20}{25}$	Geography:	$\frac{80}{100}$
Music:	$\frac{3}{5}$	Art:	$\frac{9}{10}$

4. Write these fractions and percentages on the number lines.

(a) $\frac{3}{10}$, 50%, $\frac{90}{100}$, 70%

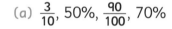

(b) $\frac{4}{5}$, 90%, $\frac{2}{10}$, 60%

(c) 75%, $\frac{1}{4}$, $\frac{9}{10}$, 40%

5. Change these percentages to fractions.

Per cent means per 100, so 37% is 37 out of 100 or $\frac{37}{100}$.

(a) $43\% = \frac{\square}{100}$ (b) $7\% = \frac{\square}{\square}$ (c) $99\% = \frac{\square}{\square}$ (d) $71\% = \frac{\square}{\square}$ (e) $1\% = \frac{\square}{\square}$

We can simplify the answer sometimes.

For example: 35% → $\frac{35}{100} \div \frac{5}{5} = \frac{7}{20}$ ←

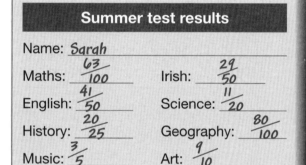

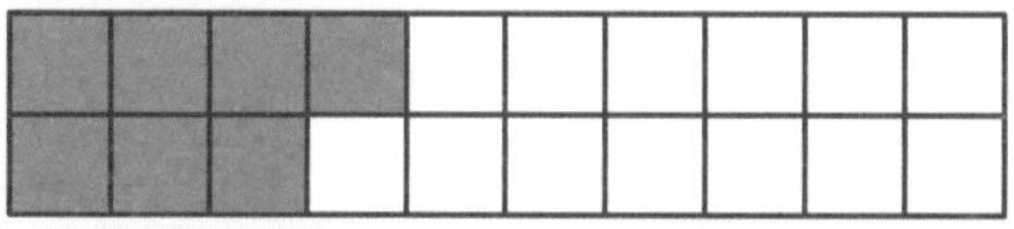

6. Now change these percentages to fractions and simplify.

(a) 50% = _____ (b) 20% = _____ (c) 8% = _____ (d) 45% = _____

(e) 4% = _____ (f) 90% = _____ (g) 75% = _____ (h) 36% = _____

Calculating percentages

1. Write <, > or = in each ◯.

(a) 40% ◯ $\frac{4}{10}$ (b) $\frac{2}{20}$ ◯ 2% (c) 45% ◯ $\frac{3}{5}$ (d) $\frac{2}{50}$ ◯ 2%

(e) $\frac{1}{10}$ ◯ 1% (f) $\frac{35}{100}$ ◯ 30% (g) 25% ◯ $\frac{1}{5}$ (h) $\frac{8}{100}$ ◯ 9%

2. Six free-takers scored the following percentages of their kicks. What fraction did each miss?

(a) Jack scored 90%. (b) Linda scored 80%.
(c) Sally scored 95%. (d) Liam scored 75%.
(e) Marie scored 83%. (f) Shane scored 88%.

3. Match a percentage from the top row with a fraction from the bottom row.

100%	15%	2%	75%	9%	4%	50%	10%
$\frac{9}{100}$	$\frac{1}{10}$	$\frac{1}{2}$	$\frac{2}{2}$	$\frac{3}{20}$	$\frac{2}{50}$	$\frac{1}{50}$	$\frac{3}{4}$

4. Add the following fractions and write the answers as percentages.

(a) $\frac{1}{10} + \frac{3}{100} =$ ____% (b) $\frac{3}{10} + \frac{7}{100} =$ ____% (c) $\frac{4}{10} + \frac{1}{100} =$ ____% (d) $\frac{7}{10} + \frac{6}{100} =$ ____%

5. Write these percentages as tenths and hundredths.

(a) 17% = $\frac{\square}{10} + \frac{\square}{100}$ (b) 29% = $\frac{\square}{10} + \frac{\square}{100}$ (c) 51% = $\frac{\square}{10} + \frac{\square}{100}$ (d) 96% = $\frac{\square}{10} + \frac{\square}{100}$

We can find a percentage of a number by changing the percentage to a fraction first.

A Jimmy drank 30% of a litre carton of milk after a race. He drank:

30% → $\frac{30}{100} = \frac{3}{10}$

Find $\frac{3}{10}$ of a litre.

$\frac{10}{10}$ = 1,000ml
$\frac{1}{10}$ = 100ml
$\frac{3}{10}$ = 300ml

B Sally spent 75% of her €12 buying a cinema ticket. It cost:

75% → $\frac{75}{100} = \frac{3}{4}$

Find $\frac{3}{4}$ of €12.

$\frac{4}{4}$ = €12
$\frac{1}{4}$ = €3
$\frac{3}{4}$ = €9

6. Now work these out by changing the percentages to fractions first.

(a) 90% of 10 ____ (b) 50% of 20 ____ (c) 20% of 15 ____ (d) 43% of 100 ____

(e) 25% of 8 ____ (f) 14% of 50 ____ (g) 40% of 25 ____ (h) 75% of 40 ____

7. There are 40 children in a youth club. How many of them do each of the following if...

(a) 25% cycle to the club? ____ (b) 50% walk to the club? ____
(c) 30% play hurling? ____ (d) 75% run home? ____
(e) 90% swim once a week? ____ (f) 45% play table tennis? ____

Percentages – Problem-solving

1. **Children's Book Club**

Seven children are each reading the same novel that is 200 pages long. Work out how many pages each has read.

(a) Eve is 50% finished. (b) Cathy has 30% read. (c) Mark has 40% read.
(d) Tony has 10% still to read. (e) Joan has 75% read. (f) Eoin has read 65%.
(g) Claire read 50% of the book on Saturday and 20% on Sunday.

2. **If the children read the same percentages of a 300-page book, how many pages of this new book would each have read?**

(a) _____ (b) _____ (c) _____ (d) _____ (e) _____ (f) _____ (g) _____

3. **Four people are competing in a 180km cycle race. Find how many kilometres each has cycled already.**

(a) Feargal has completed 50% of the race. (b) Shane is 75% of the way there.
(c) Diarmuid has 10% still to go. (d) Ruairí has 60% still to go.

4. **Peter, Elaine and Zeta won a total of €500 in a raffle. Peter got 40% of the money while Elaine and Zeta got equal amounts. How much money did each get?**

(a) **Peter = €_____** (b) **Elaine = €_____** (c) **Zeta = €_____**

5. **Use the following information to complete the school football league table below. (A win is worth 2 points, a draw is worth 1 point.)**

(a) Kilshanny NS won 75% of their games, drew 10% and lost the rest. They scored 80 goals and had 50% of that number scored against them.

(b) Killard Educate Together won 10 games and drew 50% as many games as they won. They scored 80% of the number of goals Kilshanny scored and conceded 25% fewer goals than they themselves scored.

(c) Gaelscoil Naomh Bríd lost 40% of their games, while the number they won was equal to the number they drew. They scored two goals per game on average and conceded 70% of the number they scored.

Team	Played	Won	Drew	Lost	Goals for	Goals against	Points
Kilshanny NS	20				80		
Killard Educate Together	20						
Gaelscoil Naomh Bríd	20						

Challenge Ella, Jack and Ava were doing a school project of 30 pages. Ella did six pages, Jack did nine pages and Ava did the rest. What percentage of the project pages did each complete? Ella = _____, Jack = _____, Ava = _____.

Chapter 20: Time

The importance of time

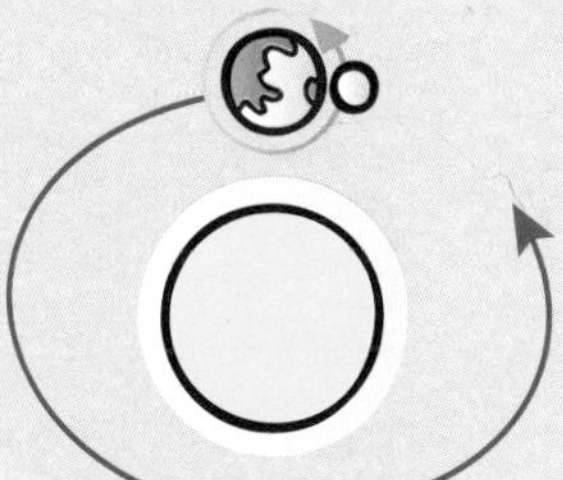

Many years ago, a famous Italian mathematician and astronomer called Galileo proved that the Earth was not the centre of the universe. The Earth spins on its axis **once** every **24 hours**. While it is spinning, it is also going around (orbiting) the Sun. It takes a **year** to complete one orbit.

Time is measured in seconds, minutes, hours, days, weeks, months and years. Our lives are controlled greatly by time and the passage of time.

Examples: time to get up, to go to school or work, have our lunch, times and lengths of television programmes, bus and train timetables, departure and arrival times at airports, etc.

1. In ancient times, it was decided to divide a day into 24 hours and an hour into 60 minutes because there were lots of factors for each.

(a) List all the factors of 24.

(b) Work out how many minutes there are in these fractions of 60 minutes.

(i) $\frac{1}{2}$ = ____	(ii) $\frac{1}{3}$ = ____	(iii) $\frac{1}{4}$ = ____	(iv) $\frac{1}{5}$ = ____	(v) $\frac{1}{6}$ = ____
(vi) $\frac{1}{10}$ = ____	(vii) $\frac{1}{12}$ = ____	(viii) $\frac{1}{20}$ = ____	(ix) $\frac{1}{30}$ = ____	(x) $\frac{1}{60}$ = ____

2. How long do these events take to happen? Match.

(a)	Earth to spin (rotate once)	(i)	about 3 minutes
(b)	one full Moon to the next	(ii)	a full day
(c)	hurling match	(iii)	about six hours
(d)	day in school	(iv)	about 10 seconds
(e)	planet Earth to travel around the Sun	(v)	about 29 days
(f)	brush your teeth	(vi)	about half an hour
(g)	eat your dinner	(vii)	70 minutes
(h)	sneeze once	(viii)	about one hour
(i)	an Olympic runner to run 100m	(ix)	one year
(j)	fly from Dublin to London	(x)	one second

3. Colour match the times in the top row with those in the bottom row.

(a) 93 mins	(b) 210 mins	(c) 170 mins	(d) 185 mins	(e) 75 mins	(f) 103 mins
$1\frac{1}{4}$ hours	2 hrs 50 mins	1 hr 33 mins	$3\frac{1}{2}$ hours	3 hrs 5 mins	1 hr 43 mins

Challenge A train journey took 2 hours and 25 minutes. Write this time in:

(a) minutes: ____ minutes

(b) hours and a fraction of an hour: ____ hours

Adding and subtracting hours and minutes

1. Add the hours and minutes.

Example:
hrs	mins
2	47
+ 3	3,1 9
5	86
→ 6	26

(a)
hrs	mins
3	43
+ 3	29
	72

(b)
hrs	mins
2	56
+ 3	17

(c)
hrs	mins
4	41
+ 3	34

(d)
hrs	mins
2	46
+ 0	38

2. Now try these.

(a)
hrs	mins
1	26
2	35
+ 3	28

(b)
hrs	mins
2	27
3	35
+ 2	19

(c)
hrs	mins
1	24
4	09
+ 2	43

(d)
hrs	mins
2	14
3	17
+ 1	31

(e)
hrs	mins
2	36
1	48
+ 2	26

3. Subtract the hours and minutes. You will have to regroup one hour as 60 minutes.

Example:
hrs	mins
3,4	7,9 19
- 2	43
1	36

(a)
hrs	mins
2,3	8 6, 26
- 1	48

(b)
hrs	mins
4	32
- 1	45

(c)
hrs	mins
6	37
- 3	64

(d)
hrs	mins
8	35
- 2	46

4. Now try these. Note: Sometimes you will not have to regroup one hour to minutes.

(a)
hrs	mins
5	53
- 1	28

(b)
hrs	mins
8	47
- 5	29

(c)
hrs	mins
6	25
- 4	43

(d)
hrs	mins
9	44
- 3	38

(e)
hrs	mins
7	35
- 4	47

5. Now try these addition and subtraction two-step questions.

(a) (2 hrs 35 mins + 3 hrs 17 mins) – 4 hrs 59 mins = _____ hrs _____ mins

(b) (3 hrs 45 mins + 4 hrs 38 mins) – 5 hrs 46 mins = _____ hrs _____ mins

(c) (8 hrs 23 mins + 6 hrs 39 mins) – 3 hrs 47 mins = _____ hrs _____ mins

(d) (7 hrs 49 mins – 5 hrs 26 mins) + 6 hrs 53 mins = _____ hrs _____ mins

(e) (8 hrs 24 mins – 4 hrs 42 mins) + 3 hrs 37 mins = _____ hrs _____ mins

(f) (9 hrs 16 mins – 7 hrs 48 mins) + 5 hrs 56 mins = _____ hrs _____ mins

Challenge A bus journey to Cork took 195 minutes. A train journey took 2 hrs 48 mins.

(a) How much faster was the train? _____ minutes

(b) How much time would a person save over five journeys by taking the train instead of the bus? _____ minutes

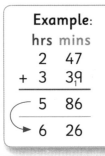

Time – am and pm

12 midnight | 2.00am | 4.00am | 6.00am | 8.00am | 10.00am | 12 noon | 2.00pm | 4.00pm | 6.00pm | 8.00pm | 10.00pm | 12 midnight

AM = Ante Meridiem = Before noon | **PM** = Post Meridiem = Afternoon

00:00 | 02:00 | 04:00 | 06:00 | 08:00 | 10:00 | 12:00 | 14:00 | 16:00 | 18:00 | 20:00 | 22:00 | 00:00

am means 'after midnight' until midday. It is also called the **first half** of the day.

1. (a) List five things that happen in **am** times.

(b) Now list five things that happen in **pm** times.

pm means 'past midday' until midnight. It is also called the **second half** of the day.

2. Write the following times using am and pm.

(a) 10 past midnight 12.10am

(b) $\frac{1}{4}$ to midday ______

(c) 20 past 4 in the morning ______

(d) 25 to 6 in the evening ______

(e) 10 to 4 in the afternoon ______

(f) 25 past midday ______

(g) 10 to 6 in the morning ______

(h) 28 mins to 7 in the evening ______

(i) 20 mins to 1 at night ______

This clock shows 10.25am.

We need am and pm because analogue clocks can only show 12 hours. Digital clocks show all 24 hours in a day. With digital clocks, we do not need to use am or pm as they show us how much time has elapsed since midnight (00:00).

Most bus times, train times, mobile phones, times of flights, television programmes and cinema times use the 24-hour system.

Examples:

(i) 6.30am → 06:30

(ii) 12.05pm → 12:05

(iii) 2.53pm → 14:53

(iv) 12.01am → 00:01

(v) 7.25pm → 19:25

(vi) 11.35pm → 23:35

3. Write these times using the 24-hour clock system (digital time).

(a) 3.15am [:] (b) 1.25pm [:] (c) 9.35am [:] (d) 3.20pm [:]

(e) 9.20pm [:] (f) 5.40am [:] (g) 7.45pm [:] (h) 9.50pm [:]

4. Now write these digital times using the am and pm system.

(a) 06:05 = ______ (b) 14:40 = ______ (c) 08:18 = ______ (d) 15:46 = ______

(e) 12:34 = ______ (f) 17:17 = ______ (g) 22:05 = ______ (h) 23:56 = ______

(i) 07:01 = ______ (j) 13:26 = ______ (k) 18:19 = ______ (l) 23:12 = ______

Challenge A nature programme is due to start at 17:05. The time shown on Susan's watch is half past four in the afternoon. How long must she wait before the programme starts? ______ minutes

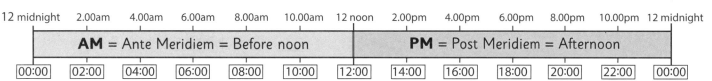

Time – One-minute intervals

1. Write or draw hands to show these times in three different ways.

Example: (i) 3.15pm (ii)  (iii) 15:15

(a) (i) ________ pm (ii)  (iii) [:]

(b) (i) ________ am (ii)  (iii) 00:17

(c) (i) 7.45pm (ii)  (iii) [:]

(d) (i) ________ pm (ii)  (iii) 20:20

(e) (i) 2.43pm (ii)  (iii) [:]

(f) (i) ________ pm (ii)  (iii) 23:59

(g) (i) ________ pm (ii)  (iii) [:]

Calculating time in your head: How many hours and minutes are there from 03:37 → 08:11?

Step 1: Count minutes to next hour.

Step 2: Count remaining minutes.

Step 3: Count on the hours.

 + 23 mins →  + 11 mins →  + 4 hours → 

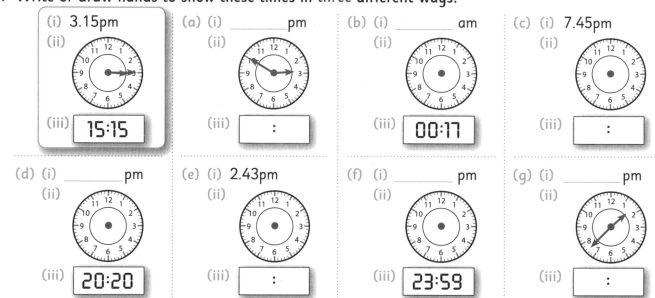

03:37 → 04:00 → 04:11 → 08:11

23 mins + 11 mins + 4 hours = 4 hours 34 minutes

2. Do these in your head. How many hours and minutes are there from...

(a) 14:49 to 19:12?

(b) 4.31am to 11.05pm?

(c) midnight to 8.41am?

(d) 06:45 to 13:53?

(e) 11.50am to 3.55pm?

(f) $\frac{1}{4}$ past midday to 6.35pm?

3.

ALIEN INVASION		**FILM LENGTH:**	**129 MINS**
	SCREENING TIMES:	**12:45 15:40**	**18:25 21:00**

(a) For how many hours and minutes does the film last?

(b) John went to see the first screening. At what time did the film finish?

(c) Jackie finishes work at 4.37pm. For how long will she have to wait until the next screening?

(d) The projectionist was on duty for all four screenings. For how long was she on duty?

(e) The ticket office opened half an hour before the first screening and remained open for 30 minutes after the last screening started. For how long was it open?

(f) The ticket seller was paid €10 per hour. How much did she earn in a day?

Timetables

1. Fill in your timetable for a day using the 24-hour clock system.

(a) How long do you take to get ready in the morning?

(b) In hours and minutes, how long is your school day?

(c) What activity do you spend most time at after you arrive home from school?

(d) How much time altogether do you spend travelling to and from school?

(e) How many hours and minutes do you spend in bed?

(f) How much time is there from the time school finishes until you go to bed?

Timetable

:	Get up	:	School finishes
:	Finish breakfast	:	Arrive home
:	Leave house	:	
:	Arrive at school	:	
:	School starts	:	
:	Lunch break	:	Go to bed

Write three activities you do when you arrive home in each blank space above.

2. This is a bus timetable for the Cork City to Dublin Airport route.

	Departure times				
	Bus 1	**Bus 2**	**Bus 3**	**Bus 4**	**Bus 5**
Cork City	06:15	07:35	09:15	11:45	14:35
Fermoy	——	08:12	09:52	12:21	15:17
Cashel	——	08:57	10:38	13:06	16:04
Dublin (O'Connell St)	——	10:23	12:05	——	17:32
Dublin Airport	08:57	10:48	12:32	14:53	18:05

(a) Why do you think the times are shown in the 24-hour clock system?

(b) How long does Bus 1 take to complete the journey?

(c) How long does each of the other buses take to complete the journey?

(d) Which is the 2nd fastest bus to complete the journey?

(e) Why do you think that Bus 4 does not go to O'Connell Street, Dublin?

(f) Why do you think the first bus does not stop on the way?

(g) Sam's flight leaves at 15:37. He needs to check in two hours before departure. He lives in Cork City. What is the latest bus he should take?

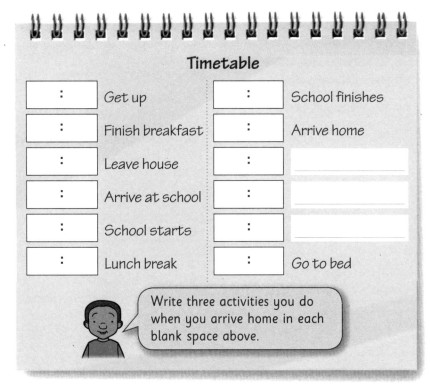

(h) Aprile took Bus 5. Her flight departs at 20:17. How long had she to wait at the airport before departure?

Challenge Priscilla is travelling from Cork City and wants to check in two hours before her flight at 17:15. She already knows there will be a 25-minute detour. Which is the latest bus she could take? ______

Television guide

Here is part of a television station's guide to programmes.

Television guide	
08:30	Morning News
09:15	The J.P. Show
10:10	Doctor Liam
11:15	Wild Nature
12:00	Midday News
12:25	Boynton Beach
13:10	Albany Square (film)
15:05	The Pranksters
15:43	Country House
16:17	Judge Jacinta
17:45	News
18:20	Cartoons
18:55	Weather
19:01	Football Live
21:08	Live with Jennifer
22:17	Sportogram

1. How long is the 'Morning News'? ________

2. At what time does 'The J.P. Show' finish? ________

3. How long does 'Boynton Beach' last? ________

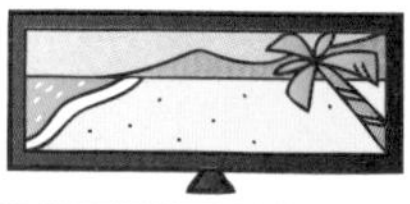

4. How long does the film 'Albany Square' last? ________

5. 'Judge Jacinta' lasts for ________ minutes.

6. Josephine watched 'Doctor Liam' and 'Country House'. How long did she spend watching television? ________

7. Dad and Ella watched 'Football Live'. How long did they each spend watching television? ________

8. How long did 'Live with Jennifer' last? ________

9. 

Mam watched 'Doctor Liam' and 'Albany Square'. How long did she spend watching television? ________

10. There were three news programmes. What was the total time taken up by them? ________

11. Write the time 'Sportogram' starts using the am and pm system. ________

12. If it is now 5.43pm, how long has Donna to wait for 'Cartoons' to start? ________

13. Grandma watched 'Wild Nature', 'Boynton Beach' and 'Albany Square'. How long altogether did she spend watching television? ________

14. 

Freda and Frank watched 'Cartoons', 'Football Live' and 'Live with Jennifer'. How long altogether did they each spend watching television? ________

15. For how long altogether was the television station open from the beginning of the first programme to the end of 'Live with Jennifer'? ________

Challenge Emer watched television from 9.15am until the end of **Boynton Beach**. Joey began watching at 5.45pm until the end of **Football Live**.

(a) Who spent longer watching television? ________

(b) How much longer? ________

Time – Problem-solving

1. Write each of these 24-hour times as am or pm times.

(a) 05:43 (b) 11:17 (c) 15:40 (d) 19:54 (e) 23:23

2. Write each of these am and pm times using the 24-hour system.

(a) 12.17am (b) 9.25am (c) 1.53pm (d) 5.38pm (e) 10.22pm

3. Write these analogue times in the 24-hour system.

(a) 25 past midnight (b) 20 to 8 in the morning (c) 25 to 4 in the afternoon

(d) 23 mins to 6 in the evening (e) 34 mins to 11 at night (f) 27 mins past 10 at night

4. A bus journey to Galway takes 2 hrs 17 mins. At what time did each bus reach its destination if these were the starting times?

(a) 07:35 (b) 09:54 (c) 13:46 (d) 08:39

(e) 17:28 (f) 19:52 (g) 21:37 (h) 20:18

5. A film lasts 113 minutes. What were the five starting times of the film if the following were the finishing times?

(a) 11:20 (b) 14:05 (c) 16:42 (d) 19:27 (e) 22:05

6.

A group of hill-walkers began their hike at 8.25am. They completed their hike at 15:08. How long did they spend hiking? ____________

7. Sam went to bed at 7.40pm. If he had arisen at 06:48 that morning, how long was he 'up and about'? ____________

8.

A football match started at $\frac{1}{4}$ to 3 in the afternoon. It finished 109 minutes later. At what time did the match finish? (Give the answer using the 24-hour system.) [:]

9. Ursula has booked a flight from Dublin Airport to Spain leaving at 13:34. Check-in is two hours before departure. If it takes her 47 minutes to get to the airport, what is the latest time she should leave home? [:]

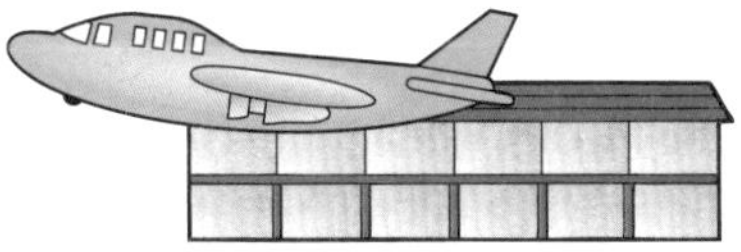

10. Ellie spends a total of 68 minutes travelling to and from work each day. How many hours and minutes does she spend travelling if she works a five-day week? ____________

11. Dad went to bed at 22:25 on Monday. He got up for work at 07:15 on Tuesday. How long did he spend in bed? ____________

Challenge

Kate spent 2 hrs 28 mins working on a school project. She spent 79 minutes at swimming training and she spent from 15:20 to 17:12 reading in the library. How long altogether did she spend doing the three activities? ____ hours ____ minutes

Chapter 21: Area

Area is the amount of space covered by a 2-D shape.

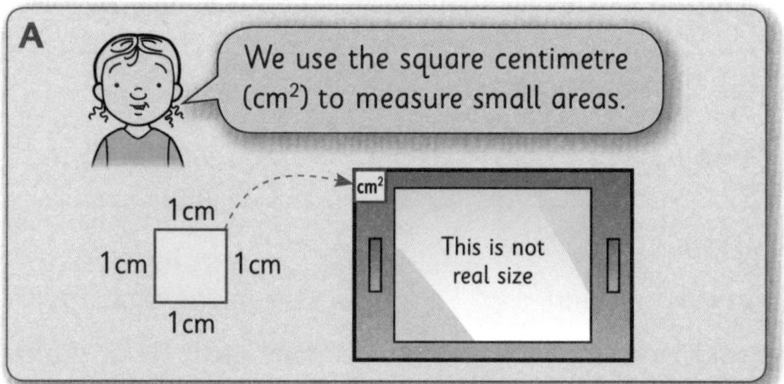
A
We use the square centimetre (cm^2) to measure small areas.
1cm
1cm
1cm
1cm
cm^2
This is not real size

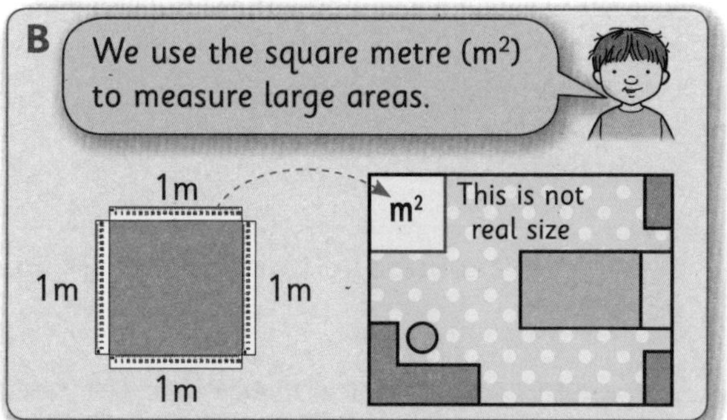
B
We use the square metre (m^2) to measure large areas.
1m
1m
1m
1m
m^2
This is not real size

1. Would you measure the area of the following in cm^2 or m^2? (They are not real size.)

(a) 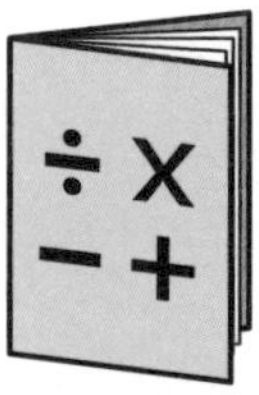
÷ ×
− +

(b) 

(c) 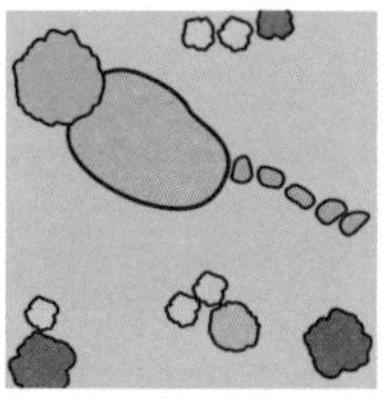

(d) 

(e) 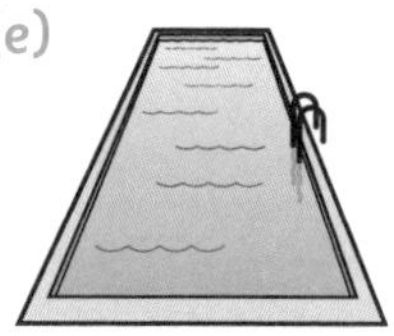

(f) 

(g) 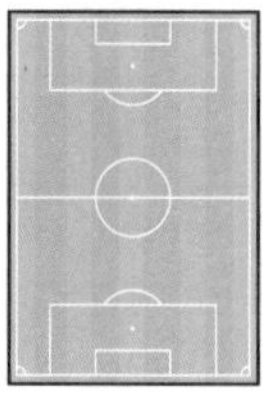

(h) 

(i) 

(j) 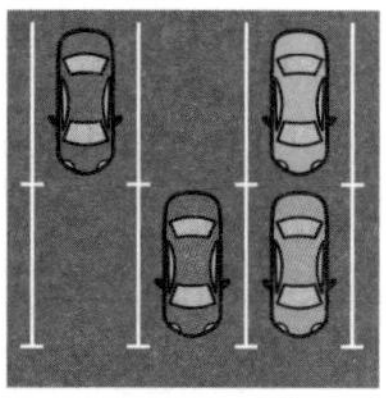

2. What is the area of each shape? Each □ represents $1cm^2$.

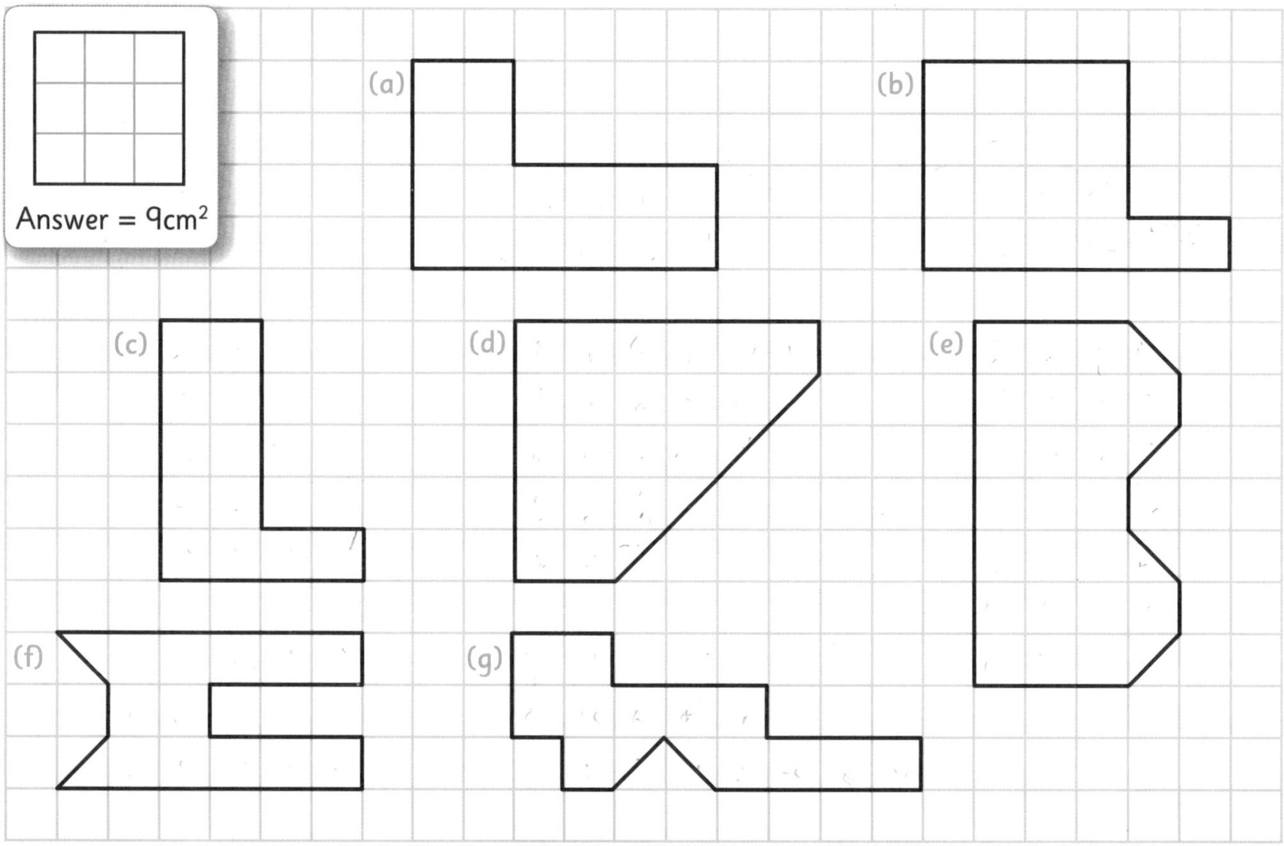
Answer = $9cm^2$
(a)
(b)
(c)
(d)
(e)
(f)
(g)

STRAND **Measures** STRAND UNIT/ELEMENT *Area*

LANGUAGE *Area, space, 2-D shape, centimetre square, cm^2, metre square, m^2, perimeter, distance, around, length, width, method, multiply, divide, calculate, total, greatest, smallest*

Area and perimeter

Remember:  **Area** is the space covered by a 2-D shape.

Perimeter is the distance around the 2-D shape. 

1. Look at this picture of a dog. It has been made using pentominoes. Fill in the grid.
   Each ☐ represents $1cm^2$.

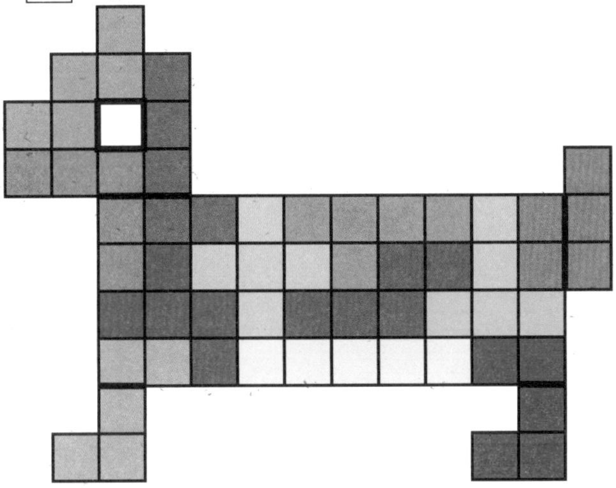

Body Part	Area	Perimeter
Head		
Eye		
Body		
Tail		
Leg (×2)		
Whole dog		

2. Using cm^2 paper, draw shapes that have the following areas.
   (a) $6cm^2$ (b) $10cm^2$ (c) $14cm^2$ (d) $15cm^2$ (e) $18cm^2$ (f) $28cm^2$

3. These three shapes are placed on top of each other.

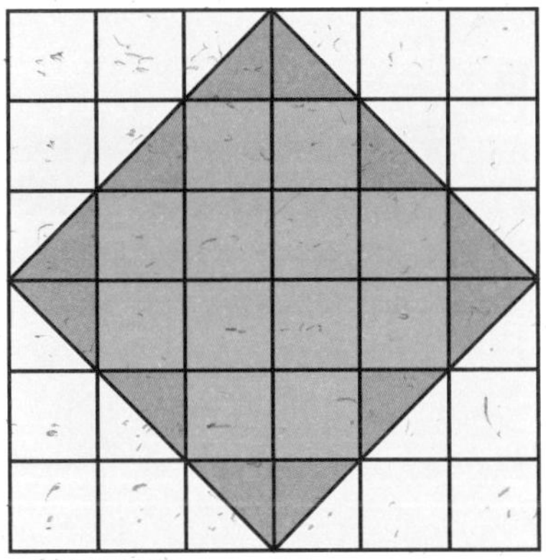

☐ represents $1cm^2$.

(a) What is the area of the **complete**:
   (i) yellow square ______; (ii) green cross ______;
   (iii) blue section? ______

(b) What is the perimeter of the (i) green cross ______;
   (ii) yellow square? ______

(c) What fraction of the blue section is covered by the green cross? ______

(d) What 2-D shape outline has the blue section? ______

(e) What fraction of the yellow square does the cross cover? ______

4. Sofia wrote her name on cm^2 paper. What is the (a) area and (b) perimeter of each letter?

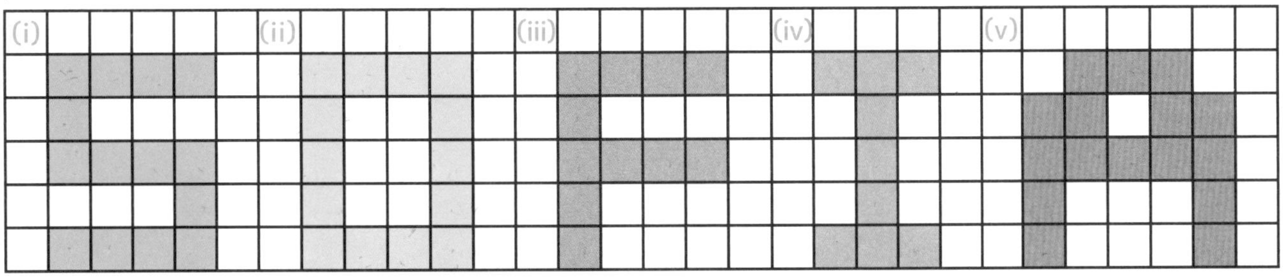

Challenge Write your own name on cm^2 paper.
Calculate the (a) area and (b) perimeter of each letter. (a) ______ (b) ______

Area – Rectangular shapes

There is an easier way of finding the area of rectangular shapes!

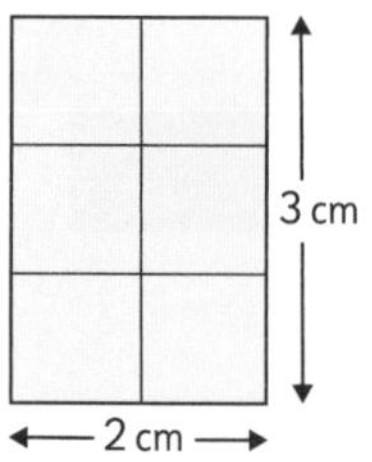

length = 3cm
width = 2cm
There are 3 rows of 2cm^2.
That makes a total of 6cm^2.

Area = 6cm^2

1. Follow the steps to find the area of each of these shapes. (Each ☐ represents 1cm^2.)

(a)

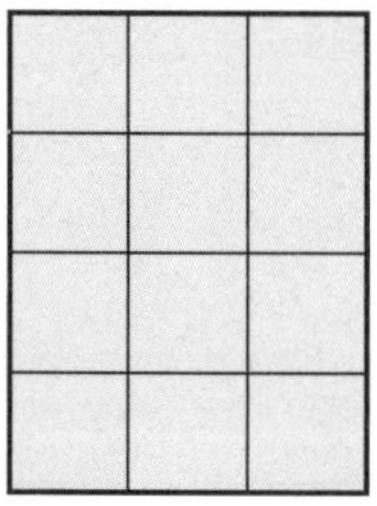

length = ______ cm

width = ______ cm

There are ______ rows of ______ cm^2.

That makes a total of ______ cm^2.

area = ______ cm^2

(b)

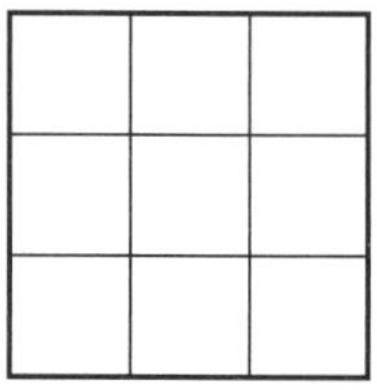

(c)

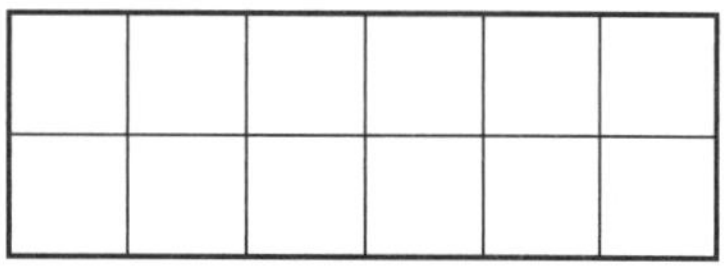

(d)

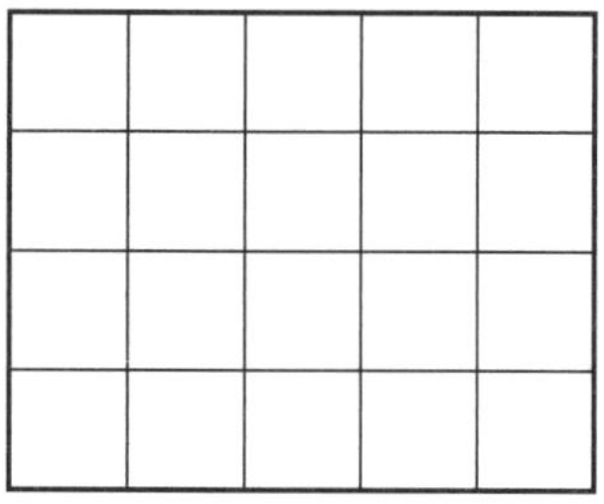

(e)

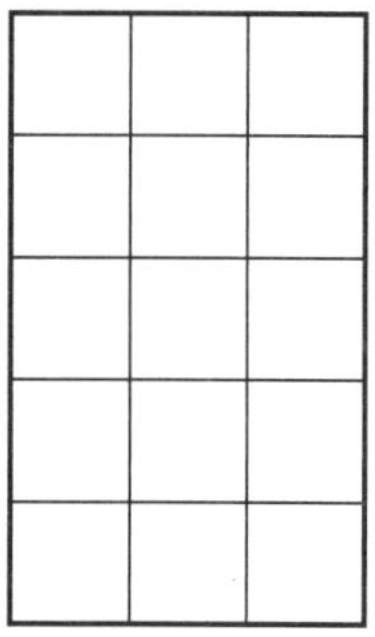

2. Draw the following rectangles onto cm^2 paper. Find the area of each.

	Length	Width
(a)	5cm	2cm
(b)	4cm	1cm

	Length	Width
(c)	6cm	9cm
(d)	6cm	4cm

	Length	Width
(e)	3cm	8cm
(f)	9cm	8cm

Have you figured out the quick way to calculate the area? It is simply: → length × width or width × length

3. Use the quick method to calculate the area of the following. Each ☐ represents 1cm^2.

(a)

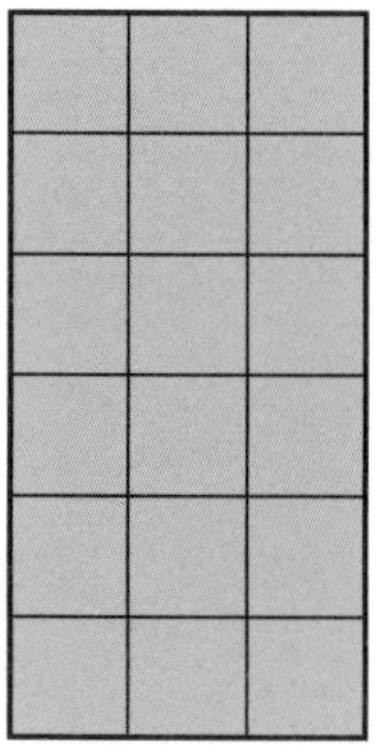

(b)

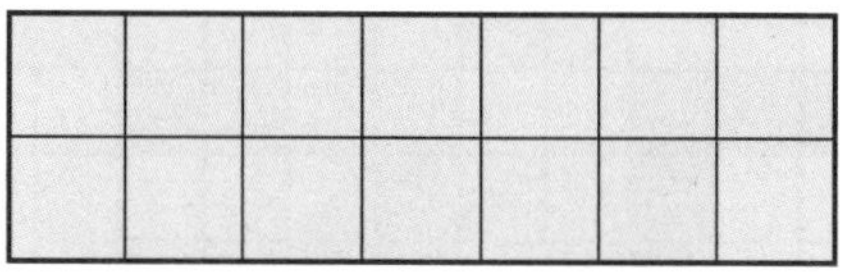

(c)

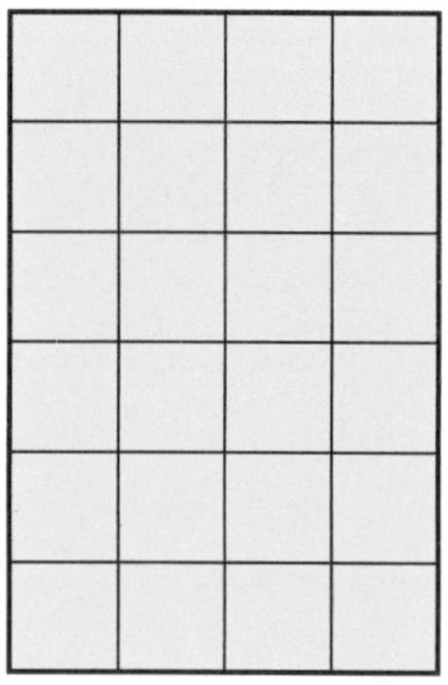

(d)

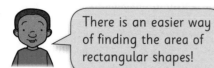

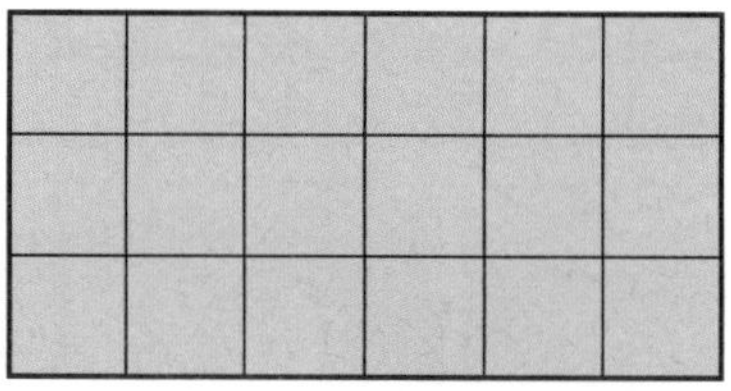

Area and perimeter

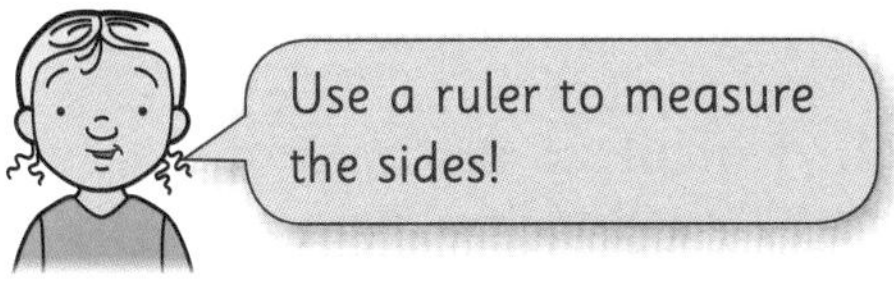

1. Find the (i) length; (ii) width; (iii) area and (iv) perimeter of the following shapes.

(a)

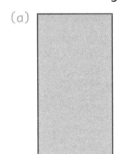

length = ______ cm
width = ______ cm
area = ______ cm^2
perimeter = ______ cm

(b)

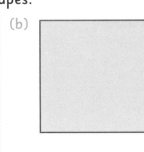

length = ______ cm
width = ______ cm
area = ______ cm^2
perimeter = ______ cm

(c)

length = ______ cm
width = ______ cm
area = ______ cm^2
perimeter = ______ cm

(d)

length = ______ cm
width = ______ cm
area = ______ cm^2
perimeter = ______ cm

2. Calculate the area of each of the following.

(a)

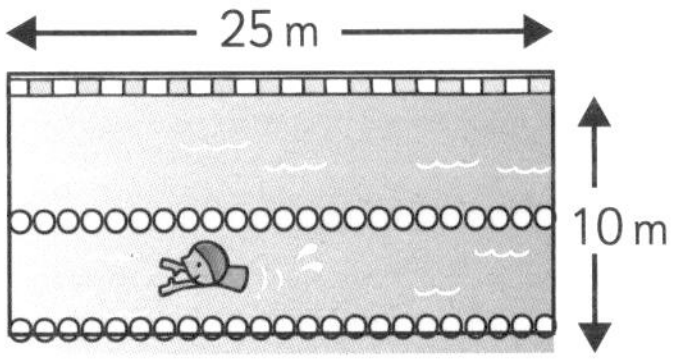

(b)

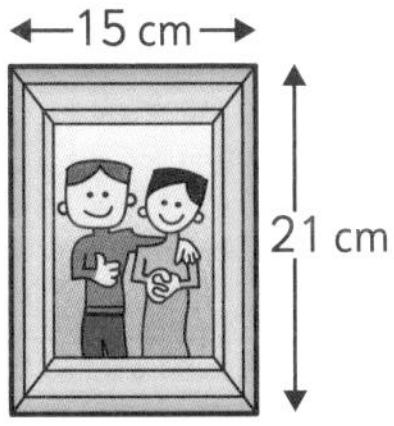

(c)

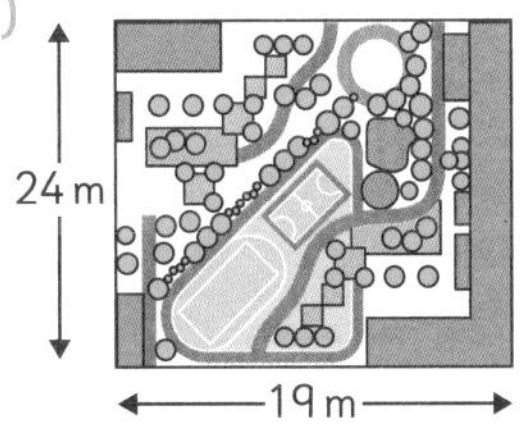

(d)

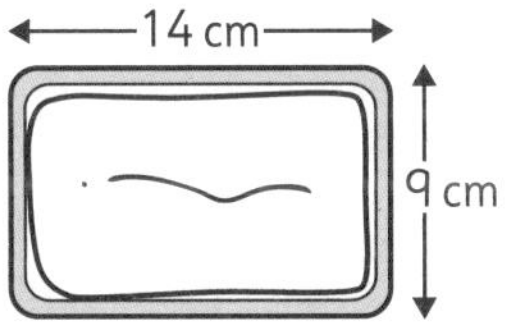

3. Look at this square facecloth.
   (a) Calculate its perimeter. ______ cm
   (b) Calculate its area. ______ cm^2
   (c) If four facecloths were laid out on a table to make a square, what would be the length of its perimeter? ______ cm

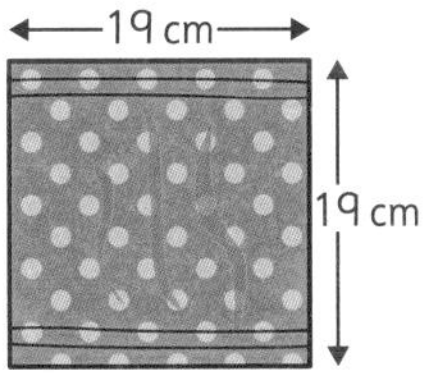

4. (a) $1m^2$ of paving stones costs €23. How much would it cost to pave this patio? €______
   (b) How much less than €500 is the cost of the paving? €______

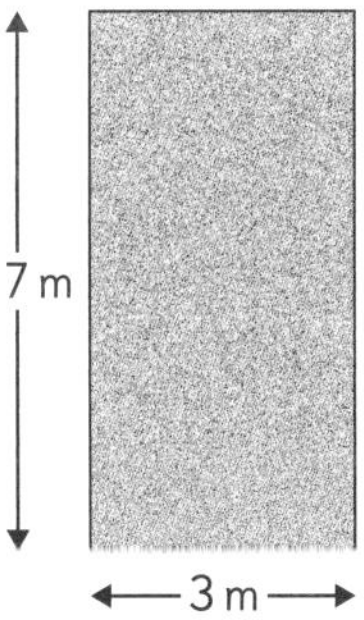

5.

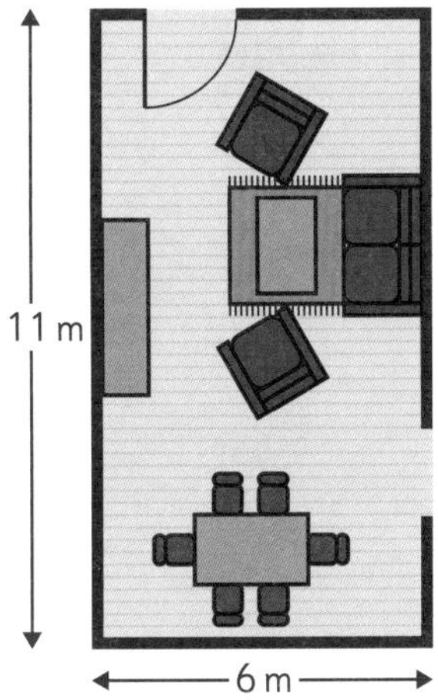

(a) Seán wants to put coving around the ceiling of his living room. What length of coving does he need?
(b) Coving costs €7 per metre. How much would the coving cost?
(c) Carpet costs €16 per m^2. How much would it cost Seán to buy new carpet for the whole living room?
(d) What change would he get from €1,500 if he bought the carpet?

Challenge

Find the area of one triangle.

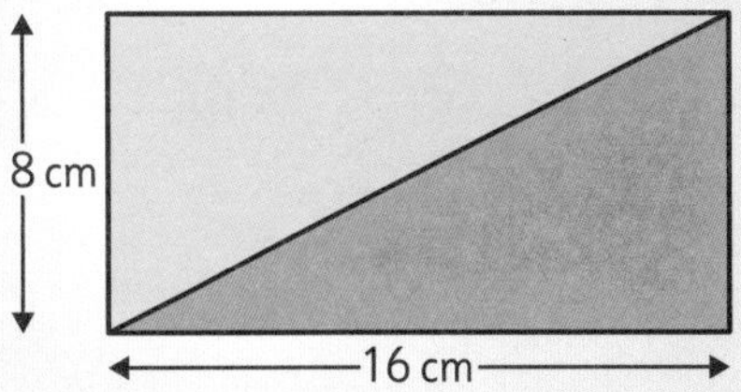

area = ______ cm^2

Area and perimeter – Multiplication method

1. Calculate the area of the following rectangles.

	Length	Width
(a)	11cm	5cm
(b)	7m	6m
(c)	8cm	12cm
(d)	9cm	3·5cm

	Length	Width
(e)	17cm	3cm
(f)	95m	15m
(g)	19m	7m
(h)	8cm	16cm

	Length	Width
(i)	13cm	15cm
(j)	24cm	17cm
(k)	32m	21m
(l)	39·5cm	36cm

2. Calculate the length or width of the following rectangles.

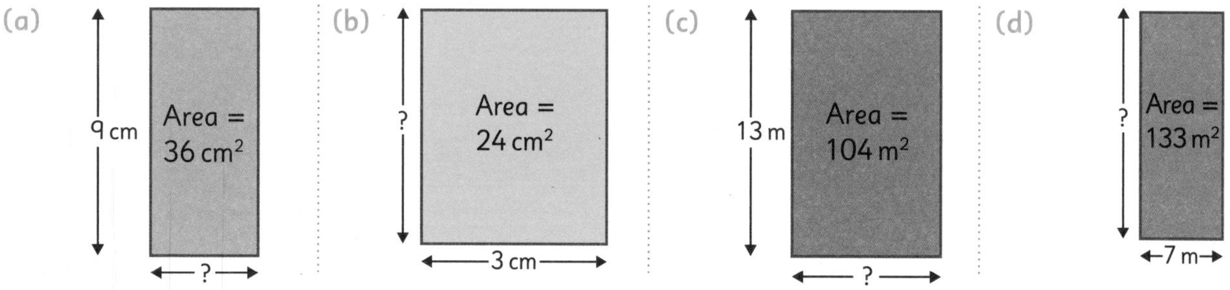

3. Calculate the perimeter of the following rectangles.

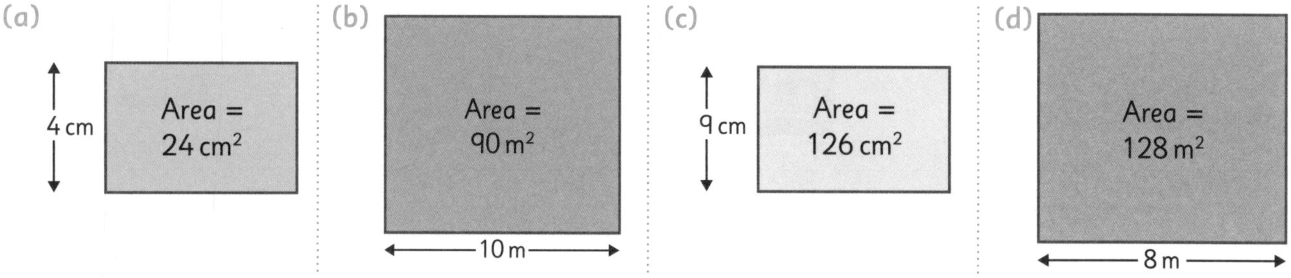

4. Calculate the area of the following rectangles.

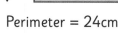

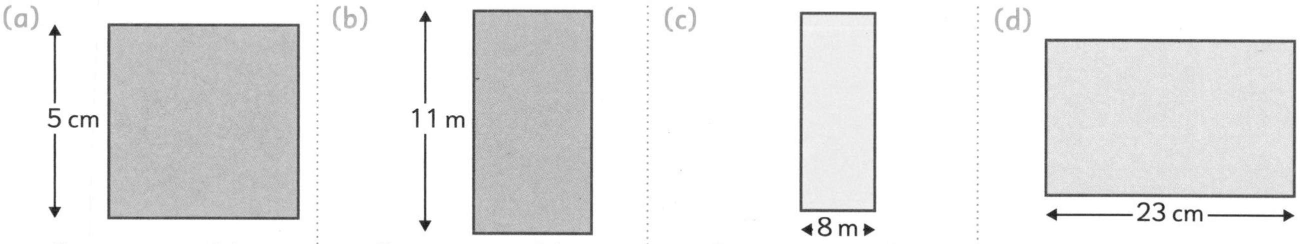

(a) Perimeter = 24cm (b) Perimeter = 34m (c) Perimeter = 58m (d) Perimeter = 74cm

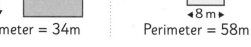

5. Complete these tables.

	Length	Width	Area	Perimeter
(a)	9cm	3cm		
(b)	6cm		30cm²	
(c)		7cm	63cm²	
(d)	8cm			28cm

	Length	Width	Area	Perimeter
(e)	11m	8m		
(f)	15m		180m²	
(g)		13m	312m²	
(h)		14m		58m

Area – Irregular shapes

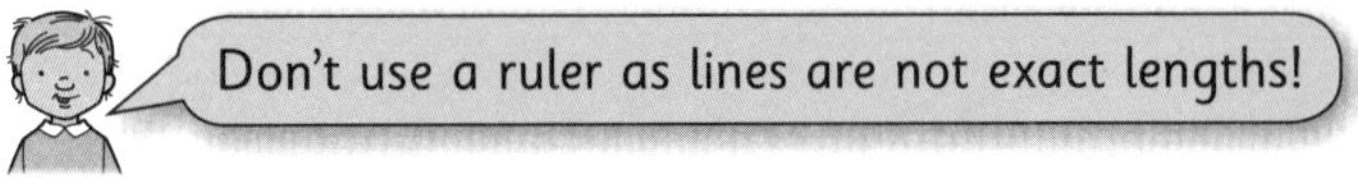

1. Use the information provided to calculate the lengths of sides x and y in each of the following shapes.

(a)

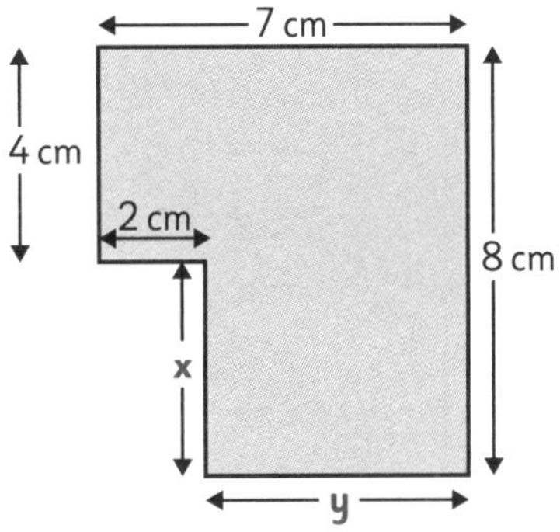

(b)

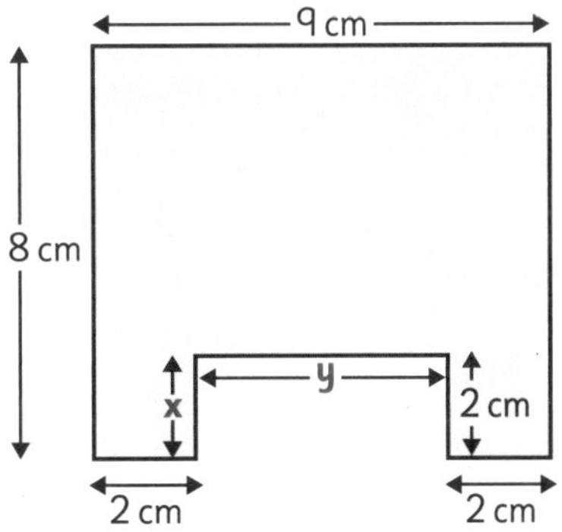

(c)

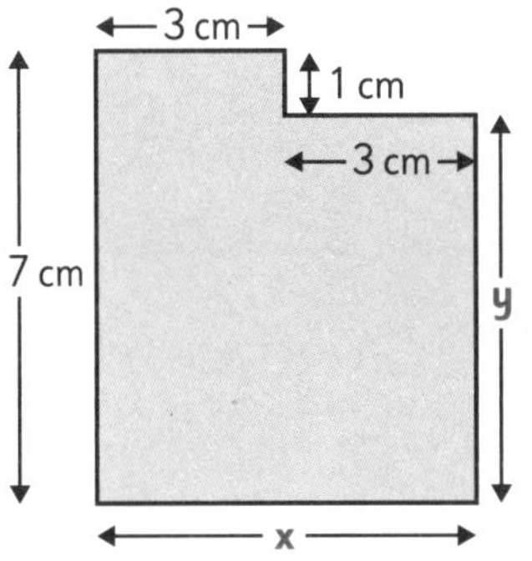

Finding the area of more challenging shapes

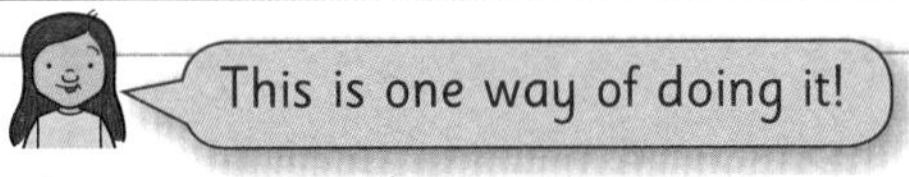

Step 1

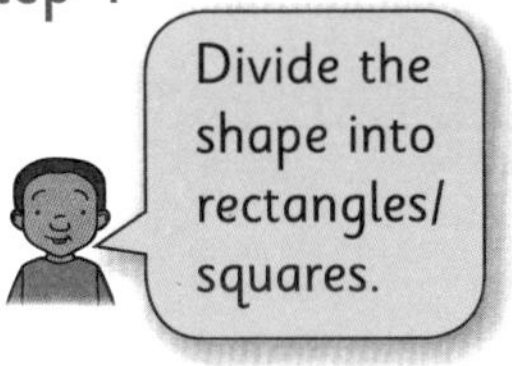

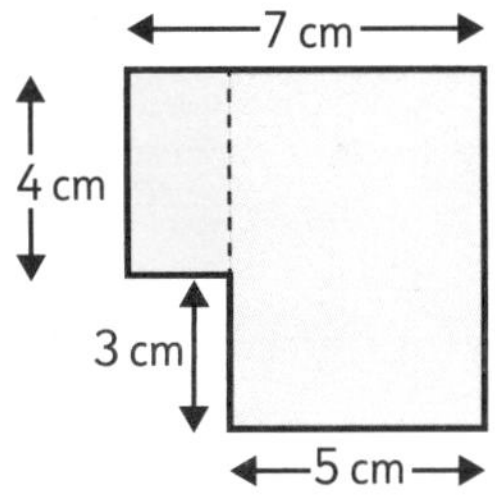

Step 2

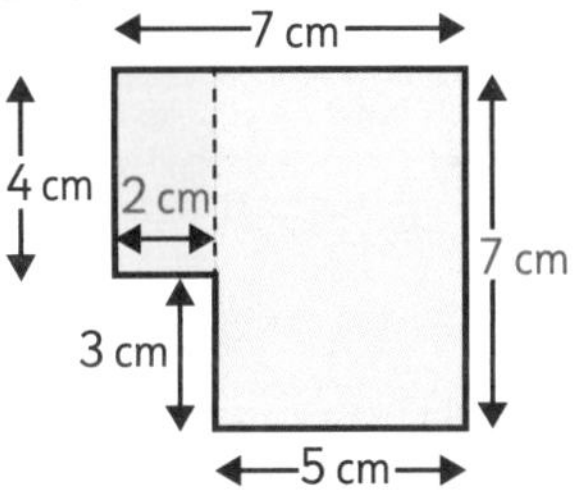

Step 3

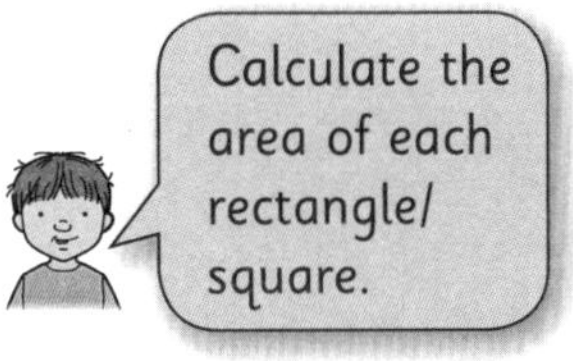

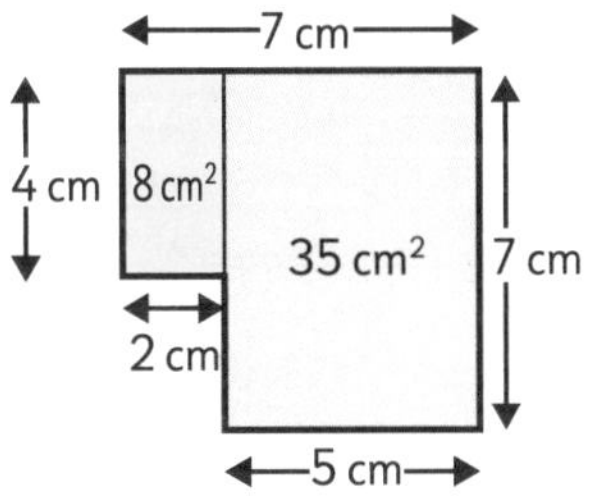

Step 4

$35cm^2 + 8cm^2 = 43cm^2$

$$\begin{array}{r} 35cm^2 \\ +\ 8cm^2 \\ \hline 43cm^2 \end{array}$$

2. Find the (i) perimeter and (ii) area of each of the following shapes.

(a)

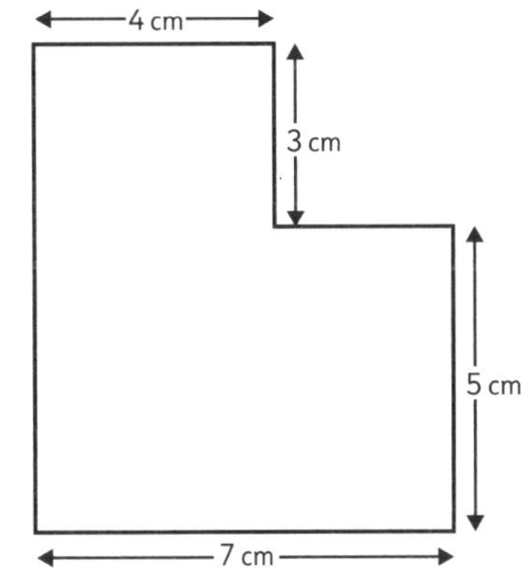

(b)

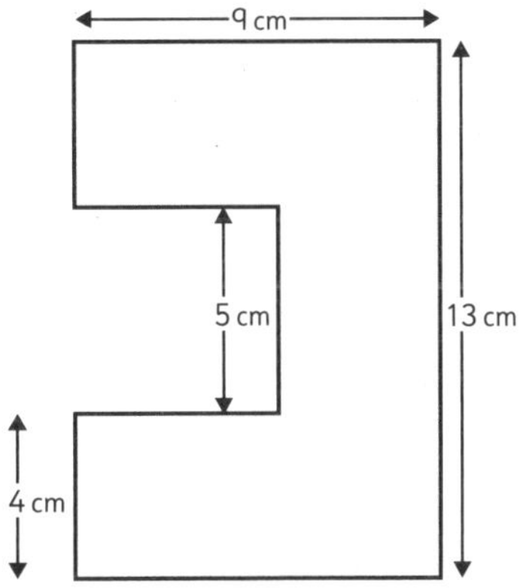

(c)

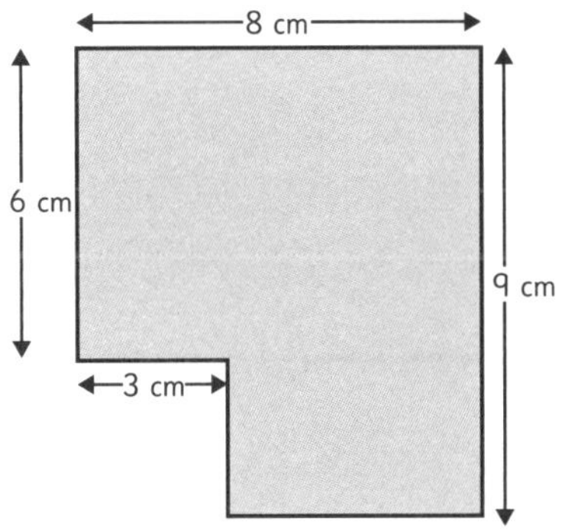

(d)

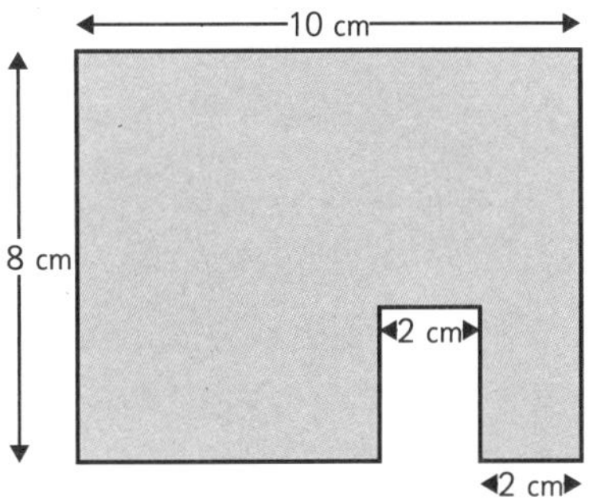

(e)

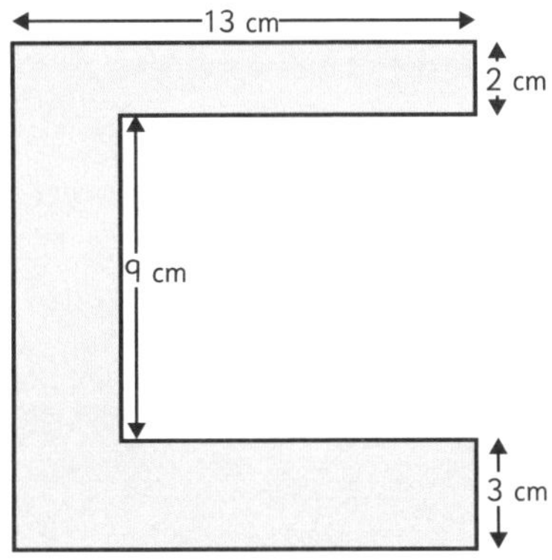

(f)

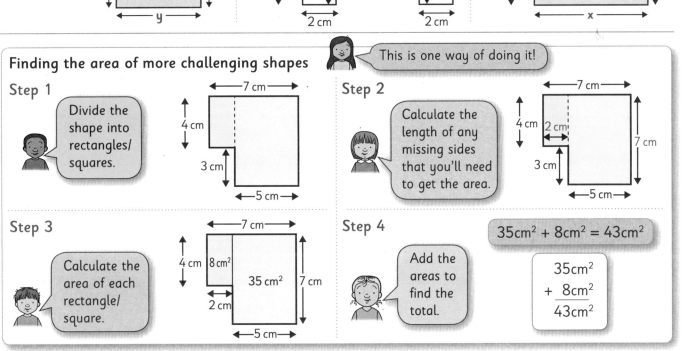

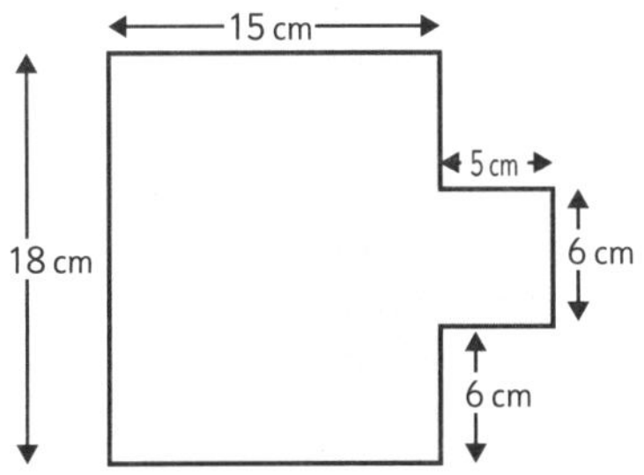

Area – Bronze Age site

A group of archaeologists excavated a Bronze Age site. The map below shows a small patch of the site where six spearheads were uncovered and divided into zones.

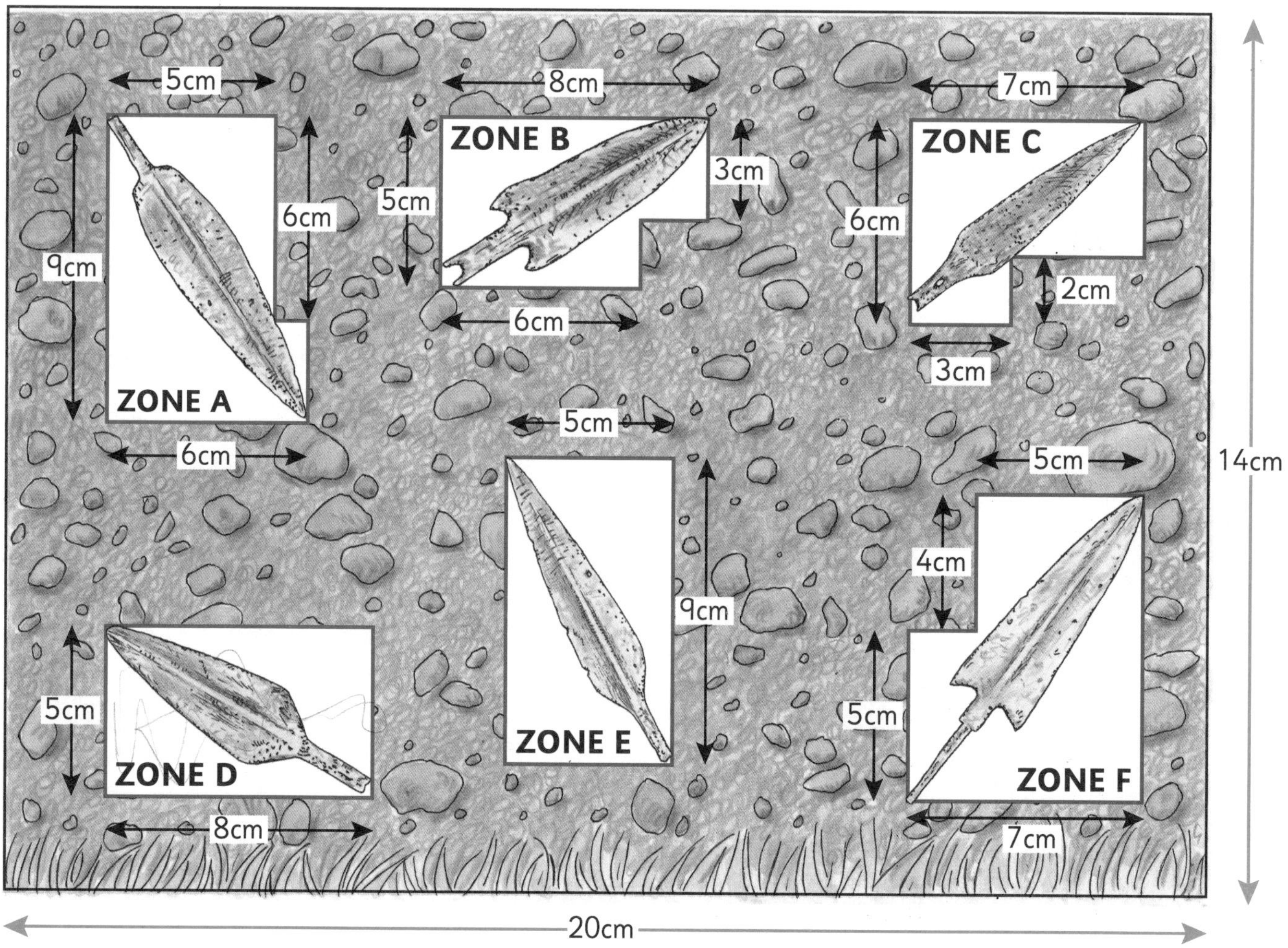

1. What is the (i) perimeter and (ii) area of this small patch of the excavated site?

2. Fill in the grid.

Zone	Perimeter	Area
A		
B		
C		

Zone	Perimeter	Area
D		
E		
F		

3. Which zones have the (i) greatest and (ii) smallest area?

4. Which zones have the (i) longest and (ii) shortest perimeter?

5. Which three zones have the same perimeter?

Challenge What is the area of the patch not included in any of the six zones? ____ cm^2

A quick look back 6

LOOK BACK

1. 

A pencil is 87mm long. Write the length in cm using a decimal point.

_______ cm

2. Write 3m 39cm as metres using a decimal point.

_______ m

3. 

Ann walked 3·495km. Write the distance she walked in metres.

_______ m

4. The side of a square is 19cm in length. What is the perimeter of the square?

_______ cm

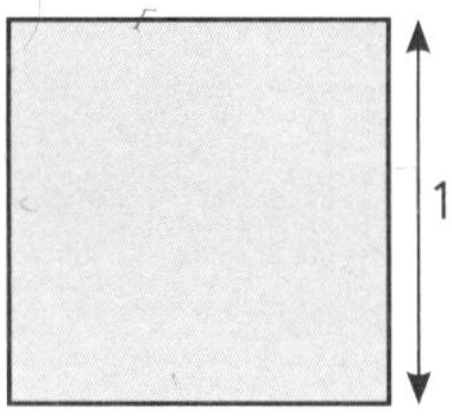

5. Write $\frac{1}{4}$ in decimal form. _______

6. Paul spent 20% of his €40 buying a cap. The cap cost

€_______ .

7. What must be added to 3·992 to make 4? Give your answer in decimal form.

____

8. Write $\frac{13}{50}$ as a percentage. _______

9. 

Julie had €36. She spent 75% of it buying a dress. How much did the dress cost?

€_______

10. Simplify this fraction:

$\frac{36}{100} \div \frac{\square}{4} = \frac{9}{\square}$

11. Liam spent $\frac{1}{4}$ of his €40 on a sliotar and 30% of it on a hurley.

He spent € _______ altogether.

12. Jerry drank 85% of a litre of water. How many ml of water were left?

_______ ml

13. 

Rónán read 60% of a 400-page book one week and finished it the next week. How many pages did he read the second week?

_______ pages

14. Write 172 minutes as hours and minutes.

_______ hours and _______ minutes

15. Write 20 minutes past 5 in the afternoon in digital form.

[:]

16. 

A soccer match started at 3.00pm. The match finished 112 minutes later. Write the finishing time in digital form.

[:]

17. 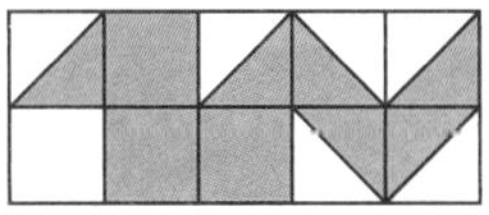

What is the area of the coloured part of this shape if a side of each small square represents 1cm?

_______ cm^2

18. A rectangle is 9cm long and has an area of $72cm^2$. What length is its perimeter?

_______ cm

19. How many minutes are there from 11:47 to 13:20 ?

_______ minutes

20. Ring the biggest amount.

39% 0·42 $\frac{2}{5}$ $\frac{41}{100}$

Chapter 22: Percentages 2

A quick revision of fractions and decimals

A Write $\frac{2}{5}$ in decimal form.

Method (i): $\frac{2}{5} \rightarrow 5\overline{)2{\cdot}0}$ = 0·4 (quotient 0·4)

Method (ii): $\frac{2}{5} \times \frac{2}{2} \rightarrow \frac{4}{10}$ = 0·4

B Write 4·056 in fraction form.

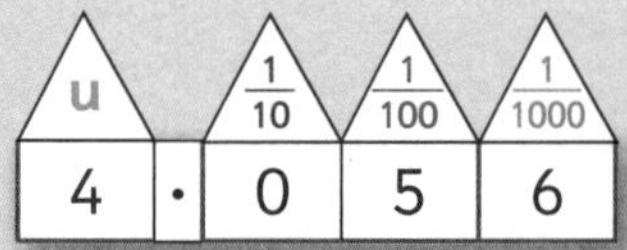

$\rightarrow 4\frac{056}{1000} = 4\frac{56}{1000}$

1. Fill in the missing decimal or fraction. (Simplify where possible.)

(a) $\frac{99}{100}$ = ______ (b) 7·8 = 7 $\frac{\square}{\square}$ (c) $5\frac{23}{1000}$ = ______ (d) $11\frac{11}{1000}$ = ______ (e) 5·2 = 5 $\frac{\square}{\square}$

A quick revision of fractions and percentages

Remember: Per cent means per hundred or out of a hundred!

A Write $\frac{3}{4}$ as a percentage.

$\frac{3}{4} \times \frac{25}{25} \rightarrow \frac{75}{100}$ = 75%

B Write 60% as a fraction and simplify.

60% $\rightarrow \frac{60}{100} \rightarrow \frac{6}{10} \div \frac{2}{2} = \frac{3}{5}$

2. Write the missing percentage or fraction (simplify).

(a) 80% = $\frac{\square}{\square}$ (b) $\frac{2}{5}$ = ______ (c) 4% = ______ (d) $\frac{1}{20}$ = ______ (e) $\frac{6}{25}$ = ______

Decimals and percentages

A $\frac{10}{100}$ = 0·10 = 10% **B** $\frac{49}{100}$ = 0·49 = 49% **C** $\frac{1}{100}$ = 0·01 = 1%

(a) Converting decimals to percentages: Multiply by 100: 0·23 × 100 = 23% (Move digits 2 places.) ←

(b) Converting percentages to decimals: Divide by 100: 99% ÷ 100 = 0·99 (Move digits 2 places.) →

3. Write the missing decimal or percentage.

(a) 23% = ______ (b) 0·90 = ______ (c) 0·8 = ______ (d) 70% = ______ (e) 7% = ______

(f) 0·01 = ______ (g) 0·4 = ______ (h) 3% = ______ (i) 0·1 = ______ (j) 1·0 = ______

4. What (i) fraction; (ii) decimal and (iii) percentage of each of these shapes is coloured?

(a)

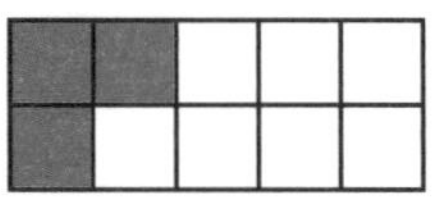

(i) Fraction ______
(ii) Decimal ______
(iii) Percentage ______

(b)

(i) Fraction ______
(ii) Decimal ______
(iii) Percentage ______

(c)

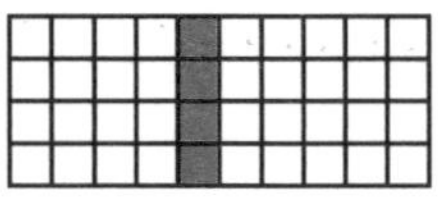

(i) Fraction ______
(ii) Decimal ______
(iii) Percentage ______

(d)

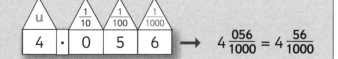

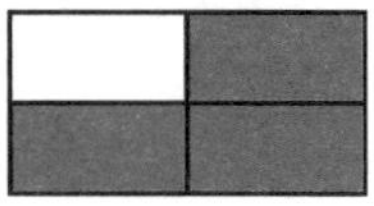

(i) Fraction ______
(ii) Decimal ______
(iii) Percentage ______

STRAND **Number** STRAND UNIT/ELEMENT *Decimals and percentages*
LANGUAGE *Per cent, percentage, fraction, decimal, units, tenths, hundredths, simplify, calculator, horizontal bar-line graph, pie chart, increase/decrease*

Percentages 2 – Grids and blocks

1. Complete this table.

Fraction	$\frac{5}{100}$	$\frac{29}{100}$			$\frac{1}{10}$			$\frac{6}{10}$	
Decimal	0·05		0·5			0·01			0·4
Percentage	5%			99%			100%		

2. Ring the **odd one out** in each of these groups.

(a) 10%, 0·01, $\frac{1}{10}$ (b) $\frac{9}{100}$, 90%, 0·9 (c) 0·6, 6%, $\frac{6}{100}$ (d) $\frac{4}{10}$, 0·4, 4%

(e) 50%, 0·5, $\frac{5}{100}$ (f) $\frac{1}{4}$, 20%, 0·25 (g) $\frac{7}{100}$, 7%, 0·7 (h) 0·06, 60%, $\frac{3}{5}$

3. Put each fraction, decimal and percentage in the proper block. The **largest** values go in the bottom row; the **smallest** in the top row.

(a) 0·004, $\frac{4}{10}$, $\frac{4}{100}$, 4%, $\frac{4}{1000}$, 40%, 0·04, 0·4, $\frac{40}{100}$

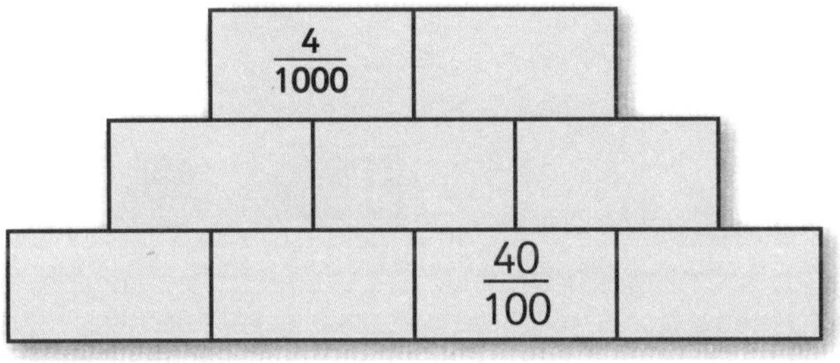

(b) 1·0, 10%, 1%, $\frac{10}{10}$, 0·01, $\frac{100}{100}$, 0·1, $\frac{1}{10}$, 100%

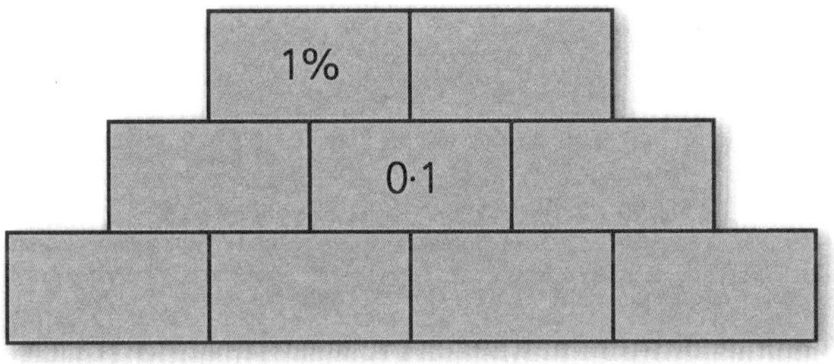

4. Gary, Cathy and Kim had a high jump competition. They each had three jumps. Mark their scores on the metre sticks with the first letter of their names.

(a) First jumps

Gary: $\frac{30}{100}$m

Cathy: 0·5m

Kim: 40% of 1m

(b) Second jumps

Gary: $\frac{2}{5}$m

Cathy: 0·65m

Kim: 75% of 1m

(c) Third jumps

Gary: 80% of 1m

Cathy: 0·9m

Kim: $\frac{68}{100}$m

5. Calculating decimals and percentages (Change the decimal or percentage to a fraction first.)

(a) 20% of 15 (b) 0·1 of 50 (c) 50% of 22 (d) 0·25 of 20 (e) 0·90 of 20

(f) 5% of 40 (g) 0·5 of 50 (h) 75% of 28 (i) 0·6 of 30 (j) 30% of 30

6. The Mizen Head weather station has recorded the number of rainy days for the following months. Record the data on the bar-line graph.

(a) February (28 days): 75% rainy days.
(b) April: 0·5 days had rain.
(c) June: 20% of days had rain.
(d) September: 30% rainy days.
(e) November: 60% of days had rain.

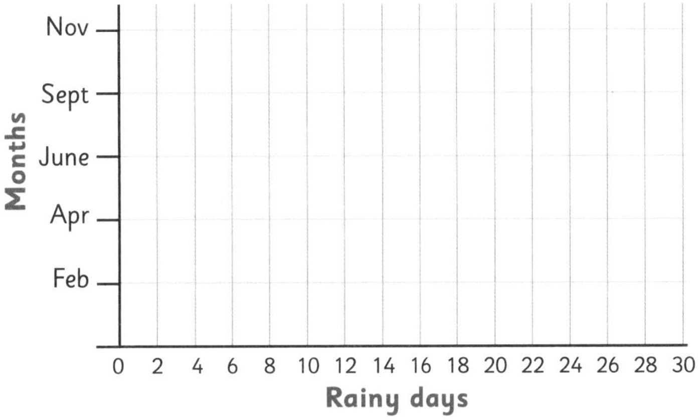

Percentages 2 – Problems

Remember: There are 360° in a circle. Calculate each sport as a fraction of 360°.

1. This pie chart shows the favourite sports of a group of 60 children.

Hurling: 0·5; Soccer, 20%; Rugby: 5%; Gaelic football: 0·15; Swimming: 10%

Find how many children selected each sport (use fractions to help you).

(a) Hurling: ____

(b) Soccer: ____

(c) Swimming: ____

(d) Rugby: ____

(e) Gaelic football: ____

Favourite Sports

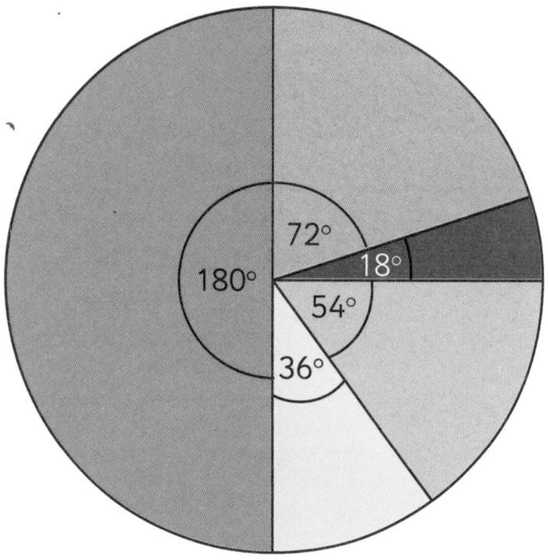

Key:
- = Hurling
- = Soccer
- = Rugby
- = Gaelic football
- = Swimming

2. Solve the following.

(a) 20% of 100m	(b) $\frac{1}{2}$ of 1kg	(c) 0·1 of a litre
(d) 37% of €1	(e) 0·6 of €200	(f) 0·75 of 2kg
(g) 80% of 1km	(h) 25% of 1 litre	(i) 50% of 1 hour
(j) 30% of 10cm	(k) 0·1 of an hour	(l) $\frac{30}{100}$ of a metre

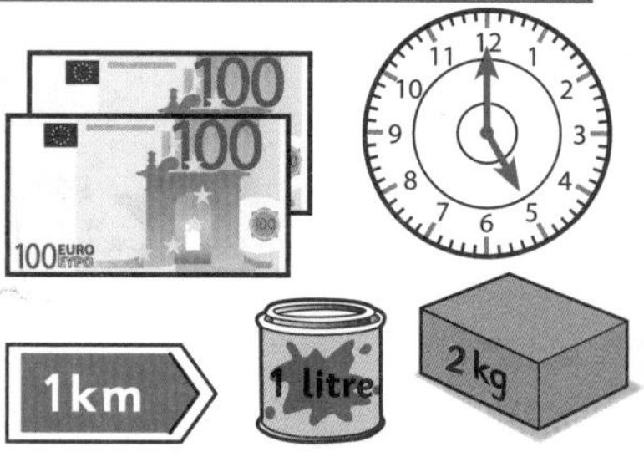

3. Fun facts

(a) 20% of Ireland's population is children aged between 0 and 14. If 4·5 million people live in Ireland, how many of them are:

(i) children (0–14)? ____

(ii) over 14? ____

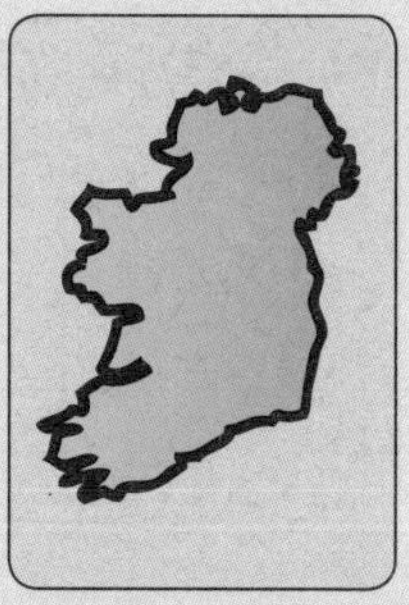

(b) In the USA, children spend, on average, 0·25 of the full day online.

(i) How many hours is that? ____

(ii) How many hours are left for sleeping, school, etc.? ____

(c) A cheetah's top speed is 120km per hour (120km/h). An Olympic sprinter can reach 40% of this speed. What is the top speed of an Olympic sprinter in km/h? ____

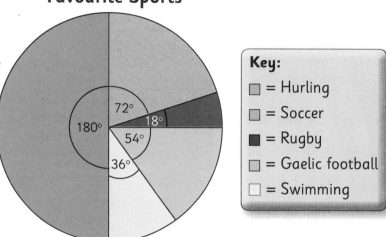

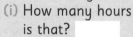

(d) A blue whale calf can weigh up to 2,700kg at birth. The average adult man weighs 0·03 of that amount. (i) How much does the average man weigh? ____ kg

(ii) What % of the calf's weight would seven men weigh? ____

4. Paul ran 0·7 of a km and Paula ran 80% of a km. How many metres further did Paula run than Paul? ____ m

Challenge Henry drank 0·25 of two litres, Harry drank 75% of a litre and Harriet drank $\frac{4}{5}$ of a litre of water. How many millilitres did each drink?

(a) Henry ____ ml (b) Harry ____ ml (c) Harriet ____ ml

Percentages 2 – Find the full amount

Joe spent 25% of his money buying a 'Spook Land' comic.
How much money had Joe at first?

25% ⟶ $\frac{1}{4}$ = €1, so €1 €1 €1 €1 = €4 (€1 × 4)

Short way

25% = $\frac{1}{4}$

$\frac{1}{4}$ = €1

$\frac{4}{4}$ = €4

1. Find the full amount if:

(a) 50% = 6	(b) 0·1 = 2	(c) 20% = 6	(d) 75% = 15	(e) 0·3 = 9
(f) 0·01 = 4	(g) 0·9 = 90	(h) 40% = 8	(i) 2% = 10	(j) 0·40 = 4

2. A baker used 40% of a bag of flour to bake baguettes. If he used 600g, how much flour is in a full bag? ____ g

3. 

30% of the children in a class are 10 years old. The other 21 children are 11 years old. How many children are there in the class? ____

4. Mary walks 20% of the journey to school and gets a bus for the rest of the way. Her total journey is 2·5km. How far does she travel on the bus? ____ km

5. Gillian scored 0·75 of the frees she took in a camogie match. If she took 16 frees altogether, how many did she miss? ____

6. 

0·7 of the hens in an enclosure are grey. If there are 63 grey hens, how many hens are there altogether? ____

7. 90% of the apples in a box are red and the rest are green. If there are 72 red apples, how many apples are there altogether? ____

8. Ethan has watched 40% of a film. The film lasts for 1 hour and 10 minutes altogether. How many minutes of the film has he seen? ____

9. 

Jan got €20 from her granddad for her birthday. If she spent 0·3 of the money buying a book, what was the cost of the book? € ____

10. A shopkeeper sold 0·5 of this box of oranges on Friday and 20% of it on Saturday. How many oranges were still left in the box? ____

11. 

Lily ran a total of 35km between Saturday and Sunday. She ran 0·6 of it on Saturday. How many km did she run on Sunday? ____ km

12. Gerry ate 0·5 of the blueberries on Monday and 25% of the blueberries on Tuesday. If he ate 48 blueberries altogether, how many were in the box at first? ____

13. 

Ariana ate 0·45 of the grapes and Alex ate 35% of them. If there were 18 grapes left, how many were in the container at first? ____

Challenge Joe took 0·35 of the strawberries. Jane took $\frac{2}{5}$ of them and Kim took 20%. What percentage of the strawberries were left? ____

Percentages 2 – Increasing and decreasing

Increasing and decreasing by a decimal or percentage

A Increase 12 by 0·25 of itself:

0·25 or $\frac{1}{4}$ of 12 = 3

→ 12 + 3 = 15

B Decrease 20 by 40% of itself:

40% or $\frac{2}{5}$ of 20 = 8

→ 20 – 8 = 12

1. Try these yourself.

(a) Increase 10 by 20% of itself. ______

(b) Decrease 18 by 0·5 of itself. ______

(c) Decrease 20 by 25% of itself. ______

(d) Increase 4 by 0·75 of itself. ______

(e) Decrease 100 by 13% of itself. ______

(f) Increase 200 by 0·4 of itself. ______

(g) Increase 200 by 1% of itself. ______

(h) Decrease 100 by 0·25 of itself. ______

(i) Increase 9 by 100% of itself. ______

(j) Increase 80 by 0·05 of itself. ______

2. Ciarán's pay was €10 per hour. He got a pay rise of 25%.
How much per hour is he getting now? €______ per hour

3.

Tara usually spent 50 minutes doing her homework.
One evening, she had to finish a project and this increased her time by 50%.
How long did she spend at her homework that evening? ______

4. There were 20 people in a queue waiting to buy tickets. Some of them got tired and left. As a result, the queue decreased by 30%. How many remained in the queue? ______

5.

A farmer had 100 sheep.
When new lambs were born, her flock increased by 73%.
What is the size of her flock now? ______

6. If 20% of the 135 passengers on an aeroplane to Sydney disembarked at the Dubai stop-over, how many were still on the plane? ______

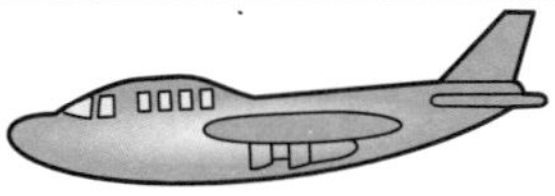

7.

A joiner was making 204 pieces of furniture each month. He bought new machinery and he now produces 25% more pieces. How many pieces of furniture is he now making per month? ______

8. Chrissie ran 750m. Claire ran 20% further than Chrissie.
How far in total did the two girls run? ______ m

9.

Andrew had €12·80. Shane had 30% less than that.
How much did they have altogether? €______

Challenge There were 380 spectators at a football match. 0·25 of them left at half-time and 30% left before the match was over. How many spectators remained until the end of the match? ______

Chapter 23: Directed numbers

Look at this vault. Some of the safety deposit boxes are above ground level, embedded in rock. Other boxes are below ground level, safely buried in earth and mud. Each box can only be opened by a unique key held by the vault-owner. The boxes hold interesting valuables.

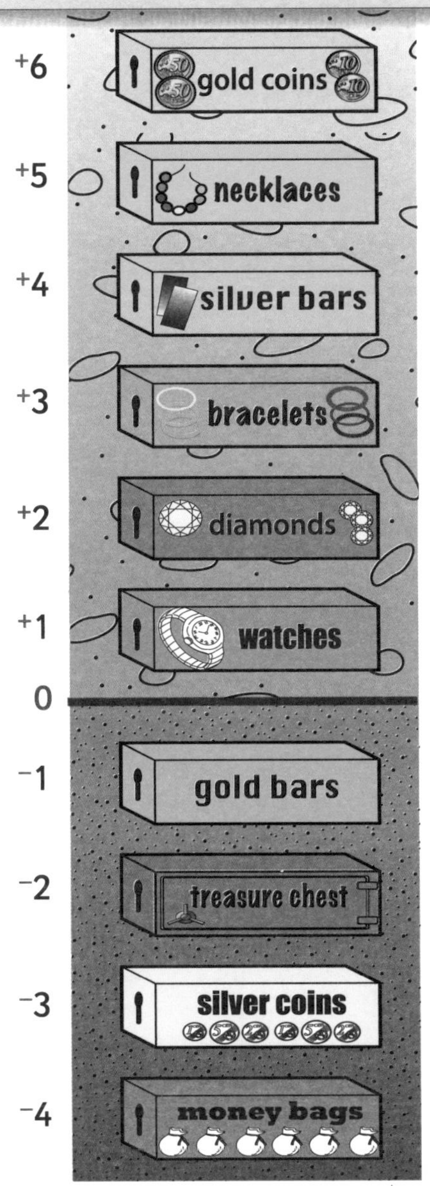

A **positive** number is **greater** than zero.
A **negative** number is **less** than zero.

Levels above 0 (ground level) are written with a positive (or plus) sign. $^{+}6$ is called positive 6 or plus 6.

Levels below 0 (ground level) are written with a negative (or minus) sign. $^{-}3$ is called negative 3 or minus 3.

The vault-owner is on level $^{+}3$. He wants to go to the vault that has the treasure chest. Which level must he go to? Is it $^{+}2$ or $^{-}2$?

1. **Complete.**
   - (a) How many levels are above ground level? ______
   - (b) What treasure is at level $^{+}6$? ______
   - (c) How many levels are below ground level? ______
   - (d) What treasure is at level $^{+}4$? ______
   - (e) What treasure is at level $^{+}1$? ______
   - (f) What treasure is at level $^{-}1$? ______
   - (g) What treasure is at level $^{-}4$? ______
   - (h) What treasure is at level $^{-}3$? ______
   - (i) What treasure is at level $^{-}2$? ______

2. **Write the missing numbers for the levels on the following number line.**

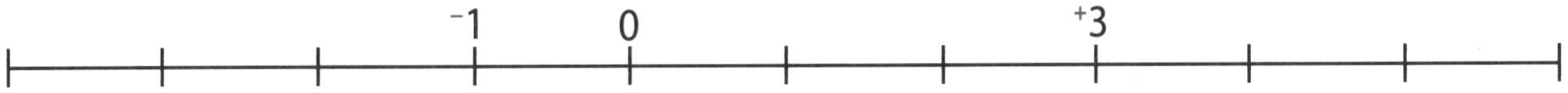

3. **How many levels are there between…**

(a) $^{+}3$ and $^{+}5$? ______	(b) $^{+}1$ and $^{+}3$? ______	(c) $^{+}1$ and $^{+}6$? ______
(d) $^{+}1$ and $^{-}1$? ______	(e) $^{+}2$ and $^{-}2$? ______	(f) $^{+}3$ and $^{-}3$? ______
(g) $^{-}2$ and $^{+}4$? ______	(h) $^{-}3$ and $^{+}5$? ______	(i) $^{-}4$ and $^{+}6$? ______

Directed numbers – Thermometer

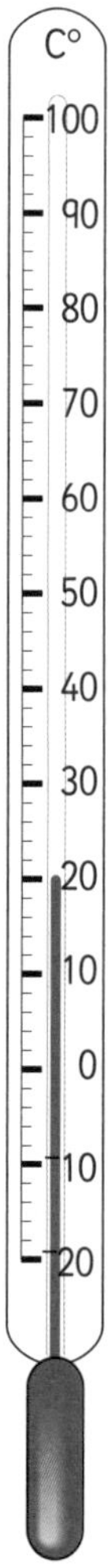

Celsius (C) is a scale for measuring temperature. Weather temperatures are given in degrees (°) Celsius (C). 10 degrees Celsius is written as 10°C.

Maths Facts Water freezes at 0°C; water boils at 100°C. Our average body temperature is 37°C. Negative temperatures are below freezing (0°C). Positive temperatures are above freezing.

1. Colour the correct temperature in °C on each thermometer.

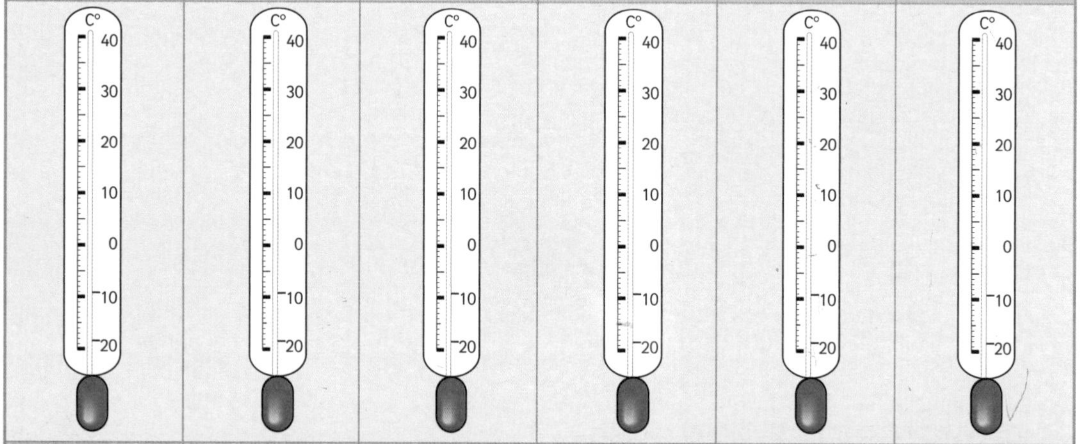

A	B	C	D	E	F
10°C	Average body temperature	Freezing point of water	15° below freezing point	⁻20°C	25° above freezing point

2. Now show the above temperatures on the following number line. Write the correct capital letters in the spaces.

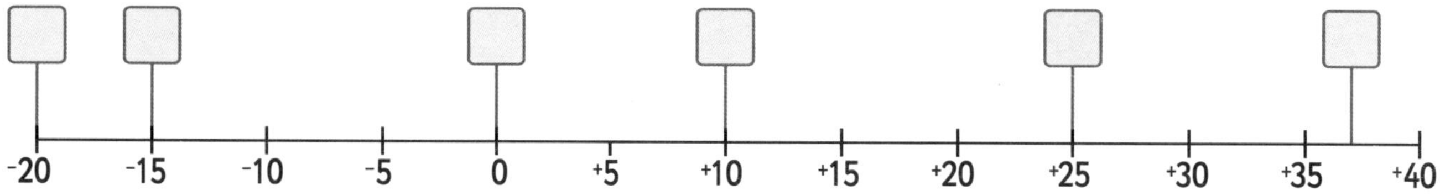

(a) Which thermometer shows the highest temperature? ________

(b) Which thermometer shows the lowest temperature? ________

(c) Which thermometer shows 0°C? ________

(d) What is the difference in degrees between thermometers:

(i) C and F? ______	(ii) C and E? ______	(iii) A and B? ______	(iv) A and E? ______
(v) E and F? ______	(vi) D and E? ______	(vii) E and B? ______	(viii) B and F? ______

Challenge

One summer in Ireland, the hottest temperature was ⁺29°C. The coldest temperature in Ireland that winter was ⁻12°C. What is the difference between the two temperatures? ______ °C

Directed numbers – City temperatures

These are the temperatures in the following cities at midday one day in December.

New York: ⁻1°C	Dublin: 5°C	Helsinki: ⁻2°C	Oslo: ⁻8°C
Cape Town: 27°C	Cork: 6°C	Cairo: 22°C	Rome: 13°C
Moscow: ⁻11°C	Winnipeg: ⁻14°C	Tokyo: 11°C	Hong Kong: 18°C

1. Which city has the highest temperature? ____________
2. Which city has the lowest temperature? ____________
3. What is the difference between the temperatures in Rome and Dublin? ____ °C
4. What is the difference between the temperatures in Dublin and Cork? ____ °C

5. How much warmer is it in Tokyo than in Winnipeg? ____ °C
6. How much colder is it in Rome than in Cape Town? ____ °C
7. What is the difference between the temperatures in Moscow and Helsinki? ____ °C
8. Which city is warmer: Helsinki or Winnipeg? ____________
9. Which city is colder: Moscow or Oslo? ____________

10. How much colder is Winnipeg than Oslo? ____ °C
11. How much warmer is Cork than New York? ____ °C
12. What is the difference between the temperatures in Tokyo and Moscow? ____ °C
13. What is the difference between the temperatures in Rome and Cork? ____ °C
14. How much warmer is it in Cairo than in Hong Kong? ____ °C
15. What is the difference between the highest and the lowest temperature listed? ____ °C
16. Complete the following grid by increasing or decreasing the **original** temperatures, as required.

City	Cork 6°C	New York ⁻1°C	Cape Town 27°C	Oslo ⁻8°C	Helsinki ⁻2°C	Hong Kong 18°C	Winnipeg ⁻14°C
Increase the temperature by 5°C.							
Decrease the temperature by 3°C.							
Increase the temperature by 15°C.							
Decrease the temperature by 13°C.							

Directed numbers – League tables

There are 12 teams in the Animal Premier League. The table below shows the positions of the top eight teams in the league. You will add four extra teams to the list later.

> **Key**
> **POS** = Position; **P** = Games played; **W** = Wins; **D** = Draws; **L** = Losses; **F** = Goals for; **A** = Goals against; **GD** = Goal difference; **Pts** = Points.

Each team gets **3** points for winning, **1** point for a draw and **0** points for losing.

Animal Premier League Table

POS	Team	P	W	D	L	F	A	GD	Pts
1	Crying Monkeys	33	28	4	1	82	16	66	88
2	Happy Bears	33	18	7	8	45	30		
3	Rebel Giraffes	33	19	3	11	55	50		
4	United Birds	33		9		57	40	17	54
5	Flying Tigers	33	15	7	11	40	35	5	52
6	Jumping Cows	33	14			41	34	7	48
7	Slimy Fish	33	8	11	14	29	42	−13	35
8	Leaping Lions	33	9	6	18	41	57		
9									
10									
11									
12									

1. Fill in the goal difference and points for 'Happy Bears' and 'Rebel Giraffes'.
2. Fill in the games won and lost by 'United Birds'.
3. Fill in the number of games that 'Jumping Cows' has (a) drawn ________ and (b) lost ________.
4. Fill in the goal difference and points for 'Leaping Lions'.

5. The bottom four teams in the league are 'Barking Dogs', 'Proud Penguins', 'Clever Cats' and 'Skipping Kangaroos'. Complete the **table below**. Based on this information, place the teams in order from 9–12 on the **Animal Premier League Table** above.
   Now complete the rest of the table above.

POS	Team	P	W	D	L	F	A	GD	PTS
	Barking Dogs	33	6	12	15	36	57	−11	
	Proud Penguins	33	8	7	18	34	55		31
	Clever Cats	33	7	7	19	33	59		
	Skipping Kangaroos	33	8	7	18	38	56		

Chapter 24: Fractions, decimals, percentages

1. Get cracking to refresh what you already know!

(a) 0·2 of 30 = ______ (b) 75% of 40 = ______ (c) $\frac{9}{1000}$ = 0·______

(d) If 40% = 4, 100% = ______. (e) Increase 25 by 40%: ______

(f) Write these in order starting with the smallest: 4%, $\frac{4}{1000}$, 0·44. ______ ______ ______

(g) Which is the odd one out: $\frac{3}{4}$, 0·075, 75%? ______ (h) Write 3·029 in fraction form: ______

(i) 0·8 of 40 = ______ (j) If 2% = 10, find 100%. ______ (k) 75% of an hour = ______

(l) $\frac{17}{20}$ = ______ % (m) $\frac{1}{25}$ = ______ % (n) Simplify the fraction that equals 0·12: ______

Sale prices

We calculate a sale price the same way we calculate a decrease.

Example:

Decrease by 40% → $\frac{40}{100}$ → $\frac{4}{10} = \frac{2}{5}$

$\frac{2}{5}$ of €60 = €24

Sale price: €60 – €24 = €36

Short way

$\frac{5}{5}$ = €60

$\frac{1}{5}$ = €12

$\frac{3}{5}$ = €36

2. Calculate these sale prices.

(a) Was €20, now 50% off: €______

(b) Original price €10, sale price 30% off: €______

(c) Old price €2, sale discount 25%: €______

(d) Was €80, reduced by 15%: €______

(e) 8% off original price of €200: €______

(f) 33% off original price of €100: €______

---

3. Winter sports sale (The equipment is colour-coded to help you.)

Find the sale price of all items:

(a) Skis: €______

(b) Ski poles: €______

(c) Woolly hat: €______

(d) Snowboard helmet: €______

(e) Gloves: €______

(f) Base layer: €______

(g) Jacket: €______

(h) Ski goggles: €______

(i) Snowboard: €______

(j) Boots: €______

Percentage (%) extra free

We calculate % extra free the same way as we calculate an increase.

Increase by $\frac{40}{100} \rightarrow \frac{4}{10} \rightarrow \frac{2}{5}$ of 1kg = 400g

New weight: 1kg + 400g = 1·4kg

Short way

$\frac{5}{5} \rightarrow$ 1kg = 1,000g

$\frac{1}{5} \rightarrow \frac{1}{5}$kg = 200g

$\frac{7}{5} \rightarrow \frac{7}{5}$kg = 1,400g
= 1·4kg

1. Now work out the new amount of each of these.

(a) 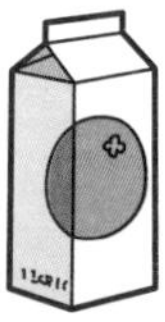
Was 1 litre,
now 20% extra free. _____ l

(b) 
Was pack of 10,
now 50% extra free. _____

(c) 
Old box = 2kg,
new box contains
25% extra free. _____ kg

(d) 

1·5 litres of frozen yoghurt,
new carton contains
10% extra free. _____ l

Percentage (%) extra free

Find the new cost of **one**.

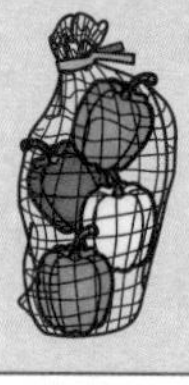

A pack of four peppers was €1·80.
Now 50% extra free.
How much does one pepper cost now?

→

We get 50% more peppers. 50% of 4 = 2.
We now get six peppers for €1·80.

$6\overline{)\text{€}1{\cdot}80}$
€0·30

One pepper costs 30c now.

2. Now do these.

(a) 

A tin of five tennis balls costs €12. Now 20% extra free. How much does one tennis ball now cost? € _____

(b) 

Bananas were four for €1. Now 25% extra free. One banana now costs _____ c or € _____.

(c) 

A six-pack of stickers now has 50% extra free. How much does one pack of stickers now cost?
_____ c or € _____

(d) 

A net of 10 oranges costs €2·80. The net now has 40% extra free. How much does one orange now cost? € _____

3. How much of a tip did each customer leave at each of these eateries?

(a) RECEIPT
Bob's BBQ
bill €109

Paid €10% tip.
Tip: € _____

(b) RECEIPT
Tina's Tapas
total due
€91·60

Gave tip of 20%.
Tip: € _____

(c) RECEIPT
Greg's Grill
total €80·56

Tipped 25%.
Tip: € _____

(d) RECEIPT
DAN'S DINER
AMOUNT
€120

Tipped 15%.
Tip: € _____

(e) RECEIPT
Barry's Burritos
total bill
€75·00

Gave 12% tip.
Tip: € _____

Changing fractions to decimals and percentages

We can change **any fraction** to a **decimal** or **percentage** by dividing the **numerator** by the **denominator**.

Example 1:

$$\frac{3}{4} = 4\overline{)\,3{\cdot}00}\ \text{(quotient } 0{\cdot}75) = 75\%$$

Example 2:

$$\frac{11}{20} = 20\overline{)\,11{\cdot}00}\ \text{(quotient } 0{\cdot}55) = 55\%$$

Example 3:

$$\frac{19}{25} = 25\overline{)\,19{\cdot}00}\ \text{(quotient } 0{\cdot}76) = 76\%$$

1. Now write these as (i) decimals and then as (ii) percentages.

(a) $\frac{2}{5}$ = (i) _____ (ii) _____

(b) $\frac{1}{4}$ = (i) _____ (ii) _____

(c) $\frac{17}{20}$ = (i) _____ (ii) _____

(d) $\frac{17}{25}$ = (i) _____ (ii) _____

(e) $\frac{13}{20}$ = (i) _____ (ii) _____

The calculator can do these a faster way. Always estimate first!

Example: $\frac{13}{20}$ = ☆ To do this, key the following into your calculator: [1] [3] [÷] [2] [0] [%]

The calculator gives the answer 65 ⟶ 65% or 0·65.

We don't have to press [=] when doing percentages on **most** calculators.

2. Have a go at these using the quick calculator method. Estimate first to see if the answer is >, = or < 0·5 (50%).

(a) $\frac{1}{2}$ = _____ (b) $\frac{3}{4}$ = _____ (c) $\frac{59}{100}$ = _____ (d) $\frac{47}{50}$ = _____ (e) $\frac{3}{25}$ = _____ (f) $\frac{4}{5}$ = _____

Using your calculator to change any fraction to a percentage or decimal with remainders

How do we change $\frac{1}{3}$ into a percentage and decimal?

Estimate first to see if the answer is >, = or < 0·5 (50%).

$3\overline{)\,1{\cdot}000}$ (quotient 0·333) or calculator method: [1] [÷] [3] [%] ⟶ 33·3333 ⟶

We usually only use 2 or 3 decimal places for percentages, so:

$\frac{1}{3}$ = 33·33%

3. Now write these as percentages using the quick calculator method. We only need 3 decimal places.

(a) $\frac{1}{6}$ = _____ (b) $\frac{1}{9}$ = _____ (c) $\frac{1}{12}$ = _____ (d) $\frac{1}{8}$ = _____ (e) $\frac{2}{3}$ = _____

(f) $\frac{5}{9}$ = _____ (g) $\frac{7}{12}$ = _____ (h) $\frac{5}{6}$ = _____ (i) $\frac{3}{8}$ = _____ (j) $\frac{7}{9}$ = _____

4. Aaron had €8. He spent €5 on a healthy burger. First write this information as a fraction. Then use a calculator to find (a) what decimal and (b) what percentage of his money he spent.

5. 

Eli spent $\frac{5}{12}$ of his money buying a hurley. Write (a) what decimal (to three places) and (b) what percentage of his money he spent. Estimate first.

Challenge

Use 3 decimal places.

Rachel spent $\frac{7}{12}$ of her money. Robert spent $\frac{11}{16}$ of his money.

What (i) decimal fraction and (ii) percentage of their money did each spend?

Rachel: (i) _____ (ii) _____ Robert: (i) _____ (ii) _____

Fractions, decimals, percentages – Use your calculator!

1. Each of these children got €100 for their birthdays. List their names in order starting with the one who spent the least percentage of their money. Estimate first.

(a) Janet spent $\frac{4}{9}$ of her money.

(b) Fred spent $\frac{7}{16}$ of his money.

(c) Rob had $\frac{1}{3}$ of his money left.

(d) Ava used $\frac{7}{12}$ of her money.

(i) ______ (ii) ______ (iii) ______ (iv) ______

Expressing a number as a percentage of another

We can see that $\frac{2}{5}$ of the tins of soup are missing.
What percentage of them is missing?
Estimate first to see if the answer is >, = or < 0·5 (50%).

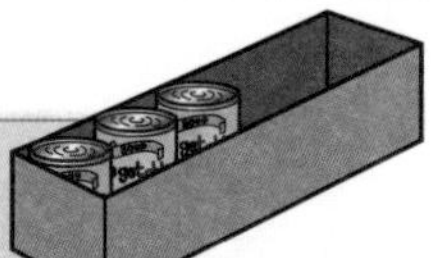

Quick way

$\frac{2}{_1\not{5}} \times \frac{\not{100}^{20}}{1} = \frac{40}{1} = 40\%$

Use your calculator, key in: 2 ÷ 5 % ⟶ 40. So 40% of them are missing.

2. Write a word sentence using percentages to explain each of these pictures.

(a)

(b)

(c)

(d)

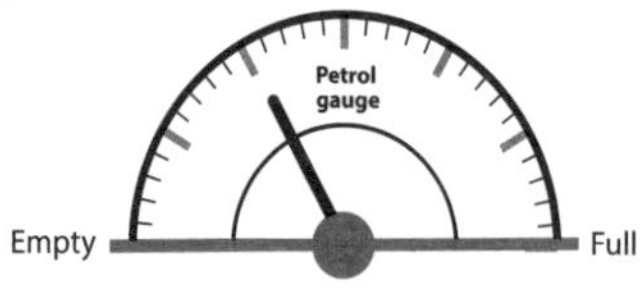

Now draw two pictures of your own and get your partner to make up a sentence for each.

3. Use your calculator to help you write each of these in order starting with the smallest.

(a) $\frac{5}{9}$, 0·57, 57·5%

(b) 39%, $\frac{5}{16}$, $\frac{8}{25}$

(c) 0·42, 40%, $\frac{5}{12}$

(d) $\frac{1}{12}$, 13%, $\frac{3}{16}$

(e) 0·85, $\frac{11}{12}$, $\frac{2}{3}$

(f) 99%, $\frac{24}{25}$, 0·975

(g) $\frac{2}{3}$, 62%, 0·64

(h) 0·88, 81%, $\frac{7}{8}$

(i) 78%, 0·775, $\frac{3}{4}$

4. Use a calculator to find out what percentage of sugar is in some foods that we eat. The answers might surprise you!

(a)

weight 22g
sugar 8g ______ %

(b)

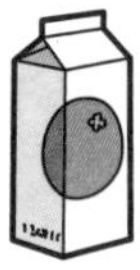

weight 240g
sugar 24g ______ %

(c)

weight 54g
sugar 28g ______ %

(d)

weight 45g
sugar 18g ______ %

Challenge Did you know that one teaspoon of sugar (or one sugar cube) contains 4g of sugar? Work out how many teaspoons of sugar are in each item in Question 4.

(a) ______ (b) ______ (c) ______ (d) ______

Increasing and decreasing

Using your calculator to calculate the percentage or decimal of a number

How much is 25% of 184?

We don't have to press [=] when doing percentages on **most** calculators.

To calculate a percentage, key in: [1] [8] [4] [×] [2] [5] [%] → 46   25% of 184 = 46

To calculate a decimal, key in: [1] [8] [4] [×] [0] [·] [2] [5] [=] → 46   0·25 of 184 = 46

1. Use the percentage method to do these. (Round each answer to the nearest whole number.)

(a) 33% of 90   (b) 17% of 83   (c) 25% of 1,024   (d) 39% of 600   (e) 5% of 945

2. Use the decimal method to do these. (Round each answer to the nearest whole number.)

(a) 0·75 of 13   (b) 0·09 of 431   (c) 0·99 of 850   (d) 0·53 of 871   (e) 0·43 of 666

Increasing or decreasing by a percentage using a calculator

A Example: Increase 130 by 45%.

100% + 45% = 145% or 1·45

(i) Percentage method, key in: [1] [3] [0] [×] [1] [4] [5] [%] → 188·5

(ii) Decimal method, key in: [1] [3] [0] [×] [1] [·] [4] [5] [=] → 188·5

B Example: Decrease 255 by 13%.

Remember,
100% – 13% = 87%.

(i) Percentage method, key in: [2] [5] [5] [×] [8] [7] [%] → 221·85

(ii) Decimal method, key in: [2] [5] [5] [×] [0] [·] [8] [7] [=] → 221·85

3. Use your calculator when doing these. (Round your answer to the nearest whole number.)

(a) Increase 8 by 25%.   (b) Decrease 18 by 50%.   (c) Reduce 20 by $\frac{1}{3}$.

(d) Increase 67 by 39%.   (e) What is 13% more than 20?   (f) 38% less than 50 is?

(g) Increase 279 by 17%.   (h) Make sixty 75% smaller.   (i) Make eighty nine 23% bigger.

(j) What number is 35% bigger than 50?   (k) Reduce 178 by 21%.

4. Use your calculator to work out the total costs below.

(a) **Restaurant bill:**

€243

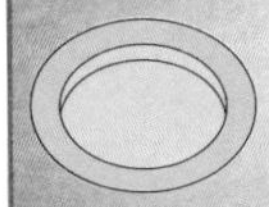

Add service charge of **13%**.

Total cost: € ______

(b) **Flight to Athens:**

€328 plus **3%** booking fee.

Total cost: € ______

(c) **Concert tickets:**

€45 each plus **4%** credit card charge on each ticket.

Two tickets cost: € ______

5. Use your calculator to help you make five fractions with a value between 50% and 75% inclusive using the numbers below.

9	7	1	8	11	4	2	16	5	3

Fractions, decimals, percentages – Review

1. Calculate the discount in money terms. Use your calculator. Only go to 2 decimal places.

(a) **Joe's Hardware**

€275
Now 15%
discount

Discount: €________

(b) **DIY Deals**

€190
12% discount now

Actual saving: €________

(c) **Swimming lessons €15 each**

Buy 5 lessons, get
15% discount.

Saving: €________

(d) **Toy Superstore**

Special offer!
11% discount on
your total bill
if you spend
over €100.

Bill before discount: €136·50
Actual discount: €________

2. How much have you learned about fractions, decimals and percentages? Complete.

(a) (i) $\frac{1}{2} + \frac{3}{4}$ ________ (ii) $2\frac{3}{4} + 3\frac{1}{8}$ ________ (iii) $2\frac{2}{3} + 1\frac{9}{12}$ ________ (iv) $3\frac{7}{8} - 1\frac{1}{4}$ ________ (v) $7\frac{1}{6} - 3\frac{2}{3}$ ________ (vi) $8\frac{5}{9} - 2\frac{2}{3}$ ________

(b) Write these improper fractions as mixed numbers in their lowest terms.

(i) $\frac{17}{3}$ (ii) $\frac{29}{6}$ (iii) $\frac{41}{7}$ (iv) $\frac{69}{8}$ (v) $\frac{88}{9}$ (vi) $\frac{73}{5}$

(c) Write in order starting with the smallest.

(i) 75%, 0·8, $\frac{3}{5}$, 0·09 (ii) 0·39, $\frac{429}{1000}$, 40%, 0·6 (iii) $\frac{47}{1000}$, 46%, $\frac{7}{10}$, 0·459

(d) Increase: (i) €40 by 10%; (ii) €60 by 20%; (iii) 0·7 by 100%; (iv) 48 by 0·25 of itself.

(e) Decrease: (i) €90 by 50%; (ii) €70 by 10%; (iii) 80 by 20%; (iv) 40 by 0·75 of itself.

3. Complete these. (Use your calculator if you wish.)

(a) 
Jenny spent $\frac{1}{3}$ of her €120 on a skateboard and 50% of what was left on kneepads. How much did she spend altogether? € ________

(b) Tony spends $\frac{1}{3}$ of a full day at work. He spends 25% as long watching television. How long does he spend watching television? ________
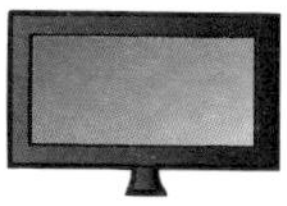

(c) 15% of the children in a youth club have black hair. 65% have brown hair. The remaining 36 children all have blonde hair. How many children have black hair? ________

(d) Tara walks $\frac{1}{8}$ of her journey to work. She travels 62·5% of her journey by train. She completes her journey by bus. If she travels 13km by bus, what distance does she travel by train? ________ km

Chapter 25: Weight

Here are some common items, people and animals with their approximate weights.
We use **grammes** and **kilogrammes** to measure weight.

Remember: 1,000g = 1kg
$1g = \frac{1}{1000}kg = 0{\cdot}001kg$

We use a variety of different weighing tools to measure weight.

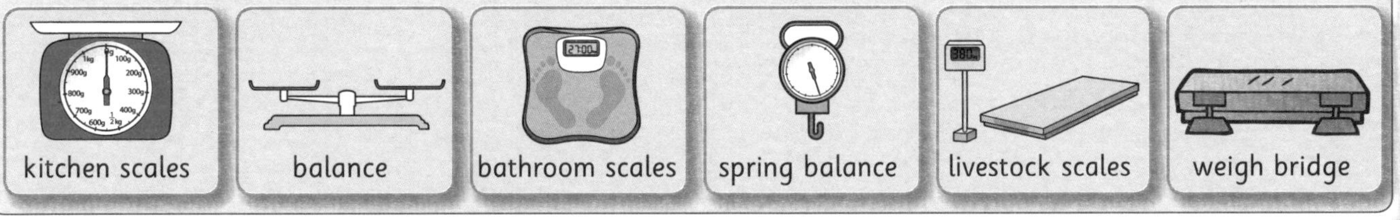

Circle what you think is the best estimate for the weight of each of these. Select the best measuring tool. Discuss.

	Approximate weight of:		Measure with:
(a)		2g 20g 220g	
(b)		600g 1·7kg 150g	
(c)		2kg 5kg 12kg	
(d)	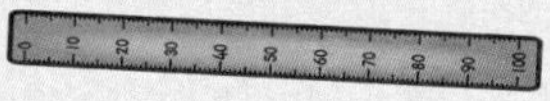	150g 15g 5g	
(e)		90kg 500kg 1,200kg	
(f)		1·1kg 270g 680g	
(g)		10g 350g 100g	
(h)		3,750kg 2,100kg 350kg	
(i)		250g 1·25kg 25g	
(j)		350g 750g 85g	

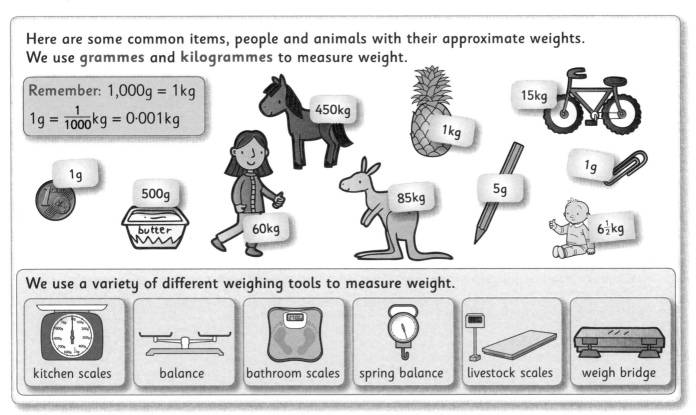

Maths Fact 110·4kg of gold was used to make a coffin for Egyptian pharaoh Tutankhamun. If half of this gold was stolen, how much would be left? ____ kg

Kilogrammes using fractions and decimals

We have seen that 1g = $\frac{1}{1000}$kg = 0·001kg.

741g = $\frac{741}{1000}$kg = 0·741kg | 34g = $\frac{34}{1000}$kg = 0·034kg | 9g = $\frac{9}{1000}$kg = 0·009kg

1. Write these grammes as fractions and decimals of kilogrammes.

4g = $\frac{4}{1000}$kg = 0·004kg

(a) 9g = ____ kg = ____ kg
(b) 14g ____ kg = ____ kg
(c) 3g = ____ kg = ____ kg
(d) 416g = ____ kg = ____ kg
(e) 228g = ____ kg = ____ kg
(f) 67g = ____ kg = ____ kg
(g) 923g = ____ kg = ____ kg
(h) 503g = ____ kg = ____ kg
(i) 156g = ____ kg = ____ kg
(j) 830g = ____ kg = ____ kg
(k) 449g = ____ kg = ____ kg

2. Write these decimal kilogramme weights as fractions of a kilogramme and as grammes.

0·047kg = $\frac{47}{1000}$kg = 47g

(a) 0·533kg = ____ kg = ____ g
(b) 0·006kg = ____ kg = ____ g
(c) 0·072kg = ____ kg = ____ g
(d) 0·272kg = ____ kg = ____ g
(e) 0·65kg = ____ kg = ____ g
(f) 0·165kg = ____ kg = ____ g
(g) 0·81kg = ____ kg = ____ g
(h) 0·01kg = ____ kg = ____ g
(i) 0·384kg = ____ kg = ____ g
(j) 0·7kg = ____ kg = ____ g
(k) 0·99kg = ____ kg = ____ g

Hot Tip! Metric systems are designed for decimals – so use them!
Fill in all the decimal places. **8·27kg = 8,270g**

4,376g = 4·376kg	3,017g = 3·017kg	5,008g = 5·008kg	8,470g = 8·470kg
2·915kg = 2,915g	4·078kg = 4,078g	8·007kg = 8,007g	9·8kg = 9,800g

3. Change these kilogramme weights to grammes.

1·859kg = 1,859g

(a) 2·736kg = ________ g
(b) 6·259kg = ________ g
(c) 4·372kg = ________ g
(d) 3·257kg = ________ g
(e) 8·057kg = ________ g
(f) 5·418kg = ________ g
(g) 6·45kg = ________ g
(h) 3·3kg = ________ g
(i) 3·709kg = ________ g
(j) 8·731kg = ________ g
(k) 5·008kg = ________ g

4. Now change these grammes to kilogrammes.

2,147g = 2·147kg

(a) 1,737g = ________ kg
(b) 1,459g = ________ kg
(c) 6,281g = ________ kg
(d) 2,046g = ________ kg
(e) 990g = ________ kg
(f) 3,553g = ________ kg
(g) 8,300g = ________ kg
(h) 6,430g = ________ kg
(i) 7,084g = ________ kg
(j) 5,308g = ________ kg
(k) 9,004g = ________ kg

Maths Fact The Indonesian Komodo dragon is the largest lizard on Earth, weighing up to 136kg. If, after one particularly large meal, the Komodo dragon's weight increased by 0·25, what would he weigh then? ________ kg

Weight: +, –, × and ÷

Paul and Niamh are going on holiday and have a baggage allowance of 30kg in total. Niamh's suitcase weighs 14kg 795g and Paul's has a weight of 15·886kg. Will they be over the baggage allowance?

Their baggage is too heavy by 0·681kg.

kg	g
14	795
+ 15	886
30	681

or

Quick way

14·795kg
+ 15·886kg
30·681kg

1. Add these weights to check if they are under the baggage allowance of 30kg.

(a) kg g: 14 634 + 15 689

(b) kg g: 16 529 + 15 737

(c) kg g: 18 326 + 11 675

(d) 19·549kg + 12·774kg

(e) 15·114kg + 13·896kg

We can subtract **kg** and **g** in the same manner as addition.

kg	g
30	681
– 14	795
15	886

or

Quick way

30·681kg
– 14·795kg
15·886kg

2. (a) kg g: 23 526 – 17 617

(b) 37·218kg – 19·338kg

(c) kg g: 16 205 – 14 117

(d) 37·772kg – 28·783kg

(e) kg g: 9 300 – 6 524

(f) 10·091kg – 8·295kg

(g) kg g: 12 431 – 6 833

(h) 20·375kg – 17·507kg

This is how we multiply and divide using **kg**.

A

kg	g
8	435
×	7
59	045

or

Quick way

8·435kg
× 7
59·045kg

B

kg g
6) 15 228
2 538

or

Quick way

6) 15·228 kg
2·538 kg

3. (a) kg g: 17 547 × 8

(b) 9·374kg × 7

(c) 26·538kg × 9

(d) kg g: 15 269 × 6

(e) kg g: 38 209 × 7

(f) 24·563kg × 8

4. (a) 6) 42·684 kg

(b) kg g: 4) 14 352

(c) kg g: 7) 56 259

(d) 8) 21·496 kg

(e) 9) 40·554 kg

5. (a) (3·975kg + 647g + 2kg 494g) × 7

(b) ($6\frac{532}{1000}$kg + 7,278g + 5kg 166g) × 8

(c) (7kg 286g + $4\frac{1}{4}$ kg + 3,669g) ÷ 5

(d) ($11\frac{249}{1000}$kg + 3kg 53g + 4·722kg) ÷ 8

(e) (16·553kg – $7\frac{654}{1000}$kg) × 9

(f) (24kg 52g – 6,655g) ÷ 9

Maths Fact

There are only 6 grammes of gold in a modern Olympic gold medal. The rest is made up of silver and copper. If each Olympic gold medal weighs 400g, write as kg the weight of other metals that make up each medal. ______ kg

Weight – Real-life problems

Solve the following problems.

1. Joe is baking a cake and the recipe tells him to use $\frac{1}{5}$kg of flour. How many grammes is that? _____ g

2. When Joe had baked his cake, it weighed 1kg 400g. He cut it into eight equal slices. What did each slice weigh in g? _____ g

3. At the Pizza Plaza, the chef has made seven pizza bases in the last hour. Each weighs 167g. What is the total weight in kg of all seven pizza bases? _____ kg

4. The Pizza Plaza got a delivery of supplies weighing 26 $\frac{726}{1000}$ kg. They used all their supplies during a seven-day festival and they used the same amount each day. How much did they use each day? _____ kg

5. A bunch of eight bananas weighs 1kg 8g. Two bananas are eaten. One weighed 0·117kg and the other weighed 126g. What is the weight of the remaining bananas in kg? _____ kg

6. 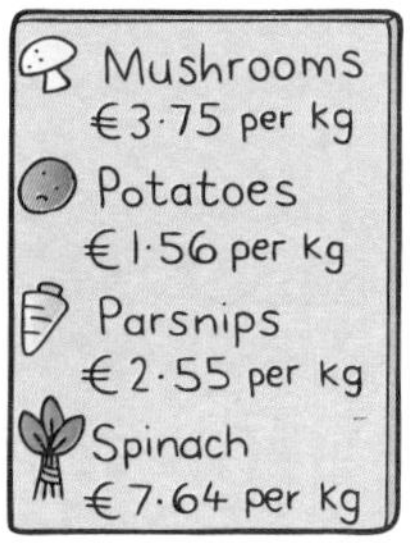

Tara went to the farmers' market and bought 200g of mushrooms, 5kg 250g of potatoes, 0·4kg of parsnips and $\frac{750}{1000}$ kg of spinach. What change did she get from €20 after her purchases? € _____

7. 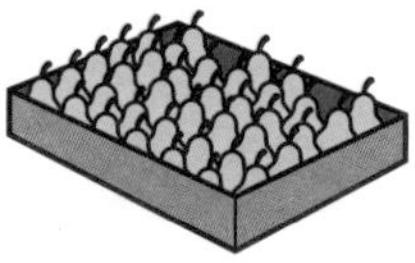

The total weight of three boxes of pears is 98·842kg. One box weighs 24$\frac{1}{2}$kg and the second box weighs 37 $\frac{593}{1000}$ kg. What is the weight of the third box? _____ kg

8. Tim weighs 13kg 223g. His older brother weighs four times this amount. How much do the two boys weigh together? _____ kg

9. 

A butcher sold 22·586kg of steak in the morning. He sold 18$\frac{3}{4}$kg in the afternoon. If he had 78kg 92g of steak at the beginning of the day, how much steak had he left at the end of the day? _____ kg

10. The zoo transported these animals to a new home: a penguin weighing 3·45kg; a giraffe weighing 527kg 675g; a chimp weighing 53·177kg and a giant tortoise weighing 168kg 680g. What was the total weight of the animals in the transport truck? _____ kg

11. A machine in a dog food factory was loaded with 20kg of meat. It filled 39 tins with 167g of meat in each tin before breaking down. What was the amount of meat left in the machine? _____ kg

Maths Fact Queen Victoria was given a wedding present of an enormous wheel of cheese weighing 450kg.

If Queen Victoria's household ate an equal amount of this cheese each day during April and consumed it all, what would have been the daily consumption? _____ kg

Weight – Food, glorious food!

When we know the cost of a certain quantity, we can then calculate the cost per kg.

A A tin of coffee costs €4·76 for 100g. How much per kg?

100g = $\frac{1}{10}$kg   €4·76
× 10
1kg ⟶ €47·60

B How much for 250g of the coffee?

250g = $\frac{1}{4}$kg   4) €47·60
250g ⟶ €11·90

C A tin of macaroni cheese costs €1·68. It holds 400g. How much per kg?

400g = €1·68
100g = 4) €1·68
€0·42 per 100g
× 10
1kg (1,000g) = €4·20

D Bolognese sauce costs €2·58 for 300g. How much per kg? 300g = €2·58

3) €2·58
€0·86 per 100g
€0·86 × 10 ⟶ €8·60 per kg

1. Complete.

	Item		Weight	Cost	Cost per kg
(a)	Chickpeas		500g	€1·29	
(b)	Tin of tomato soup		400g	€1·48	
(c)	Red cheddar cheese	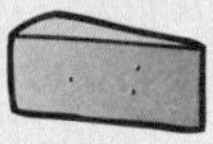	200g	€3·34	
(d)	Barbecue ribs		750g	€4·86	
(e)	Chicken goujons	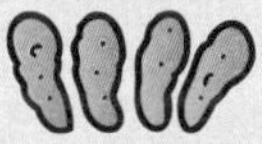	250g	€2·28	
(f)	Whole chicken	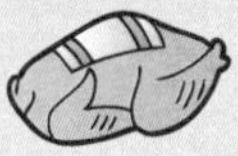	1·5kg	€5·10	
(g)	Dishwasher salt		2·25kg	€2·43	
(h)	Breakfast cereal		800g	€6·16	
(i)	Dog food mix		4kg 500g	€13·32	
(j)	Multi-pack dog food		6 × 400g	€4·80	

2. 3,630kg of food has to be brought into space to feed a crew of three people on a six-month-long visit to the International Space Station. How much is that per person per month to the nearest kg? ______ kg

Maths Fact

The T-Rex dinosaur could eat up to 227kg of meat in one bite. How much meat would be eaten by a T-Rex in 12 full-size bites? ______ kg

A quick look back 7

LOOK BACK

1. Write 0·57 as a percentage. ______ %

2. 

Alex ate 53% of the pancake. Amy ate the rest. Write how much Amy ate in decimal form.

______

3. Write 7·083 as a mixed number.

______ $\frac{\square}{\square}$

4. Ring the largest amount:

8·19   82% $\frac{4}{5}$ 7·999

5. How much is 0·6 of 300? ______

6. Ursula ran for 80% of an hour. For how many minutes did she run?

______ minutes

7. 

What is the total length of 10 straws each 16cm long?

Give your answer in metres. ______ m

8. 0·9 of a number is 198.

The number is ______ .

9. Lenny got €50 from his grandad.

He spent 30% of it on a book and 0·2 of it on a drink.

How much did he spend altogether?

€ ______

10. Increase 36kg by 50%. ______ kg

11. The temperature in Oslo one day was ⁻9° Celsius. The temperature in Dublin was ⁺15°C. What was the difference in temperature between the two cities?

______ °C

12. What is the difference between ⁻8°C and ⁺31°C? ______ °C

13. 

A scarf usually costs €15. During a sale, it was reduced by 20%. What was the sale price?

€ ______

14. A watermelon can be bought in one shop for €4·50. It costs 10% more in another shop. What is the difference in the prices? € ______

15. Write 10kg as a percentage of 50kg.

______ %

16. Write 2,173g as kilogrammes using a decimal point. ______ kg

17. 

A box of bananas weighs 8·4kg. Another box is 10% lighter. Write the difference in weight in kg.

______ kg

18. A tin of vegetable soup costs €1·20. How much would 2kg of the soup cost?

€ ______

19. What is 0·37 of 200? ______

20. Write 12kg as a percentage of 40kg.

______ %

Chapter 26: Number theory

3 × 2 = 6
↑ ↑ ↑
factor × factor = product

When we multiply two **factors**, the answer is called the **product**.

Every number has itself and 1 as factors.

7 × 9 = 63
↑ ↑ ↑
factor × factor = product

1. Find the product of each of these pairs of factors.

(a) 2 × 6 = ______ (b) 3 × 5 = ______ (c) 4 × 8 = ______ (d) 2 × 9 = ______

(e) 3 × 11 = ______ (f) 4 × 12 = ______ (g) 5 × 7 = ______ (h) 6 × 9 = ______

Some numbers have many related pairs of factors.

Each factor is only written once.

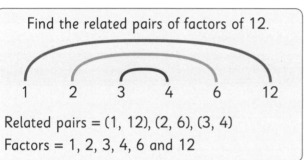

Find the related pairs of factors of 12.

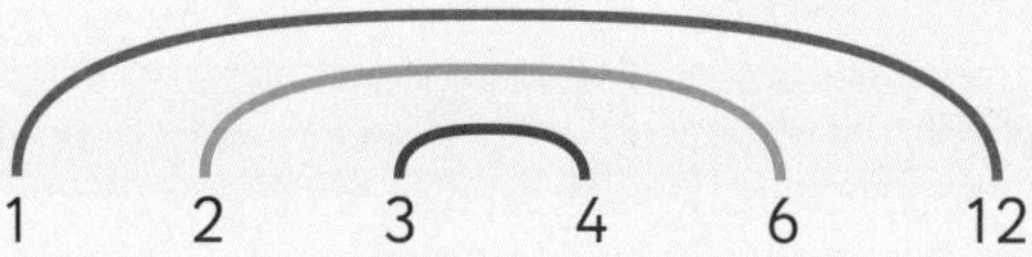

Related pairs = (1, 12), (2, 6), (3, 4)

Factors = 1, 2, 3, 4, 6 and 12

Find the related pairs of factors of 16.

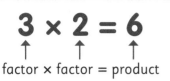

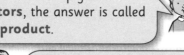

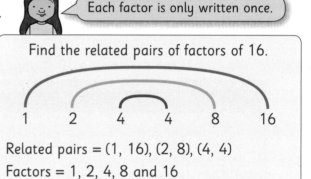

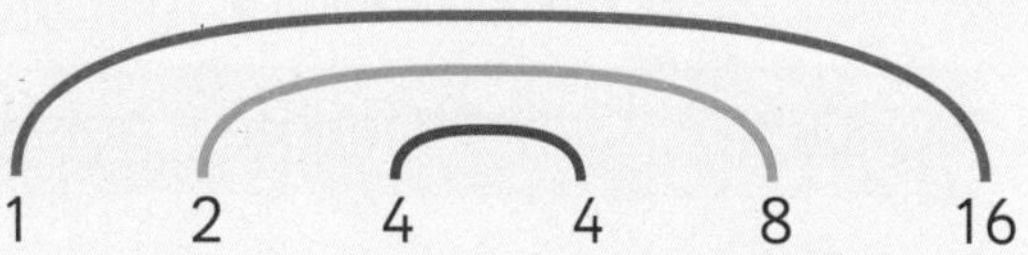

Related pairs = (1, 16), (2, 8), (4, 4)

Factors = 1, 2, 4, 8 and 16

2. (i) **Write the related pairs of factors for each of these numbers and** (ii) **order the factors starting with the smallest.**

	Number	(i) Related pairs of factors	(ii) All factors of the number
(a)	4	(1, 4), (2, 2)	1, 2, 4
(b)	9		
(c)	15		
(d)	17		
(e)	18		
(f)	24		
(g)	27		

---

3. Write true or false after each statement.

(a) The only factor of 1 is 1. ______

(b) Factor is another name for product. ______

(c) Factors of all numbers include the number itself and 0. ______

(d) The factors of 2 are 1 and 2. ______

(e) The product of 6 and 9 is 69. ______

(f) A factor is a whole number that will divide exactly into another whole number. ______

(g) 2 and 3 are factors of 6, 12, 18, 24 and 30. ______

(h) 4 and 6 are factors of 4, 6, 12, 16, 24 and 30. ______

(i) 2 is a factor of all even numbers. ______

(j) 3 is a factor of all odd numbers. ______

(k) 19 has only two factors. ______

(l) The factors of 84 are 12 and 7. ______

Multiples

We often use multiples of numbers to help us count quicker.

A

2c 4c 6c 8c 10c

The **multiples** of 2 are
2, 4, 6, 8, 10, 12, 14, 16...

B

5c 10c 15c 20c 25c

The **multiples** of 5 are
5, 10, 15, 20, 25, 30, 35, 40...

1. Write the first five multiples of each of the following numbers.

(a) 3 (b) 6 (c) 8 (d) 7 (e) 4 (f) 9 (g) 10 (h) 12 (i) 15

2. Write the 1st, 4th, 7th, 9th and 10th multiples of the following.

	Number	1st multiple	4th multiple	7th multiple	9th multiple	10th multiple
(a)	3	3				
(b)	5		20			
(c)	9			63		
(d)	11				99	
(e)	12					120
(f)	15		60			
(g)	20					
(h)	25			175		
(i)	50					

3. (a) Circle the **multiples** of 7: 7, 20, 21, 27, 35, 56, 67, 70, 75, 84.

(b) Circle the **multiples** of 8: 15, 16, 24, 29, 32, 40, 64, 68, 74, 88.

(c) Circle the **multiples** of 6: 12, 19, 30, 36, 41, 48, 54, 56, 66, 74.

(d) Circle the **multiples** of 9: 12, 18, 27, 36, 48, 63, 81, 85, 90, 93.

4. True ✓ or false ✗?

(a) 12 is a multiple of 3. ☐

(c) All multiples of 9 are not all multiples of 3. ☐

(e) The next multiple of 5 after 20 is 30. ☐

(g) 45 is a multiple of both 5 and 9. ☐

(i) 18 is a multiple of 3, 6 and 9. ☐

(k) All multiples of 4 are multiples of 2. ☐

(m) All multiples of 2 are multiples of 4. ☐

(o) All multiples of 3 are multiples of 9. ☐

(b) 3 is a multiple of 12. ☐

(d) 4 is the 2nd multiple of 2. ☐

(f) 20 is the 5th multiple of 5. ☐

(h) 49 is the 6th multiple of 7. ☐

(j) 66 is a multiple of 9. ☐

(l) 72 is a multiple of 7, 8 and 9. ☐

(n) 144 is a multiple of 2, 6 and 12. ☐

(p) 3,000 is a multiple of 30 and 300. ☐

Prime and composite numbers

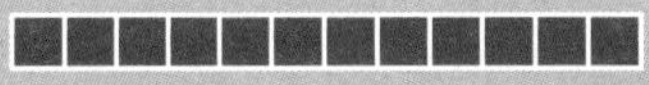

1 × 12 = 12

2 × 6 = 12

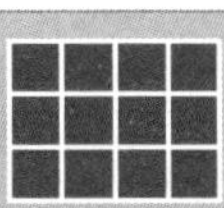

3 × 4 = 12

12 has factors 1, 2, 3, 4, 6 and 12.

If a number has more than itself and 1 as factors, it is a **composite** number, e.g. 12.

1 × 7

7 has only 2 factors.
The factors are 1 and 7 itself.

If a number has only itself and 1 as factors, it is a **prime** number, e.g. 7.

1	2	3	4	5	6	7	8	9	10
11	12	13	14	15	16	17	18	19	20
21	22	23	24	25	26	27	28	29	30
31	32	33	34	35	36	37	38	39	40
41	42	43	44	45	46	47	48	49	50
51	52	53	54	55	56	57	58	59	60
61	62	63	64	65	66	67	68	69	70
71	72	73	74	75	76	77	78	79	80
81	82	83	84	85	86	87	88	89	90
91	92	93	94	95	96	97	98	99	100

1. Finding prime numbers on a hundred square.

Eratosthenes was a famous Greek mathematician. He invented the first known method of finding prime numbers. Complete the following on the hundred square:

(a) Cross out all multiples of 2, except 2.

(b) Cross out all multiples of 3, except 3.

(c) Cross out all multiples of 5, except 5.

(d) Cross out all multiples of 7, except 7.

You are now left with the prime numbers!

The number 1 is neither a prime nor composite.

Helpful hints to determine if numbers are prime or composite

A number is divisible by a smaller number if it can be divided evenly by the smaller number without a remainder.

20 is divisible by 5.
20 ÷ 5 = 4 exactly

11 does not divide evenly by 3.
11 ÷ 3 = 3 remainder 2

Helpful divisibility tests for numbers greater than 99:

	Divisible by:	The test:	Example:
(a)	2?	If the last digit is even.	82**6** ✓ **6** is even
(b)	4?	If the last two digits are ÷ 4.	1**48** ✓ **48** ÷ 4 = 12
(c)	8?	If the last three digits are ÷ 8.	2,**456** ✓ **456** ÷ 8 = 57
(d)	5?	If the last digit is 0 or 5.	57**5** ✓ Last digit is **5**

	Divisible by:	The test:	Example:
(e)	3?	If the sum of the digits ÷ 3.	**192** ✓ **1** + **9** + **2** = 12 12 ÷ 3 = 4
(f)	6?	If tests for 2 and 3 work.	642 ✓ 642 is even 6 + 4 + 2 = 12
(g)	9?	If the sum of the digits ÷ 9.	**3,573** ✓ **3** + **5** + **7** + **3** = 18 18 ÷ 9 = 2
(h)	10?	If the last digit is 0.	5,79**0** ✓ Last digit is **0**

2. Circle the divisors of each number. Use the divisibility rules to help you!

	Number:	Divisible by:
(a)	64	(1) (2) 3 (4) 5 6 7 (8) 9 10
(b)	346	1 2 3 4 5 6 7 8 9 10
(c)	1,701	1 2 3 4 5 6 7 8 9 10

	Number:	Divisible by:
(d)	90	1 2 3 4 5 6 7 8 9 10
(e)	1,446	1 2 3 4 5 6 7 8 9 10
(f)	4,328	1 2 3 4 5 6 7 8 9 10

Prime or composite?

1. Work out whether the following numbers are **prime** or **composite**. Tick (✓) the correct box.

	Number	Prime	Composite
(a)	9		
(b)	11		
(c)	19		
(d)	26		
(e)	39		

	Number	Prime	Composite
(f)	89		
(g)	164		
(h)	197		
(i)	356		
(j)	980		

	Number	Prime	Composite
(k)	1,853		
(l)	1,848		
(m)	3,485		
(n)	3,246		
(o)	9,998		

2. Work out whether the following numbers are prime or composite. Match.

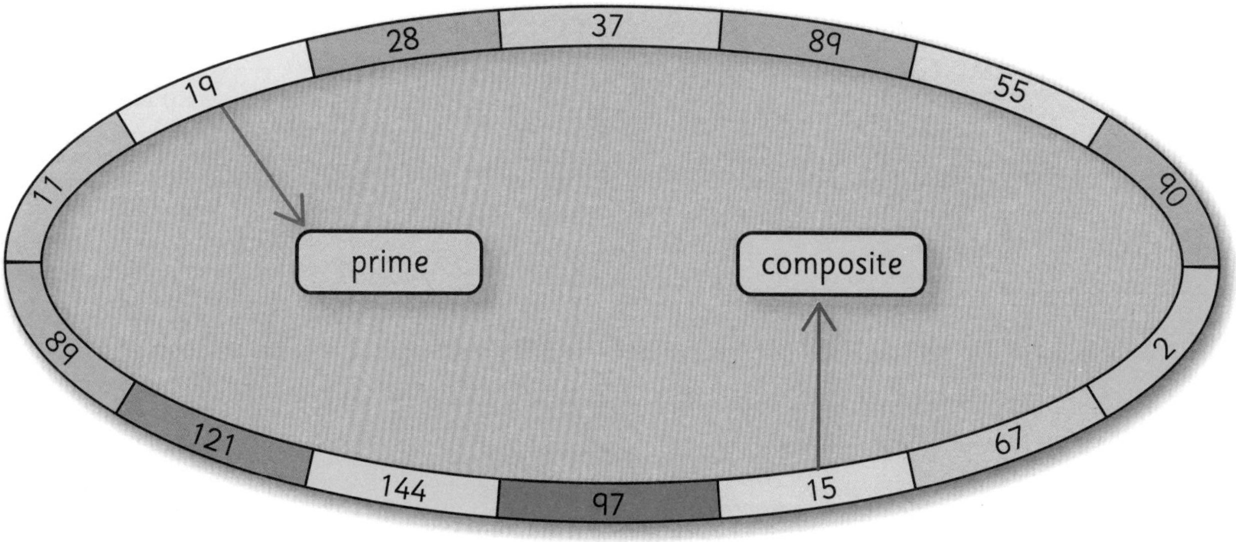

3. Circle the number in each group that is **not** a composite number.

(a) 20, 21, 22, 23, 24, 25, 26, 27.

(b) 32, 33, 34, 35, 36, 37, 38, 39, 40.

(c) 48, 49, 50, 51, 52, 53, 54, 55, 56.

(d) 74, 75, 76, 77, 78, 79, 80, 81, 82.

4. Use the rules of Eratosthenes to answer the following.

(a) How many prime numbers are there between 1 and 100? ________

(b) Find the sum of the three prime numbers between 40 and 50. ________

(c) Find the difference between the two prime numbers between 20 and 30. ________

(d) How many composite numbers are there from 1 to 100 inclusive? ________

(e) List the prime numbers between 80 and 90. ________

(f) How many even prime numbers are there between 1 and 100? ________

(g) Find the difference between the smallest and largest prime numbers on the hundred square. ________

(h) What is the smallest composite number? ________

Challenge

(a) Find two prime numbers that have a total of 60. ____ and ____

(b) Find three prime numbers that have a total of 75. ____, ____ and ____

Odd and even numbers

1. **Use your hundred square to help you complete the following.**
   (a) All odd numbers end in one of these digits: ____, ____, 5, ____, ____.
   (b) All even numbers end in one of these digits: ____, ____, ____, ____, 0.

2. **Write all the odd numbers from:**
   (a) 22 to 24 (b) 42 to 52 (c) 76 to 90 (d) 162 to 174 (e) 1,230 to 1,250

3. **Write all the even numbers from:**
   (a) 27 to 39 (b) 55 to 67 (c) 81 to 95 (d) 123 to 137 (e) 1,117 to 1,131

4. **Use two dice to complete the following. Write whether the answer is odd or even.**
   (a) odd + odd = ________ (b) odd − odd = ________ (c) odd × odd = ________
   (d) odd + even = ________ (e) odd − even = ________ (f) odd × even = ________

Goldbach, a mathematician, stated that every even number greater than 2 can be found by adding together two prime numbers. No one has ever proved his statement incorrect – if you do, you will be famous!

5. **Discover if Goldbach's statement is true for these even numbers.** (There may be more than one answer!)

Number	Prime + Prime
8	3 + 5
10	+
12	+
14	+
16	+

Number	Prime + Prime
28	+
32	+
36	+
40	+
44	+

Number	Prime + Prime
48	+
52	+
66	+
74	+
82	+

When two prime numbers are subtracted, the answer is always an even number.

17 − 11 = 6 | 29 − 17 = 10 | 53 − 37 = 14
prime − prime = even | prime − prime = even | prime − prime = even

There may be more than one answer!

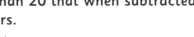

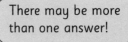

6. **Find two prime numbers less than 20 that when subtracted give the following even numbers.**
   (a) 11 − ____ = 4 (b) ____ − 13 = 6 (c) 19 − ____ = 12
   (d) ____ − ____ = 10 (e) ____ − ____ = 8 (f) ____ − ____ = 14

7. **Find two prime numbers less than 100 that when subtracted give the following even numbers.**
   (a) 31 − ____ = 20 (b) ____ − ____ = 18 (c) ____ − ____ = 16

Challenge Find two prime numbers between 100 and 150 that when subtracted, give the even number 38 as the answer. ____ and ____

Numbers with shape

A **rectangular number** can be arranged into the shape of a rectangle. Both factors must be greater than 1.

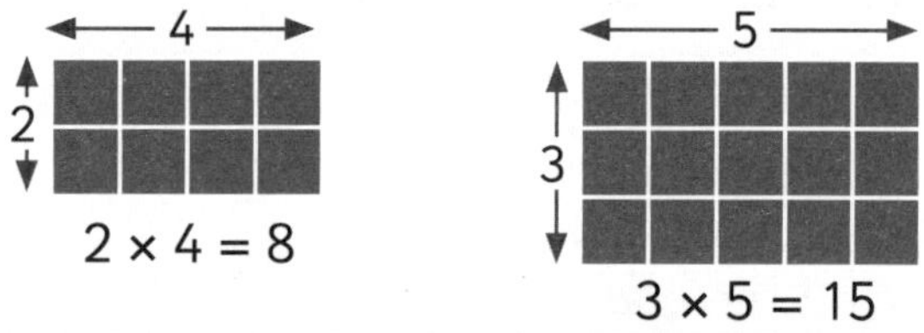

1. Draw rectangles for these rectangular numbers.

(a) 6 (b) 10 (c) 20 (d) 40
(e) 14 (f) 16 (g) 30 (h) 42

Some numbers have more than one rectangular shape. Example: 12 = 6 × 2 and 3 × 4.

2. Draw at least two rectangular shapes for each of these rectangular numbers.

(a) 18 (b) 24 (c) 36 (d) 48 (e) 12 (f) 72 (g) 100

3. Circle the rectangular numbers.

(a) 3, 5, 7, 10, 11, 14, 21, 35.
(b) 15, 17, 18, 19, 23, 29, 38, 63.
(c) 31, 33, 35, 37, 39, 41, 46, 54.
(d) 45, 47, 49, 51, 53, 59, 77, 93.

4. Circle the numbers that are not rectangular.

(a) 6, 11, 15, 17, 21, 25, 37, 43.
(b) 32, 34, 39, 43, 52, 57, 61, 67.
(c) 61, 63, 67, 39, 71, 75, 79, 83.
(d) 79, 81, 84, 89, 91, 97, 99, 101.

5.

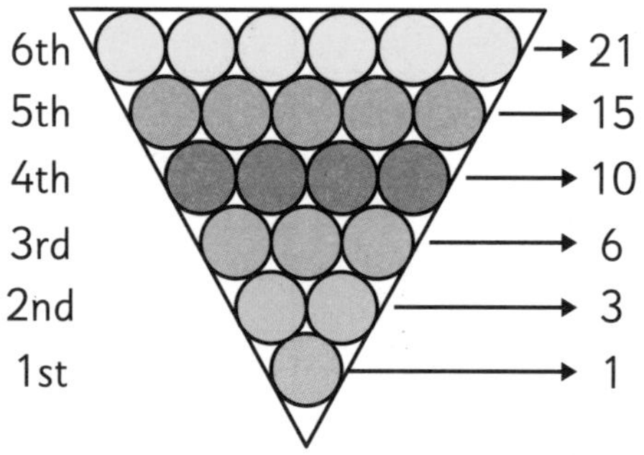

A **triangular number** can be arranged in the shape of a triangle. Do you see the pattern? Continue the pattern to find the next three triangular numbers.

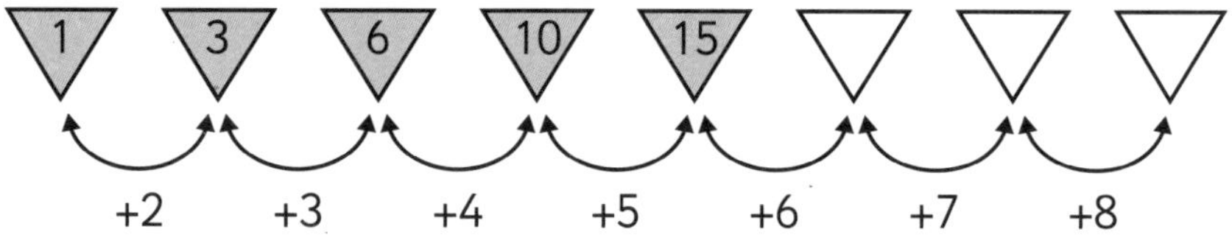

6. Complete this table showing triangular numbers. Follow the pattern. Complete the diagram.

1st	= 1	→	1
2nd	= 1 + 2	→	3
3rd	= 1 + 2 + 3	→	6
4th	=	→	10
5th	=	→	
6th	=	→	
7th	=	→	
8th	=	→	
9th	=	→	
10th	=	→	

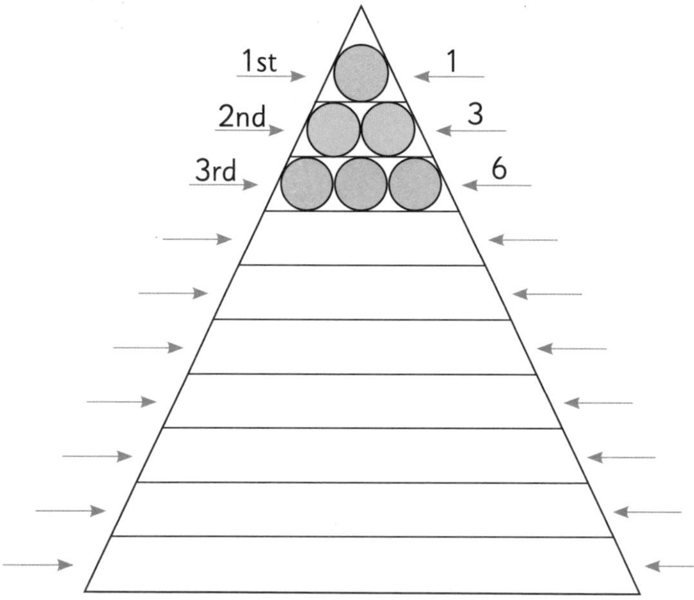

Square numbers

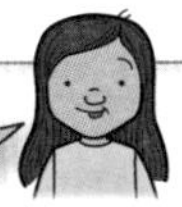

When a number is multiplied by itself, the product is a square number.

Here are the first five square numbers:

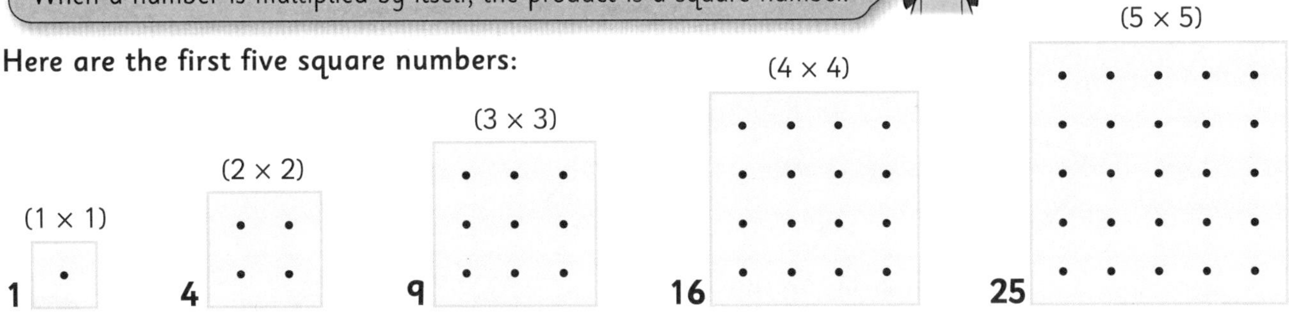

Can you see a pattern that makes it easy to calculate square numbers?

1. Now draw these six square numbers using dots as above.

(a) 6 × 6 (b) 7 × 7 (c) 8 × 8 (d) 9 × 9 (e) 10 × 10 (f) 11 × 11

2. Use your calculator to work out the following.

(a) 12th square number (b) 16th square number (c) 22nd square number

Add consecutive odd numbers. What do you notice?

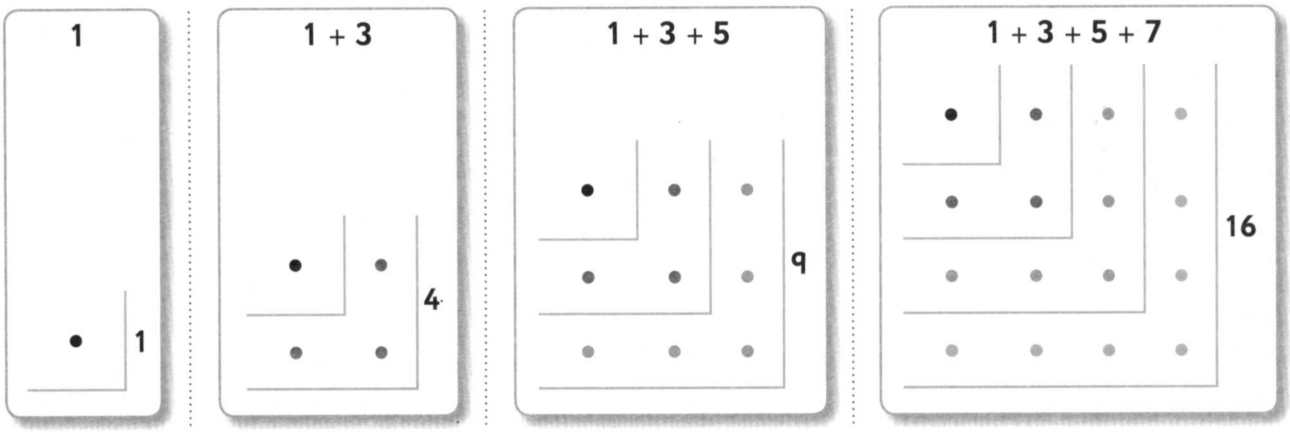

These are the first four square numbers as the sum of consecutive odd numbers.

3. Continue the dot pattern to show the remaining square numbers up to 100 as the sum of consecutive odd numbers. You may use a geoboard.

4. Complete this table.

	Consecutive odd numbers	Square numbers
1st	1	= 1 or (1 × 1)
2nd	1 + 3	= 4 or (2 × 2)
3rd	1 + 3 + 5	= 9 or (3 × 3)
4th	1 + 3 + 5 + 7	= or
5th	1 + 3 + 5 + 7 + 9	= or
6th	1 + 3 + 5 + 7 + 9 + 11	= or
7th	1 + 3 + 5 + 7 + 9 + 11 + 13	= or

Chapter 27: The circle

Parts of the circle

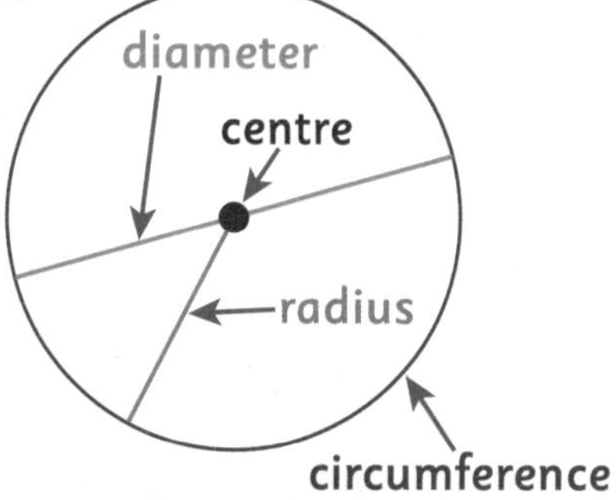

The plural of radius is radii.
It is pronounced ray-dee-eye!

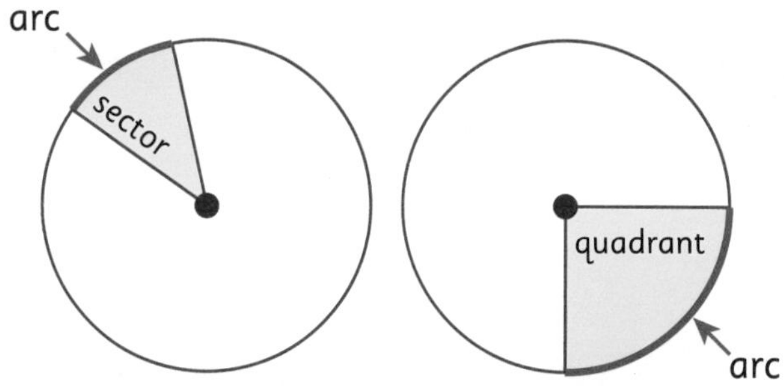

An arc is a part of the circumference.
A sector is a section of the circle made by an arc and two radii.
A quadrant is $\frac{1}{4}$ of the circle.

1. Which part of the circle does each of the following sentences describe?

(a) Any straight line from the centre to the circumference. ______________

(b) A slice of the circle between two radii. ______________

(c) The perimeter or curved side of the circle. ______________

(d) A section of the circumference. ______________

(e) The middle point inside the circle. ______________

(f) Any straight line from one side of the circle to the other, passing through the centre. ______________

(g) A sector that is exactly $\frac{1}{4}$ of the circle. ______________

2. True ✓ or false ✗?

(a) An arc is a straight line. ☐

(b) A radius is half the diameter. ☐

(c) A circle can only have one centre. ☐

(d) A diameter is a line of symmetry. ☐

(e) A diameter makes a right angle. ☐

(f) A quadrant is a sector. ☐

(g) A circle can only have one diameter. ☐

(h) A sector is always a quadrant. ☐

3. Use your protractor to measure each angle made by the sectors.

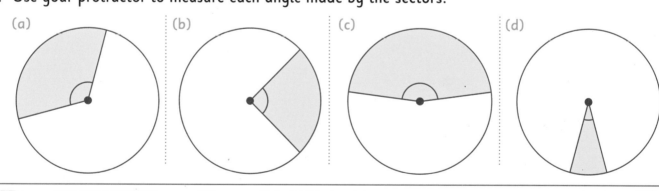

(a)

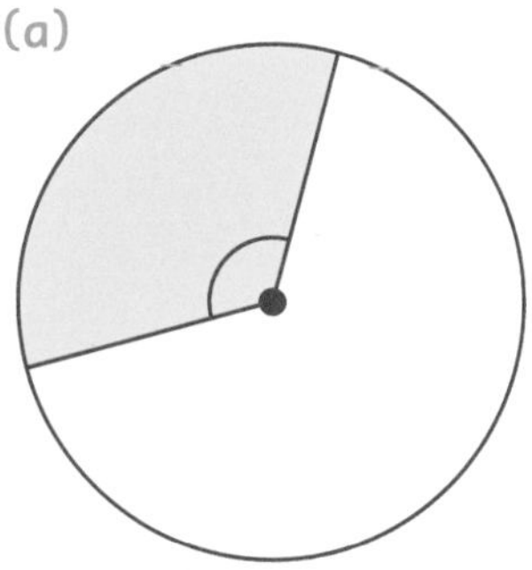

(b)

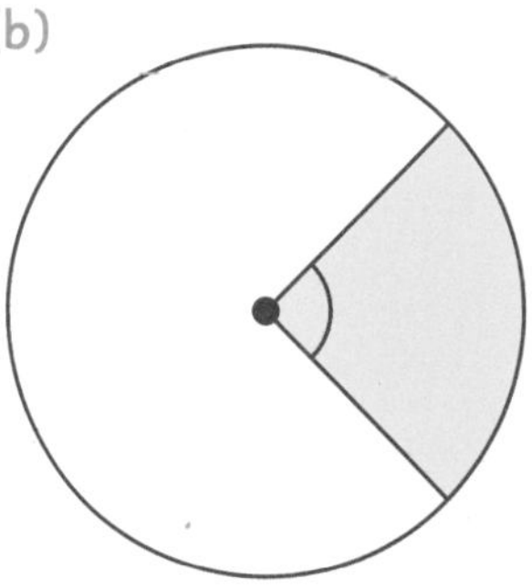

(c)

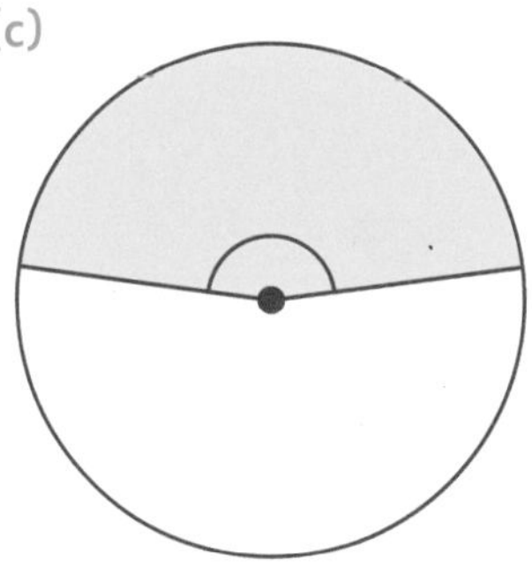

(d)

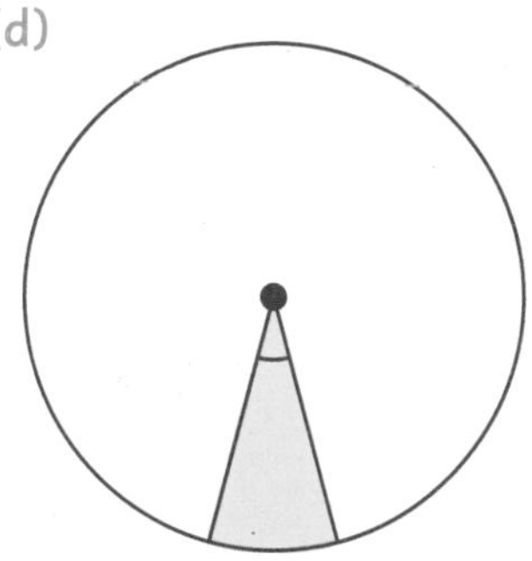

Which sector is also a quadrant?

What are two quadrants that are joined together called?

The abbreviation of the word radius is r.

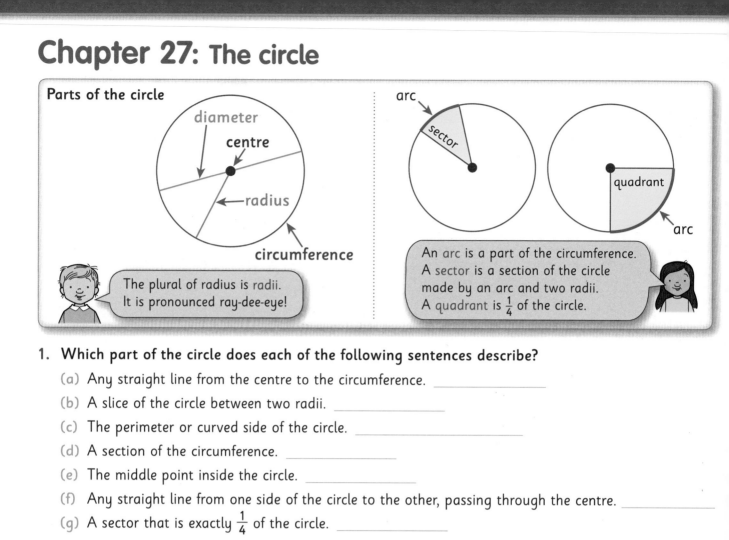

Challenge

(a) Trace around a circular object to draw a circle.

(b) Mark where you think the centre lies.

(c) Using a protractor, make a sector with an angle of 75°.

STRAND Shape and space **STRAND UNIT/ELEMENT** *2-D shapes*

LANGUAGE *Circle, centre, circumference, radius, radii, diameter, sector, quadrants, combined, compass, shorter, ruler, estimate, area, approximate, more, less*

Drawing circles

1. Look at the pictures. Answer the questions.

(a) What is the length of the **diameter** of the (i) clock; (ii) mirror; (iii) window?

(b) What is the length of the **radius** of the (i) orange; (ii) mirror; (iii) clock?

(c) What is the total length of the diameters of two such plates?

(d) How much shorter is the radius of the orange than the radius of the plate?

(e) What is the combined length of the diameter of all five objects?

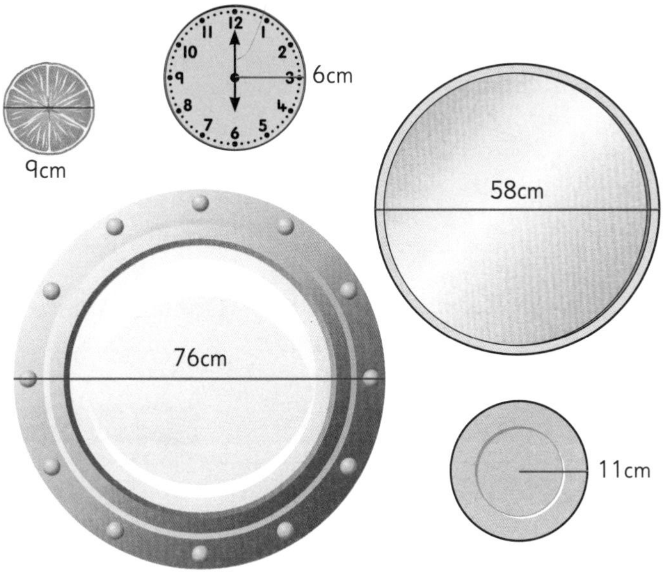

Draw a circle that has a radius of 5cm.

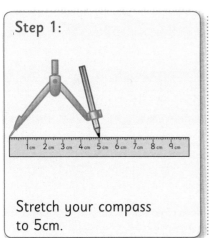

Step 1:

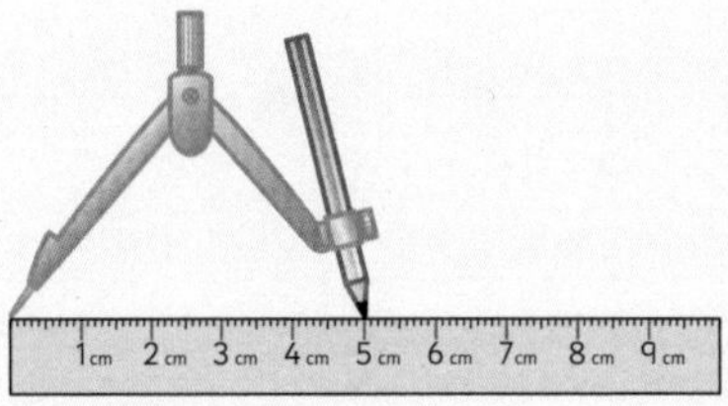

Stretch your compass to 5cm.

Step 2:

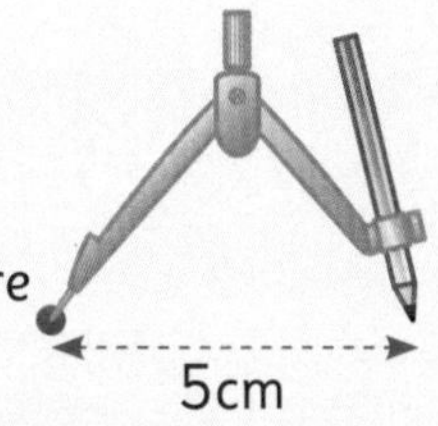

Make a centre point on your page. Place the sharp point of the compass on it.

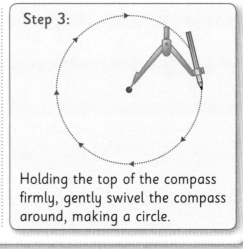

Step 3:

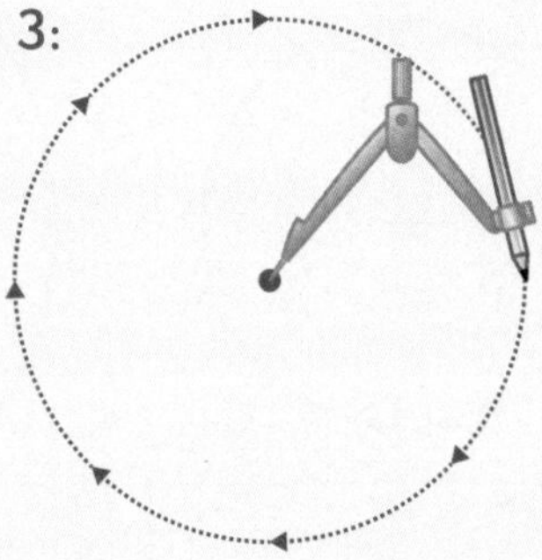

Holding the top of the compass firmly, gently swivel the compass around, making a circle.

2. Construct circles that have the following radii:

(a) 4cm (b) 6cm (c) $2\frac{1}{2}$ cm (d) 3·5cm (e) 48mm

3. Construct circles that have the following diameters:

(a) 6cm (b) 9cm (c) 4·6cm (d) 58mm (e) 10·4cm

Puzzle:

How many circles are there altogether? ______

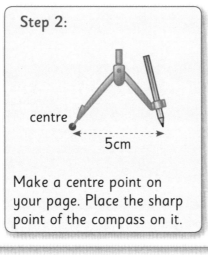

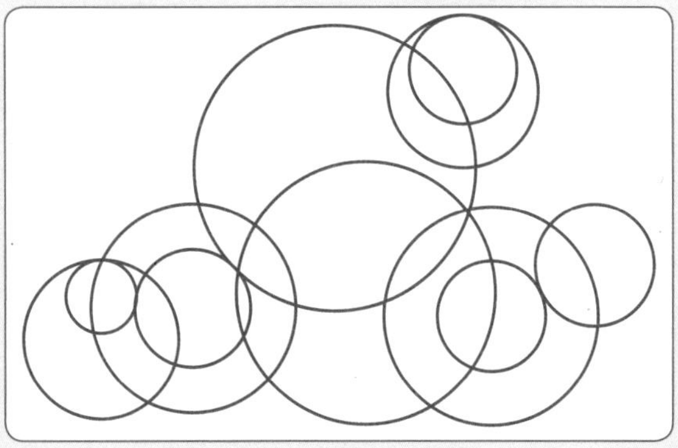

Challenge 1

Using your compass, construct a circle of radius 4·5cm. On the circle, mark in:
(a) the centre; (b) a radius; (c) the diameter; (d) a sector; (e) the circumference; (f) a quadrant.

Challenge 2

Using your compass, make your own circle puzzle. Ask your partner to count all the circles that you have drawn.

Area of a circle

Estimate the area of the circle. Each square represents 1cm^2.

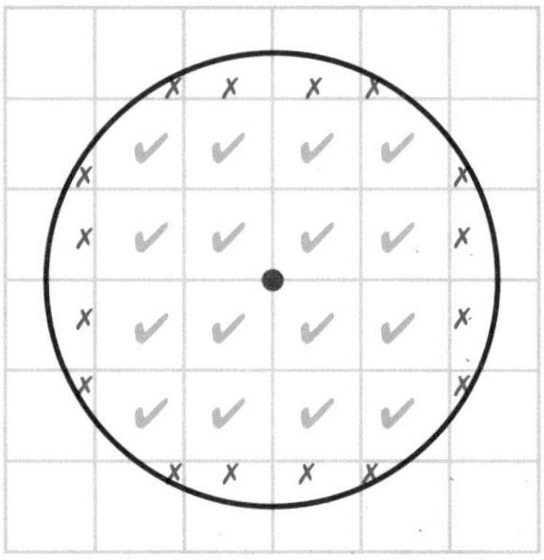

Estimating gives us the approximate area of a circle!

Count....

✓ all the full squares.

✓ half squares or more than half squares as full squares.

Don't count...

✗ squares that are less than half a square.

Answer: Area = 16cm^2

1. Calculate the (i) radius; (ii) diameter; (iii) approximate area of the following:

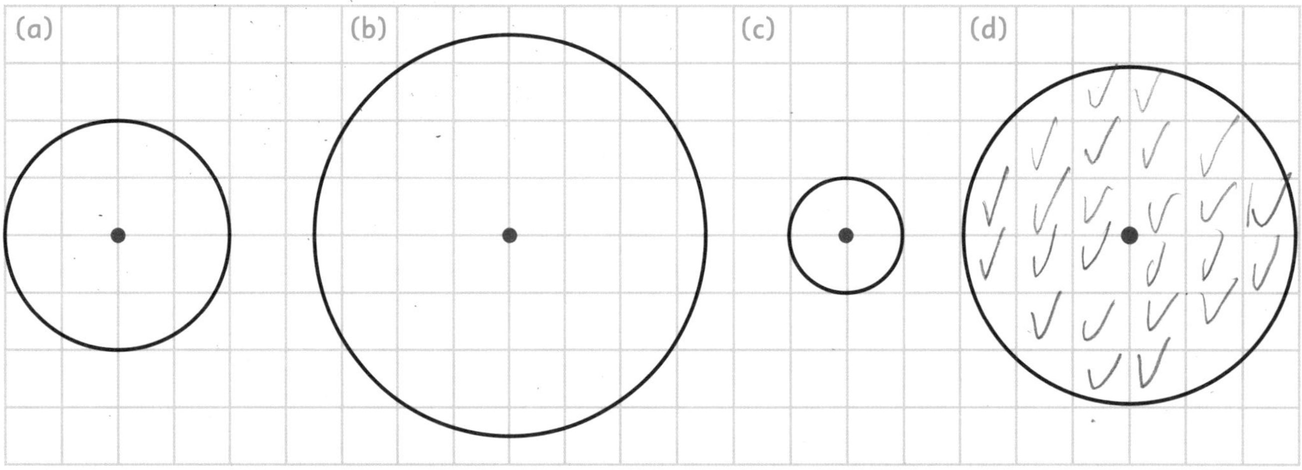

2. (a) Construct circles that have the following radii on centimetre square paper.

(i) 4cm | (ii) $4\frac{1}{2}$ cm | (iii) $2\frac{1}{2}$ cm | (iv) 5cm | (v) 5·5cm

(b) Calculate the approximate area of each circle.

3. Complete.

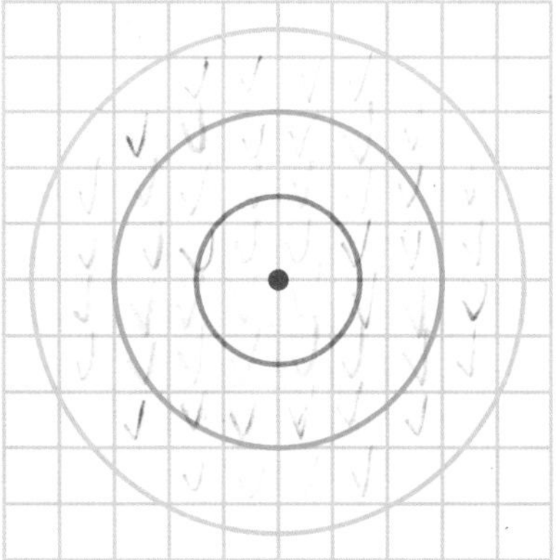

Each square represents 1cm^2.

(a) What is the radius of the blue circle?

(b) What is the diameter of the green circle?

(c) How much longer is the diameter of the blue circle than the orange circle?

(d) What is the approximate area of the (i) orange; (ii) green; (iii) blue circle?

(e) What is the combined length of the diameters of all three circles?

4. (a) What is the radius of a 5c coin?

(b) What is the approximate area of a 5c coin?

(c) What is the combined length of the diameters of four such coins?

(d) What is the approximate combined area of six such coins?

(e) What is the approximate combined area of 20 such coins?

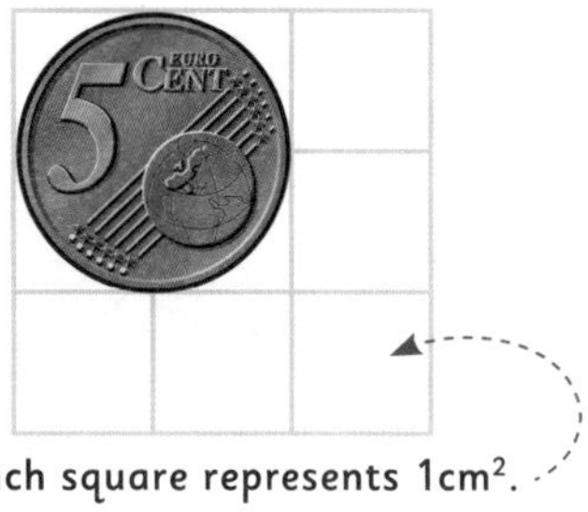

Each square represents 1cm^2.

Circular designs

Remember: Ignore parts of squares that are less than half of a full square.

1. Look at this garden plan. (□ = 1m²)

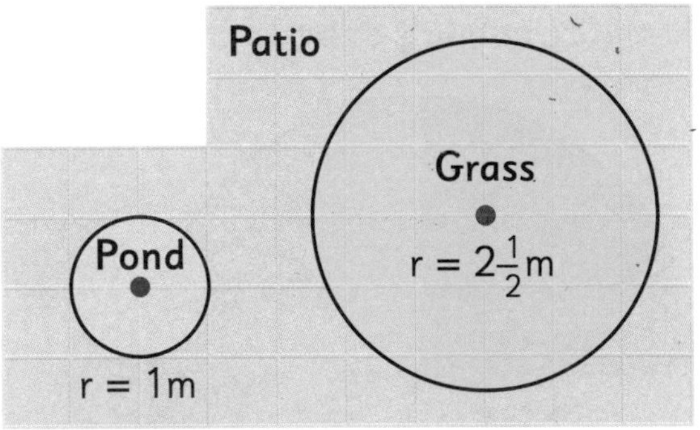

(a) What is the total area of the garden?

(b) What is the approximate area of the (i) grass; (ii) pond; (iii) patio area?

(c) If patio tiles cost €47·50 per square metre, find the approximate cost of paving this patio.

(d) How much less than €2,000 did the paving cost?

2.

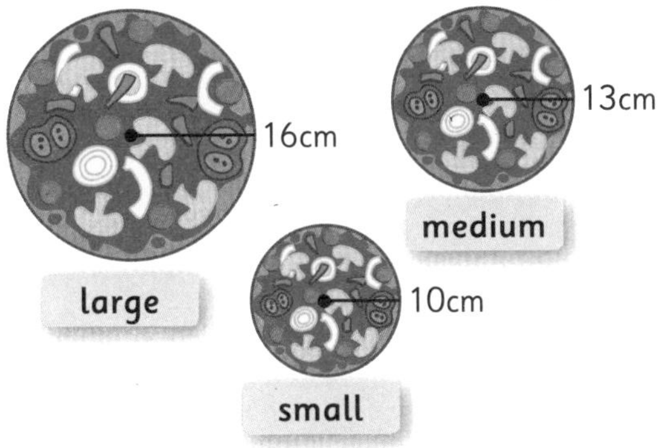

(a) What is the diameter of the (i) large pizza; (ii) medium pizza; (iii) small pizza?

(b) A family ordered five large pizzas for a party. What was the combined diameters of the pizzas in metres?

(c) The same family got a discount of €3·50. If a large pizza cost €13·20, what did the pizzas cost them?

(d) The radius of an XL (extra large) pizza is double the radius of the small pizza shown here. What is the diameter of the XL pizza?

How to create this design

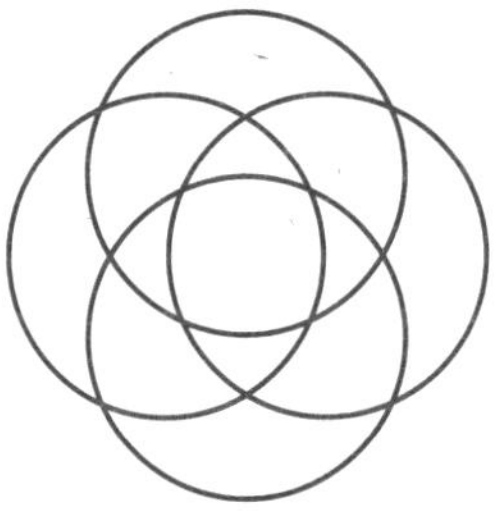

Every circle in the pattern must have the same radius.

Step 1:
Draw a circle of radius 3cm.

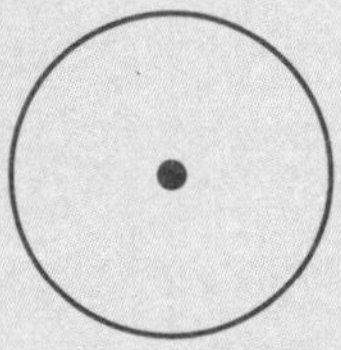

Step 2:
Mark the bottom of the circle. This will become the centre of the next circle. Draw the next circle.

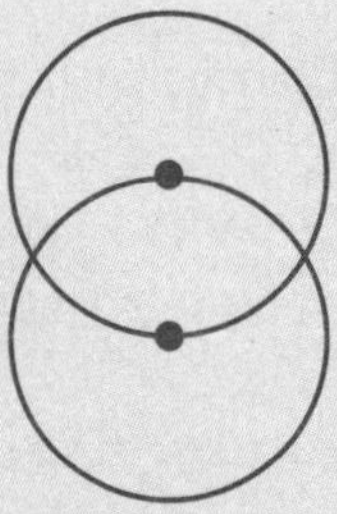

Step 3:
Mark the points where the circles intersect (meet). These points become the centres for the next circles.

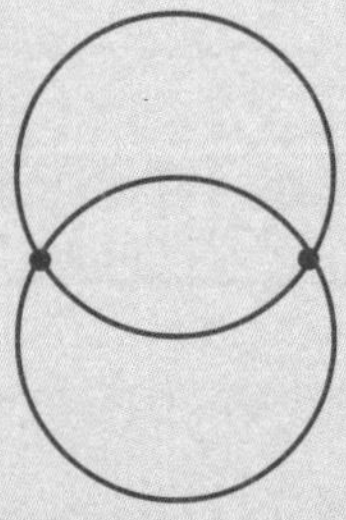

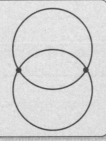

Step 4:
Draw the next circles. You can continue the pattern, making the design as big as you want!

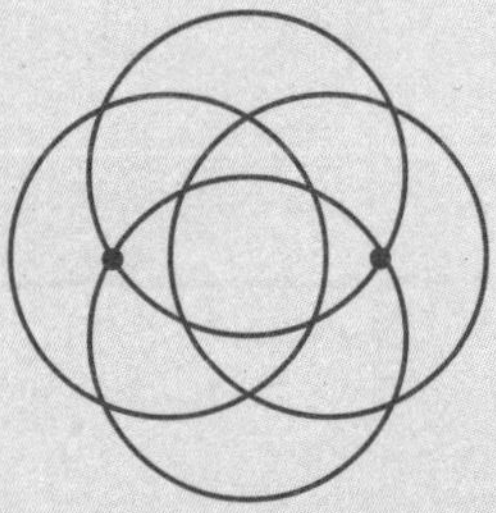

Challenge Try drawing these designs with your compass. Colour each design.

(a)

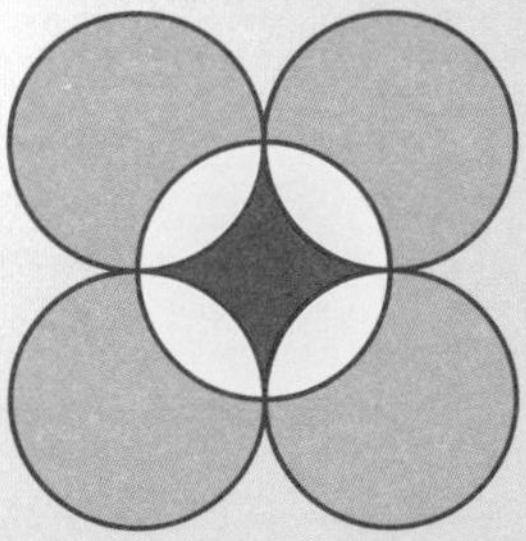

(b)

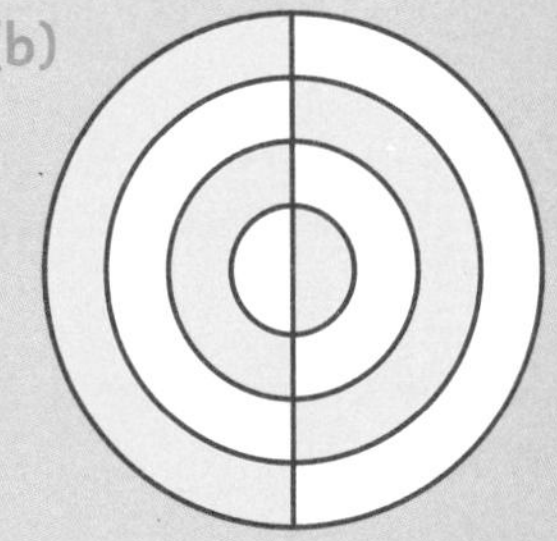

Chapter 28: Data 3 – Pie charts

Pie charts are a useful way to show data. Study these pie charts. Then answer the questions.

1. Children in an art club

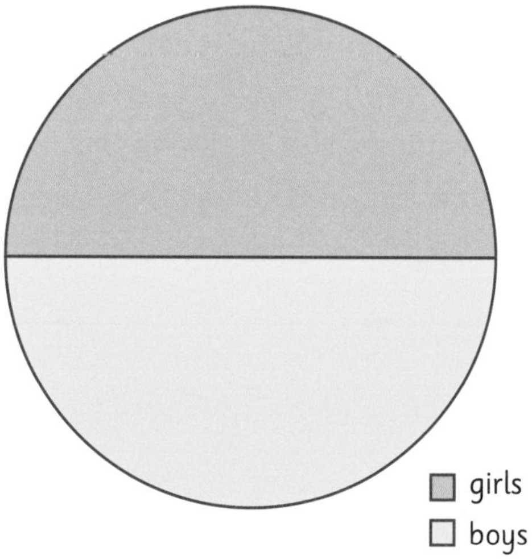

(a) If there are 30 children in the club, how many are boys?

(b) What fraction of the club members are girls?

(c) Could this pie chart represent a club of 21 children? (Give a reason.)

2. Favourite primary colour

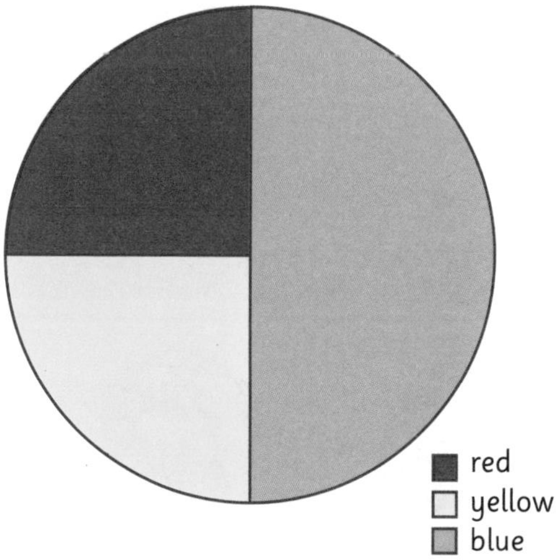

(a) What fraction of the children chose blue as their favourite colour?

(b) What fraction chose yellow?

(c) If 14 children voted for red, how many children voted for blue?

(d) How many children took part in the survey?

3. Favourite Irish attractions

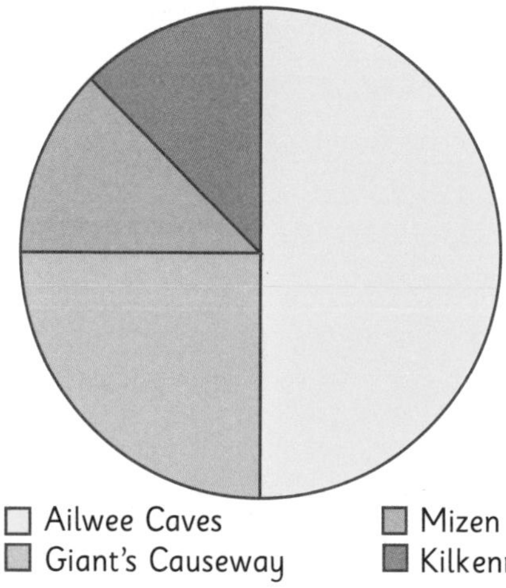

(a) Which attraction was most popular in this survey?

(b) What fraction of the children chose the Giant's Causeway?

(c) What fraction chose Kilkenny Castle?

(d) What fraction of the children altogether voted for Mizen Head and Kilkenny Castle?

(e) If 88 children voted in this survey, how many voted for Mizen Head?

Challenge

The children in Fifth Class raised €752 for their school. This pie chart shows how the money was spent:

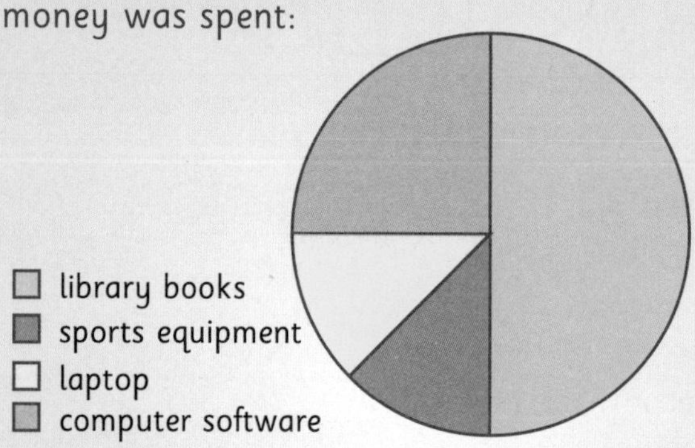

(a) What fraction of the money was spent on sports equipment? ____

(b) How much money was spent on:

(i) sports equipment? € ____

(ii) library books? € ____

(iii) computer software? € ____

(iv) laptop? € ____

STRAND **Data** **STRAND UNIT/ELEMENT** *Representing and interpreting data*

LANGUAGE *Pie chart, favourite, survey, data, represent, fraction, vote, altogether, key, percentage, calculate, degrees, sector, compare, protractor*

Data 3 – A closer look at pie charts

1. Dad used this pie chart to show how he spends his time on an average weekday.

Dad's day

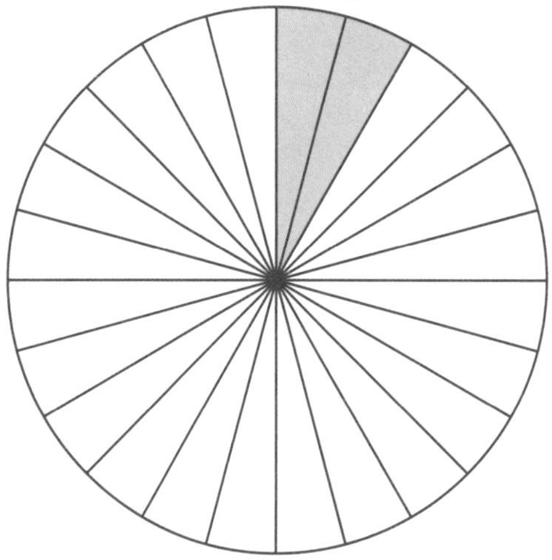

- This pie chart is divided into 24 equal pieces because there are 24 hours in a day.
- Dad spends two hours eating, so two pieces of the pie chart are coloured green.
- Each section that is coloured green is called a **sector** or slice of the pie chart.

Key:
- **green** – eating (2 hours)
- **yellow** – sleeping (6 hours)
- **blue** – working (8 hours)
- **red** – driving (3 hours)
- **purple** – family time (4 hours)
- **orange** – chores (1 hour)

(a) Draw the pie chart into your copybook. Complete it by following the key.

(b) What activities did Dad spend the (i) longest; (ii) shortest time doing?

(c) What fraction of Dad's day was spent (i) at work; (ii) sleeping; (iii) doing chores?

(d) What fraction of Dad's day was spent at work and on family time together?

(e) What percentage of Dad's day was spent (i) eating; (ii) driving; (iii) working?

Your completed pie chart from Question 1 could look like this!

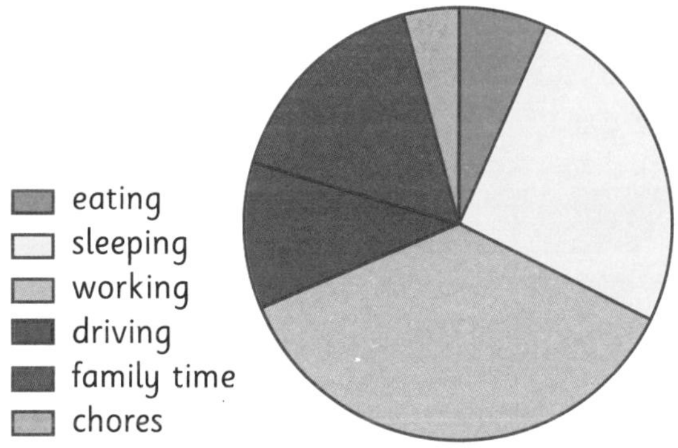

Remember, there are 360° in a circle.

How many degrees represent eating?

(a) Calculate the fraction in its simplest form → $\frac{2}{24} = \frac{1}{12}$

(b) Then find $\frac{1}{12}$ of 360°.

$360 \div 12 = 30°$ or $12\overline{)360°}$ = 30°

2. Calculate the degrees for each sector of Dad's day pie chart.

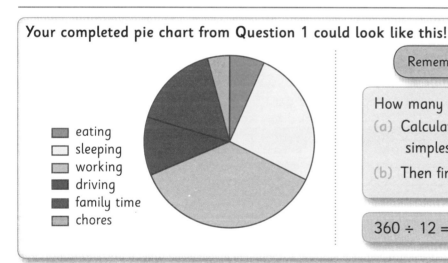

Activity	Eating	Sleeping	Working	Driving	Family time	Chores
Time in hours	2					
Fraction	$\frac{1}{12}$					
Degrees	30°					

Challenge Represent the activities done by you in a 24-hour day on a pie chart. Use full hours only for each activity.

Data 3 – Constructing pie charts

Always write the fractions in their simplest form.

1. **60 children were asked to vote for their favourite type of soup. The data will be represented on a pie chart. First you must complete the following grid.**

Soup	Vegetable	Chicken	Tomato	Potato and Leek
Votes	15	20	10	15
Fraction	$\frac{1}{4}$			
Degrees				

How to construct the pie chart:

(a) Calculate the degrees for each sector. (You did this in Question 1 above!)

(b) Use your compass to draw a circle.

(c) Draw a **radius** anywhere on the circle, this will be the base for your first angle.

(d) Use your **protractor** to construct each angle.

(e) Colour each **sector**. Give them a colour code.

(f) Give your pie chart a title.

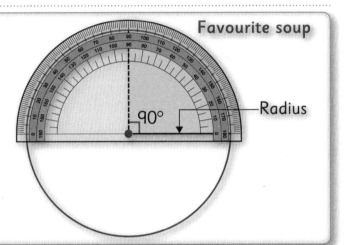

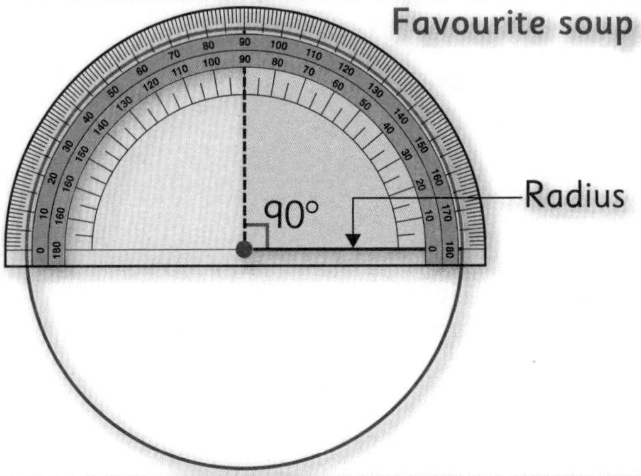

2. **Now draw a pie chart in your copybook to represent the data on favourite soups in Question 1.**

3. **20 people were asked to name their favourite flower.**

(a) Complete the following grid. (b) Represent the data on a pie chart.

Flower	Rose	Daffodil	Tulip	Crocus	Daisy
Votes	5	2	6	5	2
Fraction					
Degrees					

Challenge This grid shows the **number of coins** thrown into a wishing well one Saturday.

(a) Complete the information on the grid. (b) Represent the data on a pie chart.

Coins						
Number of coins		10	20	15	20	40
Fraction	$\frac{1}{8}$				$\frac{1}{6}$	
Degrees		30°		45°	60°	

(c) What was the total value of the money thrown into the wishing well? € ______

Data 3 – Revision

A Travelling Book Fair comes to Bracken Primary School once a year. Each of the 180 pupils gets a book. These pie charts show the types of book the children chose over the last two years.

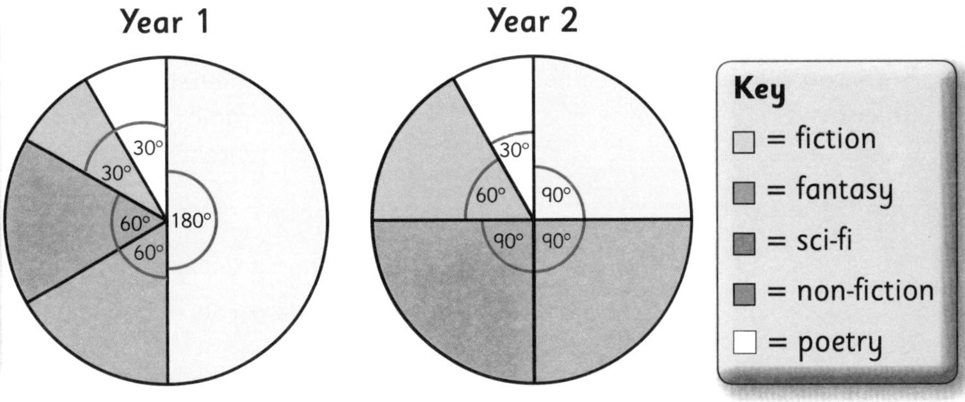

Answer the questions based on the above pie charts.

Warning! There may be more than one answer!

1. Which genre of book was most popular in (a) year 1; (b) year 2?
2. Which genre of book was least popular in (a) year 1; (b) year 2?
3. **Now copy and complete the following grids in your copybook using the information above.**

(a) *Year 1*

Genre	Fiction	Fantasy	Sci-fi	Non-fiction	Poetry
Degrees	180°				
Fraction	$\frac{1}{2}$				
Number of children	90				

(b) *Year 2*

Genre	Fiction	Fantasy	Sci-fi	Non-fiction	Poetry
Degrees	90°				
Fraction	$\frac{1}{4}$				
Number of children					

4. (a) Represent the above data on this multiple horizontal bar chart.
   (b) Write down five statements about this multiple bar chart.

Favourite genre

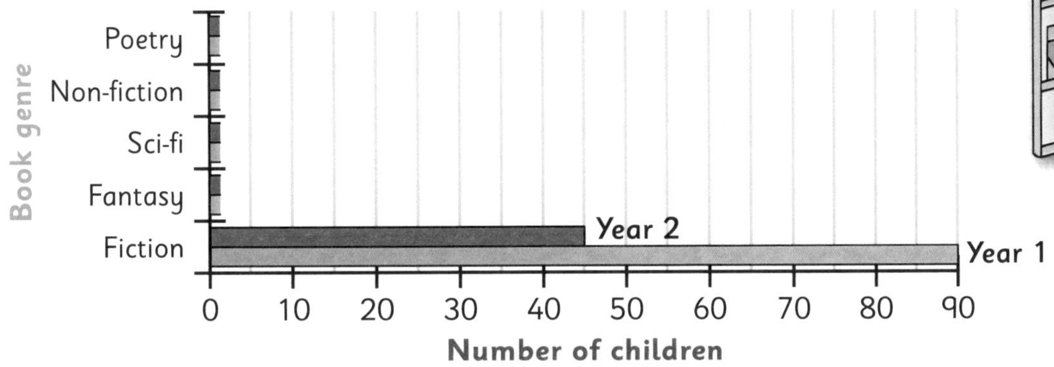

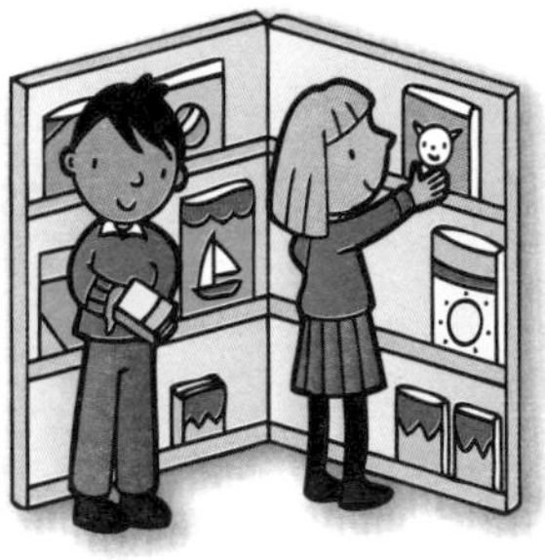

Chapter 29: Equations

Closed sentence	Open sentence
A **closed** number sentence has no **unknown** (missing) parts. It can be true or false. **Examples:** 6 + 5 = 10 (false) 7 < 12 (true) 9 × 8 = 72 (true) 5 + 3 > 8 + 3 (false)	An **open** number sentence has an **unknown** part. We use a frame □ to represent the unknown part. An open sentence can be either true or false. **Example:** □ + 5 = 10 If □ has a value of 5, then this sentence is true. If □ has a value of 4, then this sentence is false.

1. Say whether the following number sentences are closed or open.

(a) 12 + 7 = 10 (b) $\frac{81}{9}$ = 9 (c) 12 + □ = 19 (d) $\frac{54}{6}$ = □

(e) □ × 8 – 32 (f) 33 × 6 = □ (g) 23 – 11 = 12 (h) 7 × 7 = 49

(i) 5 + 4 = 6 + 3 (j) 21 – 6 = 5 × □ (k) 7 + 8 > 2 × 4 (l) 7 × 9 = 54

2. Are these closed number sentences true or false? ✓ if true, ✗ if false. Explain your answer.

(a) 14 + 12 = 26 □ (b) 19 – 5 > 18 □ (c) 3 × 6 = $\frac{36}{2}$ □

(d) 5 × 8 = 32 + 5 □ (e) 34 + 12 < 8 × 7 □ (f) 49 ÷ 7 = $\frac{54}{7}$ □

(g) $\frac{99}{3}$ > 11 × 3 □ (h) $\frac{64}{8}$ = 8 × 8 □ (i) 22 + 15 < 34 – 12 □

(j) $\frac{45}{15}$ > 2 × 0 □ (k) 42 – 5 = 46 – 1 □ (l) 6 × 7 < 3 × 33 □

Put the correct sign (<, = or >) in each ◯ to make these open number sentences true.

3. (a) 12 + 8 ◯ 20 (b) 16 – 4 ◯ 10 (c) 5 × 9 ◯ 40

(d) 5 × 3 ◯ 7 × 2 (e) $\frac{21}{7}$ ◯ 3 × 1 (f) $\frac{70}{7}$ ◯ 6 + 11

(g) 9 × 9 ◯ 100 – 19 (h) $\frac{34}{4}$ ◯ 5 + 4 (i) 112 – 9 ◯ 9 × 11

(j) 64 + 12 ◯ 80 – 4 (k) $\frac{325}{25}$ ◯ 4 × 3 (l) 22 × 3 ◯ $\frac{83}{12}$

(m) 24 ÷ 4 ◯ 36 ÷ 9 (n) 29 + 46 ◯ 100 – 23 (o) 84 – 11 ◯ 9 × 8

4. (a) 100 ÷ 10 ◯ 20 (b) 72 ÷ 9 ◯ 7 + 1 (c) 63 ÷ 7 ◯ 443

(d) 9 × 9 ◯ 100 – 20 (e) 8 × 12 ◯ 10 × 10 (f) 20 × 6 ◯ 12 × 10

(g) 99 – 23 ◯ 54 + 12 (h) 175 ÷ 25 ◯ 12 – 5 (i) 96 ÷ 8 ◯ 5 × 2

(j) 87 + 33 ◯ 11 × 10 (k) 180 ÷ 20 ◯ 5 + 4 (l) 145 – 65 ◯ 8 × 10

(m) 126 – 27 ◯ 78 + 20 (n) 96 ÷ 12 ◯ 36 – 29 (o) 186 – 30 ◯ 99 + 58

STRAND **Algebra** STRAND UNIT/ELEMENT *Equations*
LANGUAGE *Equations, closed, open, true, false, greater/less than, equal, decimals, fractions, percentages, symbols – addition, subtraction, multiplication, division, equals*

More equations

1. Put the correct operation sign (+, –, x or ÷) in each ◯ to make the number sentence true.

(a) 6 ◯ 7 = 13	(b) 19 ◯ 12 = 31	(c) 6 ◯ 5 = 30
(d) 26 ◯ 12 = 14	(e) 27 ◯ 3 = 9	(f) 42 ◯ 6 = 7
(g) 34 ◯ 10 = 340	(h) 290 ◯ 10 = 29	(i) 35 = 7 ◯ 5
(j) 63 = 9 ◯ 7	(k) 84 = 70 ◯ 14	(l) 37 = 50 ◯ 13

2. Write the correct number in each box to make the number sentence true.

(a) 5 + ☐ = 12	(b) 38 – 14 = ☐	(c) 6 × ☐ = 54	(d) $\frac{72}{☐} = 9$
(e) ☐ + 14 = 30	(f) ☐ – 12 = 37	(g) 7 × 8 = ☐	(h) $\frac{☐}{8} = 8$
(i) 112 + ☐ = 145	(j) ☐ – 73 = 99	(k) 25 × ☐ = 800	(l) $\frac{80}{5} =$ ☐
(m) 134 + ☐ = 167	(n) 143 – 57 = ☐	(o) ☐ × 3 = 135	(p) 10 – ☐ < 1

3. Ruairí has €100 to spend. Write five word problems and the five corresponding number sentences using the symbols < or > only!

Example: **Word problem:** The jacket and the T-shirt cost more than €100.

Number sentence: €96 + €32 > €100

Item	Jacket 	Jeans 	T-shirt 	Suit 	Jumper 	Shoes 
Cost	€96	€59	€32	€169	€45	€55

A number sentence that has the equals sign (=) is called an **equation**.
Example: 7 + 5 = 10 + 2.

What is on the left (7 + 5) has **the same value** as what is on the right (10 + 2).

Both sides of the scales are equal so the scales balance.

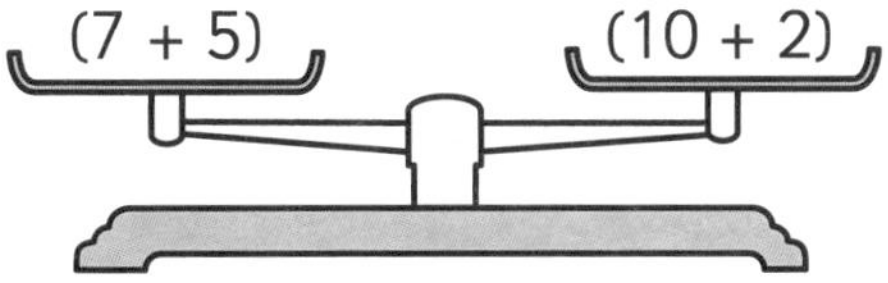

4. Write the missing numbers to complete these equations.

(a) 12 + ☐ = 16	(b) 5 + 4 = 6 + ☐	(c) 19 – 4 = 12 + ☐
(d) 36 = ☐ + 24	(e) 18 + 5 = ☐ + 13	(f) 17 + ☐ = 14 + 8
(g) 6 × 4 = 8 × ☐	(h) 22 + 6 = 18 + ☐	(i) 45 = 30 + ☐
(j) 12 + 9 = 17 + ☐	(k) $\frac{42}{6} = 1 \times$ ☐	(l) 36 + 23 = 42 + ☐

Problems as equations

1. Complete the correct open number sentence to match each word problem.

(a) Róisín ate seven portions of fruit on Monday and six portions on Tuesday. How many portions did she eat altogether?

(i) 7 – 6 = _____ (ii) 7 + 6 = _____ (iii) 7 × 6 = _____

(b) Ava swam 120m in a pool over three days. If she swam the same length each day, what length did she swim each day?

(i) 120m – 3 = _____ (ii) 120m ÷ 3 = _____ (iii) 120m × 3 = _____

(c) Marie planted eight trees. Her cousin planted five times more than Marie. How many trees did her cousin plant?

(i) 8 – 5 = _____ (ii) 8 + 5 = _____ (iii) 8 × 5 = _____

(d) Seán played the piano for 17 minutes on Monday. If he played it for 46 minutes altogether on Monday and Tuesday, how many minutes did he play on Tuesday?

(i) 46 + 17 = _____ (ii) 17 + _____ = 46 (iii) 46 ÷ 17 = _____

(e) Aisling baked 48 buns for the cake sale. If she sold 36 of them, how many were left?

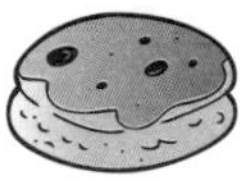

(i) 48 × 36 = _____ (ii) 48 + 36 = _____ (iii) 48 – 36 = _____

(f) Five friends ate in a restaurant. The total cost of their food was €115. They decided to divide the bill evenly. How much did each pay?

(i) €115 × 5 = _____ (ii) €115 – 5 = _____ (iii) €115 ÷ 5 = _____

2. Write each of the following word problems as equations.

	Word problem	Equation
(a)	Ciarán and his two friends earned €36 busking. They divided the money evenly among them. Each got €12.	
(b)	Sophia had 12 marbles. She then bought three times that amount. Now she has 48 marbles. 	
(c)	A cinema ticket costs €6 per child. Three children went. They paid €18 altogether. 	
(d)	There are 24 roses in the garden. Eoin will plant 14 more. When he is finished, there will be 38 roses altogether. 	
(e)	Daniel collected 18 shells on a beach. He gave his friend five of them. He has 13 left. 	
(f)	Darragh wants 21 soccer stickers. He has 14. He needs seven more. 	

3. Write a word problem for each of these equations.

(a) 9 + 3 = 12
(b) 20 – 8 = 12
(c) 6 × 5 = 30
(d) 60 ÷ 12 = 5
(e) 45 + 32 = 77
(f) 64 – 34 = 30
(g) 51 × 10 = 510
(h) 210 ÷ 3 = 70
(i) 14 + 23 + 19 = 56
(j) 22 + 34 – 12 = 44
(k) (3 × 5) + 6 = 21
(l) (25 ÷ 5) – 3 = 2

Equations – Fractions, decimals and percentages

1. Complete the following to make each of them into an equation.

(a) (i) $\frac{1}{2}$ of 64 = ____ (ii) $\frac{1}{4}$ of 96 = ____ (iii) $\frac{1}{8}$ of 184 = ____

(b) (i) $\frac{2}{3}$ of 72 = ____ (ii) $\frac{3}{4}$ of 80 = ____ (iii) $\frac{2}{9}$ of 72 = ____

(c) (i) $\frac{4}{5}$ of 85 = ____ (ii) $\frac{5}{8}$ of 64 = ____ (iii) $\frac{4}{9}$ of 108 = ____

(d) (i) 0·5 of 96 = ____ (ii) 0·9 of 320 = ____ (iii) 0·2 of 45 = ____

(e) (i) 0·25 of 360 = ____ (ii) 0·75 of 280 = ____ (iii) 0·6 of 210 = ____

(f) (i) 0·15 of 240 = ____ (ii) 0·64 of 700 = ____ (iii) 0·08 of 900 = ____

(g) (i) 10% of 540 = ____ (ii) 30% of 430 = ____ (iii) 100% of 776 = ____

(h) (i) 80% of 375 = ____ (ii) 40% of 156 = ____ (iii) 70% of 189 = ____

(i) (i) 5% of 120 = ____ (ii) 12% of 800 = ____ (iii) 64% of 550 = ____

2. You may use your calculator when solving these:

(a) $\frac{1}{4}$ of ____ = 12 (b) $\frac{1}{9}$ of ____ = 7 (c) $\frac{3}{8}$ of ____ = 42

(d) $\frac{5}{6}$ of ____ = 120 (e) $\frac{4}{5}$ of ____ = 400 (f) $\frac{5}{12}$ of ____ = 80

(g) 0·25 of ____ = 90 (h) 0·75 of ____ = 465 (i) 0·2 of ____ = 256

(j) 0·7 of ____ = 364 (k) 0·4 of ____ = 328 (l) 0·9 of ____ = 369

(m) 70% of ____ = 588 (n) 30% of ____ = 231 (o) 60% of ____ = 312

(p) 12% of ____ = 216 (q) 5% of ____ = 115 (r) 8% of ____ = 168

3. Sporty's Mega Summer Sale

Find the sale price for each of the following. Then write an equation for each one.

	Item	Original price	Reduction	Sale price	Equation
(a)	Pair of runners 	€110	10% off	€	
(b)	Tracksuit 	€73·50	20% off	€	
(c)	Football jersey 	€44	25% off	€	
(d)	Golf clubs 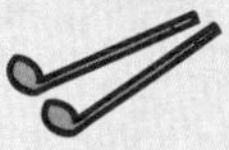	€249	$\frac{1}{3}$ off	€	
(e)	Wetsuit 	€34·88	$\frac{3}{4}$ off	€	
(f)	Hurley 	€36·24	$16\frac{2}{3}$% off	€	
(g)	Bicycle 	€275·20	$12\frac{1}{2}$% off	€	
(h)	Surfboard 	€960·70	40% off	€	

A quick look back 8

1. Write the product of the factors 7 and 8.

______

2. Write the missing **factor** of 30.

1, 2, 3, ______ 6, 10, 15, 30.

3. Write the sixth multiple of 9.

______

4. Ring the correct word:

39 is a **prime** / **composite** number.

5. Write the ninth square number.

______

6. 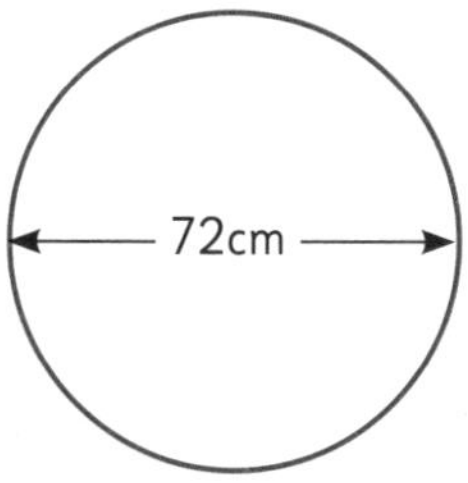

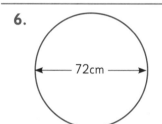

A circle has a diameter of 72cm. What length is its radius?

______ cm

7. This pie chart shows the favourite subject of 45 children. How many children prefer P.E.?

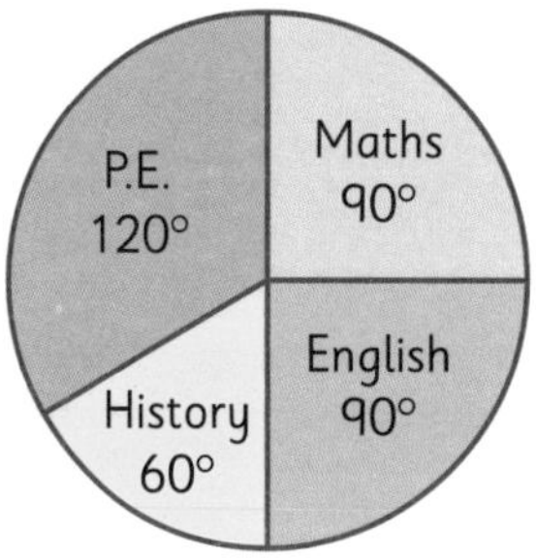

______

8. How many degrees are there in $\frac{1}{6}$ of a full turn?

______ °

9. 

There were 240 children in a school. 60% of them were girls. How many girls were there in the school?

______

10. Put the correct number into the box to make this into an equation:

45 ÷ ☐ = 12 – 3

11. Complete this equation by writing the correct digit in the box:

10% of 200 = ☐ + 9

12. 

The original price of a pair of runners was €55. During a sale, they were reduced by 20%. What was the sale price?

€ ______

13. What is the cost of 12·5kg of potatoes if 2·5kg cost €1·40?

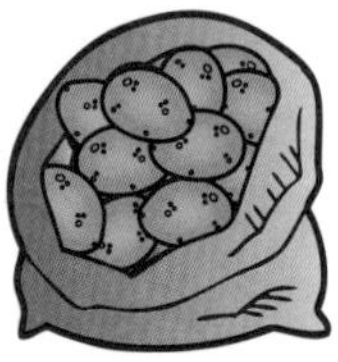

€ ______

14. Increase €85 by 100%.

€ ______

15. 0·038 × 1,000 = ______

16. Write the prime numbers between 80 and 90.

______ , ______ .

17. Joe spent $\frac{3}{4}$ of his money and Cara spent $\frac{11}{16}$ of hers. Who spent the greater fraction of their money?

______

18. $\frac{5}{8}$ of a number is 40. What is the number? ______

19. A hat usually costs €120. During a sale, it was reduced by 30%. How much did Maria save if she bought the hat during the sale?

€ ______

20. The area of a rectangle is 84cm². If its length is 12cm, what is its perimeter?

______ cm

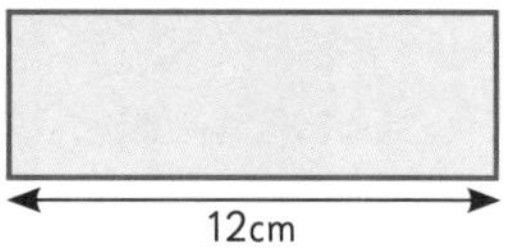

Chapter 30: 3-D shapes

Dimensions (D = Dimension)

1-D shapes have:
- length

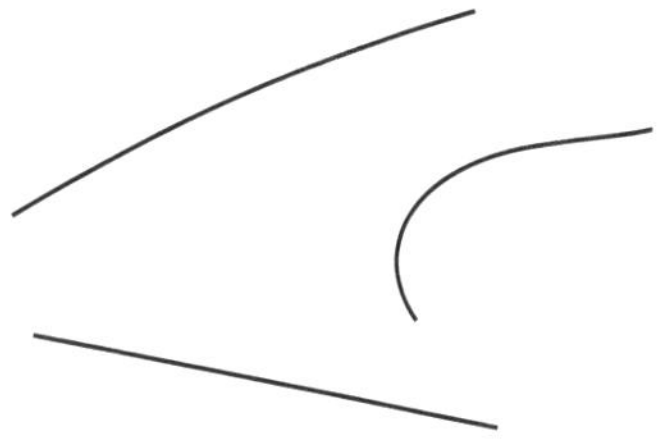

2-D shapes have:
- length
- width

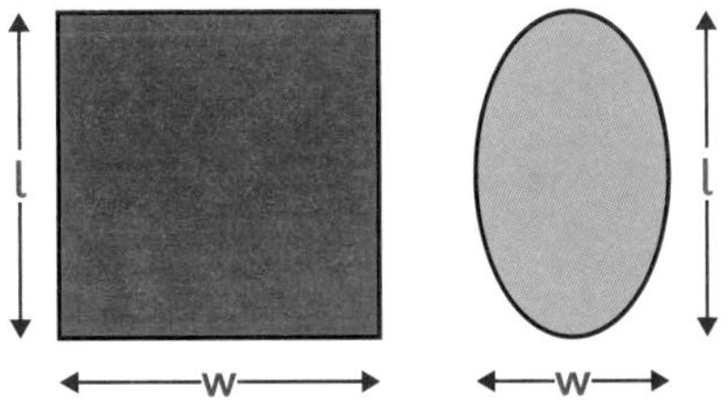

3-D shapes have:
- length
- width
- height

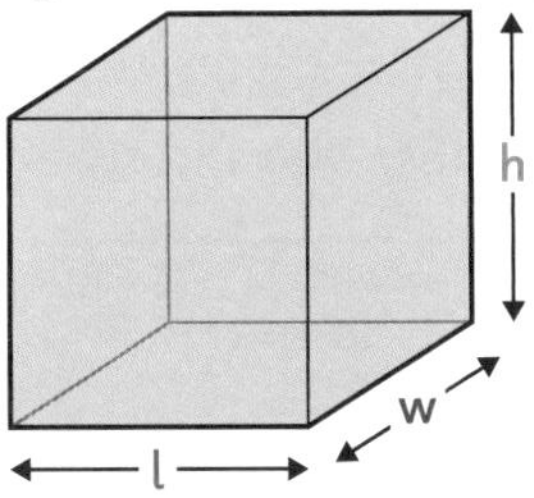

1. Choose the best word to complete each sentence.

(a) 2-D shapes are (flat/solid).

(b) 3-D shapes are (flat/solid).

(c) 1-D shapes are (lines/pictures).

(d) 2-D shapes (can/cannot) be held.

(e) 1-D shapes are (drawings/real objects).

(f) 2-D shapes (have/don't have) height.

(g) 3-D shapes have (1-D/2-D) shaped faces.

(h) 1-D shapes (can/cannot) be held.

(i) 3-D shapes (can/cannot) hold smaller objects inside them.

2. (a)
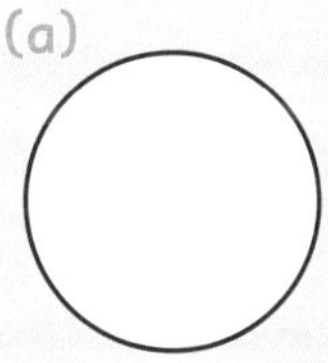
(b)
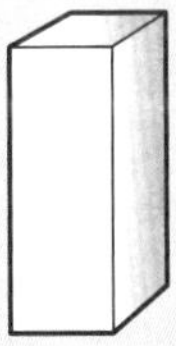
(c)
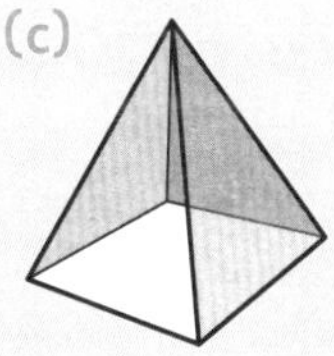
(d)
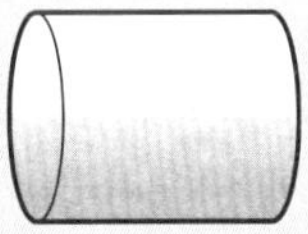
(e)
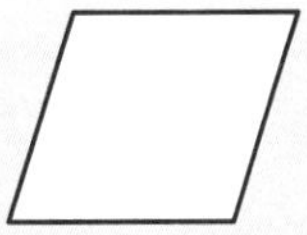
(f)
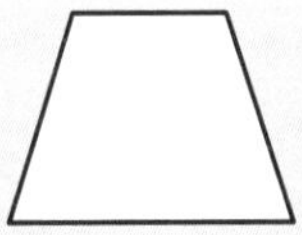
(g)
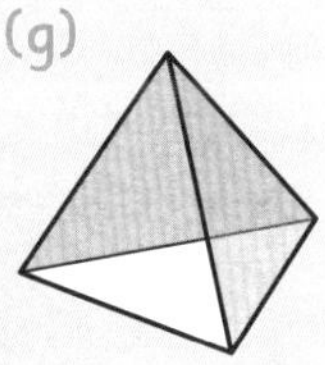
(h)
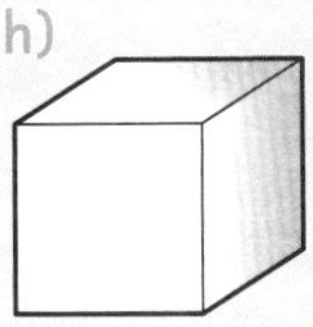
(i)
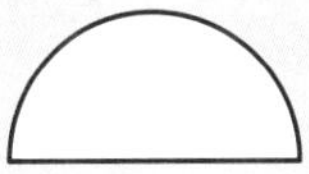
(j)
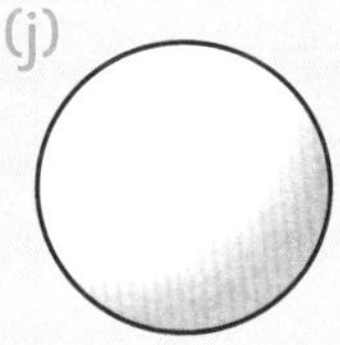
(k)
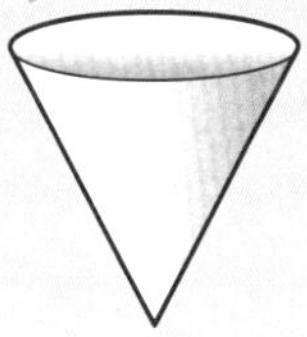
(l)
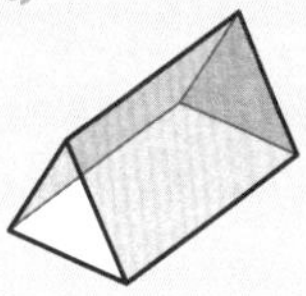
(m)
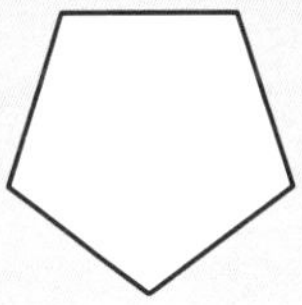
(n)
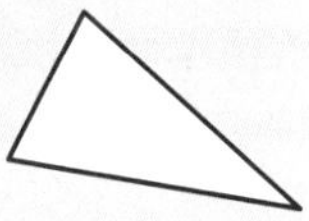

(i) Name each shape (a) – (n) above.

(ii) List all the 2-D shapes above.

(iii) List all the 3-D shapes above.

(iv) Which of the above 3-D shapes can stack?

(v) Which of the above 3-D shapes can roll?

(vi) Which two of the above 2-D shapes do not have corners? (Be careful!)

(vii) Which 3-D shape is made up of one square and four equal triangles?

Challenge

Draw the following 3-D shapes into your copybook. Label the:
- length
- width
- height

(a)
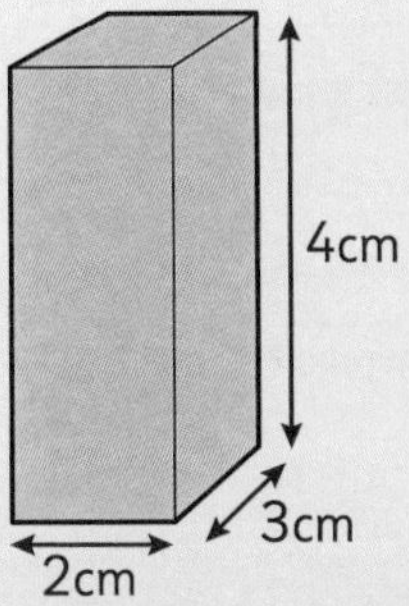

(b)
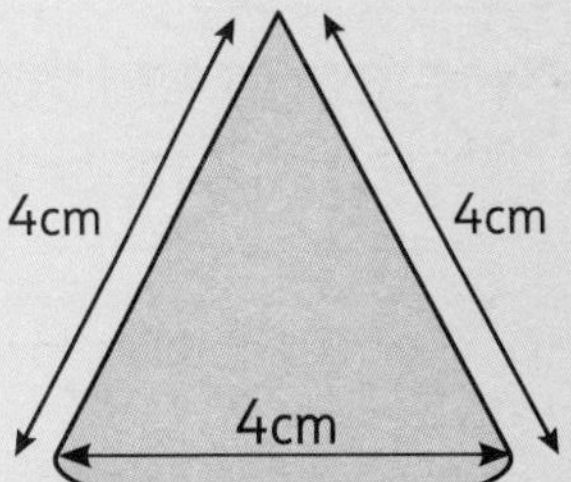

STRAND **Shape and space** STRAND UNIT/ELEMENT *3-D shapes*
LANGUAGE *Length, width, height, flat, solid, stack, regular/irregular, corners, forms, edges, vertex, vertices, skeleton, apex, tetrahedron, prism, polygon, pyramid, hemisphere, flat, solid*

161

3-D shapes – Faces, edges and vertices

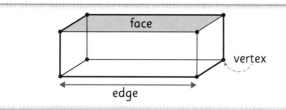

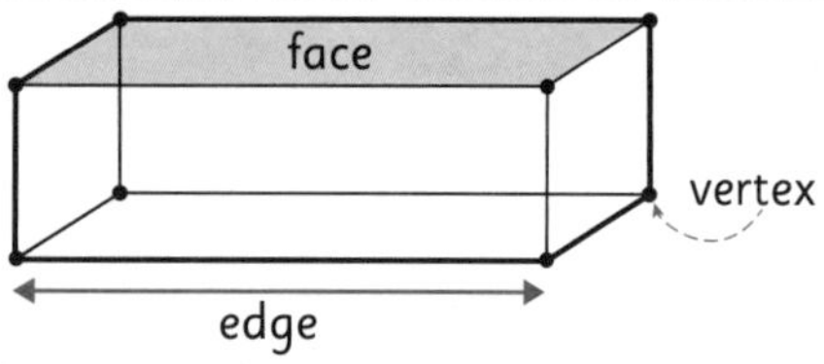

This is the skeleton of a cuboid. We can see through the skeleton. This makes it easy to count the faces, edges and vertices.

1. Complete the following table.

	Shape	Name	Number of faces	Number of edges	Number of vertices	Name the 2-D faces
(a)	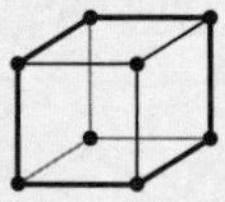	______	______	______	______	(i) ______
(b)	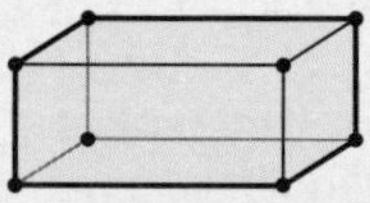	______	______	______	______	(i) ______ (ii) ______
(c)		______	______	______	______	(i) ______ (ii) ______
(d)	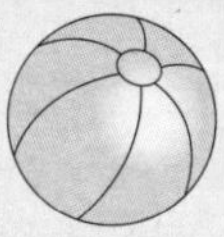	______	______	______	______	
(e)	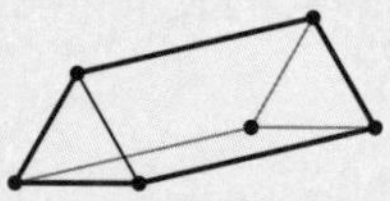	______ ______	______	______	______	(i) ______ (ii) ______
(f)	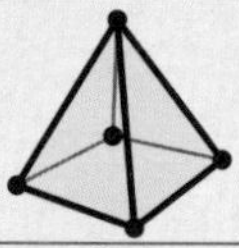	______	______	______	______	(i) ______ (ii) ______
(g)	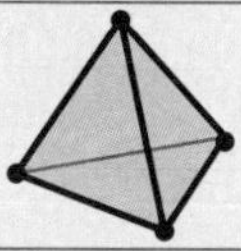	______	______	______	______	(i) ______
(h)	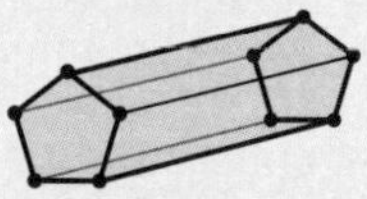	______ ______	______	______	______	(i) ______ (ii) ______
(i)	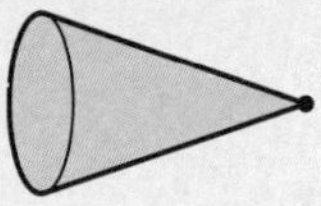	______	______	______	______	(i) Circle (ii) Rectangle

A cone has 2 faces but only 1 face has a definite name. The curved face could be folded from different shapes, e.g. triangle, square!

2. Imagine that you work as a designer of practical items.

(a) Which 3-D shape would you use to create each of the following?

(i) mug	(ii) pair of earrings	(iii) shed roof	(iv) suitcase
(v) pencil-holder	(vi) flower basket	(vii) footrest	(viii) footbridge

(b) Draw your own designs into your copybook.

Challenge Construct as many of the 3-D shape skeletons from Question 1 as you can using straws and Blu-Tack.

3-D shapes – Pyramids and prisms

Pyramids

- A pyramid is named after the shape of its **base**, e.g. square pyramid, pentagonal pyramid, etc.
- All the other faces are triangles.
- The vertex at the top of a pyramid is called the **apex**.

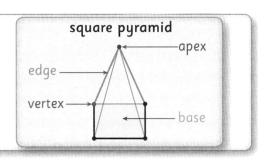

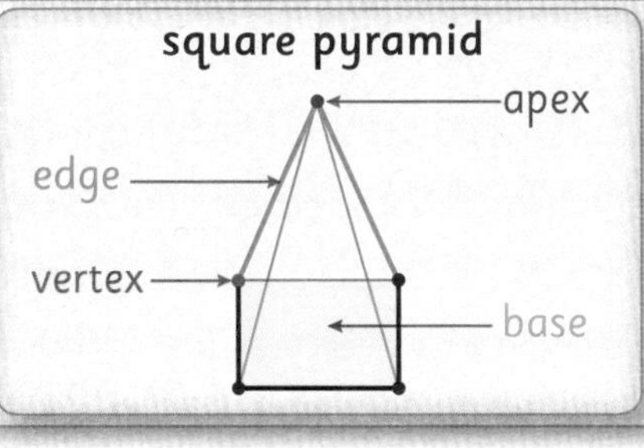

1. (a) Name each of the following pyramids.

(i) 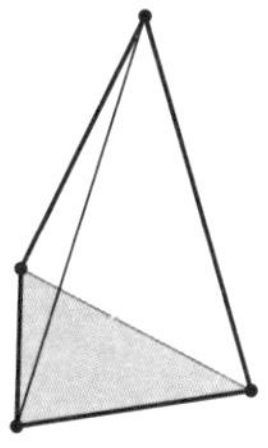

(ii) 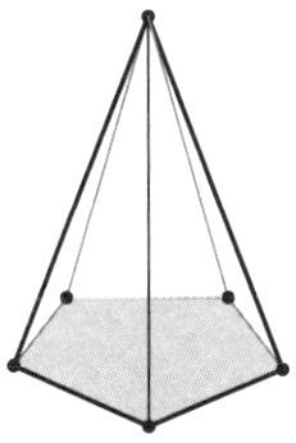

(iii) 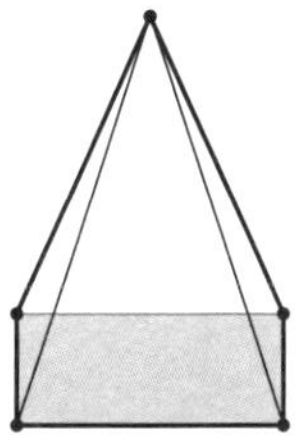

(iv) 

rectangular
hexagonal
triangular
pentagonal

(b) Trace each pyramid into your copybook. Label the **apex**, the **base**, an **edge** and a **vertex**.

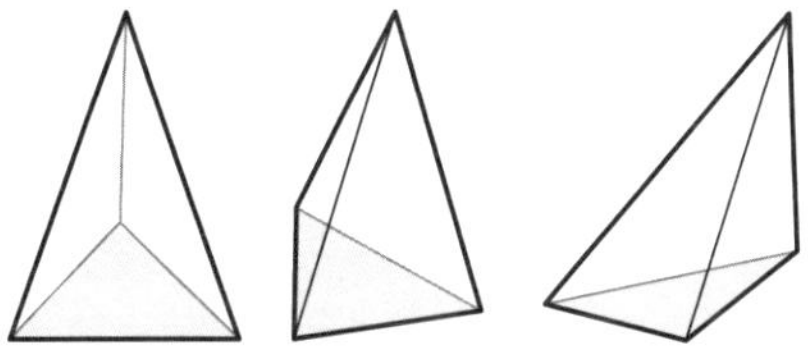

Each of these pyramids is a **tetrahedron**. Tetrahedron is a special name given to a triangular-based pyramid. We have called it a **triangular pyramid** up until now!

The plural of tetrahedron is tetrahedra.

2. **Answer these questions about the tetrahedron.**
   (a) What 2-D shape is each face?
   (b) How many (i) faces; (ii) edges; (iii) vertices (including the apex) has it?
   (c) How many edges meet at each vertex?

Prisms

A **prism** is a 3-D shape that can be cut into identical slices. Prisms have **straight edges** only. A prism, like a pyramid, is also named after the shape of its **base**.

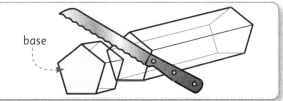

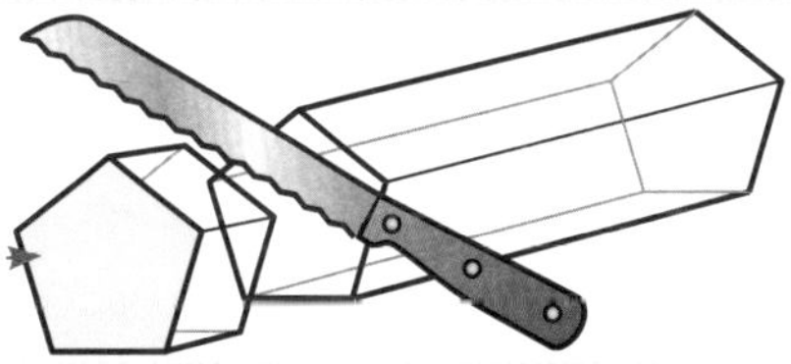

3. **Write the correct name for each of the following prisms.**

(a) 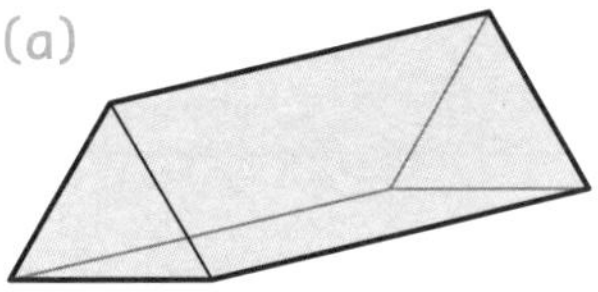

(b) 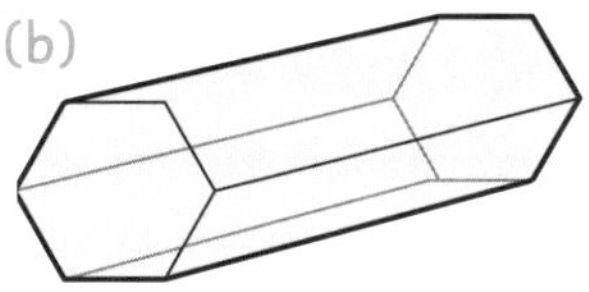

(c) 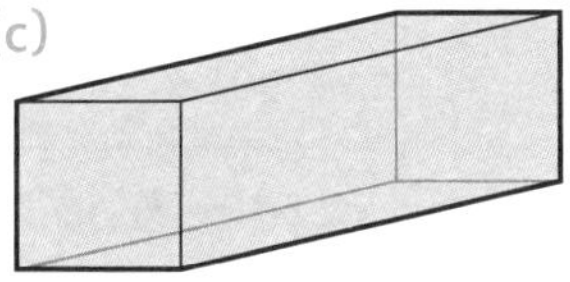

(d) 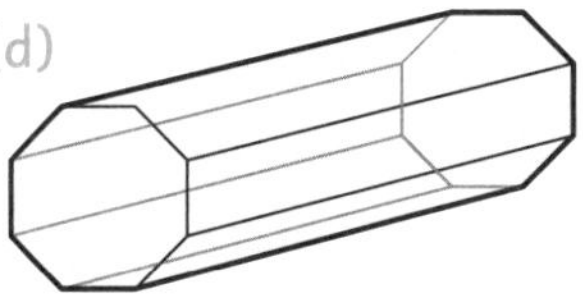

4. **Say whether the following prisms are regular or irregular.**

Remember, in regular polygons all sides are of equal length.

(a) 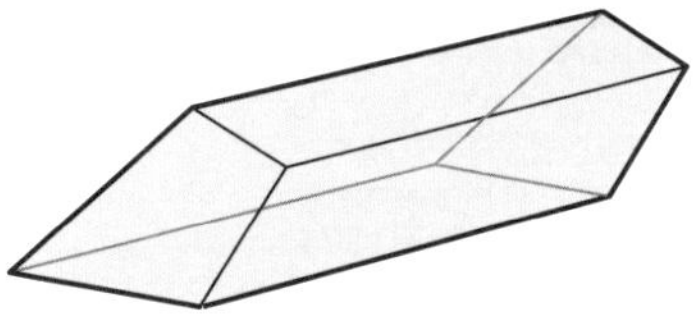

(b) 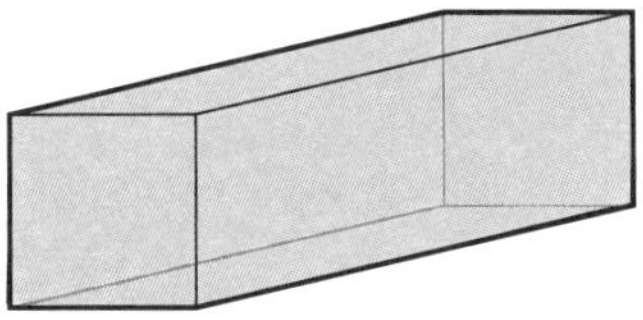

(c) 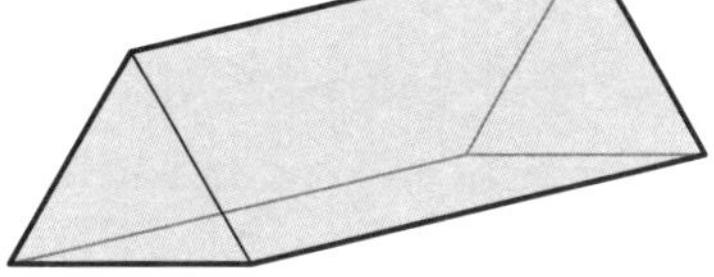

(d) 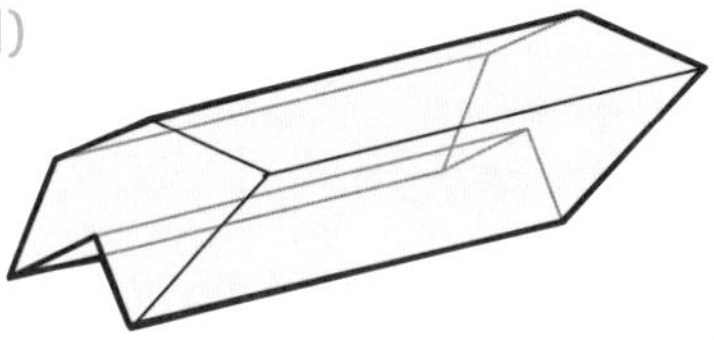

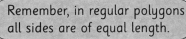

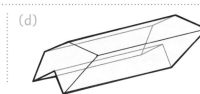

3-D shapes – Polyhedra

Polyhedra

- A polyhedron is a 3-D shape with flat faces.
- Each face is a polygon (has straight sides).
- The plural of polyhedron is polyhedra.

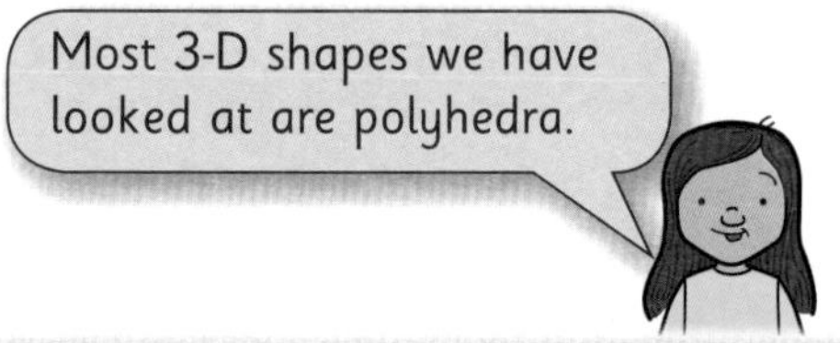

Most 3-D shapes we have looked at are polyhedra.

1. List the shapes below that are (a) polyhedra and (b) not polyhedra.

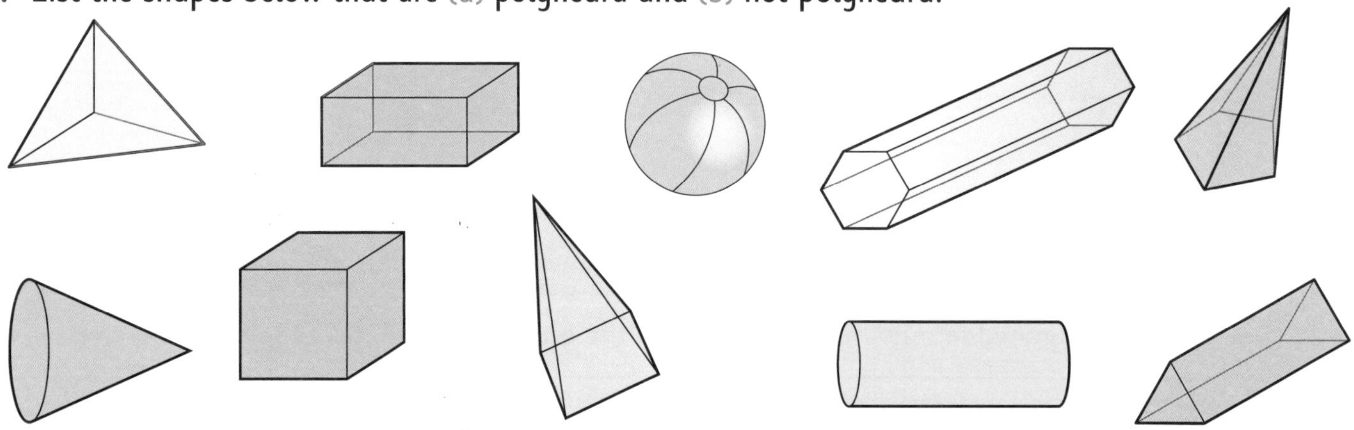

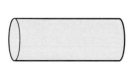

2.

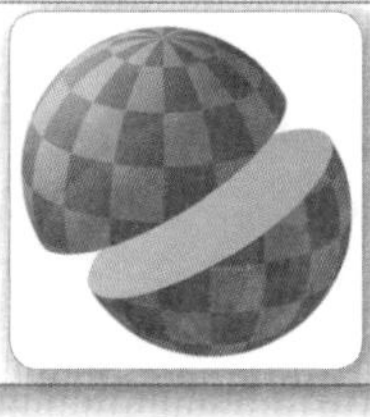

- A **sphere** can be cut into **two halves**.
- Each half is called a **hemisphere**.

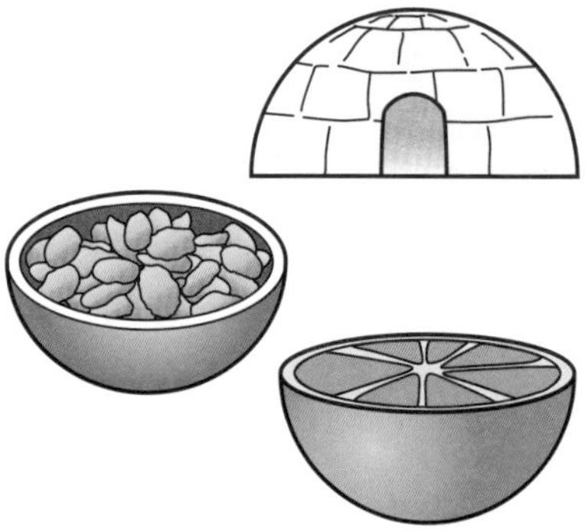

(a) Is a hemisphere a polyhedron? Give a reason for your answer.

(b) How many (i) faces; (ii) edges; (iii) vertices has a hemisphere?

(c) List five objects that are shaped like a hemisphere.

3. Regular polyhedra are made up of identical faces. Which of these familiar shapes are regular polyhedra?

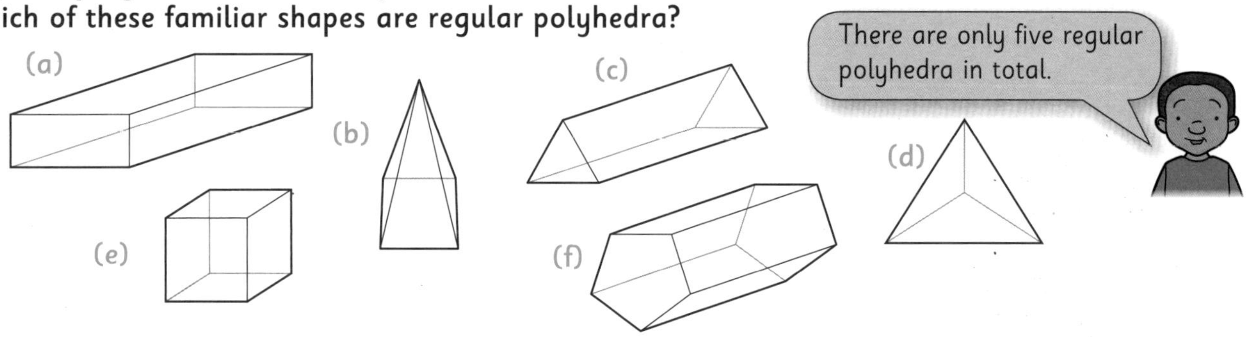

(a)
(b)
(c)
There are only five regular polyhedra in total.
(d)
(e)
(f)

4.

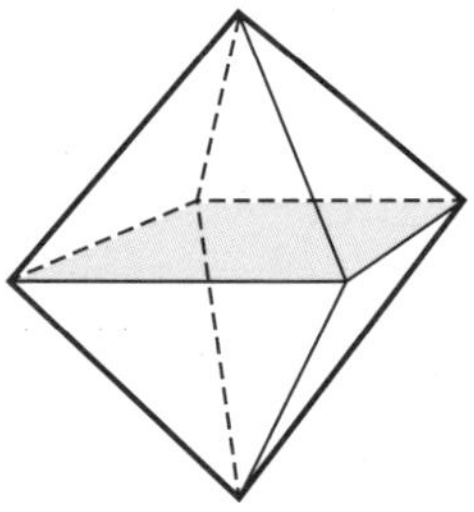

This is an octahedron.

(a) It is made up of two square p____________ with the square faces stuck together.

(b) How many faces has it?

(c) What shape is each face?

(d) Is it a regular polyhedron?

Challenge 1

Find out the names of the other two regular polyhedra.

Challenge 2 The words '**polyhedron**' and '**tetrahedron**' come from ancient Greek. Research the origins of the words '**polyhedron**' and '**tetrahedron**'.

3-D shapes in the environment

1. List all the 3-D shapes you can find in each picture.

(a)

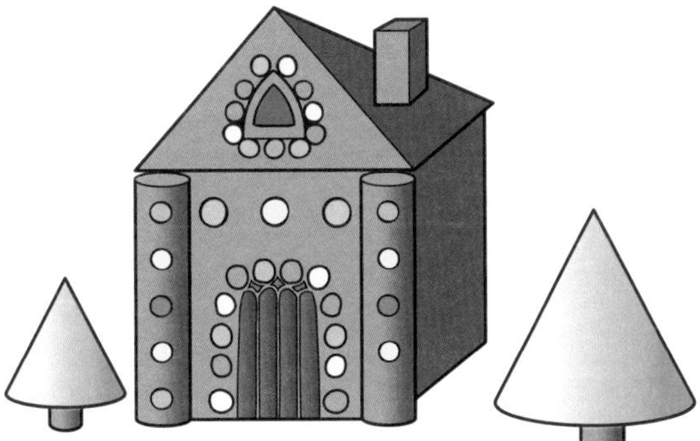

(b)

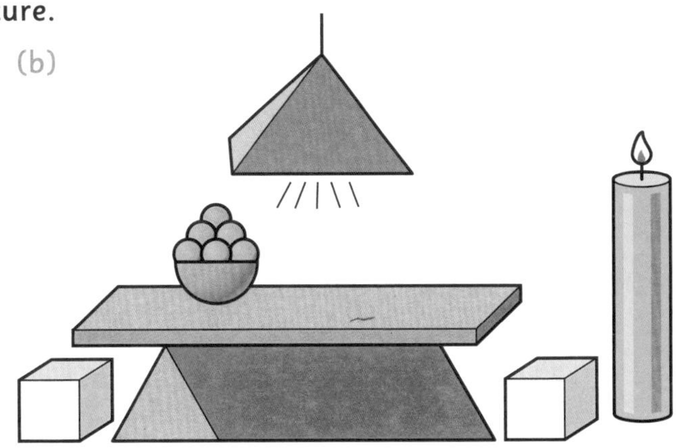

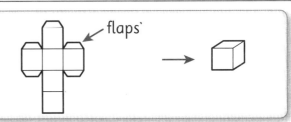

Shape nets

When a 3-D shape is flattened out, we see its net.
Sometimes flaps are added to a net.
They make it easier to glue the faces together.

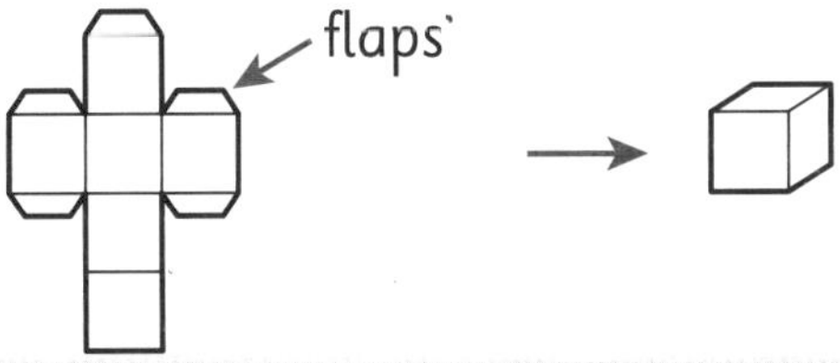

2. Colour match each net in **A** to its solid shape in **B**.

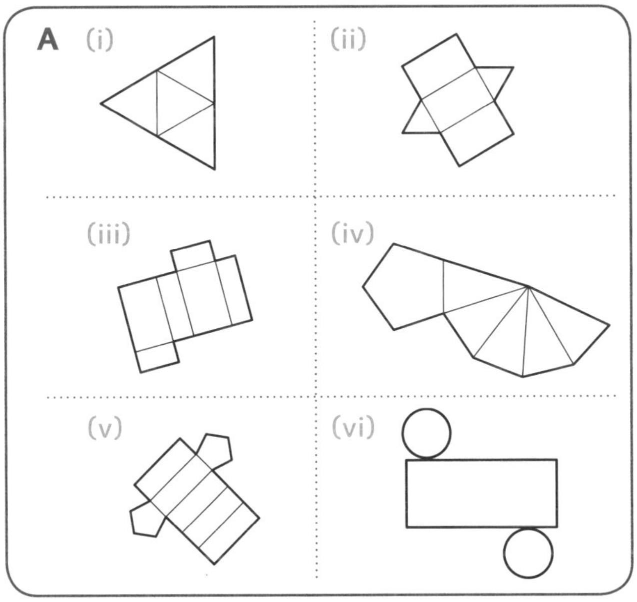

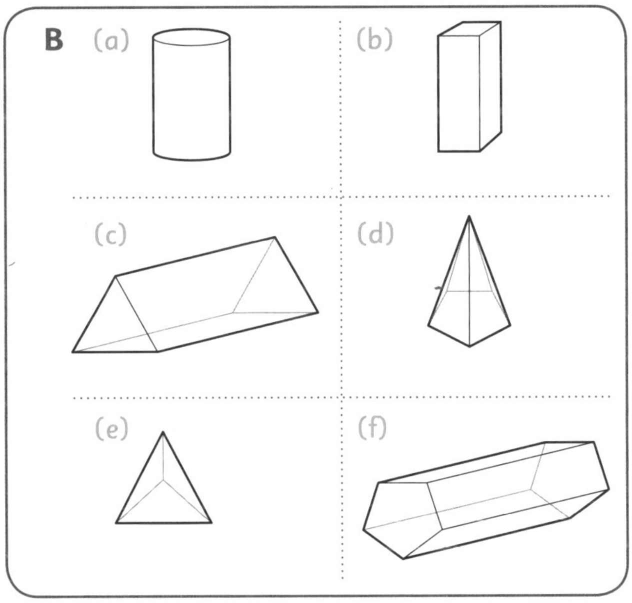

3. Which of the following nets do **not** make a tetrahedron?

(a)

(b)

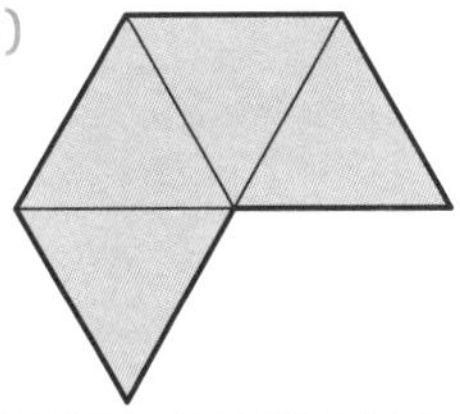

(c)

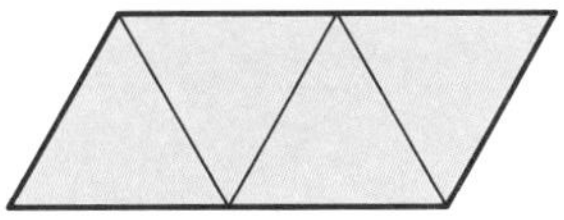

Challenge

Draw these shape nets onto card. Cut along their perimeters. Fold each one to make the original 3-D shape.

(a)

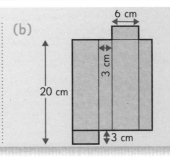

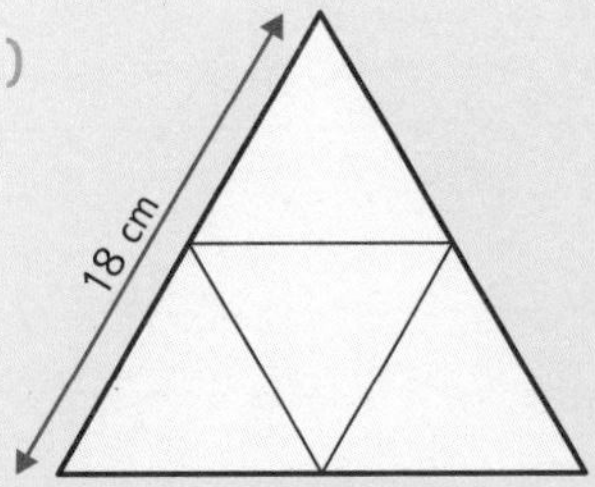

(b)

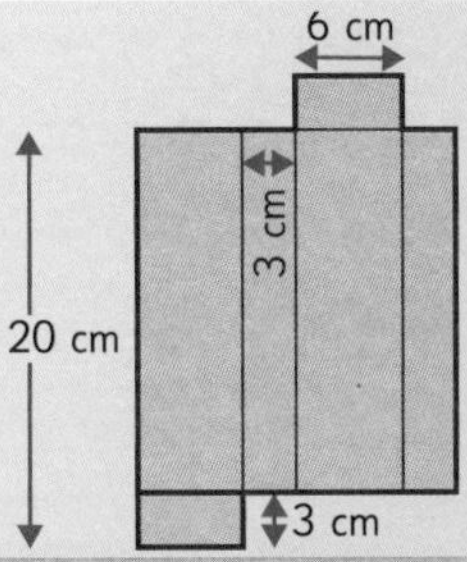

Chapter 31: Rules and properties

Order of operations

Find the cost of four children's tickets and two adults' tickets.
Write the method of calculating this in equation form.

Adults **€8**
Children **€5**
Cinema Prices

4 × €5 + 2 × €8 = ☆

Here is how three children did it.

Pat	**Sam**	**Ruth**
€5 + €8 = €13	4 × €5 = €20	€5 + 2 = €7
2 + 4 = 6	2 × €8 = €16	€4 × 7 = €28
€13 × 6 = €78	€20 + €16 = €36	€28 × €8 = €224

Who got the right answer? Explain.

Here is the order of operations we must follow:
Brackets, **M**ultiplication, **D**ivision, **A**ddition, **S**ubtraction
( ) first; **×** and **÷** next; finally **+** and **–**.

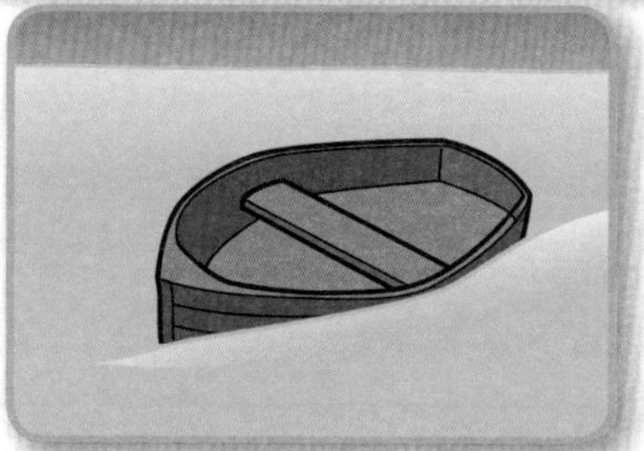

An easy way to remember is: **B**oats **M**ay **D**rift **A**t **S**ea.

1. Have a go at these. Compare the answers. What do you notice in each group?

(a) (i) 8 + 7 + 3 = ______ (ii) (3 + 7) + 8 = ______ (iii) 7 + (3 + 8) = ______

(b) (i) 19 – 5 – 3 = ______ (ii) (19 – 5) – 3 = ______ (iii) 19 – (5 – 3) = ______

(c) (i) 4 × 8 × 2 = ______ (ii) (4 × 2) × 8 = ______ (iii) 8 × (2 × 4) = ______

(d) (i) 80 ÷ 4 ÷ 2 = ______ (ii) (80 ÷ 4) ÷ 2 = ______ (iii) 80 ÷ (4 ÷ 2) = ______

(e) Complete these two sentences. Write **does** or **does not**.

(i) When doing **addition** or **multiplication**, the order of operations ______ matter.

(ii) When doing **subtraction** or **division**, the order ______ matter.

2. Now try these.

(a) 5 × (4 + 7) = ______ (b) (64 ÷ 8) × 9 = ______ (c) 14 + (18 ÷ 3) = ______

(d) 90 – (30 ÷ 6) = ______ (e) (72 ÷ 8) – 9 = ______ (f) 84 – (6 × 5) = ______

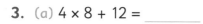

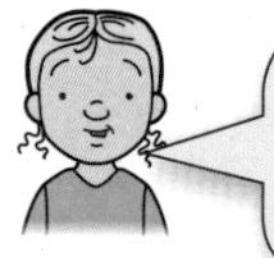

When **×** and **÷** are in the same number sentence (equation), start with the one that appears **first** (on the left) and continue as we do when reading a word sentence.

Example: 54 ÷ 6 × 8
(54 ÷ 6) × 8

3. (a) 4 × 8 + 12 = ______ (b) 35 – 14 ÷ 2 = ______ (c) 64 ÷ 8 + 24 = ______

(d) 36 ÷ 3 × 7 = ______ (e) 16 + 48 ÷ 8 = ______ (f) 24·6 ÷ 3 × 2 = ______

(g) 3 × 6 ÷ 2 = ______ (h) 90 ÷ 9 × 5 = ______ (i) 6·5 ÷ 5 × 7 = ______

(j) 5·6 × 24 + 16 = ______ (k) 6·3 – 2·47 × 16 = ______ (l) 7·02 ÷ 27 + 6·87 = ______

(m) 6·84 ÷ 19 × 24 = ______ (n) 3·76 ÷ 8 + 36 = ______ (o) 1·26 ÷ 7 + 34 = ______

STRAND **Algebra** **STRAND UNIT/ELEMENT** *Rules and properties*
LANGUAGE *Operations, addition, subtraction, multiplication, division, equation, brackets, number sentence, compare, solve, examine, patterns, sequence, missing terms, Pascal's triangle*

Rules and properties – Problem-solving

1. Complete these.

(a) 8 × 3 + 2·7 = ____

(b) 3·6 + 72 ÷ 8 = ____

(c) 48 ÷ 8 × 6 = ____

(d) 7 × 10 ÷ 2 = ____

(e) 30·5 ÷ 5 × 4 = ____

(f) 6 + 3 × 8 + 2 = ____

(g) 59 + 6 ÷ 3 + 14 – 8 = ____

(h) 63 ÷ 9 + 8 – 11 = ____

(i) (12 – 7) + 3 + 18 ÷ 9 = ____

2. Put the correct operation sign (+, –, ×, ÷) in the ◯ to calculate each answer.

(a) David bought two adult stand tickets and three children's tickets.
Find the total cost of the tickets.

2 ◯ €35 ◯ 3 ◯ €5 = €____

(b) Cara bought four stand tickets but later gave one back. Find the final cost of the tickets.

4 ◯ €35 – €35 = €____

(c) Adrian bought five terrace tickets and four children's tickets.
Find the total cost of the tickets.

5 ◯ €20 ◯ 4 ◯ €5 = €____

(d) Later Adrian returned one of his terrace tickets.
How much altogether did he spend on tickets?

5 ◯ €20 ◯ 4 ◯ €5 ◯ €20 = €____

3. Put the correct operation sign (+, –, ×, ÷) in the ◯ and then calculate each answer.

(a) Eileen bought two teas and three rolls.
How much did she spend?

2 ◯ €1·50 ◯ 3 ◯ €3·55 = €____

(b) Tina bought two coffees, three sandwiches and one roll. What was the cost of her bill?

2 × €1·75 ◯ 3 × €3·25 ◯ €3·55 = €____

(c) Paul bought one coffee and three wraps but decided to return one of the wraps. How much did he spend?

€1·75 ◯ 3 ◯ €2·80 ◯ €2·80 = €____

COFFEE SHOP
PRICES

TEA ~ €1·50
COFFEE ~ €1·75
SANDWICH ~ €3·25
WRAP ~ €2·80
ROLL ~ €3·55

Rules and properties – Pattern

1. Examine these patterns. Draw the next **two** terms for each.

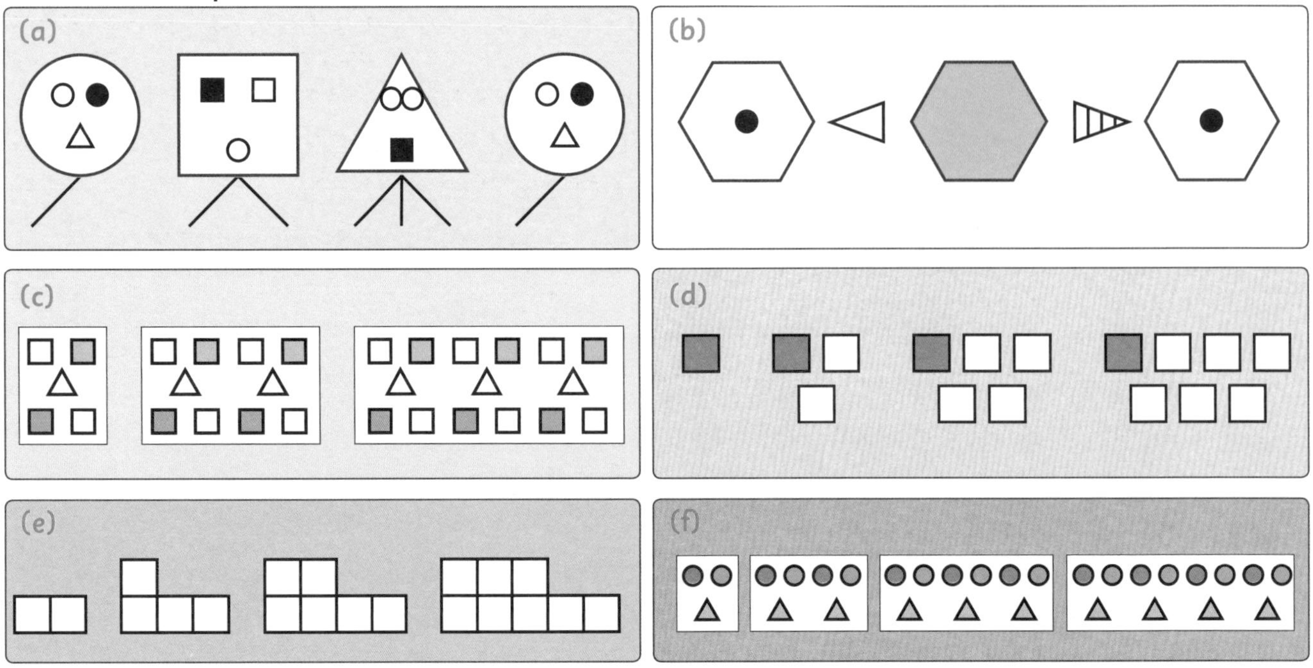

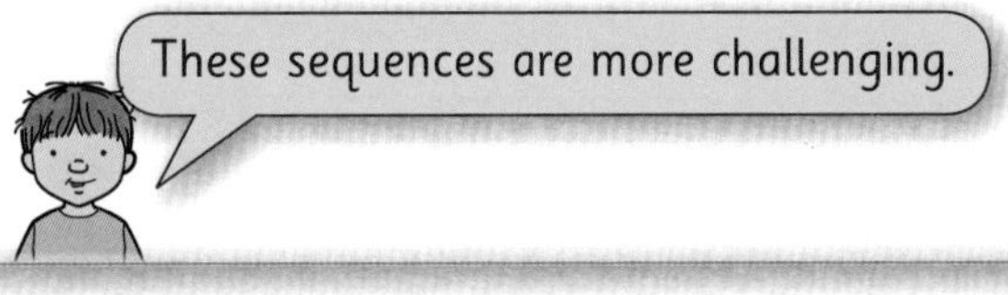

56, 55, 53, 50, 46, 41, 35
−1 −2 −3 −4 −5 −6

2. Examine each sequence carefully and find the pattern. Write the next **three** terms for each. Use your calculator to help you.

(a) 6, 11, 17, 24, 32…
(b) 1, 2, 5, 10, 17…
(c) 1, 3, 7, 13, 21…
(d) 500, 480, 460, 440…
(e) 19, 20, 22, 25, 29, 34…
(f) 1, 2, 4, 8, 16…
(g) 1, 5, 13, 25, 41…
(h) 4, 16, 64, 256…
(i) 2·3, 4·6, 9·2, 18·4…

3. Fill in the missing terms in each sequence.

(a) 17, ____, 31, 38, ____, 52.
(b) 45, ____, 69, ____, ____, 105.
(c) 63, ____, 55, 51, ____, ____.
(d) 128, 64, ____, 16, ____, 4.
(e) 3·5, 5, ____, ____, 9·5, ____.
(f) 24·8, 22·6, ____, ____, 16, ____.
(g) 73, 72, 70, ____, 63, ____.
(h) ____, ____, ____, $7\frac{3}{4}$, $7\frac{1}{2}$, $7\frac{1}{4}$.

Work out the answers to these. Examine the pattern. You may use your calculator.

4. (a) 1 × 9 = 10 – 1
(b) 2 × 9 = 20 – 2
(c) 3 × 9 = 30 – 3
(d) 4 × 9 = 40 – 4
(e) 5 × 9 = 50 – 5

5. (a) 5 × 5 = ____
(b) 15 × 15 = ____
(c) 25 × 25 = ____
(d) 35 × 35 = ____
(e) 45 × 45 = ____

6. (a) (1 × 9) + 2 = ____
(b) (12 × 9) + 3 = ____
(c) (123 × 9) + 4 = ____
(d) (1,234 × 9) + 5 = ____
(e) (12,345 × 9) + 6 = ____

Use the pattern to perdict the next term.

4. (f) 6 × 9 = ____

5. (f) 55 × 55 = ____

6. (f) (123,456 × 9) + 7 = ____

More patterns

Tropical storms are named after girls and boys. The names are listed alphabetically in the order that they occur. Only 21 letters of the alphabet are actually used on six separate lists. These lists are repeated cyclically (in a cycle). The following are the first four names in each list:

2015	2016	2017	2018	2019	2020
Ana	Alex	Arlene	Alberto	Andrea	Arthur
Bill	Bonnie	Bret	Beryl	Barry	Bertha
Claudette	Colin	Cindy	Chris	Chantal	Cristobal
Danny	Danielle	Don	Debby	Dorian	Dolly

The letters Q, U, X, Y and Z are not used to name tropical storms.

1. (a) Name the first tropical storm of 2015. ____________
   (b) What letter will be used for the 5th storm of 2017? ____________
   (c) What is the next year that the first tropical storm will be named Ana? ____________
   (d) What name is used for the 4th storm of 2020? ____________
   (e) What is the next year that the 2nd tropical storm will be named Bret? ____________
   (f) What is the next year that the 3rd tropical storm will be named Chantal? ____________

2. **Now complete the following table.**

	2028	2030	2050	2063	2074
1st storm	Alex				
2nd storm					
3rd storm					
4th storm					

Pascal's triangle
Pascal's triangle was discovered by a French mathematician Blaise Pascal in the 17th century.

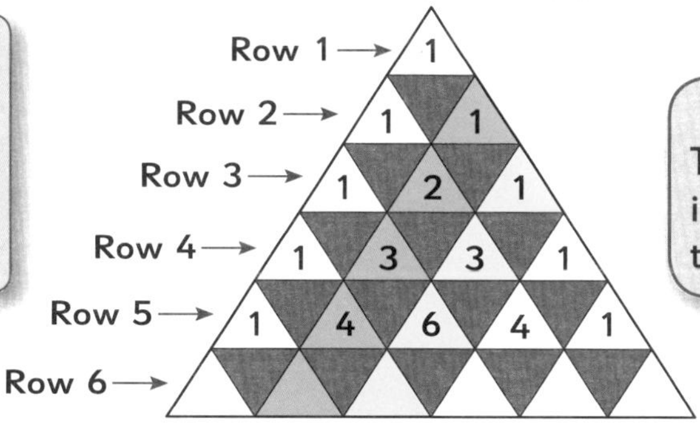

Hint!
The total for the numbers in each row is **double** the previous row!

3. **Examine the triangle above carefully.**
   (a) Fill in the numbers that are missing from the 6th row.
   (b) What pattern do the green numbers make?
   (c) What pattern do the yellow numbers make?
   (d) Find the sum of the numbers in each row of the completed Pascal's triangle above.
   (e) Find the sum of all the numbers in Pascal's triangle above.

Challenge
(a) Write the numbers that would appear in rows 7 and 8.
(b) Predict what the sum of the numbers on rows 7 and 8 will be.
(c) Then find the sum of the numbers to see if you predicted correctly.

Chapter 32: Capacity

We use **litres (l)** and **millilitres (ml)** to measure the capacity of containers. Capacity means the amount a container can hold.

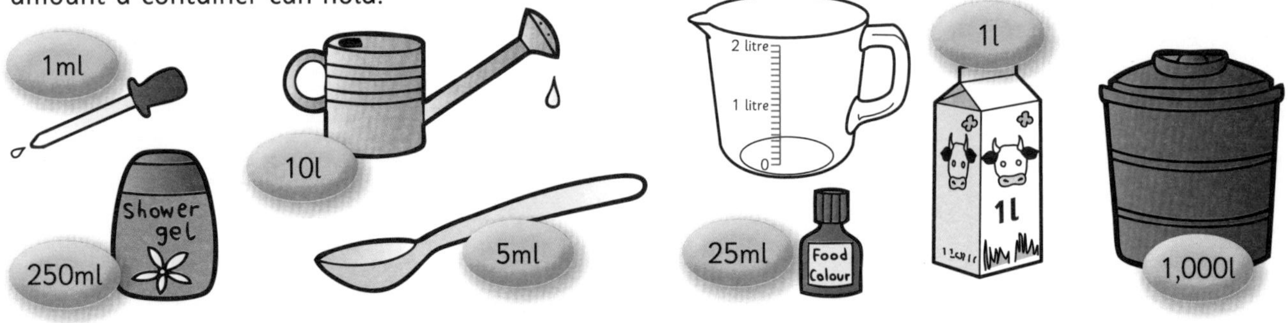

1. Circle what you think is the best estimate of the capacity of each of these containers.

Remember: 1,000ml = 1l **Remember:** 1ml = 0·001l

Approximate capacity of:			
(a) A tablespoon	5ml	15ml	30ml
(b) A large soft drink bottle	100ml	2l	8l
(c) A garden bucket	10l	10ml	1,000ml
(d) A bottle of fabric conditioner	25ml	250ml	$2\frac{1}{2}$ l
(e) An orange juice carton	1l	10ml	40ml
(f) The fuel tank of a mid-range car	2l	70l	240l
(g) An attic water tank	100l	3,000l	500l

2. A bottle of vinegar holds 250ml. How much vinegar will five bottles hold?

(a) _____ml or (b) _____l and _____ml

3.

A garage showroom has five new cars on display. 20 litres of fuel are poured in equal quantities into the fuel tanks of these cars. How much fuel is poured into each fuel tank? _____l

Maths Fact Your salivary glands produce about 1·5 litres of fluid in your mouth every day. About how many days would it take you to produce 30 litres of fluid? _____

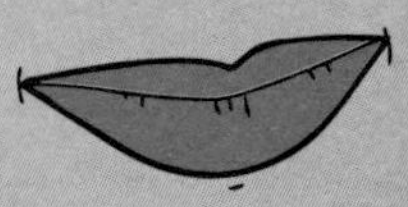

Challenge

(a) How many of the small bottles are needed to hold the same amount as three of the large bottles? _____

(b) A large bottle of paint costs €2·36. A small bottle costs €1·47. How much altogether for 3 large and 2 small bottles of paint? € _____

(c) How much altogether for 2 large and 3 small bottles of paint? € _____

STRAND **Measures** STRAND UNIT/ELEMENT *Capacity*

LANGUAGE *Capacity, container, litre, millilitre, estimate, measure, fractions, decimals, graduated jugs, addition, subtraction, multiplication, division, change, identical*

Litres and millilitres

Remember: $1ml = \frac{1}{1000}l = 0{\cdot}001l$

$468ml = \frac{468}{1000}l = 0{\cdot}468l$ $79ml = \frac{79}{1000}l = 0{\cdot}079l$ $3ml = \frac{3}{1000}l = 0{\cdot}003l$

1. Write these **millilitres** as litres in fraction and in decimal form.

$7ml = \frac{7}{1000}l = 0{\cdot}007l$

(a) 5ml = ____ = ____
(b) 18ml = ____ = ____
(c) 2ml = ____ = ____
(d) 75ml = ____ = ____
(e) 146ml = ____ = ____
(f) 420ml = ____ = ____
(g) 902ml = ____ = ____
(h) 700ml = ____ = ____

2. Now write these **litre** measures as **millilitres**. (First write them as fractions of a litre.)

$0{\cdot}009l = \frac{9}{1000}l = 9ml$

(a) 0·003l = ____ = ____
(b) 0·051l = ____ = ____
(c) 0·004l = ____ = ____
(d) 0·267l = ____ = ____
(e) $0{\cdot}03l = \frac{3}{100}l =$ ____
(f) 0·680l = ____ = ____
(g) 0·104l = ____ = ____
(h) 0·92l = ____ = ____

Remember: The metric system is quite easy when we use decimal places. →

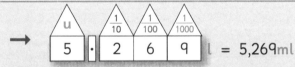

u		$\frac{1}{10}$	$\frac{1}{100}$	$\frac{1}{1000}$	
5	·	2	6	9	l = 5,269ml

6,149ml → 6·149l
5,039ml → 5·039l
7,004ml → 7·004l
2·235l → 2,235ml
6·095l → 6,095ml
4·008l → 4,008ml

3. Change these litre measures to **millilitres**.

3·472l = 3,472ml

(a) 4·159l = ________ ml
(b) 5·75l = ________ ml
(c) 6·258l = ________ ml
(d) 25·703l = ________ ml
(e) 16·03l = ________ ml
(f) 7·372l = ________ ml
(g) 9·29l = ________ ml
(h) 2·2l = ________ ml

4. Now write these **millilitres** as **litres**.

4,809ml = 4·809l

(a) 3,561ml = ________ l
(b) 4,247ml = ________ l
(c) 8,420ml = ________ l
(d) 2,049ml = ________ l
(e) 6,070ml = ________ l
(f) 319ml = ________ l
(g) 53ml = ________ l
(h) 2,264ml = ________ l

Maths Fact 9,100 litres of water can be stored by a large Saguaro Cactus. For how many weeks would the water of this Saguaro Cactus last if 25 litres were drained off each day? ____

Using measures

We use **graduated** jugs or cylinders to accurately measure the amount of liquid in a container.

A This graduated jug has a capacity of _____. It now contains 300ml of liquid.

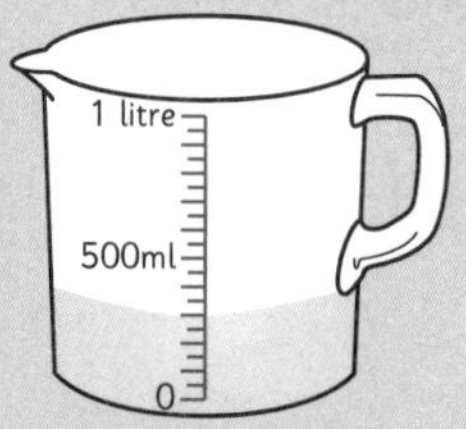

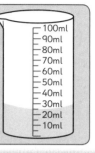

B This graduated cylinder has a capacity of _____. It now contains 25ml of liquid.

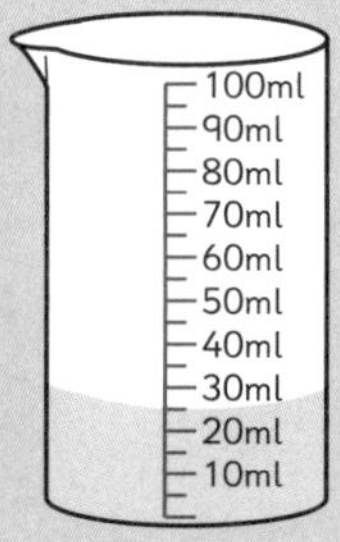

1. Read these graduated measures and write the correct measure of fluid in each.

(a)

(b)
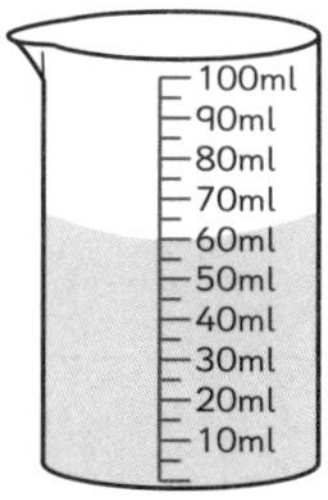

(c)
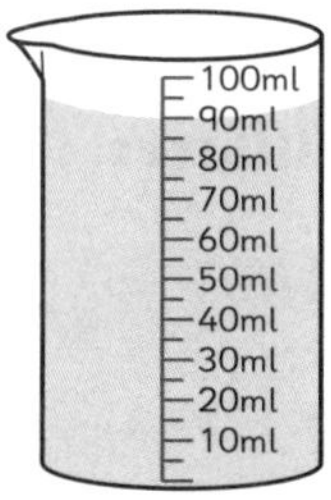

(d)
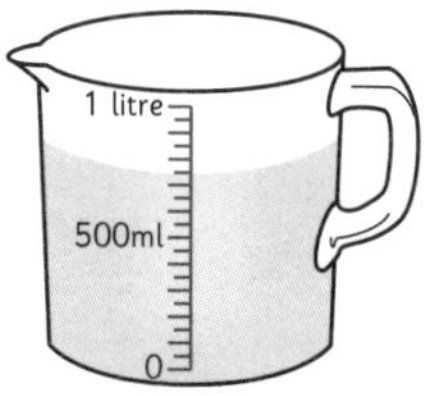

(e)
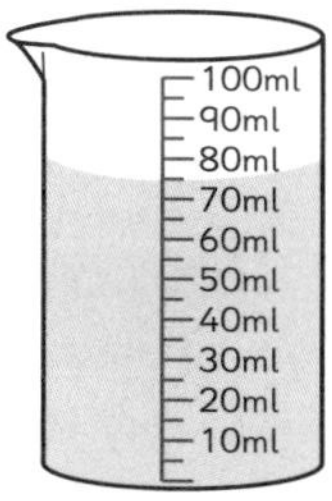

2. Draw the correct amount of fluid in each of these containers.

(a)

200ml

(b)
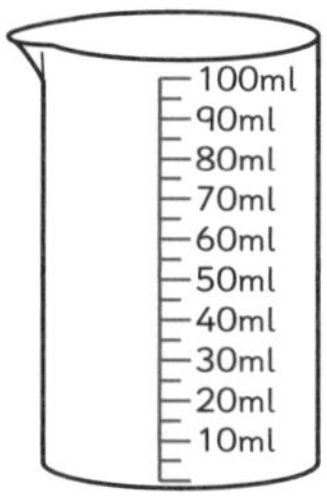

70ml

(c)
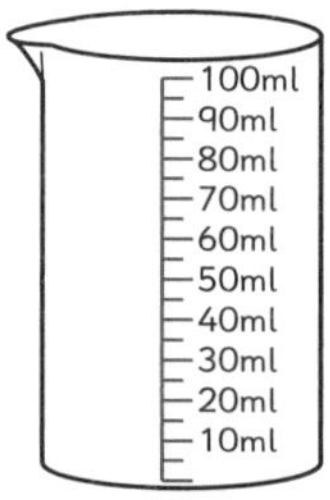

95ml

(d)
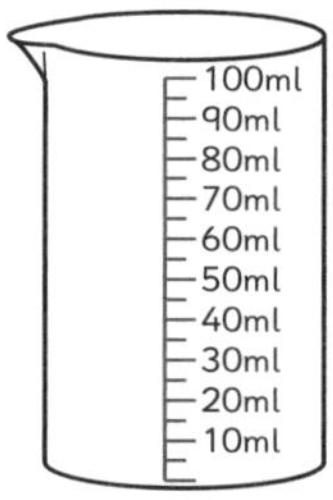

30ml

(e)

150ml

3. Use three colours to top up each container to the level of fluid asked for in (i) to (iii) of (a), (b), (c) and (d) below. Write the total volume for each.

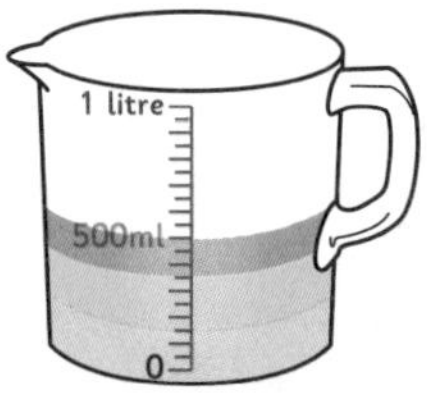

(i) 150ml
(ii) 0·2l
(iii) 0·15l
Total: 500ml

(a)
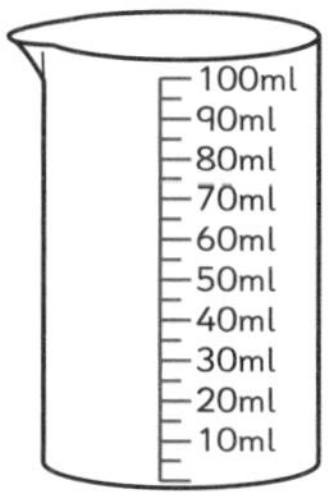

(i) 20ml
(ii) 45ml
(iii) 0·02l
Total: _____

(b)
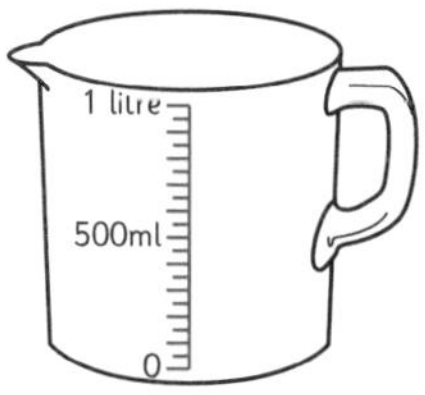

(i) 0·3l
(ii) 250ml
(iii) 0·25l
Total: _____

(c)
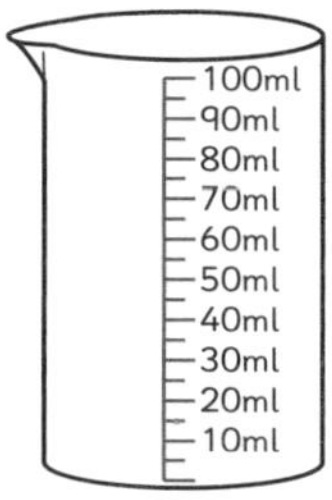

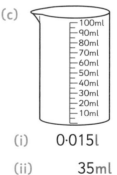

(i) 0·015l
(ii) 35ml
(iii) 0·030l
Total: _____

(d)

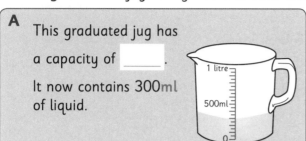

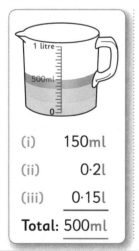

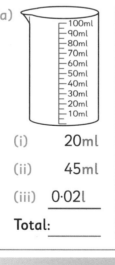

(i) 250ml
(ii) 0·35l
(iii) 0·3l
Total: _____

Maths Fact

In some parts of the Atacama Desert in Chile, an average of 1 millilitre of rain falls per year. At this rate of rainfall in the Atacama Desert, write the amount of rain that would have fallen over a 500-year period:

(a) as ml and (b) as a decimal fraction of a litre. (a) _____ (b) _____

Capacity – Addition and subtraction

A gardener's watering can contains 3·425l of water. 1·439l of plant food is added. How much liquid is in the can now?

$$\begin{array}{r} 3\cdot425\,l \\ +\ 1\cdot43_19\,l \\ \hline 4\cdot864\,l \end{array}$$

1. Now do these.

(a) $\begin{array}{r} 6\cdot258\,l \\ +\ 2\cdot574\,l \\ \hline \end{array}$
(b) $\begin{array}{r} 5\cdot376\,l \\ +\ 2\cdot979\,l \\ \hline \end{array}$
(c) $\begin{array}{r} 23\cdot573\,l \\ +\ 8\cdot759\,l \\ \hline \end{array}$
(d) $\begin{array}{r} 15\cdot782\,l \\ +\ 8\cdot769\,l \\ \hline \end{array}$
(e) $\begin{array}{r} 35\cdot058\,l \\ +\ 8\cdot975\,l \\ \hline \end{array}$

A large bottle of fabric conditioner holds $2\frac{1}{2}$ l. Mark did seven washes using 30ml for each wash. How much conditioner was left?

$2\frac{1}{2}\,l = 2\cdot5\,l$ →

$30\text{ml} \times 7 = 210\text{ml}$ →

$$\begin{array}{r} 2\cdot500\,l \\ -\ 0\cdot210\,l \\ \hline 2\cdot290\,l \end{array}$$

2. Now try these.

(a) $\begin{array}{r} 3\cdot350\,l \\ -\ 1\cdot490\,l \\ \hline \end{array}$
(b) $\begin{array}{r} 5\cdot620\,l \\ -\ 2\cdot655\,l \\ \hline \end{array}$
(c) $\begin{array}{r} 4\cdot247\,l \\ -\ 1\cdot555\,l \\ \hline \end{array}$
(d) $\begin{array}{r} 10\cdot320\,l \\ -\ 6\cdot505\,l \\ \hline \end{array}$
(e) $\begin{array}{r} 12\cdot243\,l \\ -\ 9\cdot785\,l \\ \hline \end{array}$

3. Try these next. Be careful with the signs!

(a) $\begin{array}{r} 5\cdot116\,l \\ -\ 0\cdot258\,l \\ \hline \end{array}$
(b) $\begin{array}{r} 3\cdot865\,l \\ +\ 2\cdot368\,l \\ \hline \end{array}$
(c) $\begin{array}{r} 10\cdot075\,l \\ -\ 7\cdot299\,l \\ \hline \end{array}$
(d) $\begin{array}{r} 8\cdot200\,l \\ -\ 3\cdot545\,l \\ \hline \end{array}$
(e) $\begin{array}{r} 15\cdot735\,l \\ +\ 7\cdot687\,l \\ \hline \end{array}$

4. An oil tank holding 57·36l was topped up to a total of 846·77l. How much extra fuel was added? _____ l

5. What was the total amount of milk produced by two goats if one produced 2·734 litres and the other 1·997 litres? _____ l

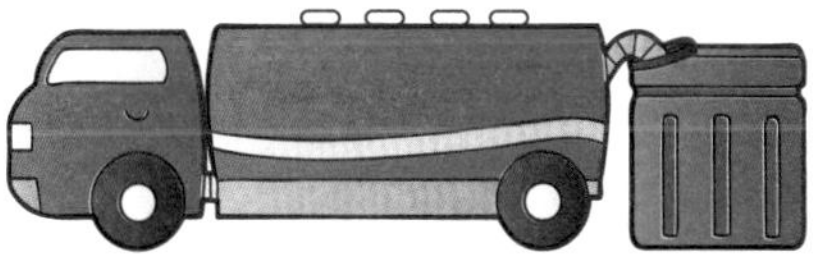

6. A small bottling factory produced 60·7l of juice in the first hour. It produced 18·936l less in the second hour.

(a) How many litres were produced in the second hour? _____ l

(b) How many litres of juice were produced altogether over the two hours? _____ l

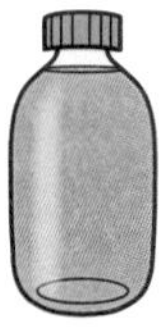

Maths Fact Explorers Wills and Burke brought 272 litres of rum across Australia on their 1860–61 expedition. The rum was for their camels to drink. How many camels did Burke and Wills have if each camel carried 68 litres? [____]

Capacity – Multiplication and division

$$8 \cdot 486\,l \times 18 = \boxed{\star}$$

```
        8 · 4 8 6 l
    ×         1 8
    6 7 8 8 8
    8 4 8 6 0
  1 5 2 · 7 4 8 l
```

```
        0 · 2 7 2 l
  16 ) 4 · 3 5 2 l
        3 2 ↓
        1 1 5
        1 1 2 ↓
            3 2
            3 2
            0 0
```

$$4 \cdot 352\,l \div 16 = \boxed{\star}$$

This is how we multiply and divide using litres. Be sure to keep the decimal point under or over itself.

1. Write 2,415ml as litres in decimal form and multiply by:

 (a) 9 (b) 12 (c) 16 (d) 27 (e) 38 (f) 42 (g) 58 (h) 69

2. Change 7,296ml to litres and divide by:

 (a) 8 _____ (b) 12 _____ (c) 16 _____ (d) 24 _____ (e) 48 _____

3. These are the prices charged in a new juice bar.
Each drink contains 500ml.
Work out the price for each mixture.

		(a)	(b)	(c)	(d)	(e)
Apple	50c per 100ml	250ml	—	—	—	150ml
Orange	60c per 100ml	—	300ml	125ml	—	75ml
Pear	45c per 100ml	—	—	—	300ml	—
Lime	80c per 100ml	—	—	125ml	75ml	75ml
Blackberry	66c per 100ml	250ml	—	—	—	50ml
Pineapple	72c per 100ml	—	200ml	250ml	125ml	150ml
Total cost of drinks:		€ ____	€ ____	€ ____	€ ____	€ ____

4. Create and cost your own fruit juice of 500ml from the above juices and prices. Make three in total.

5. A bottle of olive oil holds 250ml. There were 13 of these bottles stacked on a shelf. Seven of them were knocked off and got broken. How much olive oil altogether was left on the shelf? _____ l

6. Circle the biggest volume in each group.

 (a) 720ml 0·7l $\frac{73}{100}$l (b) 1·35l 1,400ml $1\frac{43}{1000}$ l (c) $7\frac{1}{4}$ l 7,030ml 7·29l

 (d) 45ml 0·054l $\frac{53}{1000}$l (e) 9,100ml $9\frac{2}{10}$l 9·025l (f) 8·37l $8\frac{3}{4}$ l 8·085l

Maths Fact If all the water in the world could fit into a four-litre jug, the fresh water available would amount to just one tablespoon. How many litres of water would be needed to produce 10 tablespoons of fresh water? _____ l

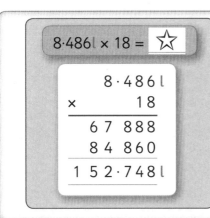

Capacity – A little bit of everything

1. Add or subtract to complete these.

(a) $\begin{array}{r} 8 \cdot 146\,l \\ -\ 6 \cdot 258\,l \\ \hline \end{array}$

(b) $\begin{array}{r} 5l\ 866\,ml \\ +\ 3l\ 975\,ml \\ \hline \end{array}$

(c) $\begin{array}{r} 10 \cdot 095\,l \\ -\ \ 9 \cdot 298\,l \\ \hline \end{array}$

(d) $\begin{array}{r} 5l\ 280\,ml \\ -\ 3l\ 645\,ml \\ \hline \end{array}$

(e) $\begin{array}{r} 12 \cdot 737\,l \\ +\ \ 7 \cdot 364\,l \\ \hline \end{array}$

2. Write 675ml as a decimal and multiply by:

(a) 8 (b) 13 (c) 47 (d) 63

3. Write 9l 540ml as a decimal and divide by:

(a) 6 (b) 9 (c) 15 (d) 36

4. Attach these labels to the container that you think is best suited to it.

 235ml
 $2\frac{1}{2}$ l
 1·7l
 9l
 450 ml
 210l

5. Circle the bigger volume of each pair of the following.

(a) 1,720ml 0·7l (b) 1·35l 1,400ml (c) $7\frac{1}{2}$ l 7,030ml (d) 9,100ml $9\frac{2}{10}$ l

6. A bottle of medicine holds 230ml. Paul has been told by his doctor to take two 5ml teaspoons of medicine three times a day for a week. How much medicine will be left in the bottle when he is finished? _____ ml

7. A 2l bottle of orange juice is shared equally among the 16 children at a party. How many ml does each child get? _____ ml

8. An oil tanker holds 15,000l of oil. The driver delivered 955l, 1,270l and 1,019l while making three deliveries. How many litres of oil were left in the tanker? _____ l

9. A domestic oil tank holds 1,000l. If 137l, 98l, 126l and 119l are used over a four-week period, what is the value of the oil left in the tank if oil costs 83c per litre? €_____

10. The fuel tank of a car holds 45l 370ml of diesel.

The fuel tank of a truck holds 38·75l more than the car.

(a) How much fuel does the truck hold? _____ l

(b) What is the total capacity of fuel that can be held by the two vehicles? _____ l

Maths Fact 475·8l of fuel are used to move the space shuttle crawler-transporter a distance of 1·6km. How many litres of fuel would be used to move the crawler-transporter a distance of 8km? [____] l

Capacity – H_2O

1. We should drink two litres of water a day. How many litres would you drink in the decade 2020 to 2029 if you followed this advice? (Don't forget to allow for leap years!) ______ l

2020, 2024 and 2028 are leap years.

2. A healthy human kidney (the organ that filters fluids) can process 900ml of fluid every hour. How much fluid will it process between 11:00 and 12:30? ______ l

3. A litre of water weighs 1kg. How many litres of water are equal to a weight of $2\frac{3}{5}$ kg? ______ l
Write this as ml. ______ ml

4. **Frozen water is 9% lighter than liquid water. What is the weight of:**
(a) 10l of frozen water? ______ kg (b) 8l of frozen water? ______ kg (c) 32l of frozen water? ______ kg

5. **An average bath uses 80l of water. An average shower uses 7l of water per minute. An average power shower uses 25l per minute. Compare and write in order the amounts of water used starting with the least if a person spends 4 minutes in the shower.**
(a) ______________ (b) ______________ (c) ______________

It takes 10l of water to produce a sheet of A4 paper.
It takes 30l of water to produce a cup of tea.
It takes 140l of water to produce a cup of coffee.
It takes 200l of water to produce a can of cola.
It takes 7,000l of water to produce one barrel of crude oil.
It takes 25,700l of water to produce a day's food for a family of four.

PAPER
A4

6. **How many litres of water are needed to produce:**
   (a) a 32-page A4 scrapbook?
   (b) eight cups of tea?
   (c) 35 cups of tea?
   (d) three dozen boxes of 24 cans?
   (e) four barrels of crude oil?
   (f) food for a family of four for a fortnight?
   (g) five cups of tea and three cups of coffee?
   (h) three cans of cola and 12 cups of tea?
   (i) a 64-page A4 book?
   (j) four cans of cola and three cups of coffee?
   (k) seven barrels of crude oil?

7. **Complete the following.**
   (a) How many cups of coffee are produced from (i) 280ml; (ii) 700ml; (iii) 1·4l of water?
   (b) How many barrels of crude oil are produced from (i) 21,000l; (ii) 35,000l of water?
   (c) An A4 pad of paper took 2,000l of water to produce. How many pages are in this pad?
   (d) It took 150l of water to produce the amount of tea that is in the teapot. How many cups of tea is this?

Maths Fact

An old-fashioned toilet cistern could use up to 12l of water per flush! How many litres would have been used by that type of cistern in three dozen flushes? ______ l

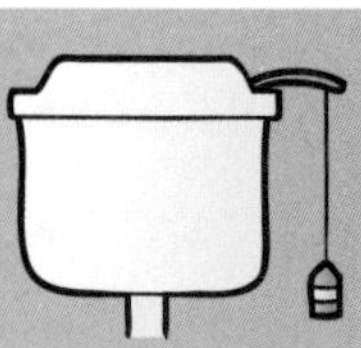

Chapter 33: Chance

Chance deals with the **possibility** that something might or might not happen. Other words for possibility are **probability** or **likelihood**.

impossible · certain · even chance · unlikely · possible · likely

Write one of the labels from the list above for each of the following statements.

1. The 10th of May will fall on Thursday. ____________

MAY						
Mon	Tue	Wed	Thu	Fri	Sat	Sun
	1	2	3	4	5	6
7	8	9	10	11	12	13
14	15	16	17	18	19	20
21	22	23	24	25	26	27
28	29	30	31			

2. Friday May 4th will fall after Saturday May 5th. ____________

3. If you buy a lottery ticket, you will win a major prize. ____________

4. If a drinking glass falls off a table, it will break. ____________

5. Bernie will roll an even number. ____________

6. Bernie will roll an odd number. ____________

Answer each of these statements in the same manner as above.

7. It will rain during the first week of January. ____________

8. The school bus will not run tomorrow. ____________

9. The next baby born in the maternity hospital will be female. ____________

10. The Olympic Games will be held in London again. ____________

11. When sharing a deck of cards equally among four people, each will get a picture card. ____________

12. You will see penguins if you go on an Arctic expedition. ____________

13. The next Taoiseach of Ireland will be a woman. ____________

14. The season of spring comes immediately after winter. ____________

15. Ireland will win the next men's Rugby World Cup. ____________

Activity: Write a statement of your own for each of the labels at the top of the page.

Maths Fact 25% of the medicines that we use contain ingredients that come from rainforest plants or animals. What is the chance that the medicine the doctor prescribes for you will contain ingredients from a rainforest plant or animal in (i) fraction form and (ii) decimal form? (i) ______ (ii) ______

STRAND Data **STRAND UNIT/ELEMENT** *Chance*

LANGUAGE *Possibility, likelihood, probability, chances, impossible, likely, unlikely, possible, even chance, tails, heads, coin, spinners*

Chance – Likelihood

1. Timmy travelled from Galway to Dublin to visit his cousin who was having an operation in the children's hospital.

impossible	**unlikely**	**even chance**
possible	**likely**	**certain**

Which of the above phrases has the greatest likelihood of being true in the following sentences?

(a) Timmy came to Dublin by car. ______________

(b) He drove the car himself. ______________

(c) Timmy's cousin is a girl. ______________

(d) Timmy came to Dublin by train. ______________

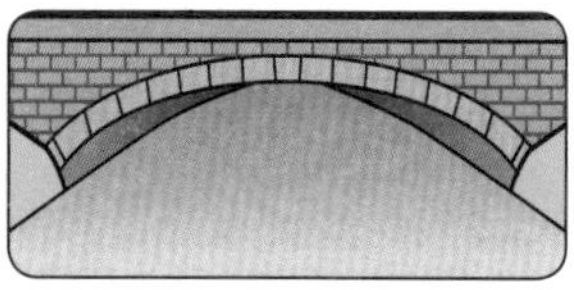

(e) He crossed a bridge on the way to Dublin. ______________

(f) He travelled on a Saturday. ______________

(g) The operation was a success. ______________

(h) Timmy will travel back to Galway in a space shuttle. ______________

(i) Timmy's cousin was glad to see him. ______________

(j) Timmy brought a cow with him to the hospital. ______________

2.

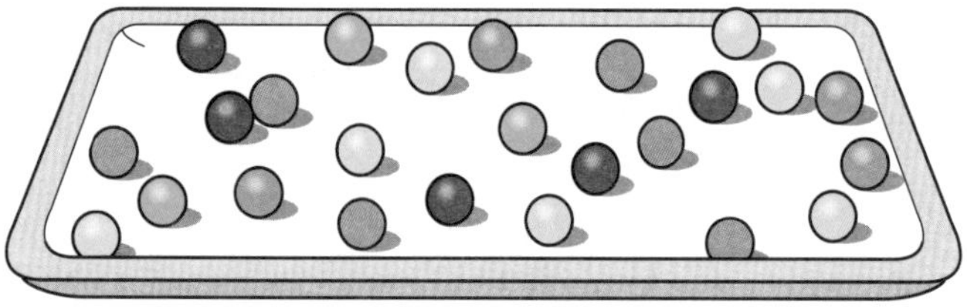

(a) How many red balls are there? ________

(b) How many green balls are there? ________

(c) How many blue balls are there? ________

(d) How many yellow balls are there? ________

(e) How many pink balls are there? ________

(f) How many balls are there altogether? ________

---

3. Work out the chances of the following happening if the balls from Q.2 were placed in an opaque bag and one pulled from the bag. The first one has been done for you.

(a) What is the likelihood of pulling a blue ball out of the bag? Four out of 25 or $\frac{4}{25}$.

(b) What is the probability of pulling a red ball out of the bag? ______________

(c) What is the chance of pulling a yellow ball out of the bag? ______________

(d) What is the chance of pulling a pink ball out of the bag? ______________

(e) What is the chance of pulling a green ball out of the bag? ______________

(f) What is the chance of pulling a black ball out of the bag? ______________

(g) What is the likelihood of pulling out either a yellow or a green ball? ______________

(h) What is the chance of pulling a pink or green ball out of the bag? ______________

(i) What is the likelihood of pulling a blue or pink ball out of the bag? ______________

(j) What is the likelihood of pulling a red, green or blue ball out of the bag? ______________

(k) What is the likelihood of pulling a yellow, pink or green ball out of the bag? ______________

Maths Fact In America, the chances of a man being colour-blind are 1 out of 12.
How many from a group of 96 would be expected to be colour-blind? ________

Chance – Recording scores

An Irish euro coin has a harp on one of its faces. We call it **tails**. The opposite side we call **heads**.

When we toss a euro coin, we have a one in two chance of getting tails and a one in two chance of getting heads.

This is known as a 50:50 chance or an even chance.

1. **Laura took a euro coin and tossed it 50 times. She recorded her results on this chart.**

Tails/Heads	Tally	Total	Fraction
Tails	卌 卌 卌 卌 卌 III	28	$\frac{28}{50}$
Heads	卌 卌 卌 卌 II	22	$\frac{22}{50}$

Try this activity with a partner. First predict what you think your results will be. Take 10 turns while your partner records the score. Then swap around. Be sure to record your results separately. Take 50 turns each in total.

Repeat the exercise with a different size coin. Will you get different results? Compare your results with other pairs of children.

2. Now try this activity with two coins. Again work with a partner. Take 10 turns. Your partner should record the score. Then swap around and your partner does the activity. Take 50 turns each.

Result	Tally	Total	Fraction
Two tails			
Two heads			
Head & tail			

(a) How many times did you toss two tails? _____ Partner's result: _____

(b) How many times did you toss two heads? _____ Partner's result: _____

(c) How many combinations of heads and tails did you record? _____ Partner's result: _____

(d) Did your results match your expectation? _____

(e) Compare your results with a few other pairs of children in your class.

(f) What would you expect your results to be if you and your partner took 100 turns each?

(g) Will your results be consistent? Explain.

Maths Fact 1 The probability of being born with 11 fingers or toes is 1 in 500. At this rate, how many people would you expect to have 11 fingers or toes in a group of 55,000? _____

Maths Fact 2 The chances of getting a hole-in-one at golf are 1 in 5,000. At this rate, how many people would be needed to ensure that nine holes-in-one were scored? _____

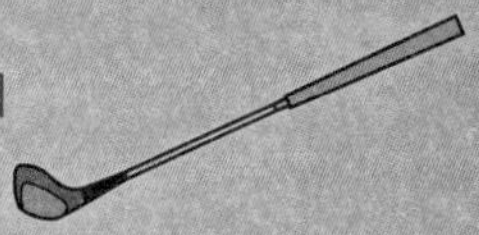

Chance – Fractions and percentages

Example:
What is the chance of the spinner stopping on **pink**?
The chance of the spinner stopping on **pink** is 1:5 or $\frac{1}{5}$.

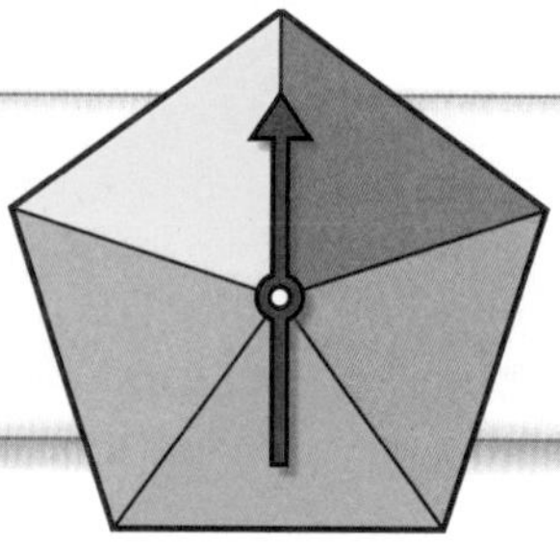

1. Write the answers to these as ratios and as fractions.

(a) What is the likelihood of the spinner stopping on yellow or blue? ___ : ___ or ___
(b) What is the probability of the spinner not stopping on green? ___ : ___ or ___
(c) What is the likelihood of the spinner not stopping on either orange or blue? ___ : ___ or ___
(d) What is the chance of the spinner stopping on blue? ___ : ___ or ___
(e) Is there an even chance of stopping on either yellow or green? (yes/no) ___
(f) What is the likelihood of the spinner not stopping on green or yellow? ___ : ___ or ___
(g) Is it equally likely that the spinner might stop on either pink or blue? (yes/no) ___

2.

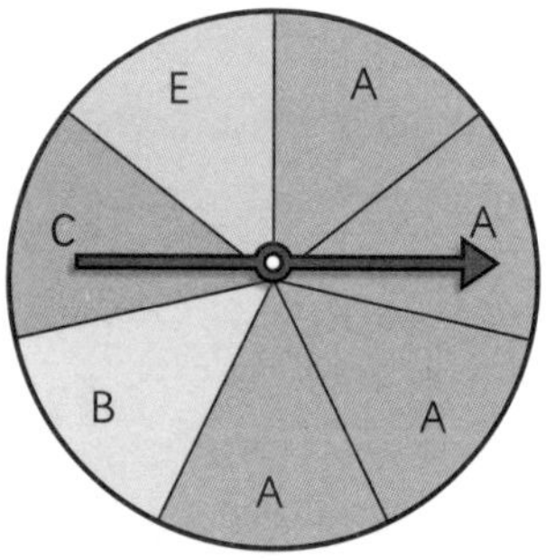

(a) What is the chance of the spinner stopping on C? ___ : ___ or ___
(b) What is the likelihood of the spinner stopping on E? ___ : ___ or ___
(c) What is the probability of the spinner stopping on C or E? ___ : ___ or ___
(d) What is the chance of the spinner not stopping on A? ___ : ___ or ___
(e) What is the probability of not stopping on B or C? ___ : ___ or ___
(f) Is there an even chance that it might stop on either C or A? (yes/no) ___
(g) What is the chance that it will not stop on B? ___ : ___ or ___

---

3. (a) What is the probability of the spinner stopping on C? ___ : ___ or ___
(b) What is the chance of the spinner not stopping on C or E? ___ : ___ or ___
(c) What is the likelihood of the spinner stopping on C or E? ___ : ___ or ___
(d) What is the chance of the spinner not stopping on C? ___ : ___ or ___
(e) Is there an even chance of stopping on either B or E? (yes/no)
(f) What is the probability of the spinner not stopping on A or B? ___ : ___ or ___

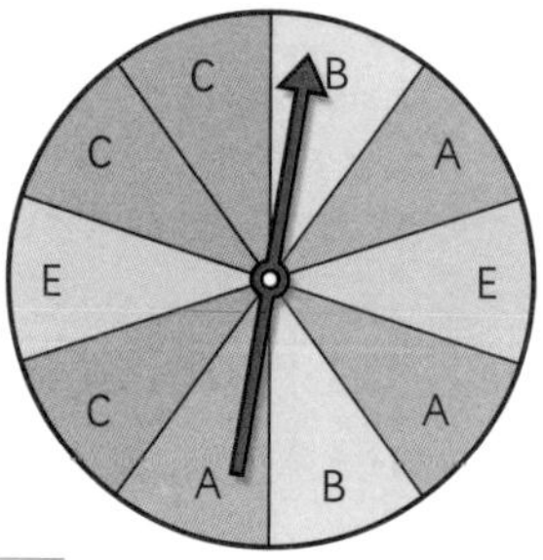

---

4. If all 10 cards are shuffled and then placed face-down on a table...

(a) ...what is the chance of picking the 2 of diamonds? ___ : ___ or ___ %
(b) ...what is the chance of picking an odd number? ___ : ___ or ___ %
(c) ...what is the chance of picking an even number? ___ : ___ or ___ %
(d) ...what is the chance of picking a multiple of five? ___ : ___ or ___ %
(e) ...what is the chance of picking a multiple of two? ___ : ___ or ___ %

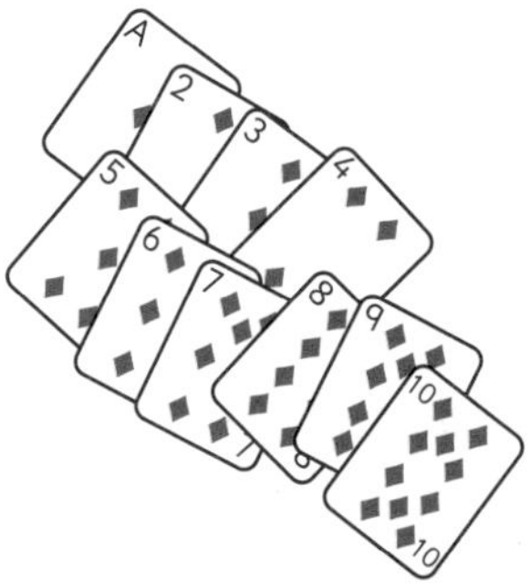

Maths Fact The chances of living to be 100 years old are 1 in 10,000.
How many 100-year-olds would be expected to be living in a city of (a) 40,000 people and (b) 200,000 people? (a) ___ (b) ___

Chance – Rolling dice

It is possible to work out the probability of any outcome when all the outcomes of the event are equally likely.

There are six possible outcomes when you roll a regular die: 1, 2, 3, 4, 5 or 6.

There is only one 5, therefore the chance of rolling a 5 is 1:6 or $\frac{1}{6}$.

There are three even numbers so the chance of rolling an even number is 3:6 or $\frac{3}{6}$ or 50%.

1. What is the probability of rolling:

(a) an odd number? ______ (b) a number less than 4? ______ (c) the number 8? ______

(d) a multiple of 2? ______ (e) a square number? ______ (f) a triangular number? ______

2. Roll a 6-sided die 36 times. Use tally marks to record the outcomes. Show your results on a vertical bar-line graph. First predict what you think the outcome will be.

	Frequency table		
	Prediction	Tally	Outcome
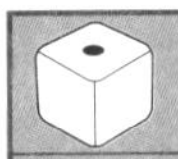			

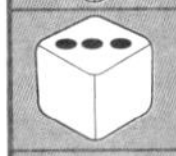			

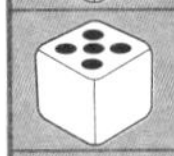			

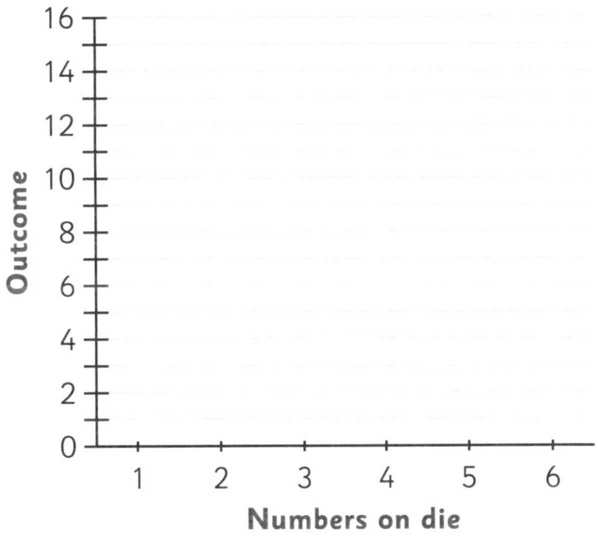

Did your predictions come close to the tally? ______

3. In this experiment, you have only one spin of the Animal Spinner. What is the chance of stopping on the following?

(a) a dog: ☐ in ☐ or $\frac{1}{12}$

(b) a cat: ☐ in ☐ or ______

(c) a cow: ☐ in ☐ or ______

(d) a sheep: ☐ in ☐ or ______

(e) a goat: ☐ in ☐ or ______

(f) a horse: ☐ in ☐ or ______

(g) a goat or a sheep: ☐ in ☐ or ______

(h) a horse or a dog: ☐ in ☐ or ______

(i) a pig or a cat: ☐ in ☐ or ______

(j) a sheep or a cat: ☐ in ☐ or ______

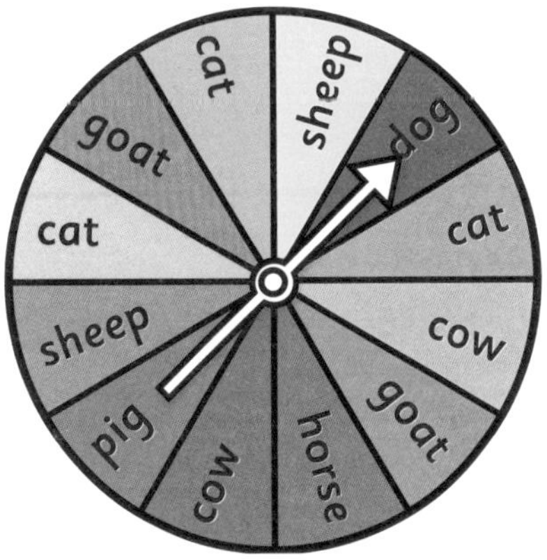

Animal Spinner

Maths Fact If you are an American, the chances are 1 in 150 that you are in jail! How many Americans are likely to be in jail from a town with 7,500 inhabitants? ______

More chance

Events are **equally likely** if they have the same chance of happening.
We can use equally likely outcomes to work out probabilities.

100 tickets are sold for a raffle. With one ticket, your chance of winning is 1:100 or $\frac{1}{100}$.
With five tickets, your chance of winning goes up to 5:100 or $\frac{5}{100}$ or $\frac{1}{20}$ or 5%.

1. (a) What is your chance of winning with 10 tickets? ____ : ____ or ____ %

(b) What is the possibility of you winning if you hold 20 tickets? ____ : ____ or ____ %

(c) What is the chance of you being a winner if you bought 15 tickets? ____ : ____ or ____ %

2. Take a pack of playing cards and shuffle them.

(a) Cut the pack and record the colour on each cut using a tally. Reshuffle the cards each time. Discuss the results with a partner after 20 cuts.

Frequency table	
Red	
Black	

(b) How many reds would you predict after (i) 30 cuts; (ii) 50 cuts; (iii) 80 cuts?

3. (a) Perform the same experiment over 40 cuts, but this time record the suits picked.

Suit	Tally	Outcomes
♥		
♦		
♣		
♠		

(b) Show your results on a horizontal bar-line graph.

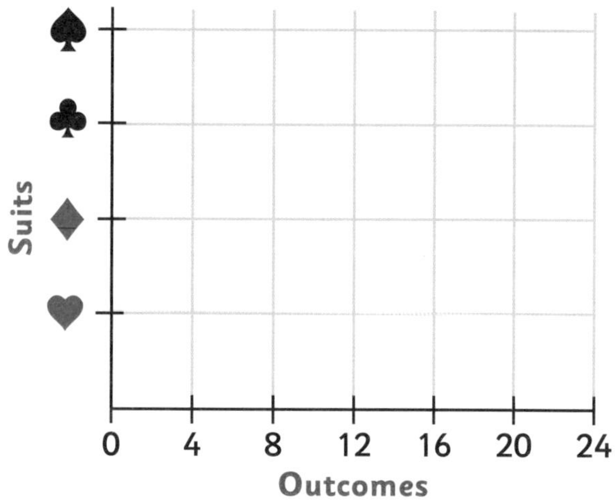

Discuss the results with a partner. Compare your results.

(c) Now predict the number of diamonds out of 100 cuts. ______

(d) How many picture cards would you expect from 100 cuts? ______

(e) How many aces would you predict from 100 cuts? ______

(f) How many fives would you predict from 100 cuts? ______

Maths Fact The odds (chances) are that 1 in 10 people are allergic to dust mites. At these odds, how many people in a village of 340 people could be allergic to dust mites? ______

A quick look back 9

LOOK BACK

1. This shape is called a ________.

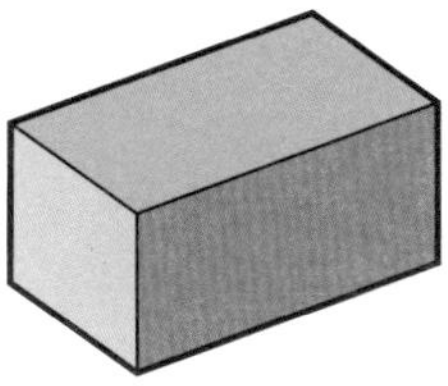

2. How many edges has a cuboid?

____

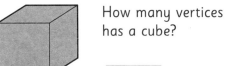

3. How many vertices has a cube?

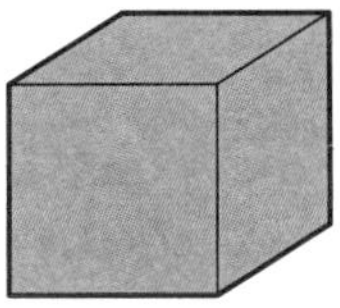

____

4. How many faces has an octahedron?

____

5. Supply the missing word below.

We can ________ and multiply numbers in any order.

6. Order does matter when we are doing subtraction or ________.

7. Remembering the sentence 'Boats may drift at sea', complete this sentence:

$6 \times 4 + 5 =$ ________

8. Now complete this number sentence.

$36 - 21 \div 7 =$ ________

9. Solve:

$40{\cdot}5 \div 5 + 1{\cdot}4 \times 6 =$ ________

10. There are 35 children in a class. One day, 20% of them were absent. How many were present?

____

11. 25% of the pie chart represents 30 chickens. How many chickens altogether does the pie chart represent?

____

12. $(4{\cdot}8 \div 4) + 2{\cdot}1 \times 5 =$ ________

13. Write the next term in this sequence:

1·7, 3·2, 4·7, 6·2, ________

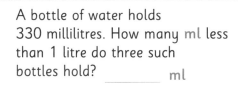

14. A bottle of water holds 330 millilitres. How many ml less than 1 litre do three such bottles hold? ________ ml

15. A bucket holds 15 litres of water. When 3·5l and 3·05l were taken from the bucket, how much water was left? ________ l

16. There are 5 red marbles, 6 yellow marbles and 4 blue marbles in the bag. What are the chances of selecting a yellow marble while blindfolded?

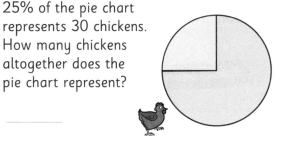

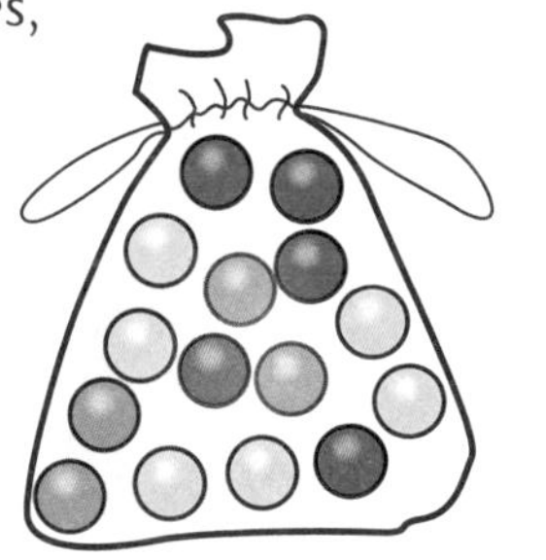

____

17. On an 8-sided spinner, 5 sections are blue, 1 green and 2 red. Which colour is the spinner most likely to stop on?

____

18. Increase 200ml by 100%. ________

19. Write the next term in this sequence:

12·8, 10·4, 8, 5·6, ________

20. $\frac{3}{8} \times 6 =$ ________ $= \frac{\square}{\square}$

Chapter 34: Animalmathics – Dublin Zoo

Entrance prices: Adult €16·50 | Child €11·80

Special offer – Family tickets: 2 adults + 2 children €46·50 | 2 adults + 3 children €51 | 2 adults + 4 children €54·50

1. How much would you save by buying a family ticket instead of individual tickets? Fill in the grid. You may use your calculator to check your answers.

		Family ticket price	Individual total	Amount saved
(a)	2 adults + 2 children			
(b)	2 adults + 3 children			
(c)	2 adults + 4 children			

2. (a) Dublin Zoo opened in 1831. How many years has it been open? _____

(b) In 1844, the first giraffe arrived at Dublin Zoo. He died 25 years later. In what year did he die? _____

(c) Sheila was the last African Lion at Dublin Zoo. She died in 2012 at the age of 25. What year was she born? _____

(d) A hippopotamus born in 1986 died in 2007. What age was he when he died? _____

3. A survey done recently by Dublin Zoo showed the Zoo's most popular animals as voted by visitors to the Zoo. Draw a vertical bar-line graph to show this information. Start with the red panda at 1 and continue in order to number 11 (hippopotamus).

1. Red Panda 20%
2. Elephant 13%
3. Tiger 12%
4. Giraffe 10%
5. Penguin 10%
6. Gorilla 9%
7. Meerkat 6%
8. Orangutan 5%
9. Wolf 4%
10. Lion 3%
11. Hippopotamus 2%

The percentages are rounded to the nearest per cent.

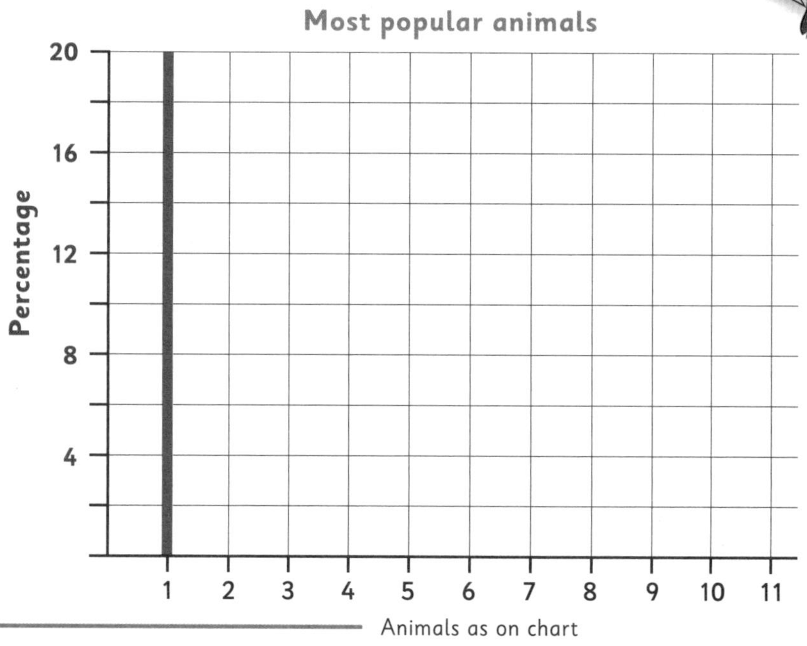

4. Write a number sentence and find the total cost of the following from the Dublin Zoo shop.

	Items	Number sentence	Total cost €
(a)	2 orangutans and 3 zebras	(2 × €6·50) + (3 × €8·50) =	
(b)	1 penguin, 2 gorillas and 5 zebras		
(c)	3 orangutans and 4 gorillas		
(d)	6 zebras, 7 penguins, 2 orangutans		

5.

Opening Times			
March to September	**Opening**	**Closing**	**Last Admission**
Monday to Sunday	9.30am	6.00pm	5.00pm

(a) For how many minutes is the zoo open each day? ______

(b) What is 6.00pm in the 24-hour clock? ___ : ___

(c) If you arrived at the zoo at 11.07am and stayed until 3.33pm, for how many minutes would you have been there? ______

6. Find the total cost of each of the following orders from the Zoo Café.

(a) 3 teas, 2 coffees and 4 sandwiches.

(b) 4 coffees, 3 sparkling waters and 5 sandwiches.

(c) 5 water, 3 cones and 5 sandwiches.

(d) 2 coffees, 5 teas and 6 sandwiches.

(e) 4 teas, 2 sandwiches and 6 cones.

ZOO CAFÉ

tea **€1·90**
coffee **€2·20**
sparkling water **€0·75**

ZOO CAFÉ

sandwich **€3·25**
cone **€1·50**
soup **€4·50**

7.

Pat bought seven toy orangutans costing €6·50 each.
Henry bought four zebras costing €8·50 each.
How much did they spend altogether?
Write as a number sentence and solve.

Challenge 1

In 1855, Dublin Zoo bought its first pair of lions. If an average lion weighs 124kg, what is the weight of four pairs of lions? ______ kg

Challenge 2

Joan bought five toy penguins costing €9 each. Pam bought eight toy gorillas at €12 each. Who spent more and how much more did she spend? Write as a number sentence and solve. ______

A quick look back 10

LOOK BACK

1. Make 47 a hundred times bigger.

____

2. The average of three numbers is 33. Two of the numbers are 46 and 37, what is the third number?

____

3. A regular hexagon has _______ lines of symmetry.

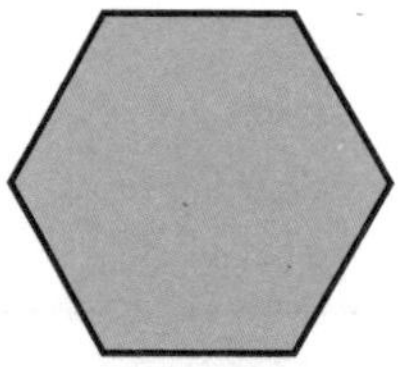

4. Ring the fraction that has the same value as $\frac{3}{4}$:

$\frac{3}{8}$, $\frac{5}{6}$, $\frac{9}{12}$, $\frac{7}{10}$, $\frac{8}{12}$

5. $\frac{2}{3} + \frac{3}{6} = \frac{\square}{\square}$

6. Write the missing number:

$\frac{45}{54} \div \frac{\square}{9} = \frac{5}{6}$

7. If I divide 96kg by 12, I get _______ kg.

8. 58·37 × 1,000 = _______

9. Cereal costs €2·40 for 750 grammes. How much would 6kg of cereal cost?

€ _______

10. 

Anita paid €200 for a dress. Tess got her dress for 25% less. How much did the two dresses cost?

€ _______

11. Add 4,006 to 52,970. _______

12. 63 ÷ 1,000 = _______

13. What name do we call this angle?

____

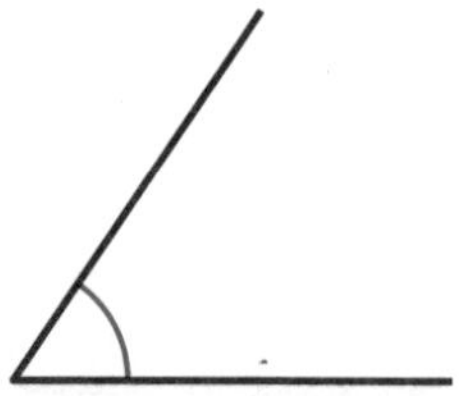

14. Pears cost €3·60 per bag of six. A bag of nine costs €4·50. How much would I save per pear if I bought the better value pears? € _______

15. 

There were 60 plums in a box. Niall took 40% of them and Henry took 45% of them. How many plums were left?

____

16. Increase €84 by 50%.

€ _______

17. A film started at 11:35. It lasted for 114 minutes. At what time did it end?

___ : ___

18. A train left Dublin for Galway at 14:35. The journey took 145 minutes. At what time did it reach Galway?

___ : ___

19. By how much is the 7 in 670 greater than the 7 in 6·073?

____

20. A restaurant bill was €44·50. 10% service charge was added. What was the total cost?

€ _______